PARATRANSIT
IN AMERICA

PARATRANSIT IN AMERICA

Redefining Mass Transportation

ROBERT CERVERO

Westport, Connecticut
London

Library of Congress Cataloging-in-Publication Data

Cervero, Robert.
   Paratransit in America : redefining mass transportation / Robert
Cervero.
      p.   cm.
   Includes bibliographical references and index.
   ISBN 0–275–95725–X (alk. paper)
   1. Paratransit services—United States.   I. Title.
HE308.C47   1997
388.3′2—dc20   96–21246

British Library Cataloguing in Publication Data is available.

Library of Congress Catalog Card Number: 96–21246
ISBN: 0–275–95725–X

First published in 1997

Praeger Publishers, 88 Post Road West, Westport, CT 06881
An imprint of Greenwood Publishing Group, Inc.

Printed in the United States of America

The paper used in this book complies with the
Permanent Paper Standard issued by the National
Information Standards Organization (Z39.48–1984).

10 9 8 7 6 5 4 3 2 1

Contents

Photo Essay A. follows page 84.

Illustrations

Figures

Preface

During the late 1980s while working in Indonesia, I discovered the joys of para-transit. I had to. For the first extended period of my adult life I was without a car. I was, in the words of transportation planners, a "transit-dependent." I came to rely heavily on the pedal-powered becaks, three-wheel bajajs, converted Toyota Kijang utility vehicles, and 24-seat minibuses of Jakarta, Bandung, and Pekan-baru to get around. And to my surprise, I was able to go from anywhere to everywhere in relative comfort (more so than by public bus) and in a friendly environment where passengers smiled and engaged in small talk. And the fares were incredibly cheap. Paratransit's success in Indonesia and many developing countries of the world lies, to a significant degree, in hard-working, indepen-dent, owner-operators whose livelihoods depend on being efficient and delivering reliable, good-quality services. Driven by the profit motive, jitney and minibus drivers aggressively seek out new and expanding markets, contain costs, and innovate as necessary (like a Jakarta bajaj driver who guaranteed arrival at my destination within ten minutes or the ride was free; I ended up paying). It is the element of competition, combined with some of the advantages of small-vehicle transportation—more frequent services, fewer stops, faster boarding and unload-ing, curb-to-curb delivery—that are behind the success of paratransit in many parts of the developing world.

Upon returning to the States to resume my life as an academic, the contrast in how I traveled couldn't have been more striking. Once again I was hauling my lonesome in a motorized 6,000-pound steel cage to go almost anywhere more than a half mile away. I found comfort only in the fact that I was behaving rationally —except when heading to downtown San Francisco, Berkeley, or Oakland, where I live, there really are few alternatives to quickly getting somewhere other than driving. In fact, the only time I found myself patronizing paratransit was when heading to the San Francisco International airport via dial-a-ride vans. Why aren't commercial shuttle vans available to reach other major destinations—like a college campus, a sports stadium, or a suburban mall? Must the choices always be limited either to driving or taking a fixed-route, fixed-schedule public bus? Is it possible to transplant some features of successful paratransit services in the developing world to American cities? In probing these questions, it quickly became apparent that as a society, we in the United States have introduced public policies and organized institutions in ways that form significant barriers to free-enterprise paratransit. Heavy-handed regulations, public bus monopolies, and the prevalence of free parking are examples. Yet, growing public concerns over the sustainability of an auto-dominated urban transportation system, the influx of immigrants who have experience riding paratransit in Latin America and Asia, and trends toward privatization in other public sectors have created a window of opportunity for expanding paratransit options in the United States. The challenge of growing a commercial paratransit sector in American cities is immense, but not insurmountable. It is this challenge that gave birth to this book.

The book is divided into three parts. The first part studies the anatomy of the paratransit industry, primarily in the United States but also abroad, examining its service features, markets, and overall performance. Case studies from across the United States and parts of Latin America and Southeast Asia are presented in this pursuit. Part 2 of the book explores the regulatory and institutional environments that have shaped America's fledgling paratransit sector in recent decades. How public policies, from regulations controlling market entry to subsidy support of public transportation, have affected paratransit's performance are probed. The final part of the book looks to the future, exploring how advanced communications technologies and public policy reforms, like market-rate pricing, might stimulate commercial paratransit services in the twenty-first century. A recommended action agenda concludes the book.

I owe a debt of gratitude to many organizations and individuals who made this book possible. The U.S. Environmental Protection Agency provided funding to support many of the U.S. case studies presented in this volume. I particularly thank Will Schroeer from EPA for his belief in this project and for his critical but helpful advice along the way. The California Department of Transportation and the University of California Transportation Center (UCTC), under the Transit Research Program, also provided grant support for examining the potential of smart paratransit. I particularly thank Melvin Webber, Director of UCTC, for his encouragement to write this book, and his enlightened thinking about the potential transferability of paratransit lessons from abroad to the United States. A grant from the Pacific Rim Exchange Program of the University of California helped support my field work on paratransit in Indonesia and other parts of Asia. The Reason Foundation of Southern California, under the direction of Robert Poole, provided a small grant for studying the paratransit regulatory environment of greater Los Angeles.

A number of my students at Berkeley provided valuable research assistance throughout the project. Tom Kirk contributed toward the preparation of the case materials for Mexico City, New York, San Diego, and Berkeley, as well as the study of federal regulations and their affects on paratransit. Alfred Round assisted with the preparation of the chapter on paratransit technologies. Karma Reid, Doug Mount, Arthur Gillespie, and Anthony Brinckman also assisted on different phases of the project.

Numerous individuals kindly gave us their time and provided valuable assistance in the course of conducting the case-study field work, and we thank them all. Though there are too many people to list individually, among those who were particularly generous with their time were C. Kenneth Orski of the Urban Mobility Corporation, Barbara Lupo with the Metropolitan Transit Development Board in San Diego, Robert Behnke of Aegis Transportation Information Systems, Peter Bisbecos of the City of Indianapolis, Danny Alvarez with the Metro-Dade Transit Agency, Robert Strauss of the California Public Utilities Commission, Mitch Rauss of SuperShuttle, Inc., John Kindt of Prime Time, Inc., John Hall with the Black and White Cab Company in Little Rock, John Stone of North Carolina State University, Cliff Slater of Maui Divers in Honolulu, Barry Klein of Citizens for Jitneys in Houston, Pamela Henderson of Kids Kabs in Michigan, Rob Hainsworth of the National Child Transportation Association, Jeff Becker with Tidewater Regional Transit, Wade Lawson with South Jersey Transportation Authority, Bill Penman of the Atlantic City Jitney Association, William Considine of the New York City Taxi and Limousine Commission, Kenneth Schriffrin of the New York City Transit Authority, Gabriel Rodriguez of the Puerto Rico Department of Transportation and Public Works, Kunchit Phiu-Nual of Chulalongkorn University in Bangkok, and Hector Antanano with the Dirección General de Auto Transporte Urbano in Mexico City.

I also owe a great deal of thanks to the excellent staff at the Institute of Urban and Regional Development at UC Berkeley who helped with the production of this manuscript. David Van Arnam went well beyond the call of duty in helping with the formatting, copyediting, and word processing of the book. Chris Amado, Martha Conway, and Dianna Jacobs helped with scanning photographic images and paste-ups. Miho Rahm and Barbara Hadenfeldt helped me manage the resources necessary to carry out this work in innumerable ways. And Jane Sterzinger very capably prepared most of the maps shown in this book.

Lastly, I thank my wife, Sophia, and my children, Christopher and Alexandria, for their support and tolerance of my sometimes hectic work schedule. I am fortunate to have a partner and kids who love taking a microbus to the local market and catching a minibus into the city during our visits to Jakarta. So far, I haven't succeeded in explaining to my four-year-old, Chris, why he can't do likewise in the Bay Area. The best I've come up with is "maybe one day." I truly hope so.

Robert Cervero
January 1996

PARATRANSIT IN AMERICA

PART I

PARATRANSIT SERVICE OPTIONS, MARKETS, AND PERFORMANCE

CHAPTER 1

Paratransit in America: Past, Present, and Prospects

INTRODUCTION

Paratransit has the potential to produce substantial mobility and environmental benefits by attracting large numbers of urban trips that otherwise would be made by private automobile. Experiments with shared-ride taxis and jitney services in Seattle, San Diego, Indianapolis, and several other U.S. cities in the late 1970s and 1980s demonstrated there is a market demand for frequent, on-call, and sometimes door-to-door services that are cheaper than exclusive-ride taxis and sometimes even public transit (Frankena and Paulter, 1984; Cervero, 1985). Importantly, these types of services blend the best features of mass transit (i.e., multiple occupancy) and the private automobile (i.e., flexible, on-call, point-to-point services). Because of allegations of unfair competition and "cream skimming," however, many local and state authorities introduced or tightened regulations over the past three decades that effectively banned competitive, free-enterprise paratransit from most American cities. In addition, labor protection legislation, such as the 13(c) provision of the Federal Transit Act, as well as capital and operating subsidies to public transit have placed private paratransit operators at a competitive disadvantage, limiting most to specialized, contract services such as for the elderly and disabled.

Despite these regulatory and economic barriers, some paratransit entrepreneurs have carved out market niches that earn them profits and provide valuable transportation services. Today, New York City has the largest number of commuter vans of any American city—an estimated 2,400 to 5,000 vehicles (seating 14 to 20 passengers) operate, both legally and illegally, on semifixed routes and variable schedules to subway stops and as connectors to Manhattan. Surveys show that over three-quarters of New York's commuter van customers are former transit riders who value having a guaranteed seat and speedy, dependable services. Miami currently has the second largest paratransit market in the continental United States—at its height in the early 1990s, around 500 vans carried some 50,000 riders each weekday (around one-third of Metrobus ridership). Many users are recent immigrants from Cuba and the West Indies who find jitney-vans a more familiar and congenial form of travel than bus transit. Surveys show Miami's jitneys have successfully carved out an independent market niche rather than siphoning customers from public transit—67 percent of survey respondents said they were drawn to jitneys because they got them to their destinations faster and 23 percent said they were less expensive (Urban Mobility Corporation, 1992). Following Hurricane Andrew in August 1992, over 200 independent jitney owner-operators were recruited to provide fixed-route van services to South Dade County residents.

Besides New York and Miami, private vans and minibuses currently provide valuable feeder services to rail stations or bus terminals in San Francisco, San Jose, San Diego, and other cities. Some serve largely transit-captive markets, such as the San Ysidro jitneys that operate between the Mexican border and worksites in south San Diego County. Shared-ride taxis that are technically illegal yet tolerated by public authorities also thrive in poor, minority inner-city neighborhoods in Baltimore, Boston, Chicago, Omaha, and dozens of other U.S. cities, many providing on-call connections to supermarkets and shopping malls. Other private paratransit services cater mainly to middle-class or professional white-collar customers—such as San Francisco's sole surviving jitney serving the downtown financial district, Berkeley's racetrack taxi pool, Atlantic City's jitney vans that parallel the boardwalk and casinos, and Washington, D.C.'s venerable shared-ride taxicabs. The most extensive and popular form of private paratransit serving middle-class America is the airport shuttle-van, which in the case of the Los Angeles and San Francisco airports currently handle about 15 percent of all ground-access trips. With the exceptions of New York, Miami, and a few other large cities, commercial shuttle vans have so far avoided serving other major activity centers—downtowns, edge cities, shopping malls, college campuses, and sports stadia, for example—because of unreceptive market conditions, like free parking and competition from subsidized public transit services. Of course, outside the United States, free-enterprise minibuses, jitneys, and three-wheelers ply their trade throughout the streets of many third-world megacities, like Jakarta, Bangkok, and Mexico City. In many of these places, paratransit is the workhorse of the local mass transit system, carrying over half of all transit trips.

This book examines the potential for private, free-enterprise paratransit services to provide a respectable transportation alternative to the private automobile in U.S. cities. If legalized and allowed to freely compete in a nondistorted marketplace, paratransit, I believe, could lure hundreds of thousands of commuters and motorists out of their cars each day, producing real and lasting mobility and environmental benefits. In many instances, paratransit could operate at a lower cost per passenger-mile than conventional bus transit and without any kind of subsidy support. Competition from private paratransit providers, moreover, could over the long run induce the kinds of efficiency gains and service reforms that would improve the overall financial health of America's struggling public transportation sector.

This book also examines regulatory and economic barriers that currently stifle commercial paratransit services in the United States. Regulations governing urban transportation have been built up, layer by layer, over time to the point where today they represent significant obstacles to market penetration and service innovations. Entry and service restrictions are placed on taxis in most U.S. cities, while jitneys, shared-ride taxis, and most other for-profit ridesharing services have generally been regulated out of existence. In most states, inter-city services, like commercial shuttle vans and private buspools, fall under the purview of state regulators, who historically have overly protected longtime operators and imposed stringent insurance and safety requirements on new entrants. In some places, participation in employer-sponsored vanpooling is effectively limited to coworkers. In general, laws aimed at protecting taxi firms and public transit agencies from head-to-head competition are inconsistent with the need to foster a wider range of door-to-door transportation options to the private automobile.

In addition, "hidden" subsidies to motorists, like free parking and unpriced traffic congestion, and overt subsidies to public transit operators have created a "nonlevel playing field," making it nearly impossible for commercial paratransit to compete. Possible ways of reducing or eliminating these barriers as a means of stimulating commercial paratransit services in the United States are also explored in this book. Particular attention is given to identifying ways of creating a more entrepreneurial and competitive environment for urban transportation services in keeping with the growing interest in advancing market-based transportation policies.

POTENTIAL BENEFITS OF COMMERCIAL PARATRANSIT

Expanded commercial paratransit services would produce at least six important benefits: (1) increase travel choices; (2) enhance mobility; (3) improve environmental conditions; (4) impose a market discipline on public transportation; (5) make poor neighborhoods more accessible; and (6) help stimulate advanced transit technologies.

Increase Travel Choices

Commercial paratransit would increase the mix and overall quality of transportation options in U.S. cities, thereby prompting some people to leave their cars at home and share rides instead. Most Americans have only one or two reasonable alternatives when traveling other than by car—either bus or taxi. Yet the past several decades have taught us that the provision of fixed-route, uniform-quality bus services will not lure significant numbers of people out of their cars. There is tremendous diversity in travel preferences—some want fast, comfortable services and are willing to pay a premium fare for them, while others are satisfied to travel more slowly and give up some comfort in return for a break at the farebox. Increasing choices increases the odds of enticing commuters to switch their mode of travel.

The importance of service features is well known within the transportation field. Studies consistently show that commuters are far more sensitive to the quality of transportation services than price levels—that is, they are most likely to change their travel behavior, and perhaps switch modes, given dramatic changes in travel times and comfort levels. Transit riders tend to be at least twice as responsive to service changes (such as more frequent headways) than to lower fares (Mayworm et al., 1980). Factors such as reliability of schedules, assurances of getting a seat, and safety have proven to be key determinants of what modes travelers choose. Commuters particularly abhor time spent walking to a bus stop, waiting, and transferring. As American cities continue to suburbanize at a rapid pace and trip origins and destinations spread in all directions, only flexible transportation services that connect people from "anywhere to everywhere," akin to the private automobile, stand a reasonable chance of competing in the marketplace.

Small vehicles provide a number of service advantages over bigger buses: they take less time to load and unload, they arrive more often, and they stop less frequently (Glaister, 1986; Banister and Mackett, 1990).[1] They are also more maneuverable in busy traffic and can accelerate and decelerate faster. Studies show that passengers also tend to feel more secure in a smaller vehicle where everyone is close to the driver (Gomez-Ibanez and Meyer, 1990), and surveys show that minibus riders enjoy the "camaraderie" and "friendliness" of being in smaller vehicles (Prentice, 1987).

Mobility Benefits

To the degree that paratransit services induce modal shifts from cars to minibuses, shuttle vans, jitneys, and commuter buses, second-order benefits would accrue, mainly in the form of increased mobility and improved environmental conditions. Rapid increases in automobile travel, coupled with limited road expansion, have brought unprecedented levels of traffic congestion in U.S. cities in recent years, especially in the suburbs. For the 39 largest U.S. metropolises, the number of lane-miles of expressways and major arterials combined increased just 13.7 percent during the 1980s, while vehicle miles driven rose 31.4 percent (Federal Highway Administration, 1995). Community opposition, environmental regulations, building moratoria, and funding shortages all contributed to the slowdown in new highway construction, while suburbanization, rising incomes, and more women in the labor force helped to fuel automobile travel. With the growth in auto trips outpacing the growth in road capacity, traffic delays rose sharply, by 57 percent from 1985 to 1988 according to one estimate (Johnson, 1993). The social costs of traffic congestion are difficult to measure, though they can be substantial, including wasted time and energy, air pollution, accidents, lost economic productivity, stress, and a declining quality of life. Some estimates place the social costs of highway congestion in the United States at $73 billion per year (in 1988 dollars), or 2 percent of gross national product (GNP) (Rowand, 1989). A study by the Texas Transportation Institute (Lomax et al., 1991) estimated that congestion costs each driver $375 annually (in 1990 dollars) in extra fuel and maintenance expenses.

Environmental Benefits

There is probably no issue today that is driving transportation policy making as much as concerns over air quality. Photochemical smog remains a serious problem in more than 100 U.S. cities, with the worst conditions in California and the industrial areas of the northeast. At extreme levels, smog can impair visibility, damage crops, and threaten human health.

In America, air pollution is largely a product of an auto-dependent society. Between 30 and 40 percent of man-made hydrocarbon and nitrogen-oxide emissions, two of the chief precursors to the formation of photochemical smog, and around two-thirds of carbon monoxide emissions come from the tailpipes of cars. Nationwide, the damage costs attributable to auto-related air pollution has been placed at around $10 billion annually according to one estimate (MacKenzie et al., 1992) and around 2 cents per vehicle mile travel according to another (Small and Kazimi, 1994). Despite much cleaner automobiles (1993 cars emitted 80 percent less pollution than the typical 1970 model) and trip reduction mandates, air quality in many urban areas has improved little and in some places has deteriorated. This is because these measures have largely been swamped by the growth in vehicle population, number of trips, and miles driven, especially in slow-moving traffic.

A study by the Environmental Defense Fund estimated that the expansion of commercial paratransit services in Southern California, coupled with average congestion charges of $3 per round trip, would reduce vehicle-miles-travelled (VMT) by 1.8 percent from the year 2010 baseline estimates (Cameron, 1991). This would in turn lead to a 2.2 percent reduction in carbon monoxide (CO) and reactive organic gases (ROG). Another study estimated that the shift of 5 percent of airport access trips from cars to shared-ride vans in the greater Los Angeles area over the past decade has eliminated some 84 tons of pollutants per year (Poole and Griffin, 1994).

Shuttle van and jitney runs to rail transit stations, such as currently found in New York, Miami, and San Jose, can yield important air quality benefits. The majority of access trips to suburban rail transit stations in the U.S. are made by solo-drivers who park-and-ride. For San Francisco's Bay Area Rapid Transit (BART) system, a 1993 onboard ridership survey found that around 70 percent of access trips to suburban stations were by private automobile (Cervero, 1995). For a three-mile automobile trip, the typical distance driven to access a suburban BART park-and-ride lot, around 84 percent of hydro-carbon (HC) emissions and

54 percent of oxides of nitrogen (NOx) emissions are due to cold starts (inefficient cold engines during the first few minutes of driving) and hot evaporative soaks (California Air Resources Board, 1989).[2] Park-and-ride transit trips do very little to improve air quality as long as an internal combustion engine is used to reach stations. Converting more of these access trips to higher occupancy vehicles (i.e., "paratransit-and-ride") would enable electrified rail transit to produce the kinds of environmental benefits it is supposed to.

The Clean Air Act Amendments of 1990 (CAAA) and the Intermodal Surface Transportation Efficiency Act of 1991 (ISTEA) explicitly encourage the expansion of transit services, including paratransit, in urban areas which violate national clean air standards. Recently some air quality management agencies have moved toward market-based strategies versus employer-targeted trip reduction regulations as a more efficient means of achieving clean air mandates.[3] The U.S. Environmental Protection Agency (EPA) has also recently issued guidelines that provide for more flexibility in how states and regions prepare Employee Commute Options (ECO) plans for nonattainment areas. In general, trends toward market-based strategies and greater flexibility in developing transportation programs that conform to air quality requirements work in favor of expanded commercial paratransit services.

In addition to air quality gains, the shift of motorists to shared-ride paratransit would yield other environmental benefits, including reduced emissions of greenhouse gases, less noise pollution, and energy conservation. While minibuses and vans emit more pollutants and noise and consume more fuel than standard cars, paratransit's high average occupancies would yield net environmental benefits. A 1988 study by the Congressional Budget Office, for example, found that commuter vans require only 37 percent as much energy per passenger-mile as a bus and only 30 percent as much as a light-rail transit system (accounting for full energy expenditures, including facility construction).

More Efficient and Economical Public Transit Services

Commercial paratransit has proven itself to be a comparatively cost-effective mode. Some of the cost savings come from high passenger loads and more frequent passenger turnover. Commercial paratransit operations also average lower labor input costs. Many services are owned, operated, and maintained by a single, often very hard-working, person. These "one-man" operations usually have no overhead, nor labor-related expenses for health insurance, worker's compensation insurance, or retirement benefits. Even for larger firms, paratransit drivers are typically nonunionized and earn far less per hour than public transit employees. Accounting for full costs, including facility construction, one study found that, on average, commuter vans cost 64 per cent less than bus transit per passenger mile and 91 percent less than heavy rail transit (Congressional Budget Office, 1988).[4]

Competitive paratransit would impose a much-needed market discipline on America's public transit industry, forcing bus operators to contain costs and increase productivity in order to effectively compete for customers. Since 1970, America's public transit industry has been plagued by rising operating deficits and declining productivity, by virtually any measure, despite the infusion of billions of dollars in operating assistance annually. Federal, state, and local subsidies to public transit operations jumped from $132 million in 1970 to over $10 billion in 1992. This aid has produced relatively little payoff—nationwide transit ridership has remained fairly stagnant over the past three decades, at around 7 to 8 billion passenger trips (ignoring transfers) annually. Meanwhile, highway travel has risen from 570 billion miles a year in 1970 to over 2 trillion miles in 1990 (Federal Highway Administration, 1995). Transit's market share of motorized trips in U.S. cities has slipped from around 5 percent in 1970 to under 3 percent in 1990 (Pucher, 1995). Studies show that a large share of government subsides has been consumed by higher labor costs, less service output per worker, and the unbusinesslike expansion of services into low-density, suburban markets (Sale and Green, 1978; Cervero, 1983). Between 1975 and 1985, for instance, transit labor productivity dropped sharply from 13,618 vehicle miles of service per worker to 9,364. As critics of transit subsidies had feared, operating assistance was not spurring ridership increases but instead was leading to lax management practices and overly generous wage settlements. Perhaps more troubling, the underwriting of public transit services and creation of a protected public monopoly have prevented higher quality paratransit options from gaining a market foothold.

Experiences show that increased competition can induce public transit operators to become more productive and efficient. In the Norfolk, Virginia area, the Tidewater Transit District Commission (TTDC) began competitively contracting selected suburban services to private minibus operators who provided door-to-door, dial-a-ride service in 1979. TTDC drivers agreed to form a nonunionized class of minibus operators earning lower wages, allowing TTDC to eventually win back the dial-a-ride services and operate them in-house in 1984. In the Tidewater area, Houston, and other U.S. cities, increased competition has prodded public transit agencies to concentrate mainly on serving high-density, high-volume corridors which enjoy economies of scale.

Private vans and buspools would also provide peak-hour supplements to public transit operators, relieving them of the need to expand costly peak-hour services. Studies consistently show that it costs two to three times more to run buses during rush hours than at other times, largely because of restrictive union work rules that guarantee eight hours' pay and provide split-shift wage premiums (Cervero, 1988). In Singapore, the area licensing scheme that charges motorists for entering the downtown area during peak hours has relied heavily on shared-ride taxis and expanded private buspools to absorb those priced off roads, thus holding the public transit system to a much more manageable scale. By supplementing bus runs at peak hours and serving other markets, such as senior citizens and those with physical disabilities, at other hours, commercial paratransit operators would be in a position to use vehicles efficiently throughout the day.

The few comparative studies of commercial paratransit versus subsidized public transit have shown paratransit to be an economic asset, eliminating the need for government subsidies and relieving public transit companies of their costly peak period burdens. For example, Manila's 60,000 jeepneys (converted U.S. army jeeps that each serve up to 12 riders on semifixed routes) are the mainstay of the city's transportation system, carrying around 60 percent of all peak-period passenger trips. Manila's jeepneys cost 16 percent less per seat mile than standard buses and generally provide a higher quality service (e.g., greater reliability, shorter waits) at a lower fare (Roth and Wynne, 1982). Manila's jeepney operators, moreover, have historically been the last to petition for fare increases. Almost all turn a profit where public transit authorities are unable to.

Improved Services for Poor Neighborhoods

An expanded commercial paratransit sector would also increase mobility in poor neighborhoods. One of the most troubling effects of an increasingly auto-dependent society are the social injustices that result from physically and socially isolating significant segments of American society. Those who are too poor, disabled, young, or old to own or drive a car are effectively left out of many of society's offerings. For older Americans, it can mean loneliness and inadequate attention to medical needs. For the inner-city poor, it often means isolation from job opportunities, what has been called the "spatial mismatch" problem (Kain, 1994). Today, two out of every three jobs in large metropolitan areas are being created in the suburbs. A study of commuting in Philadelphia, Chicago, and Los Angeles found that unequal accessibility to jobs explained nearly half of the difference in employment rates between black and white teenagers (Ihlanfeldt and Sjoquist, 1989). Besides poor transit services, the study suggested black youths lacked information about jobs farther away and were not inclined to seek jobs in "unfamiliar areas."

While public transit authorities have gotten into the business of running reverse-commute services in greater Philadelphia, Milwaukee, St. Louis, and other U.S. cities, even more popular are the illegal jitneys and van shuttles that ply their trade in many low-income neighborhoods across America. For inner-city residents who cannot afford to own a car, shared-ride jitneys and vans that provide low-priced, curb-to-curb service are among the next best thing. In Philadelphia, as many as 1,500 "hacks," or illegal shared-ride cabs, cruise between poor neighborhoods, supermarkets, and retail strips. In New York City, well over 10,000 illegal van operators provide feeder connections between low-income neighborhoods and rail transit stations (see Chapter 2). Such services not only vastly increase the accessibility of the urban poor and the number of potential work sites within a 45-minute commute but also reduce the cost of vehicle ownership and usage (which is especially high in inner-city neighbor-hoods because of high insurance premiums).

Stimulating the paratransit sector could aid the poor financially. Mark Frankena and Paul Paulter (1986, p. 3) note that "the low-income population spends higher shares of their income, and often simply more dollars, on taxis than does the high-income population." Another advantage, according to Peter Suzuki (1995, p. 130), is that commercial paratransit operators "are more willing to travel to neighborhoods that medallion cab drivers consider to be too dangerous." In a competitive marketplace, firms might also compete for patrons in poor neighborhoods during off-peak hours when there is a surplus of unused vehicles.

One concern about possibly cracking down on illegal paratransit services and forcing them to meet insurance, indemnity, and vehicle fitness standards is that this would end up inflating fares, hurting the poor financially. Some argue that illicit operations function usefully as third-world like paratransit in a society that sets first-world like standards on all common-carrier services. One way to help offset fare impacts of legalizing "gypsy" shared-ride cabs and clandestine jitneys would be through a system of user-side subsidies and vouchers targeted at the poor, perhaps administered through community-based human services programs.

Stimulate the Development of Advanced Transportation Technologies

Expanded commercial transit could also help speed up the development of advanced transportation technologies. In order to gain a competitive edge, com-mercial transit operators might try to introduce automated technologies like satellite-based vehicle tracking and dispatching systems that can be used to opti-mize routing, avoid detours, reduce deadheading, and inform waiting customers of expected vehicle arrival times. Small-scale paratransit services might be the dominant consumer of advanced transit technologies since they, unlike fixed-route bus services, are better able to alter routing in response to real-time infor-mation on vehicle locations. Moreover, commercial fleets of vans lend them-selves to alternative fuels (including battery power) far more readily than indi-vidually owned cars and even commercial buses. In states like California, where the state air control board has mandated that at least 10 percent of new car sales in the year 2003 be Zero Emission Vehicles (ZEVs), neighborhood jitneys and vans could be important assets; by providing short-haul, limited-range services, shared-ride minivans and sedans using conventional lead-acid batteries could prove to be one of the most cost-effective forms of ZEVs.

The marriage of conventional shared-ride paratransit services and Advanced Public Transit Systems (APTS) technologies, like satellite-based vehicle locator systems, might eventually spawn a kind of "smart paratransit." In some German cities, paratransit vehicles with on-board terminals are linked to central compu-ters, allowing shared-ride taxis and minibuses to be dispatched to customers wait-ing at suburban rail stations and in rural areas. Ridership on these "Call-a-Bus" services has increased between 36 percent and 80 percent above the fixed-route bus services they replaced in several German metropolises. Average passenger waiting times of seven minutes have been reported, and most paratransit operators are recovering 80 percent of full costs through the farebox, a rate that is two to three times higher than what most U.S. suburban transit services recover (Benke, 1993).

In response to a target set by the Southern California Association of Governments of achieving a 19 percent transit modal split by the year 2010 for the greater Los Angeles area, one recent study proposed a system of 60,000 "smart shuttles" that would function mainly as feeders to Metrorail stations (Urban Innovations Group, 1993). The smart shuttles would have capacities of four to eight passengers, would rely on an extensive network of High-Occupancy-Vehicle (HOV) lanes to gain a speed advantage, and would take advantage of advanced tracking and dispatching systems to optimize vehicle routing.

Melvin Webber (1994) envisages automated technologies one day allowing a virtual laissez-faire of shared-ride transportation services. Under Webber's scheme, people belonging to a "shared-ride co-op" would dial a transportation help line, say "711," wherein a central computer would direct the nearest passing motorist who also belongs to the co-op, is heading in the same direction, and is willing to fill an empty seat for a fee, to pick up the waiting customer. If none is found, the nearest publicly or privately owned bus, van, or taxi would be sent to the caller's front door.

POTENTIAL DRAWBACKS OF COMMERCIAL PARATRANSIT

The chief arguments against open competition in the urban transportation sector are that public transit systems are natural monopolies and that excessive competition would jeopardize public safety and welfare. With a true natural monopoly, like water utilities, average costs decline with output, meaning that a single firm can provide consumers the least-cost service, providing, of course, that regulation prohibits the firm from raising prices to monopoly profit levels (Kahn, 1971). In general, the natural monopoly argument for regulating entry into the urban commuter bus and van service market has little foundation. Studies have consistently shown that with the exception of rapid rail operations and very high-demand corridors, most mass transportation services operate under constant, and for most big operators, declining returns to scale (Lee and Steedman, 1970; Wells et al., 1972; Williams, 1979; Viton, 1981). A study of 73 U.S. public bus systems found that each additional bus added slightly more than 2 cents to the per vehicle hour cost of service (Keough, 1989). For bus transit, average unit costs generally increase with fleet size because big transit operators tend to be in big cities where buses usually run slower, living costs (and thus wages) and overheads are higher, and unions are more powerful (Lave, 1991).[5] Thus, in large U.S. cities where paratransit would likely have the greatest market potential, the natural monopoly argument against commercial transit competition is the weakest.

Another usual argument against paratransit is that free market conditions will lead to cutthroat competition, as with the taxi wars during the Great Depression when regulations were eventually introduced. While excessive competition (e.g., queue hopping, pestering, price gouging of tourists) occurred, at times, at airports and cab stands at major hotels in San Diego, Seattle, and several other cities that deregulated taxis in the early 1980s, no such problems were encountered with general-hail and advanced-reservation services in these cities (Frankena and Paulter, 1984). Taxi operators competed fiercely for airport customers because these patrons are the most "transit-dependent," owing to the high parking rates at airports that deter many air travelers from parking over extended periods of time. If commercial rates were charged for parking elsewhere in cities with deregulated taxis, particularly at the workplace, then it is likely that cabbies would not have fought so strenuously for airport customers; rather, competition would have been less concentrated (and thus not as excessive). In an environment of market-based pricing and universal parking charges, predatory and cutthroat competition would be less of a problem.

Another argument against commercial paratransit is that if numerous competitors were allowed into the urban transportation market, they would "skim the cream" by taking the most lucrative routes and leaving the unprofitable ones. However, a single transportation company, the argument goes, would operate in the public interest by operating both money-making and money-losing services, a practice commonly called cross-subsidization. This situation is most often alleged to occur when a common carrier is forced to serve low-density areas or nonpeak times, but faces competition, legal or otherwise, during peak periods and in high-volume areas. To ensure high levels of transportation services throughout an urban region, then, regulators argue that the public has an obligation to protect carriers from excessive competition and ensure that they receive a fair return on investment.

Because public transit operators incur deficits for almost every route they operate, it would not appear that there is any cream to skim in today's urban transit sector. By serving trips without any public subsidies, if anything, commercial paratransit services would help skim some of the deficits public operators might otherwise incur. Rather than being ruthless predators, paratransit providers would actually aid transit agencies by relieving them of high-cost services, improving service quality in the process.[6]

Lastly, in many third-world settings where entrepreneurial paratransit services thrive, drivers are all too often overly aggressive and disobey traffic rules. Many are frequently criticized for reckless driving, cutting off cars to pick up fares, blocking lanes to load and unload passengers, overloading and operating unsafe vehicles, and excessive cruising for customers (Morgridge, 1983; Kirby et al., 1986). Such problems, however, are more related to lax enforcement than to oversupply. Rather than restricting market entry and thus stifling competition, the preferred response to unruly driving behavior is stepped-up enforcement and stiffer sanctions and fines. Of course, there will always be a need for some degree of regulation to ensure that vehicles and drivers meet fitness and safety standards. However, this should not be at the expense of restricting market entry and exit, service practices (as long as they are safe), and pricing.

CLASSES AND EXISTING SCOPE OF PARATRANSIT

The term *paratransit* was coined in the 1970s to describe the full spectrum of transportation options that fall between the private automobile and the conventional bus. Like automobiles, many paratransit services are flexible and ubiquitous, connecting multiple places within a region, but at a price far below a taxi. And like bus transit, paratransit is an efficient user of road space and energy resources because of its high average loads.

The range of paratransit options is summarized in Table 1.1. These options, discussed in this section, comprise a mix of service types and configurations, passenger-carrying levels, market orientations, and levels of regulatory control. One basic distinction is whether services are purely commercial, open to the general public, or sponsored by employers (perhaps as part of a trip-reduction program) or developers. Some services, like many dial-a-ride vans, are highly specialized, restricted to certain clientele, such as the elderly and handicapped. Another basic distinction is whether services respond to immediate requests made by phone or curbside hail (such as shared-ride taxis, dial-a-ride vans), or are prearranged services (like commuter buses and vanpools).

Unfortunately, there are no comprehensive data sources that provide national statistics on paratransit ridership, so defining the existing mobility role of paratransit is largely guesswork. It is thought to be fairly small in the larger scheme of things. Supply-side statistics provide some insights. Nationwide, there were 16,471 demand-responsive vehicles (mainly vans), 19,491 intercity buses, and some 32,000 taxicabs in operation in 1990; in total, then, there were around 68,000 (mainly private-sector) vehicles that fall into our definition of paratransit. This, however, is a small fraction of the 143.5 million registered automobiles, 59,500 public buses, and 380,000 school buses that operated in 1990 (U.S. Department of Transportation, 1995). In 1992, 79 million unlinked trips were served by demand-responsive vehicles operated or contracted by public transit agencies, or a little less than 1 percent of the 8.52 billion total transit trips made that year. Last, the Nationwide Personal Transportation Survey (NPTS) provides travel diaries on trips by members of some 45,000 randomly sample U.S. households. Last conducted in 1990, NPTS records trips by type of vehicle and trip purpose, although there is no way to separate out trips by private, public, or for-hire vehicles. Table 1.2 shows the distribution of 1990 trips by three passenger vehicles that include commercial paratransit carriers—passenger vans, bus transit, and taxis—as well as all other modes (mainly private automobiles), broken down by trip purpose. For work trips, a significant share of passenger

Table 1.1.
Typology of Paratransit Services

	Service Types	Service Config- uration	Typical Passen- ger Loads	Primary Markets	Typical Regula- tory Juris- diction	Degree of Regula- tory Restric- tiveness
Commercial Services						
•*Shared-Ride Taxis*	On demand, hail request	Many-to-many	3-4	Downtown, airports, train stations	City	High
•*Dial-a-ride*						
–Specialized	On demand, phone request	Many-to-many	6-10	Elderly, handi-capped, poor	City/ State	Low
–Airport Shuttles	On demand, phone & hail request	Few-to-one	6-10	Air travelers	State	Low to moderate
•*Jitneys*						
–Circulators	Regular route, fixed stops	Fixed route/ loop (one to one)	6-15	Employees, low income, specialized	City	Moderate to high
–Transit feeders	Regular route, hail request	Many-to-one	6-15	Employees, low income	City	Moderate to high
–Areawide	Semi-regular route, hail request	Many-to-many	6-15	Low income, recent immi-grants	City	Moderate to high
•*Commuter Vans*	Pre-arranged, scheduled	Few-to-one	10-60	Commuters	State	Low
Employer- and Developer-Sponsored Services						
•*Shuttles*	Pre-arranged, regular route	Fixed route/ loop (often one-to-one)	15-30	Commuters, students	Local/ State	Low
•*Vanpools*	Pre-arranged, scheduled	Many-to-one	6-15	Commuters	State	Low
•*Buspools*	Pre-arranged, scheduled	Few-to-one	30-60	Commuters	State	Low

van travel likely includes employer-sponsored vanpools and more informal, shared-ride arrangements. The vast majority of bus transit commutes occurred on publicly owned and operated vehicles. Taxis handled only around 1 in 1,000 motorized trips in 1990. Excluding vanpools, the share of nationwide commercial paratransit trips is probably not much higher than this number. Of course, within metropolitan areas, paratransit's role is more significant, and in a few large

Table 1.2.
Distribution of Motorized Trips in United States Metropolitan Areas
by Modes That Include Commercial Paratransit Carriers and by Trip Purpose, 1991

	Work	Shop	Social/ Recreation	Other	All Types
Passenger Van	4.0	4.7	5.4	5.8	5.2
Bus Transit	2.2	0.8	0.8	1.3	1.4
Taxi	0.2	0.1	0.2	0.2	0.2
Other Modes	93.6	94.4	92.7	92.7	93.2
Total	100.0	100.0	100.0	100.0	100.0

Source: 1990-91 Nationwide Personal Transportation Survey, Data Files

east coast cities, notably New York and Miami, paratransit's market share of total trips is thought to be as high as 2 to 3 percent.

Shared-Ride Services

Shared-ride taxis, dial-a-ride vans, and jitneys comprise a class of paratransit services that carry moderate passenger loads and are demand responsive. A basic distinction is how demand is served: shared-ride taxis respond to either phone or curbside requests, dial-a-ride vans typically require phone reservations, and jitneys respond only to curbside hails.

Shared-Ride Taxis

While governments have over the years been quite solicitous of carpools and vanpools, they have generally been reluctant to extend the ride-sharing concept to taxis by allowing them to pick up more than one party. Whether taxis can serve multiple passengers is a local prerogative since taxi permits are almost universally regulated at the municipal level. Shared-ride taxis flourished in Washington, D.C., during World War II, when cab drivers displayed destination signs in their front windows and folks along the route would hail the cabs going their way. Riders saved money, drivers got multiple fares for a single trip, and scarce wartime resources were efficiently used. In 1974, Washington again adopted a version of taxi ride-sharing, primarily in response to gasoline shortages, and has retained the program ever since. In Southern California, shared-ride taxi services are restricted to downtown Los Angeles and Burbank.[7] Atlanta and Boston likewise permit downtown taxi-sharing. New York City allows shared-ride taxis only at taxistands, and taxipooling from downtown to airports occurs in Chicago, Denver, Seattle, and several other cities. Outside Washington, D.C., ride-sharing makes up a minuscule portion of taxi trips in most U.S. cities, partly because these programs are not widely marketed.

As in Washington, D.C., use of the shared-ride concept outside of downtown requires some price decontrols to allow flat or zonal fares rather than distance metering so that riders are not overcharged when drivers deviate from a route to drop off other customers. Since some passengers would prefer to avoid even modest delays caused by picking up other fares, a mix of exclusive-ride and shared-ride taxis is the best way to satisfy the riding public's preferences.

U.S. experiences with substituting shared-ride taxis for fixed-route bus services on a contract basis have been encouraging. In Phoenix, the local transit authority contracted with a taxi company to replace minimal-level Sunday fixed-route bus services in the early 1980s—an arrangement that saved over $700,000 in the first year. In the Norfolk–Virginia Beach area, shared-ride taxis that replaced poorly patronized bus routes in suburban and semi-rural areas led to a $16 per hour cost savings (Becker and Echols, 1983). These costs savings stemmed from using lower paid, usually nonunionized, drivers as well as the relaxation of restrictive work rules.

Dial-a-Ride Vans

Dial-a-ride vans operate just like shared-ride taxis except vehicles are bigger (normally 6 to 12 seats) and customers typically request rides by telephone instead of curbside hail. Dial-a-ride vans gained popularity in the 1970s when the Urban Mass Transportation Administration (UMTA) sponsored over 20 demonstration programs in typically small cities like Davenport, Iowa, and El Cajon, California. These services proved to be costly per passenger relative to shared-ride taxis because their drivers earned more per hour and average loads were light. In some cases, a travel voucher program was set up to give senior citizens, disabled individuals, and other participants a choice of whether to travel by bus, shared-ride taxi, or dial-a-van. Such user-side subsidies are an efficient way to underwrite the travel expense of the transportation needy while also promoting healthy competition among different service-providers. While human services agencies and community-based organizations still operate door-to-door van services throughout the United States, over time many of these services have been consolidated within a regional transit authority. With the passage of the Americans with Disabilities Act (ADA) in 1990, dial-a-ride services sponsored by public transit agencies (usually on a contractual basis) jumped from 14,610 vans carrying 59 million passengers in 1984 to 23,220 vans hauling 75 million passengers in 1993 (American Public Transit Association, 1995). The Orange County Transportation Association operates one of the largest publicly sponsored dial-a-ride van service in the country, serving mainly elderly, disabled, and low-income individuals with several hundred vans on a contractual basis. Pace Transit, serving the suburbs and exurbs of the Chicago region, also contracts out dial-a-ride services available to the general public in over 20 townships.

The most successful commercial dial-a-ride operations in the United States are the private shuttle vans that serve mainly airports but sometimes also other

depots like train stations and ferry terminals. Competing private companies provide on-call, door-to-door service between airports and a handful of destinations,
at fares about half that of exclusive-ride taxis. The pioneer provider of airport
van service is SuperShuttle International, which first began running vans to the
Los Angeles International Airport in 1985. Today, the company has expanded
operations to metropolitan San Diego, San Francisco–Oakland, and Sacramento
on the West Coast, Dallas and Miami in the Sunbelt, and Philadelphia and Baltimore on the East Coast, operating over 700 vans and 100 sedans.[8] In 1992,
SuperShuttle served about 110,000 passenger trips a month in Southern California with a fleet of 170 vans, cornering around 45 percent of the shared-ride airport ground transportation market.

Because of SuperShuttle's success, numerous imitators, mainly independent
owner-operators, have entered Southern California's airport shuttle market, in
large part because California's Public Utility Commission relaxed restrictions on
market entry. Between 1987 and 1991, for example, the number of firms providing van service to Los Angeles's international airport (LAX) and the Burbank
airport jumped from 16 to 38. Some problems of overcompetition (e.g., battles
over curb space, complaints of nonpickups, overcharging) resulted, however,
prompting airport authorities to enforce more stringent rules (e.g., mandatory
queues, fines, etc.). Still, less than 1 percent of shuttle van passengers have filed
complaints to California's Public Utilities Commission. Overall, airport shuttle
operators have managed to carve out a large but unserved market niche: people
who don't want to drive to the airport and want a gap-bridger between public
transportation and taxi-limousine services.

Jitneys and Commercial Vans

Jitneys further extend the shared-ride concept by carrying up to 15 passengers,[9] usually in a van or station wagon, over a semifixed route on a fairly
regular basis. Jitneys typically operate along major thoroughfares, make numerous pickups and drop-offs anywhere along a route, and, sometimes for an extra
charge, will make a slight detour to take someone to their front door. Popular
early in this century, jitneys were banned in most U.S. cities around World War I,
victims of trolley operators' charges of cream skimming and unfair competition
(Eckert and Hilton, 1972).

From a service standpoint, jitneys are essentially mini versions of standard
line-haul, fixed-route bus services; besides being privately operated and using
smaller vehicles, they differ from most line-haul services in that they stop anywhere along a route, don't follow a set schedule, and will make slight route
deviations. Relative to conventional bus routes, jitneys tend to come by more
frequently and stop less often since vehicles are smaller.

Maria Lombardo (1994) has defined five different, though not mutually
exclusive, functions performed by jitneys. Jitneys can act as *capacity enhancers*,
helping to relieve overcrowding and passenger overflow (i.e., passengers left at

the bus stop when buses are full). They can also function as *service extenders*, such as providing additional services in low-density areas where existing bus operations fall below minimal standards set by transit authorities. As capacity enhancers or service extenders, jitneys would typically be competitively bid by a public transit operator, as they currently are in Houston. A third role is as a *transit feeder*, typically connecting residential areas to crosstown bus or rail routes, or connecting transit stops to workplaces, shopping malls, and campuses. A fourth role is providing *community-based transit*, connecting residents of lower-income neighborhoods to medical centers, shopping stores, community centers, and other destinations not too far away. The final function is jitneys that operate as *activity center connectors*, circulating in and around employment centers, shopping malls, sports stadia, tourist attractions, and so on. In practice, these last three functions—transit feeders, community-based transit, and activity center connectors—are normally performed by commercial (e.g., noncontracted) jitney operators and are not always legal.

Table 1.1 defines jitney services slightly differently, according to how services are configured and the kinds of markets served. These three more generic types of jitney services collapse together some of the categories identified by Lombardo, as discussed above. One basic type of jitney is a circulator, which typically follows a fixed, circular route within a neighborhood or activity center. Most community-based jitneys operating in poor neighborhoods are circulators, looping between residences, shops, and other destinations. Atlantic City's jitneys, the nation's oldest publicly sanctioned operation, also function as circulators, running mainly up and down Pacific Avenue, ferrying workers, tourists, and others to nearby casinos, restaurants, and shops. A second basic type of jitney service functions as transit feeders, providing a many-to-one service—that is, connecting multiple origins to a single place. Rail systems in Miami, San Francisco, San Jose, and San Diego feature privately operated jitney vans that funnel to and from transit stations, mainly during commuting hours.

The final class is what I call areawide jitneys, normally operating between multiple origins and destinations within a subregion on a fairly regular basis. In many third-world cities, most jitney services are many-to-many and areawide. In the United States, New York and Miami have the most extensive areawide jitney-van services, serving mainly recent immigrant populations from the West Indies. Demand for these services is so great that most operate illegally and often openly. New York City's thriving commercial jitney industry is run mainly by Caribbean immigrants for Caribbean immigrants. Some vans operate between housing projects in the Queens and rail terminuses, while others haul commuters throughout the five boroughs, including Manhattan. Surveys show that 95 percent of New York's jitney passengers are former transit riders who value having a guaranteed seat and speedy, dependable services (Mitchell, 1992). Many independent "gypsies" are un- or underinsured, do not meet vehicle driver certification requirements, and adjust fares according to perceived market demands. Some are predatory, picking up radio calls and stealing prospective customers

from authorized taxis. Political pressure to crack down on these illegal operators ebbs and flows; however, for the most part authorities have tended to look
the other way rather than openly confront them.

Commuter Vans and Buspools

In contrast to other commercial shared-ride modes, commuter vans and buses
provide prearranged, scheduled services and are usually targeted at large employment sites, in particular downtown white- and pink-collar office districts. Like a
traditional employer-based vanpool, commuter buses provide few (origins) to one
(destination) services; yet because they rely on paid drivers, they tend to cost
more per passenger trip than vanpools. (Some commuter vans and buses serve
multiple work sites and thus are technically few-to-few.) Commuter services
tend to be quite posh, with riders enjoying comfortable seats with headrests,
ample leg room, and a temperature-controlled environ. For this, they pay premium fares, sometimes as high as $15 per day. Compared with the cost and
stress of driving during congested periods and paying for downtown parking,
however, most patrons feel commuter vans and buses are a bargain.

Many commercial vanpools and buspools serve planned communities, like
Reston in northern Virginia, Columbia between Baltimore and Washington, D.C.,
and the Woodlands, north of Houston. In the case of the Woodlands, over 15
percent of employed residents got to work by commuter bus or vanpools in
1990, many on Houston's extensive HOV network. Southern California has the
nation's largest supply of private, unsubsidized commuter bus services. At its
height in the late 1980s, over a dozen private carriers operated nearly 100 commuter runs each workday, many focused on large aerospace and high-technology
employment centers in western Los Angeles and the San Fernando Valley (e.g.,
Warner Center, Burbank Media District). Some of the largest companies operate routes of 30 to 50 miles in length. Commuter bus operators have been able to
turn a profit because they utilize labor more productively (e.g., providing charter
services during off-peak hours) and pay lower compensation rates than Southern
California public transit agencies. In addition, private drivers typically receive
no split-time premiums or guaranteed pay, and far fewer fringe benefits than their
public sector counterparts.

Unlike most commercial paratransit services, state rather than local regulatory
authorities maintain jurisdiction over intercity common-carrier van and bus services. Prospective commuter van and bus operators must first obtain a certificate
of "public convenience and necessity" from state regulators before initiating
services. When competing bus services exist, or another operator alleges unfair
competition, in many cases the new entrant must demonstrate that existing
services are inadequate to serve the market, or that a new operation will in some
way materially improve quality of services. Transit agencies often jealously
protect their service territories, even when new services do not constitute a direct
threat. Local transit, taxi, and intercity bus competitors are usually involved in

the review of service applications, and any one of the reviewers can often protest loudly enough to block market entry. Private van and bus operators are also at a competitive disadvantage when public transit agencies preempt the best markets. And in spite of their substantially lower costs, many private providers have a hard time competing with transit fares that cover only 30 to 40 percent of operating costs (and often just 10 to 20 percent of full costs, including capital depreciation). Proposed cuts in federal transit subsidies, however, could over time reduce these fiscal distortions.

Employer- and Developer-sponsored Shuttles, Vanpools, and Bus Services

Because they are promoted by state and federal air quality and transportation legislation, employer- and developer-sponsored shuttles, vanpools, and bus services are the least regulated and encumbered of all paratransit services. Employer-based vans and buses almost exclusively serve commuter markets and connect to a single workplace destination. Normally, the driver is one of the commuters, and receives no pay or a modest sum; this holds down costs. (Employer vanpools are also immune to the high unit costs associated with diurnal peaking of work trips since no split-time pay penalties are incurred.) In exchange, drivers normally are allowed personal use of vehicles during evenings and on weekends. Employer-based vans and buses are often sponsored by large firms, office parks, and Transportation Management Associations (TMAs); pooling workforces is sometimes necessary in forming a critical mass of workers who live close enough to each other to allow efficient routing and scheduling.

In response to Regulation XV trip reduction requirement (mandated by the South Coast Air Quality Management District), commercial vanpools have proliferated in Southern California during the past decade. In 1994, Commuter Transportation Services, Inc. (CTS),[10] a nonprofit corporation that provides ride-matching services, monitored over 2,000 vanpools in the region. Over 50 Southern California employers with 1,000 or more workers currently underwrite the costs of employee vanpools. Another form of employer-sponsored paratransit are shuttle vans that connect rail stations to work sites. In the San Francisco Bay Area, over 100 employer-sponsored shuttle vans tie into transit stations on the BART heavy rail system, Santa Clara County light-rail system, and CalTrain commuter rail system each workday. Nine different light-rail shuttle runs in Santa Clara County carry around 20,000 passengers daily, making up 5 percent of all rail access trips in the county. In other parts of the country, notably Montgomery County, Maryland, and central New Jersey, private developers have financed shuttles as a precondition to acquiring building permits.

In most states, employer- and developer-sponsored vanpools seating 15 or fewer passengers and operated by a driver headed to work are exempt from state certification requirements (as long as drivers have a chauffeur's license). States have jurisdiction, then, only when for-profit vanpools and subscription buses seek entry into the marketplace.

Nationwide, vehicle pooling has steadily lost its market share of work trips, falling from 20 percent in 1980 to just over 13 percent in 1990 (Pisarski, 1992). Among the factors eroding vanpooling's ridership base, and working against employer-sponsored programs in particular, are decentralization, especially of employment sites; declining average firm sizes (thus making ride-matching more difficult within firms); expansion of variable work hours (partly in response to local trip reduction requirements); part-time homeworking, which further complicates rematching; and the fact that most commutes are too short to attract vanpoolers. The only trend favorable to vanpooling is the increased mileage of HOV lanes, which grew from five miles (Bay Bridge and Lincoln tunnel) in 1970 to 378 centerlane miles in 1992 and is forecasted to exceed 900 centerlane miles in the year 2000 (Turnbull, 1992). The movement to create High-Occupancy Toll (HOT) lanes that allow free passage for vanpools (e.g., California's State Route 91, which opened between Riverside and Orange Counties in late 1995) could further stimulate the shuttle van sector in highly congested areas.

Commercial Paratransit

This book concentrates on the market opportunities and regulatory barriers related to what I call *commercial paratransit* and what others have called *entrepreneurial*, or *free-enterprise*, or *competitive paratransit*. The essence of commercial paratransit is the provision of unsubsidized, for-profit services by entrepreneurs or private firms that are open to the general public. Commercial paratransit, as I have defined it, then, excludes services competitively contracted by public transit agencies (and thus subsidized) as well as specialized and restricted services (e.g., exclusively for the elderly and handicapped or those mandated by the Americans with Disabilities, or ADA, Act). While commercial paratransit includes airport shuttle vans, I devote less attention to these services in this book since they are so well established and are in abundant supply. Technically, commercial paratransit does not include employer-sponsored or developer-supported services since these are normally restricted to employees or tenants and underwritten by firms. However, some employer-sponsored shuttle vans, particularly in Santa Clara County, California, do allow nonemployees to ride vans and involve no public subsidies. One might think of these as quasi-commercial paratransit services; as such, they are examined.

The focus of this work, then, is on nonairport, non-ADA, noncontracted, and non-employer-subsidized paratransit services—that is, shared-ride taxis, jitneys, private minibuses, dial-a-ride vans, and subscription van and bus services. These are services for which, I believe, there is a potentially large market demand that is suppressed by an overly restricted regulatory environment and market distortions. In particular, these services engender the kinds of features that would make them competitive with the private automobile in contemporary American life, especially to the degree that various market distortions (e.g., free parking, underpricing) are removed. They remain the "neglected options" identified by Ronald Kirby et al. (1974) in their seminal book on paratransit, *Paratransit: Neglected Options for Urban Mobility.*

In sum, paratransit represents a host of hybrid modes between the extremes of a taxi and a conventional bus. While paratransit encompasses the many options identified in Table 1.1, commercial paratransit refers to a more limited subset—competitive, free-enterprise services that are open to the general public.

EXPERIENCES WITH PARATRANSIT DEREGULATION

A central premise of this work is that America's commercial paratransit sector has been stymied by overregulation and market distortions. Several important studies have been conducted on the effects of regulatory reforms in America's taxi and jitney sectors as well as mass transit services, in general, in other countries, especially Great Britain. This section briefly highlights the key findings of these earlier studies.

Taxi and Jitney Deregulation

In the late 1970s and early 1980s, 22 U.S. cities experimented with taxi entry and fare deregulation. Also, San Diego, Los Angeles, Indianapolis, and several other cities allowed jitney services to be introduced. Most taxi reforms involved lifting or significantly raising the ceiling on taxi permits. These cities permitted ride-sharing in taxis, along with the introduction of zonal fares. Some cities also allowed exclusive-ride fares to vary. Taxi operators and transit interests fought these open-door policies, though to no avail owing to strong political leadership.

Several studies carried out in the 1980s evaluated the impacts of regulatory reforms in some cities.[11] In almost every setting, the number of firms and cab service hours increased markedly following deregulation. Between 1979 and 1983, for instance, the total number of cab permits increased by 128 percent in San Diego, 30 percent in Seattle, and around 12 percent in Portland (Oregon). Small cab companies and private owner-operators proliferated the most. In Seattle, for instance, small fleets (those with 4 to 13 cabs) increased in number from 9 to 23, whereas the share of cabs held by the three largest firms declined from 70 percent to 54 percent.

More cabs generally meant more and better service (in particular, shorter waits, fewer nonresponses to phone requests, and cleaner vehicles). Total weekly hours of cab service in San Diego, for example, increased 26 percent during the first four years after deregulation. Passenger waits at major cabstands virtually disappeared in all three places. Average waits for San Diego's radio-dispatched cabs, moreover, fell from 10 minutes to 8 minutes in the first two years of deregulation. Decontrol also led to greater market specialization, with many smaller and newer operators concentrating on hail and long-haul business and the largest and older companies going after the phone-request and package-delivery business.

Overall, fares remained essentially unchanged (in real dollars) following deregulation in most cities. In Seattle, price decontrols led to a variety of fare structures being introduced, including off-peak discounts and cut rates for repeat, advanced-reservation customers. Contrary to some fears, there were relatively few incidences of cabbies redlining or refusing to serve minority neighborhoods in U.S. cities with deregulated taxicab markets. Overall, free competition helped drive down or stabilize the costs of fares in high-volume business segments, but in some instances led to sharp fare increases for low-density areas or night services. Since most poor people reside in relatively high-density neighborhoods, the net incidence of fare decontrols was probably progressive (in terms of transfer effects among income groups).

San Diego's experiences with legalized jitneys were initially fairly successful (see Chapter 2 for more details). Between 1979 and 1983, 15 jitney companies, owning a total of 48 licensed vehicles and serving nearly 12,000 weekly customers, had entered the market. San Diego's new jitneys operated mainly on streets paralleling the light-rail trolley system (that opened in 1981) and main bus routes, concentrating on commercial strips, military bases, and tourist spots, such as hotels and airports. San Diego's jitneys and shared-ride taxis were allowed to set any fare they wanted, so long as they posted them in two-inch lettering in the front windows. For a five-mile trip from the airport to downtown San Diego, jitney fares remained about three-quarters cheaper than exclusive-ride taxi fares.

The most significant problem with taxicab and jitney deregulation in these cities was isolated incidences of price gouging, particularly at airports, where tourists unaccustomed with local taxi services were easy prey. In response, Seattle, San Diego, and several other cities reinstituted fare ceilings for airport cab services, and some cities placed moratoria on new cab permits altogether. Gradually, restrictions on taxicab supplies and pricing were reintroduced in many cases in response to complaints from established cab companies, transit authorities, and business merchants. Because of complaints from the local hospitality industry and tourist operators, during the mid- to late 1980s, San Diego officials suspended the issuance of new jitney licenses and began reregulating what a decade earlier was the most unrestricted, free-enterprise taxi market in the country.

Overall, all but 4 of the 22 U.S. cities that deregulated taxis in the late 1970s and early 1980s have since reregulated services, generally imposing limits on market entry and setting fare ceilings. Because of the market imperfections and ridership profiles that are unique to the taxi industry (e.g., numerous out-of-town customers), one study concluded that government regulations are necessary to ensure fair pricing and adequate service quality (Price Waterhouse, 1994).

Deregulation of Bus Services in Great Britain

Great Britain has pursued the most sweeping bus transit regulatory reforms to date. As a centerpiece of the Margaret Thatcher administration's privatization initiatives, there was nearly a complete deregulation of local bus fares, services, and controls over market entry and exit in all regions of the country except greater London, beginning in 1985. Also, publicly owned bus companies that had dominated local bus services were reorganized as separate for-profit corporations. The overarching goal was to create a market environment that was competitive, or at least contestable,[12] so that any monopoly profits or protection would be limited, if not eliminated.

Within several years of Britain's deregulation of local transit, the threat of contestable markets prodded most old-guard bus companies to significantly cut costs, mainly by changing work rules and winning wage concessions (typically two-tier wage scales with lower rates for newly hired drivers). Within the first full year of deregulation, total bus mileage in the nation had increased by 3.3 percent (Gomez-Ibanez and Meyer, 1990). Deregulation also stimulated new market-oriented services and innovations, in particular expansion of 12- to 25-seat minibuses. Where big buses were replaced by minibuses, customers were generally rewarded with more frequent and faster service without having to pay more (in large part because minibus drivers earned less). Not all areas of the nation enjoyed expanded services, however; as opponents of reforms had predicted, services during off-peak hours and in low-density areas fell following deregulation. Local authorities, however, typically contracted to restore services in areas bypassed by commercial operators (Balcombe et al., 1988).

On average, fares rose faster than inflation following deregulation, leading to a decline in ridership of 14 percent compared to prederegulation levels (Gomez-Ibanez and Meyer, 1993). Although many of the large incumbents suffered financial loses in the first year of deregulation, within several years most were turning a profit. And while some privatized bus services are still subsidized in Britain, proving that competition and subsidies can coexist, the prospect of government support seems to have promoted innovations by providing a protected niche for new entrants to test the waters and experiment with new services.

WHAT'S AHEAD

This book is organized as follows. The remainder of Part 1 examines the service, market, and performance features of commercial paratransit, both in the United States and abroad. Chapters 2 and 3 define commercial paratransit's market niches and experiences with unregulated services in a dozen or so U.S. cities. Both chapters also explore the market economics of paratransit—that is, aspects of demand, supply, and costs. The second chapter focuses on three of the more traditional forms of commercial paratransit available to the general public—shared-ride taxis, jitneys, and commercial vans. Detailed case studies are presented for these services in San Francisco–Berkeley, San Diego, Atlantic City, Miami, and New York City. Chapter 3 examines more specialized forms of commercial paratransit, like subscription vanpools, casual carpools, employer-sponsored shuttles, child transportation, and community-based car service. Chapter 4 reviews experiences with free-enterprise paratransit where they are most prolific—mainly in the developing countries of Asia and Latin America—and also addresses the prospect of transferring lessons from these places to the U.S. and other industrialized countries.

Part 2 of the book looks at commercial paratransit from a different angle—how regulations and public policies in the United States have shaped, and to a large degree, suppressed, the industry. Chapter 5 examines the legal, economic, and philosophical foundations for regulating private common-carrier passenger services in the U.S. Chapters 6 and 7 review and critique the existing regulatory and policy environments affecting commercial paratransit at the local and state government levels, respectively. Chapter 8 extends the analysis to the federal government level.

Part 3 looks to the future, probing the most promising frontiers for stimulating commercial paratransit in the United States. Chapter 9 explores how advanced communications technologies might be adapted to vans and minibuses to create *smart paratransit* services. Chapter 10 concludes the book by summarizing the salient findings of the study, suggesting policy reforms and discussing the implications of reforms on future paratransit practice.

NOTES

1. The time savings benefits of minibuses are partially offset by the longer time it normally takes to embark and disembark, because of higher steps and narrower entrances on minibuses.

2. A car with a cold catalytic converter emits significantly more than when the converter warms up. When the engine is turned off, fuel evaporates until the engine cools down, producing "hot soak" emissions. Cold start and hot soak emissions are independent of distance, meaning they account for a proportionally large share of emissions for short trips, such as to rail stations. For a 10-mile trip, the average 1987 model car emitted 17 grams of HC: 9 grams during the cold start, 2 grams during the hot soak, and 6 grams of running emissions. Halving the trip to five miles halves only the running emissions; total emissions are still 14 grams. Thus, halving VMT cuts emissions by only 18 percent (Kessler and Schroeer, 1995).

3. Because of mounting political pressure, high implementation costs (around $240 per employee per year), and growing resentment of unfunded federal mandates, the Los Angeles area repealed employer-based trip reduction requirements in late 1995, opting for more voluntary, market-based initiatives instead. Studies showed that mandatory trip reduction requirements were ineffective. A study of Southern California's Regulation XV employee trip reduction requirement, for instance, found only a small overall reduction

in single-occupant commuting (a 0.4 percent decline in private car miles driven) and no increase in public transit ridership (Wachs, 1993).

4. This study used total annual cost (operating cost plus annualized capital expenditures) of each transit mode, divided by the total number of passenger miles by that mode in 1985.

5. The taxi industry has some of the hallmarks of a natural monopoly. For smaller firms with fewer than 30 vehicles, there are likely no appreciable economies of scale with respect to costs. Larger firms, on the other hand, may be able to achieve some economies by computerizing record keeping and developing more extensive in-house maintenance capabilities. These economies are likely to be small, however (Gilbert and Samuels, 1982).

6. Of course, private entrepreneurs do not seek out money-losing services. Rather, they are in a position to operate services at a profit that might otherwise incur a deficit if operated by the public sector. Transit agencies resist giving up peak-hour, highly patronized services since these generate the highest farebox returns, even though studies consistently show the marginal cost of peak services are proportionally even higher (Lee and Steedman, 1970; Morlok and Viton, 1980; Cervero, 1982).

7. Since 1991, the city of Los Angeles has allowed all 1,350 registered taxicabs in the city to carry up to four passengers, including unrelated parties, within a defined area of downtown for a flat $3.50 fare. The city of Burbank has initiated a similar program, charging a flat $3.50 for shared-ride taxi services within city limits.

8. To minimize travel time, SuperShuttle limits pickup or delivery stops to no more than three per one-way trips. Inbound trips to the airport require an advanced telephone reservation; outbound trips may be either prescheduled or on demand, depending on the policies of the local airport.

9. Some jitneys use minibuses that seat up to 25 passengers, though these are more the exception than the rule. Because of the many slight variations across jitney operations, jitneys defy any precise definition.

10. In 1995, CTS was taken over by the Southern California Association of Governments, the regional planning organization for the greater Los Angeles–Orange County area.

11. See Frankena and Paulter (1984), Gelb (1983, 1984), Cervero (1984, 1985), Zerbe (1983), and Reinke (1986).

12. Economists argue that in order to create a competitive market, it is not always necessary that there be multiple competitors, but rather that incumbents believe that a challenger could easily enter their markets—that is, markets are contestable.

REFERENCES

American Public Transit Association. 1995. *1994–1994 Transit Fact Book*. Washington, D.C.: APTA.

Balcombe, R., J. Hopkin, and K. Perrett. 1988. *Bus Deregulation in Great Britain: A Review of the First Year*. Crowthorne, England: Transport and Road Research Laboratory, U.K. Department of Transportation, Research Report 161.

Banister, D., and R. Mackett. 1990. "The Minibus: Theory and Experience, and Their Implications." *Transport Reviews* 10(3): 189-214.

Becker, A., and J. Echols. 1983. "Paratransit at a Transit Agency: The Experience in Norfolk, Virginia." *Transportation Research Record* 914: 49-57.

Benke, R. 1993. *German "Smart Bus" System: Potential Application in Portland, Oregon.* Washington, D.C.: Federal Transit Administration, U.S. Department of Transportation.

California Air Resources Board. 1989. *The Air Pollution–Transportation Linkage.* Sacramento: CARB.

Cameron, M. 1991. *Transportation Efficiency: Tackling Southern California's Air Pollution and Congestion.* Los Angeles: Environmental Defense Fund and the Regional Institute of Southern California.

Cervero, R. 1982. "Transit Cross Subsidies." *Transportation Quarterly* 36(2): 377-389.

———. 1983. "Cost and Performance Effects of Transit Operating Subsidies in the United States." *International Journal of Transport Economics* 10(3): 535-562.

———. 1984. "Revitalizing Urban Transit: More Money or Less Regulation?" *Regulation* 8(3): 36-42.

———. 1985. "Deregulating Urban Transportation." *The Cato Journal* 5(1): 219-238.

———. 1988. *Transit Service Contracting: Cream-Skimming or Deficit-Skimming?* Washington, D.C.: Urban Mass Transportation Administration, U.S. Department of Transportation.

———. 1995. *Rail Access Modes and Catchment Areas for the BART System.* Berkeley: Institute of Urban and Regional Development, Monograph No. 50.

Congressional Budget Office. 1988. *New Directions for the Nation's Public Works.* Washington, D.C.: U.S. Congress, Congressional Budget Office.

Eckert, R., and G. Hilton. 1972. "The Jitneys." *Journal of Law and Economics* 15(2): 293-325.

Federal Highway Administration. 1995. *Our Nation's Highways.* Washington, D.C.: Federal Highway Administration, U.S. Department of Transportation.

Frankena, M., and P. Paulter. 1984. *An Economic Analysis of Taxicab Regulation.* Washington, D.C.: Bureau of Economics, Federal Trade Commission.

Gelb, P. 1983. *Effects of Taxi Regulatory Revision in Seattle, Washington.* Washington, D.C.: Urban Mass Transportation Administration, U.S. Department of Transportation.

———. 1983. *Effects of Taxi Regulatory Revision in San Diego, California.* Washington, D.C.: Urban Mass Transportation Administration, U.S. Department of Transportation.

———. 1984. *Effects of Taxi Regulatory Revision in Portland, Oregon: A Case Study.* Washington, D.C.: Urban Mass Transportation Administration, U.S. Department of Transportation.

Gilbert, G., and R. Samuels. 1982. *The Taxicab: An Urban Transportation Survivor.* Chapel Hill: University of North Carolina Press.

Glaister, S. 1986. "Bus Deregulation, Competition and Vehicle Size." *Journal of Transport Economics and Policy* 20(2): 217-244.

Gomez-Ibanez, J., and J. Meyer. 1990. "Privatizing and Deregulating Local Public Services: Lessons from Britain's Buses." *Journal of the American Planning Association* 56(1): 9-21.

———. 1993. *Going Private: The International Experience with Transport Privatization.* Washington, D.C.: The Brookings Institution.

Ihlanfeldt, K., and D. Sjoquist. 1989. "The Impact of Job Decentralization on the Economic Welfare of Central City Blacks." *Journal of Urban Economics* 26: 110-130.

Johnson, E. 1993. *Avoiding the Collision of Cities and Cars: Urban Transportation Policy for the Twenty-first Century*. Chicago: American Academy of Arts and Sciences.

Kahn, A. 1971. *The Economics of Regulation: Principles and Institutions*. New York: John Wiley and Sons.

Kain, J. 1994. "The Spatial Mismatch Hypothesis: Three Decades Later." *Housing Policy Debate* 3(2): 371-460.

Keough, M. 1989. *Scale Economies Among United States Bus Transit Systems*. Washington, D.C.: Urban Mass Transportation Administration, U.S. Department of Transportation.

Kessler, J., and W. Schroeer. 1995. "Meeting Mobility and Air Quality Goals: Strategies That Work." *Transportation* 22: 241-272.

Kirby, R., K. Bhatt, M. Kemp, R. McGillivray, and M. Wohl. 1974. *Paratransit: Neglected Options for Urban Mobility*. Washington, D.C.: The Urban Institute.

Kirby, R., M. Tagell, and K. Ogden. 1986. "Traffic Management in Metro Manila: Formulating Traffic Policies." *Traffic Engineering and Control* 27(5): 262-269.

Lave, C. 1991. "Measuring the Decline in Transit Productivity in the U.S." *Transportation Planning and Technology* 15(2/4): 312-326.

Lee, N., and I. Steedman. 1970. "Economies of Scale in Bus Transportation." *Journal of Transport Economics and Policy* 4: 15-28.

Lombardo, M. 1994. *The Potential for Jitneys in Los Angeles*. Los Angeles: University of California, School of Urban Planning, Master's Thesis.

Lomax, T., D. Bullard, and J. Hanks. 1991. *The Impact of Declining Mobility in Major Texas and Other U.S. Cities*. Austin: State Department of Highways and Public Transportation, Texas Transportation Institute, Research Report 431-1F.

MacKenzie, J., R. Dower, and D. Chen. 1992. *The Going Rate: What It Really Costs to Drive*. New York: World Resources Institute.

Mayworm, P., A. Lago, and J. McEnroe. 1980. *Patronage Impacts of Changes in Transit Fares and Services*. Washington, D.C.: Urban Mass Transportation Administration, U.S. Department of Transportation.

Mitchell, A. 1992. "Illegal Vans Fight Strong Guerrilla War for New York's Streets." *New York Times* (January 24): A16.

Morgridge, M. 1983. "The Jakarta Traffic Management Study: Impact of High Paratransit Flows." *Traffic Engineering and Control* 24(9): 441-448.

Morlok, E., and P. Viton. 1980. "Self-sustaining Public Transportation Services." *Transportation Policy and Decision Making* 1: 169-194.

Pickrell, D. 1985. "Rising Deficits and the Uses of Transit Subsidies in the United States." *Journal of Transport Economics and Policy* 19(3): 281-298.

Pisarski, A. 1992. *New Perspectives on Commuting*. Washington, D.C.: U.S. Department of Transportation, Federal Highway Administration.

Poole, R., and M. Griffin. 1994. *Shuttle Vans: The Overlooked Transit Alternative*. Los Angeles: Reason Foundation, Policy Study No. 176.

Prentice, R. 1987. "Minibuses or Conventional Buses? *Buses* 39(391): 441-443.

Price Waterhouse. 1994. *Shedding Light on Reinventing Government*. Washington, D.C.: Price Waterhouse.

Pucher, J. 1995. "Urban Passenger Transport in the United States and Europe: A Comparative Analysis of Public Policies: Part 2, Public Transport, Overall Comparisons and Recommendations." *Transport Reviews* 15(3): 211-227.

Reinke, D. 1986. "Update on Taxicab and Jitney Reregulation in San Diego." *Transportation Research Record* 1103: 9-11.

Roth, G., and G. Wynne. 1982. *Learning from Abroad: Free Enterprise Urban Transportation*. New Brunswick, New Jersey: Transaction Books.

Rowand, R. 1989. "You Sit, and You Wait, and You Boil." *Automotive News* (December): 25.

Sale, J., and B. Green. 1978. "Operating Costs and Performance of American Transit Systems." *Journal of the American Planning Association* 44(2): 22-27.

Small, K., and C. Kazimi. 1994. "On the Costs of Air Pollution from Motor Vehicles." Berkeley: University of California Transportation Center, Working Paper 237.

Suzuki, P. 1995. "Unregulated Taxicabs." *Transportation Quarterly* 49(1): 129-138.

Talley, W. 1990. "Paratransit Services, Contracting-Out and Cost Savings for Public Transit Firms. A Firm Specific Analysis." *Transportation Planning and Technology* 15: 13-25.

Turnbull, K. 1992. *An Assessment of High Occupancy Vehicle (HOV) Facilities in North America*. Washington, D.C.: Federal Transit Administration, U.S. Department of Transportation.

Urban Innovations Group. 1993. "Smart Shuttle Transit." Los Angeles: Southern California Association of Governments, Advanced Transportation Technology Task Force.

Urban Mobility Corporation. 1992. *The Miami Jitneys*. Washington, D.C.: Federal Transit Administration, U.S. Department of Transportation.

U.S. Department of Transportation. 1995. *National Transportation Statistics: 1995*. Washington, D.C.: Bureau of Transportation Statistics, U.S. Department of Transportation.

Viton, P. 1981. "A Translog Cost Function for Urban Bus Transit." *Journal of Industrial Economics* 29(3): 287-304.

Wachs, M. 1993. "Learning from Los Angeles: Transport, Urban Form, and Air Quality." *Transportation* 20(4): 329-354.

Webber, M. 1994. "The Marriage of Autos & Transit: How to Make Transit Popular Again." *Access* 5: 26-31.

Wells, J., N. Asher, M. Flowers, and M. Kamran. 1972. *Economic Characteristics of the Urban Public Transportation Industry*. Washington, D.C.: Institute of the Defense.

Williams, M. 1979. "Firm Size and Operating Cost in Urban Bus Transportation." *Journal of Industrial Economics* 28(2): 209-218.

Zerbe, R. 1983. "Seattle Taxis: Deregulation Hits a Pothole." *Regulation* 7(6): 43-48.

CHAPTER 2

Shared-Ride Taxis, Jitneys, and Commercial Vans

INTRODUCTION

The paratransit options most widely available to the general public, though not in all U.S. cities, are shared-ride taxis, jitneys, and their related cousins, commercial vans. This chapter examines these modes in terms of their service and price features, market characteristics, and overall performance, using a case study approach. It is followed by Chapter 3, which carries out similar analyses for more specialized paratransit services, like subscription van and buspools, child transportation, dial-a-ride vans, and neighborhood-based services. In both of these chapters, case analyses aim to highlight the unique market niches and urban mobility gaps that these paratransit modes serve. In that these two chapters focus mainly on for-profit, free-enterprise services, the undercurrent of governmental regulatory and policy issues surrounding these services are also addressed, partly as an entree into more in-depth discussions on these issues later in the book.

Through case studies, it becomes evident that the distinctions between commercial paratransit services are often blurry. Some shared-ride taxis, for all intents and purposes, operate like jitneys. Some so-called jitney runs to train stops are virtually indistinguishable from shuttle van services. Informal neighborhood transportation services are a lot like shared-ride taxis. While there are always dangers in attempting to bound in what many ways is a continuum of paratransit services, boundaries are nonetheless drawn in this and the following chapter to help sift through and organize the evidence.

SHARED-RIDE TAXI SERVICE

In the hierarchy of paratransit service coverage, shared-ride taxis, with their potential to provide many-to-many services, stand at the very top. Today, taxi ridesharing is permitted in most large U.S. cities, though it is usually restricted to downtown cabstands and major transportation terminals, like airports and inter-city train stations. It really has only been during times of gasoline rationing, such as during the Second World War and the Arab oil embargo of 1973–74, that taxi ridesharing has occurred to any significant degree. Today, taxi ridesharing is fairly rare, and where it does occur, it is usually an informal arrangement between unrelated parties waiting at cabstands heading to the same destination, most often between downtowns and airports. Over the past 50 years, the only significant commercial shared-ride taxi service in the United States existed in Little Rock, Arkansas; outside of airport access trips, taxi ridesharing by unrelated individuals is today largely limited to certain niche markets, such as during commute hours in Washington, D.C., when cabs are in short supply and point-to-point connec-tions between rail stations and major activity centers, like Berkeley, California's shared-ride taxi connections to a nearby racetrack. Subsidized shared-ride taxi services were sponsored by the federal government as demonstration projects during the 1970s, but none of these services survived once subsidy support was withdrawn.[1] Today, a handful of areas, like suburban Chicago, still rely on subsi-dized shared-ride taxis, though only for highly specialized markets, like serving elderly and disabled individuals.

Overall, even in large cities where it is permitted, taxi ride-sharing makes up less than 1 percent of all taxi trips, in part because many customers are highly time sensitive and unwilling to endure extra delays, but also because few cities have zonal fare systems or allow flat fares to be changed other than to airports. Shared-ride taxi programs are also rarely aggressively marketed; thus, few customers are aware they can save money by hooking up with others. In parts of downtown Manhattan, Los Angeles, Chicago, and Atlanta, taxi ride-sharing makes up as much as 3 to 5 percent of all internal (i.e., within downtown) motorized trips.[2] In the early 1980s, several shared-ride taxis running services between Lindbergh Field and downtown San Diego were capturing around 2 to 3 percent of the airport ground transportation market. While people informally share taxi rides and split the fares to and from airports in all cities, this practice is today most common in cities like Los Angeles, Atlanta, San Francisco, and Denver, where flat fares are charged between downtowns and airports.[3]

Little Rock's Shared-Ride Taxis

From the early 1950s until 1981, Little Rock had the most extensive shared-ride taxi service in the country. Prior to this, Little Rock's taxis provided only exclusive-ride services using meters. After several local taxi operators went bankrupt, the city granted an exclusive franchise to Black and White Cab to serve a 150-square-mile area. Because no public transit services existed at the time of this reorganization, Black and White Cab petitioned for and was granted the right to provide shared-ride services 24 hours a day, 7 days a week, using 75 vehicles. Except for emergencies, no exclusive-ride services were offered. Later, a second company, Capital Cabs, was also granted a shared-ride taxi franchise, pushing the citywide supply of cabs to around 100 (or 1 taxi per 1,500 residents). To accommodate taxipooling, Little Rock introduced a 91-zone fare system, with zones generally increasing in size with distance from downtown. By the late 1970s, the fare for travelling within a single zone was $0.65, with each additional zone costing $0.35 to enter. The average trip traversed three zones, for a fare of $1.35 (1978 dollars). The typical taxi carried two to three passengers, meaning drivers were averaging $2.70 to $4.05 per trip, a fairly good income at the time.

Key to the success of Little Rock's share-a-taxi program was the practice of vehicle leasing. Taxi drivers leased cabs on a daily basis for a flat fee, receiving radio-dispatching services and insurance coverage in return. After paying lease fees and covering expenses for gasoline and maintenance, all other revenue collected belonged to drivers. With this arrangement, drivers behaved like independent businessmen, seeking to maximize income by responding promptly to ride requests, developing customer loyalties, and searching out new niche markets. Many began concentrating on certain sectors of the city, becoming the exclusive operators for some businesses. Some operated vehicles like veritable jitneys, operating up and down busy thoroughfares, picking up and dropping off customers along the way. Also, central dispatchers became so familiar with the rhythm and pattern of local trip making that they became very efficient at linking drivers in the field to waiting customers so as to optimize routing and trip chaining.

A combination of good, reliable service quality, aggressive marketing, and economies of scale (from centralizing dispatch and maintenance services) resulted in the delivery of very cost-effective shared-ride services. In 1977, Little Rock's shared-ride taxis were hauling more than 1.7 million passengers annually (or around 11 cab trips per capita). This was 300,000 more passengers per year than the local bus system, which was established in the 1960s, carried (Hall, 1978). By 1980, an estimated 6 percent of all motorized trips in Little Rock were by shared-ride cabs. Most customers were captive users—the poor, predrivers, seniors, and disabled individuals—although significant numbers of middle-class riders could also be found, especially in and around state office buildings.

Shared-ride services came to an abrupt end when the Little Rock City Council passed an ordinance in 1981 replacing the zonal system with distance-based taximeters and stipulating that exclusive ride services be provided. Shortly thereafter, shared-ride services were eliminated altogether. A combination of factors—rising vehicle ownership rates, pressure from the public transit agency to reduce competition and stem ridership losses, and, according to some local observers, class and racial prejudices—led to the replacement of a very successful shared-ride service with a far more marginal exclusive and sometimes exclusionary taxi service.[4] Three years before Little Rock's shared-ride services were eliminated, John Hall, president of Black and White Cab, who first championed the idea of taxipooling, stated at a 1978 national conference on "Taxis as Paratransit": "In my estimation, exclusive ride would eliminate 40 percent of our riders if it was implemented today." This proved an understatement. By 1982, one year after exclusive-ride services were introduced, Black and White Cab's annual ridership fell to around 550,000 from 1,350,000 five years earlier, a drop of 60 percent. Because taximeter fares rose to a $1 flag drop and $0.90 per mile, lost ridership income was generally made up by higher per-trip revenues. Thus, Little Rock's taxi operators did not rebel against the changes. However, while taxi drivers, the local transit agency (whose ridership rose), and higher-income, choice taxi riders generally saw themselves as well off or better off, the poor and other transit dependents saw their mass transportation service options and service quality drastically curtailed as a result of the change. Societal losses also came in the form of lower mass transportation usage and market shares—citywide taxi and bus transit trips combined fell from over 3 million to around 2.5 million annual trips from 1980 to 1990; for work trips, the combined taxi and transit modal split was only around 1.5 percent in 1990, down from over 6 percent a decade earlier.[5]

In close, at its prime, Little Rock's shared-ride taxi program was a smashing success because it served a genuine market demand, local government gave it a green light, and profit-motivated taxi firms made the system work—providing frequent, on-call, reliable services; aggressively marketing the shared-ride concepts; and creating an organizational structure that tapped into economies of scale and financially rewarded drivers for maximizing productivity by filling up taxicabs. Today, Little Rock's mass transportation sector is a shadow of its past—taxi ridership is less than half what it was two decades earlier, residents (especially the inner-city poor) have fewer travel choices, and local bus services are losing market share (just 0.96 percent of 1990 commute trips were by transit) and incurring high deficits per passenger ($1.75 in 1993).[6]

Shared-Ride Taxis in the Nation's Capital

Today, Washington, D.C. is the only U.S. city that can still lay claim to having a citywide shared-ride taxi program. Taxipooling is complemented by an open marketplace that neither restricts the supply of taxis nor controls when and where they operate within the District of Columbia. Shared-ride taxis gained legitimacy when the U.S. Congress, which maintains veto power over local policies, passed a law in 1932 prohibiting the use of taximeters, installing a zone fare system instead. Today, the District contains 26 zones, with fares ranging from $2.80 for an intrazonal trip to $10.80 when traversing eight zones. Because zone fares penalize drivers when cabs sit in traffic congestion, there is a $1.50 evening peak-hour surcharge. Financially, shared-ride services benefit drivers only— each rider still pays a single passenger fare. Interjurisdictional taxi fares are set by the Washington Metropolitan Area Transportation Commission (WMATA), depending on trip destination. Nearly 90 percent of taxi trips originating in the District start from downtown (zones 1 and 2), and most trips are short haul—one to three zones (costing $2.80 to $4.40, plus tips).

Ridesharing is only allowed with the permission of the first passenger, and a deviation of more than five city blocks from the most direct route to that passenger's destination is not permitted. Given the initial passenger's destination, the driver may solicit other passengers heading in the same general vicinity. Drivers are not allowed to delay passengers by more than two minutes when recruiting a shared-ride customer, though such rules are virtually unenforceable. Because customers get no fare break for ridesharing, most District residents and workers request exclusive-ride services, though most accept taxipooling during rush hours when there is a shortage of cabs. Out-of-towners and tourists are generally more receptive to drivers' requests to pick up extra fares, both because they are unfamiliar with the system and are usually less pressed for time. Because most drivers concentrate on short-haul trips where fares turn over rapidly or hotels to serve the lucrative airport market, very little taxi ridesharing occurs in practice, other than along busy boulevards during rush hour, between major downtown destinations, and trips originating from the downtown K Street Airport Bus Terminal or Union Station (terminal for Amtrak, Metrorail, and intercity buses). Many cabbies will not leave Union Station during daylight hours until they have three passengers in the car.

The only time when shared-ride taxis have gained widespread acceptance appears to be when they were pressed into service by market forces and government decree. During the 1973–1974 gasoline shortage, the District's Public Services Commission (predecessor to today's Taxicab Commission) adopted a ridesharing policy, issuing route message signs to drivers, encouraging them to pick up multiple passengers, and marketing the importance of ridesharing as a fuel conservation strategy. Within the first month of this policy, estimated taxi ridership increased by 80,000 additional fares per day from the level of 275,000 trips per day for the previous month—a 30 percent gain (Lyons, 1983). As real gasoline prices have fallen and new transit options have emerged for intra-District trips (most notably Metrorail), taxi ridesharing has since fallen quite significantly. Although there are no hard numbers, informal interviews with a dozen or so District cabdrivers suggest that less than one in 10 off-peak trips and around two in three peak-period trips serve two or more unrelated parties.

Over the years, Washington's unrestricted, shared-ride taxi industry has come under frequent attack. A 1957 study commissioned by the U.S. Congress called for controlling supplies and replacing the zone rate system with taximeters as ways to improve service quality and reliability. Testifying before the House on behalf of restricted entry and metered fares, the General Counsel of the American Taxi Association stated that taxi operators find conditions in the District "little short of a disgrace. . . . It is the kind of condition," he testified, "that gives the entire industry a black eye."[7] Congress members—themselves consumers of services— have generally remained skeptical of repeated attempts to tighten control over District taxicabs, rejecting several proposals over the past 40 years. In comparing taxi services in the District with those of other East Coast cities, Philip Kuehl and Charles Olson (1974) found that such problems as discourteous drivers, discrimination, and overcharging were not due to Washington's open-entry, shared-ride status—other major cities had similar problems. Overall, the benefits of having

plentiful cabs at reasonable fares offset the inconveniences, like older fleets, associated with an open market in the minds of most Washingtonians.

Shared-Ride Airport Taxis

Today, ridesharing between downtowns and airports remains the largest niche
market for taxipooling, normally through informal arrangements. For a period,
before the airport shuttle van industry blossomed (see Chapter 7), some U.S. airports openly welcomed and indeed actively promoted taxi ridesharing. This was
often the case in cities where cabs were in short supply during peak hours, particularly those with notoriously restrictive limits on taxi permits, like New York City.
In 1979, a Share-a-Cab service was initiated at New York City's LaGuardia Airport. At the time, the Port Authority of New York and New Jersey faced continued problems of long queues at airport cabstands, especially on Friday and
Sunday nights when demand was at its peak. The greatest demand was among
air shuttle passenger wanting quick, low-cost transportation to Manhattan, about
eight miles to the southwest. Besides exclusive-ride taxis, few other reasonable
ground transportation options were available—limousine service was expensive
and infrequent, while public bus transit involved making connections, transferring
luggage, and for most travelers, unacceptable delays.

With Share-a-Cab, customers notified a curbside attendant of their destinations. Once three or more passengers heading to the same part of Manhattan
(anywhere south of 60th Street) had formed, a taxicab would leave a nearby queue
to serve the parties. The program was not an instant success. Drivers disliked
the voucher system (which delayed payment), and ridership was low. The program, however, was later expanded from a side terminal to the main La Guardia
terminal and vouchers were replaced by cash fares. Monthly ridership went from
5,100 in 1979 to 16,000 in 1982, then stabilized at around 7,000 from 1985 to
1988. Since at least three passengers were needed to form a shared-ride, drivers
were assured a minimum of $15 plus tips per trip (maximum of $24), compared
to $12 for the average exclusive ride trip to Manhattan (in the mid-1980s). The
program appeared to attract taxicabs into LaGuardia, evidenced by a shortening
of passenger queues. Share-a-Cab drivers were also waiting no longer for customers than exclusive-ride operators (Comsis, 1986). Overall, a nice market equi-
librium was in place.

LaGuardia's Share-a-Cab program was disbanded in 1990, a victim of
expanded airport shuttle van and bus limousine services. Since these other
ground transportation carriers were licensed through the state of New York or, in
the case of cross-state services, the Interstate Commerce Commission, they did
not face the same restrictions on supply as did New York City's taxicabs. Share-
a-Cab operators thus lost customers as competition heated up. Franchised limousine bus carriers also sought to protect their monopolistic positions and, along
with shuttle van operators, they pressured the Metropolitan Taxiboard of Trade
to discontinue the service. Formal airport taxi sharing may have a life in New

York City after all. In December 1995, a demonstration of shared-ride taxis ser-vices between JFK International Airport and Manhattan (for a set fare of $30 split among passengers) was initiated. This demonstration is testing the premise that by using smaller vehicles, shared-ride taxis can provide a higher quality service than shuttle vans by reducing the number of Manhattan stops, thus helping to fur-ther enrich airport access service options.

Berkeley's Racetrack Shared-Ride Taxi

A good example of a point-to-point shared-ride taxi that serves a unique market niche and a nonairport destination exists in the San Francisco Bay Area: the "racetrack taxi" that connects the North Berkeley Bay Area Rapid Transit (BART) station to the Golden Gate Fields racetrack. This seasonal service func-tions as a "service extender" to existing bus lines serving the racetrack. Horse race fans who ride BART can choose between a bus or a shared-ride taxi, at a fare of $2 per one-way trip, or take a more expensive ride-alone taxi (at around $10) to reach the racetrack, some four miles away (Map 2.1).[8]

Around 10 independent taxi owners operate shared-ride services during the race season. Most taxis make two to three trips in each direction daily, carrying four to five passengers per trip. Two dollars per person is charged regardless of the number of passengers, thus generating between $8 and $10 per trip, about what a cabbie would make for an exclusive-ride, metered haul. (Taxi drivers, however, usually have to backhaul with an empty cab to pick up another load of race track fans.) Shared-ride fares are set to match those of the chief competitor, AC Tran-sit's bus line 304.[9] Neither the city of Berkeley nor Albany regulate taxi fares.[10]

Approximately 150 racetrack fans arrive at the North Berkeley BART station on weekdays, and around 450 arrive on Saturdays and Sundays. Field surveys indicate that shared-ride taxis carry around 95 passengers on weekdays and around 320 on Saturdays and Sundays. Of all access trips to and from BART, then, shared-ride cabs capture over 60 percent of the weekday and over 70 percent of the weekend markets. AC Transit and exclusive-ride taxis serve the remainder.

With the same price and similar routing, shared-ride taxis generally win out over the bus competitor because of slight time savings (owing to fewer intermedi-ate stops), preferences for travelling in small groups, customer loyalty, and what one taxicab operator describes as "herd mentality." Apparently, some bettors like the camraderie of sharing cabs to Golden Gate Fields and the chance of gaining inside tips on the horses.

Based on interviews with drivers and other sources, we estimate the cost of operating shared-ride taxis by each independent operator to be around $29 per weekday (in 1994), including a prorated share of vehicle depreciation.[11] On a typical weekday, shared-ride taxi operators take home around $35 to $40 in profit; on weekends, they clear slightly more, around $50 per day.[12] Most drivers will forgo their place at the BART station or the Fields queues to respond to more lucrative dispatch calls (especially for trips to the airport). Most shared-ride

Map 2.1.
Routing of the Racetrack Taxi and AC Transit's Line 304

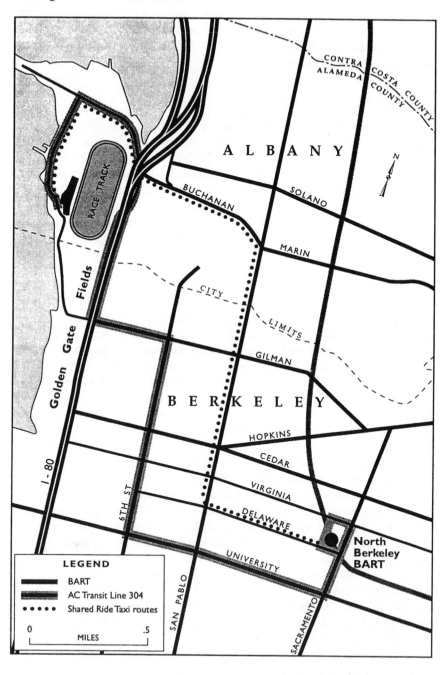

drivers we interviewed are single males who are 20 to 30 years of age and who are Sikhs from the same region in India.

Comparing cost and performance between AC Transit Line 304 and shared-ride taxis is fraught with difficulties. AC's costs, which averaged $76 per hour in 1994 (including capital deprecation but excluding debt service), are based on systemwide statistics. Jitney cost data include expenses attributable to passengers not travelling to the racetrack, such as for centralized radio-dispatch services. On an average weekday, AC Transit Line 304 costs more than three times as much per passenger trip as the shared-ride taxis (Table 2.1). For each racetrack trip served, shared-ride taxis earn about a dollar, while AC Transit's Line 304 loses about an equal amount. Fully seated shared-ride taxis also show significantly higher ridership productivity, carrying around 10 passengers more per total hour (including layover and deadhead time). Overall, the commercial racetrack taxi enjoys a significant cost and productivity advantage over its publicly supported transit competitor. Among the factors key to the racetrack taxi's success are: point-to-point service that holds down costs; destination parking charges; regular and predictable demand; customer loyalty; and a permissive local regulatory environment.

Shared-Ride Taxis: Concluding Comments

While at one time shared-ride taxi services proliferated in a handful of U.S. cities like Little Rock and Washington, D.C., for the most part taxipooling has today been reduced to very limited and specialized niche market services—mainly point-to-point runs between downtowns and airports and, in the case of Berkeley and perhaps several other cities as well, between rail stations and sports complexes. In the case of Little Rock and the LaGuardia airport run, the demise of shared-ride taxi services was mainly a function of regulation—namely, providing a protected monopoly status to shared-ride taxis' competitors. However, experiences in Washington, D.C., reveal that regulation alone is not at fault. There, increased competition from subsidized intracity bus and rail services, combined with market preference for single-ride services, have eroded shared-ride taxis' ridership base. In the absence of major technological advances that improve routing efficiency and policy shifts that eliminate transportation subsidies, it is likely that shared-ride taxis will remain a small and limited niche market service in U.S. cities.

JITNEYS

Perhaps more so that any other form of commercial paratransit, jitneys span the gamut of service options. Some, like San Francisco's downtown rail feeder, are point-to-point services, akin to a shuttle connector. Places with the most extensive legalized jitney services—Miami and Atlantic City—require jitneys to follow fixed routes and prohibit detours. Where illegal jitneys thrive—such as the

Table 2.1.

Performance Comparisons of Shared-Ride Taxis and AC Transit Services for the Golden Gate Fields Run, Average Weekday, 1994

	Operating Cost^a/ Passenger	Profit (Deficit)^a/ Passenger	Passengers/Total Service Hour
Shared-Ride Taxis	$0.90	$1.10	18.7
AC Transit Line 304	$3.01	($1.01)	9.0
Line 304 as percent of			
Shared-Ride Taxis	*234.4%*	—	*48.1%*

^{a}Cost estimates for Line 304 exclude debt service on capital purchases. Debt financing expenses are included for shared-ride taxis.

Sources: Field interviews with shared-ride operators; AC Transit, Short Range Transit Plan, Oakland, 1994; Federal Transit Administration, Transit Profiles: The Thirty Largest Agencies, For the 1993 National Transit Database Section 15 Report Year, Washington, D.C., 1994.

neighborhood-based van services discussed in Chapter 3 and Houston's illegal jitney discussed in Part 2, Chapter 6—services tend to be flexible in terms of routing and scheduling. Flexible jitneys effectively serve a paratransit corridor, deviating from main routes as demand dictates.

Jitney services were revived in Los Angeles, San Diego, and Indianapolis during the 1980s; however, in the face of competition with subsidized buses, their return was generally short-lived in these cities. In 1982, the city of Los Angeles allowed several jitney operators to ply along Wilshire Boulevard in response to a fare hike and service cuts by the Southern California Rapid Transit District (SCRTD). Jitney runs stopped within a year because operators could not match SCRTD's $0.75 fares and still cover costs (Teal and Nemer, 1986).[13] A "semilegal" jitney service has operated along King Drive and other parts of south Chicago for years, condoned by city officials, yet not fully licensed or insured (Kitch et al., 1971). In 1994, Chicago legalized fixed-route jitneys for the underserved South and West sides, although most jitney operators in these areas have chosen to remain unlicensed and uninsured in order to keep fares low and vehicles full (Suzuki, 1995).

The cases that follow highlight the three key functional roles of contemporary jitney services in the United States. San Francisco's sole surviving jitney is an example of a *rail feeder*, connecting a commuter rail terminus with the downtown Financial District. In San Diego, current jitney runs near the Mexican border function as *circulators*, connecting several large housing projects, an industrial park, and a commercial strip to the border crossing. Lastly, a network of *areawide* jitney services currently exists in Atlantic City and Miami.

The San Francisco Jitney: A Commuter Rail Feeder

Today, a privately operated 20-seat jitney minibus runs between downtown San Francisco and the Southern Pacific Transportation Depot, the northern terminus of the Peninsula CalTrain commuter rail service. Officially sanctioned by the San Francisco Police Department (SFPD) as Jitney No. 97, this is the last remnant of San Francisco's once-flourishing jitney industry. A point-to-point feeder service, Jitney No. 97 provides hints about the kinds of cost-savings measures and lean service practices that are necessary to survive in an era of public transit subsidies and heavy-handed regulation.

San Francisco's Jitneys: The Early Years

San Francisco's jitneys first appeared in 1914 to transport workers and attendees to the Panama-Pacific International Exposition. By 1915, over 1,400 private jitney operators were plying the streets of San Francisco. Complaints from streetcar operators led to a jitney ban soon thereafter; however, the Board of Supervisors lifted all restrictions in 1917 in response to a streetcar workers' strike that threatened to cripple the city. By 1918, several thousand jitneys saturated the city, primarily hauling suburbanites to downtown jobs (Belknap, 1973).

From this height, San Francisco's jitney fleet fell steadily at the hands of rising insurance rates, competition from the private automobile, and tightening rules on who could operate, when, and where. By 1950, there were 136 vehicles (mainly Cadillac limousines) hauling around 7,000 passengers per day at a 10-cents fare. Twenty years later, there were 120 vehicles operating on two routes. The major one was the "Mission" jitney—a 24-hour, seven-day-a-week service consisting of 12-seater vans and minibuses that ran along Mission Street in the Mission district, a cultural melting pot of Hispanics and other ethnic minorities. A second jitney route, comprising only around 5 percent of the jitney fleet in the early 1970s, operated between the Southern Pacific Depot and Market Street, downtown San Francisco's major thoroughfare, eight blocks to the north. Schedules along this rail feeder route generally followed the arrival and departure of commuter trains.

Throughout the postwar era, San Francisco's jitneys have been regulated by the SFPD, the same authority responsible for overseeing taxi operations. While the 1950s San Francisco jitneys were primarily limousines serving white-collar workers, by the 1970s the vehicle of choice was a van or minibus, serving a blue-collar and pink-collar clientele. The choice of vehicle was entirely up to the permit owner, provided it passed safety inspection.

Because of mounting public transit deficits and pressures to protect Municipal Railway (Muni) trolleybuses and streetcars from competition, the city issued no new jitney permits after 1972. The Mission jitney was already waning by this time; of the 116 jitneys registered to operate on Mission Street in 1973, only 52 were in action (Griffin, 1986). The Mission jitney was particularly hard hit by

BART's 1974 opening. Because city regulations required operators to charge fares at least as high as the local public transit services, jitney operators found it difficult to compete with BART's cheaper fares and faster service for intracity trips beginning and ending near BART stations.

Jitneys in the 1970s and 1980s: The Demise of an Industry

By the early 1970s, San Francisco's jitneys were mainly serving ethnic minorities from the Mission district, many of whom used to patronize jitneys when they lived in Central America and Asia. Riders were attracted by the faster services with fewer stops, the greater likelihood of getting a seat during peak hours than on a Muni bus or tram, the ability to converse with drivers and passengers in their native tongue, and lower incidences of crime than on Muni buses and trams. Along Mission Boulevard, the main thoroughfare serving the district, a jitney could be counted on to come by about once every five minutes during rush hour.

From 1972 to 1978, even though no jitney new permits were issued by the SFPD, market entry was not impossible. Permits could be bought and sold, and estimates for the going rate at the time ranged from $2,000 to $3,500. In 1978, however, voters passed Proposition K, a referendum which stipulated that permits could not be transferred or sold from one operator to another. Almost overnight, this made permits virtually worthless on the market. Permits were reverted back to the city upon the forfeiture of a permit by an operator, and, in practice, were not issued again.

An even more serious blow to San Francisco's jitney sector was the sharp increases in liability insurance premiums. In step with federal rules for interstate carriers, California raised minimum liability insurance requirements to $1.5 million in 1978 and again in 1985 to $5 million, and the city of San Francisco followed suit. Even if jitney drivers could make premium payments, because of poor vehicle conditions and relatively high accident rates, most jitney drivers could not find insurance companies who were willing to write policies. Lack of alternatives invited fraudulent insurers, and two major insurance scandals—one in 1976 and another in 1986—forced many jitnet operators into bankruptcy. Added to this was heightened police enforcement against violations like overloading (e.g., 41 in a 21-passenger bus), unsafe seating (e.g., a milk carton used as an extra seat), removal of doors to expedite alighting while in motion (cable-car style), erratic and overaggressive driving, and drivers racing one another for customers (Griffin, 1986).

By the late 1980s, virtually every San Francisco jitney had ceased operations. A 1985 editorial in the *San Francisco Chronicle* lamented the passing of "another San Francisco institution, . . . and those doughty little cars that putter up and down Mission Street." San Francisco's once-vibrant jitney industry had fallen prey to a combination of rising insurance costs, tighter regulations, fraud, and unfair competition from subsidized public transit services.

Part of the blame for the jitney's demise, however, lies within the industry itself. Over the postwar era, jitney operators in San Francisco were unable to effectively organize to protest minimum fares, routing restrictions, and rising insurance requirements. San Francisco's jitney operators were independent and often fierce competitors; thus, route associations never formed to promote the industry's interests, reduce redundancies, and coordinate services, as in much of the third world. Organizing and developing a single voice for effective advocacy proved extremely difficult.

The Sole Survivor

Today, a single jitney owner-operator remains. The sole survivor, Jesus Losa, has attained near-folklore status.[14] Every weekday, Mr. Losa drives a 1978 blue passenger bus (and a smaller blue van during off-peak hours) along Third and Fourth streets between the Southern Pacific commuter train depot and Market Street eight blocks to the north (Map 2.2). The blue bus is marked "jitney" and looks like it belongs in Tijuana or Jakarta more than the streets of San Francisco. This has not deterred professional office workers, most from upscale San Mateo County, from paying a dollar one-way fare for a five-minute lift from the train depot to their downtown jobs. Thus, in contrast to the earlier jitneys, San Francisco's sole jitney survivor serves an upmarket clientele. Loyal patrons give Mr. Losa rave reviews—in a 1988 *San Francisco Chronicle* article, one stated "I don't think I've ever missed a train with him" and another added "Jess really knows how to handle traffic" (Nolte, p. A2). Most find the jitney ride to be more dependable, faster, and more comfortable than Muni bus runs. No signs or markings designate where the jitney picks up afternoon passengers, but regulars know where to go (and nearby newspaper kiosk attendants know where to direct people who ask). An estimated 250 to 300 customers ride the six morning and six afternoon runs of Jitney No. 97. At an estimated average cost of $0.75 per passenger (versus $1.18 for Muni's motor buses), Jitney No. 97 nets around a quarter per passenger.[15]

Why is Jitney No. 97 San Francisco's sole jitney survivor? One reason is that it hauls large numbers of people a short distance, and is able to complete circuits in time to meet incoming trains. Another is that Mr. Losa runs a no-frill, low-cost service, and works hard at his trade.[16] Mr. Losa is a one-man business, driving and maintaining vehicles and taking care of all administrative chores. He has no employees, thus relieving himself of expenses for employee health insurance, worker's compensation insurance, and paid vacations. If he is sick—patrons say that is rare—the jitney simply does not run that day. Being an anomaly, Jitney No. 97 is not viewed by Muni bosses or taxi operators as a threat. Critics tolerate the jitney, and most San Franciscans are oblivious to it.

Map 2.2.
**Routing of the Jitney No. 97 Service Between the CalTrain Depot
and Market Street**

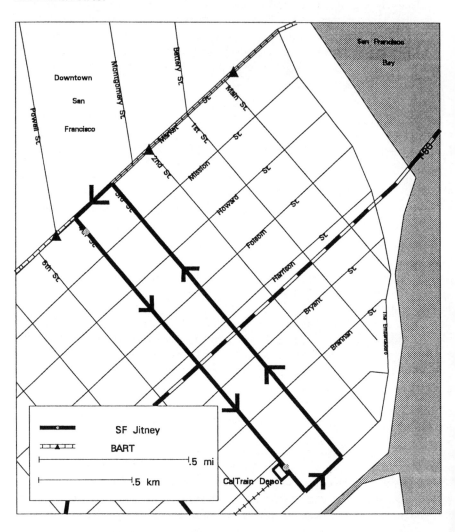

San Diego's Jitneys: Border Shuttles

Paralleling San Francisco's experiences, at the other end of the state, the San Diego region has witnessed a shake-out of the private jitney market in recent times. From a wide-ranging citywide service in the early 1980s, what was left 10 years later was largely a specialized, albeit successful, border shuttle service.

The 1980s: Rise and Fall of Citywide Jitneys

In 1979, the city of San Diego gained national attention when it legalized jitney services, in addition to deregulating taxis. With a large military and retirement population, and thousands of Mexican dayworkers streaming across the border each morning, local taxi and charter van operators saw a potential market for jitney services and pressed the City Council to revise local ordinances to accommodate them. The 1979 paratransit ordinance, which has not changed appreciably over the years, opened up the market to fixed-route jitneys seating up to 15 passengers and set no restrictions on pricing. Jitney operators only needed to file their routes and tariff plans with the city, visibly display their fares, meet minimum insurance and fitness standards, and follow rules designed to reduce loitering and fare hawking.[17]

Over the first few years, jitneys flourished in San Diego, reaching around 100 licensed vehicles operated by 15 companies in 1984. At its peak, weekly ridership eclipsed 15,000. San Diego's jitneys filled a market void, providing convenient and cheap transportation services to mainly transit dependents—military personnel, seniors, Mexican dayworkers, and the poor. Most routes concentrated on linking downtown, military bases, and the Mexican border, and a few plied along boulevards connecting to tourist areas and Lindbergh Field, the international airport just north of downtown (Reinke, 1986). A steady flow of bidirectional traffic —Mexicans heading to the city, and naval personnel, seniors, and tourists heading to the border—meant jitney vans were often full, even on weekends and evenings. Jitneys were also a bargain. In 1984, a five-mile trip from Lindbergh Field to downtown San Diego cost $3 by jitney compared to $12 by exclusive-ride taxi.

As market competition heated up, however, problems began to surface. Some jitney and bus operators complained of unscrupulous and unfair practices, especially drivers stopping at bus stops for extended periods of time and hustling fares. At the recommendation of several task forces, the city amended the paratransit ordinance to create jitney holding zones, places where vans could queue for extended periods of time. In 1988, the city transferred jurisdiction over jitneys and taxis to the Metropolitan Transit Development Board (MTDB), the regional transit planning and operating authority. Soon thereafter, a series of events— military cutbacks, economic recession, and growing competition from airport shuttles and the San Diego Trolley (which provides an economical ride from downtown to the Tijuana border)—began eroding away at jitney ridership. Complaints from the hospitality industry about overly aggressive jitney drivers led to the closure of jitney zones in tourist areas and the airport. By 1992, around 25 jitneys remained, operating in the San Ysidro portion of the city and serving the world's busiest border crossing. Today, only around 10 licensed and perhaps as many unlicensed jitney operators remain, providing short-haul services to almost exclusive Spanish-speaking customers.[18] Thus, because of increased competition (including from subsidized providers like the San Diego Trolley) and exogenous events like base closures, what 10 years earlier had been a healthy, dynamic paratransit sector was by the 1990s reduced to a very specialized and limited niche service.

San Ysidro Border Jitneys

Presently, all 10 remaining jitney licenses are for the San Ysidro border area. MTDB has capped the number of licenses for San Ysidro at 10, hoping to avoid problems of jitney overcompetition that previously plagued the city. As shown in Map 2.3, jitneys run from the border crossing along San Ysidro Boulevard, the main commercial street in the area, to a large apartment complex (Villa Nueva) and to the edge of an industrial complex, making a six-mile loop. For much of the way, the jitney route matches the Metropolitan Transit System's (MTS) Route 932.[19] Jitneys are permitted to pick up and drop off passengers at bus stops and anywhere else a curb is not painted red. Most jitneys are bubble-top Ford Econoline vans that were previously used by rental car agencies as airport shuttles and are 5 to 12 years old.

All jitney trips begin and end at the border crossing, where the San Ysidro jitneys are allotted curb space for three vehicles. Nearby is the San Diego Trolley terminal and loading zones for other private transportation services, including Tijuana shuttles, taxis, and intercity buses (Map 2.4). Jitneys queue at the border area for as long as 15 minutes or until vehicles are full. During peak hours, jitneys waiting in a holding zone 900 feet away fill curbside loading spaces once they are vacated. Quite often, however, drivers circle the border area looking for fares instead of sitting idle in the holding pen. Whenever other drivers complain to MTDB officials, police will step up enforcement, though usually only for a week or so.

Presently, the going rate for a San Ysidro jitney ride is $1, compared to $1.50 for riding public transit (bus or trolley).[20] On an average weekday, the 10 jitney vans carry around 1,000 passengers, virtually all of whom are Latinos and regular customers. Marketing is by word of mouth. Most jitney riders appear to be captive—Mexican dayworkers, kids heading to schools, low-income service workers, seniors going shopping, and so on. Many noncaptives, or choice riders, are making cross-border personal or business trips, opting to walk across the world's busiest border crossing rather than drive their cars and endure long queues at immigration checkpoints. On the Mexican side of the border, in Tijuana, an even larger collection of jitneys and shared-ride taxis await arrivers. San Ysidro's jitneys are always full when leaving the border, sometimes with standing room only. Most trips are one to two miles, and turnover is frequent. During the ride, several conversations are usually going on in Spanish, oftentimes with the driver joining in. Small talk, combined with a small vehicle, makes for an intimate ride.

Evaluating the cost performance of San Ysidro jitneys versus local bus runs is difficult because services are not directly equivalent—jitneys provide short-haul, localized services, whereas MTS line 932 is an intraregional route to downtown San Diego. Still, Route 932 is one of the highest performing public bus runs

Map 2.3.
San Ysidro Jitney and MTS 932 Routes

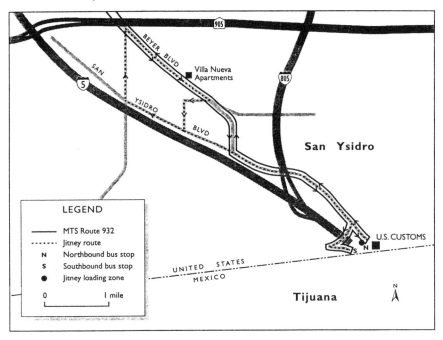

in the country, returning 83 percent of costs and incurring deficits of only 18 cents per passenger in 1994 (Table 2.2). Yet the San Ysidro jitneys outperformed Route 932, earning instead of losing 18 cents per passenger and generating revenues that exceeded full operating costs (including capital) by 22.5 percent.[21] Cost savings were mainly due to lower wages—in 1994, San Ysidro jitney drivers earned $4 to $5 per hour (and no benefits) while contracted drivers for Route 932 earned $8.31 per hour. Operating expenses for Route 932 will soon go up as the MTS replaces older buses with new, compressed natural gasoline (CNG) buses. Another factor in the jitney's performance edge, however, is higher average loads. In 1994, the 10 55-passenger coaches on Route 932 averaged just over 1,000 daily boardings and alightings at the border crossing terminal, not that much more than the 850 persons getting on and off of the 10 15-passenger jitney vans each day at the border.

In closing, in the course of a decade, the jitney industry of San Diego has gone from a fairly diverse citywide service to a highly specialized border-crossing circulator. A liberal regulatory environment helped nurture San Diego's upstart jitney industry; however, with time, the subsidization of public transit, coupled with military cutbacks and some degree of reregulation, stunted its growth. Today, San Ysidro's publicly sanctioned jitneys face increasing competition from unlicensed "gypsy"operators who provide more demand responsive service (compared to the

Map 2.4.
San Ysidro Border Station Loading Area

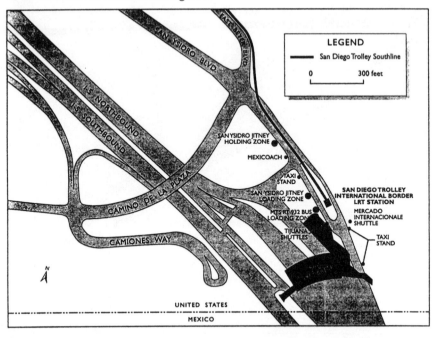

Table 2.2.
Performance Comparisons of San Ysidro Jitneys and MTS Route 932,
Average Weekday, 1994

	Operating Cost[a]/ Passenger	Profit (Deficit)[a]/ Passenger	Cost Recovery Ratio (%)
San Ysidro Jitneys	$0.82	$0.18	122.5%
MTS Route 932	$1.03	($0.18)[b]	82.9%
Route 932 as percent of Jitneys	*25.6%*	—	*47.8%*

[a] Cost estimates for Line Route 932 exclude debt service on capital purchases. Debt financing expenses are included for shared-ride taxis.
[b] Although the adult cash fare for Route 932 is $1.50, average fares are considerably lower because of the high volume of discount senior and student fares, and the use of discount passes.

Sources: Field interviews with jitney drivers; MTDB, Schedule of Base Statistics, B-10 Form, 1994; MTDB, Metropolitan San Diego Short Range Transit Plan, FY 1993-99, 1992.

15-minute average headway of jitneys queued at the border). Overall, the San Ysidro jitneys are fairly marginalized services that are tolerated by detractors and largely ignored by most San Diegans. For those who ride them every day, however, the San Ysidro jitneys have found a loyal and appreciative following.

Atlantic City's Jitneys

Atlantic City, New Jersey, has the oldest continuing jitney service in the country. Its jitneys are also among the most heavily patronized—275 trips per capita in 1995—and most tightly self-regulated transit services in North America. And unlike elsewhere, much of Atlantic City's jitney clientele consists of middle-class workers who own cars. Equally impressive, Atlantic City's jitneys provide extensive urban transit services—24 hours a day, 365 days a year—without any public subsidies.

These remarkable achievements are a product of both history and unique features of Atlantic City itself. Atlantic City's jitneys first entered the scene in March 1915, at the height of a paralyzing trolley strike. Two enterprising individuals, Frank Fairburn and S. W. Redmond, began driving their black Model T Fords up and down Atlantic Avenue, Atlantic City's main commercial strip, offering rides for a nickle. Within a year, nearly 500 jitneys of all makes and sizes were doing the same, operating when and where they chose with no regulatory constraints. Jitneys ran end-to-end along the four-mile Atlantic Avenue strip, adapting services to demand and staying out of neighboring communities so as to avoid state regulators. By late 1915, the Atlantic City and Shore Railroad, the trolley line operating along Atlantic Avenue, went into bankruptcy, a victim of jitney competition. The city responded by passing an ordinance in 1917 that forced jitneys off Atlantic Avenue and limited the number of licenses to 190, a number that has remained constant to this day. The jitneys simply moved one block to the east, on Pacific Avenue, where to this day they concentrate their trade.

Existing Jitney Services

During the first 35 years of service, passenger sedans were largely used to provide jitney services in Atlantic City. Following the second world war and to meet escalating demand, jitney sedans were replaced by 13-seat converted bread trucks, the vehicle configuration still in use today. Over the ensuing 50 years, Atlantic City's jitney services have remained essentially unchanged. Today, independent owner-operators drive their jitney minibuses along fixed routes focused on Pacific Avenue, the main thoroughfare paralleling Atlantic City's boardwalk and casino/hotel strip. A steady stream of jitneys run up and down Pacific Avenue during daylight hours, picking up and dropping off customers at designated jitney stops or when a vehicle stops at a red light. In this sense, Atlantic City's jitneys operate pretty much like conventional buses, though they follow no set schedules, a somewhat academic point since services are so frequent (averaging 2-3 minute headways along Pacific Avenue during busy periods and 5-6-minute headways other times from 6:00 A.M. to 6:00 P.M.). Today, Atlantic City has three fixed jitney routes (Map 2.5).

What most distinguishes Atlantic City's jitneys from conventional transit is that the driver is also the vehicle owner. By city ordinance, no subcontracting is

Map 2.5.
Atlantic City's Jitney Routes

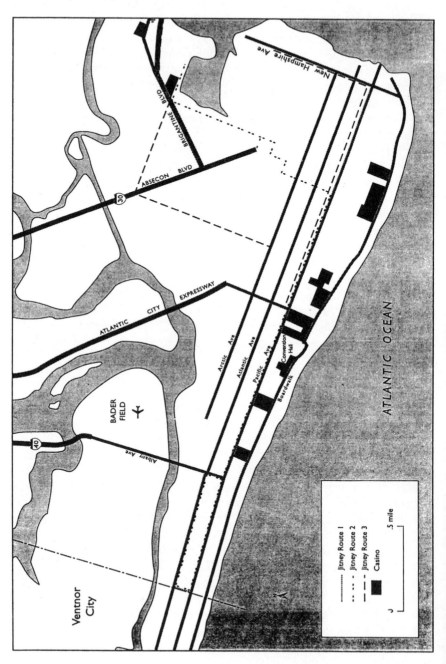

allowed. If a owner-driver is sick, the jitney vehicle does not operate that day. How much income owner-operators make comes down largely to how industrious and enterprising they are. Drivers tend to move briskly up and down Pacific Avenue, aided by synchronized traffic signals. They work hard at filling up seats, currently priced at $1.50 per trip.[22] City ordinances prevent standees, so key to financial success is frequent customer turnover. When pulling up to jitney stops, drivers stick out fingers to show the number of available seats; when vehicles are full, they indicate this with a sign hung on the windshield. Drivers tend to accelerate and decelerate quickly, trying to beat other drivers in the quest for customers. While this can at times make for an uncomfortable ride, especially for seniors (e.g., standard practice is to move as soon as the door is closed and traffic lights turn green, regardless of whether the customer is seated), it also results in high vehicle efficiency—high loads per revenue mile of service.

Key to rapid customer turnover and efficient operations is the unique nature —both spatially and temporally—of travel demand in Atlantic City. Situated on a barrier island 48 blocks long and 15 blocks wide, Atlantic City has a compact and accessible settlement pattern. Its waterfront is dotted with casinos, hotels, restaurants, and other tourist attractions. A significant share of the city's work-force is headed to these destinations on a regular basis. This makes for very efficient bidirectional travel, minimal deadheading, and frequent on-off movements along the well-defined four-mile Pacific-Atlantic Avenue corridor. As 24-hour businesses, moreover, casinos attract employees and customers all hours of the day. Tourists also tend to provide a year-round customer base, including on weekends and in the late evening. Thus, Atlantic City's jitneys are not burdened by the extreme peaking problems that plague most American transit operations. Overall, Atlantic City provides a near-perfect operating environment for jitneys —frequent seat turnovers spread over numerous hours.

Today, Atlantic City's jitney ridership stands at around 11 million trips annually. This averages to some 63,000 annual trips per jitney vehicle—a higher level of vehicle utilization than that achieved by New Jersey Transit's bus division, which averaged 57,500 passengers per vehicle (for statewide urbanized services, including those under contract) using much higher capacity buses. (New Jersey Transit operates buses along Atlantic Avenue, though its market is primarily Atlantic City workers living in surrounding communities making intercity trips; also providing intercity services are some 1,200 daily casino buses and commuter rail services.) Since casino gambling was legalized in Atlantic City in the early 1980s, jitney ridership has increased by about 3 percent annually. Most patrons are regular customers who work at casinos, hotels, and business establishments along the Pacific-Atlantic Avenue corridor. That they loyally patronize the jitneys—despite fairly cheap commercial parking rates of around $2 to $3 per day and the absence of much traffic congestion in Atlantic City—is a testament to the jitney's superior quality of service.

It is because of high productivity that mass transit services in Atlantic City are essentially nonsubsidized. Drivers earn enough profit to maintain a middle-class lifestyle, though without having to work inordinately long hours.[23] Drivers work hard while on the job but are rewarded with plenty of leisure time—at least three days off and typically no more than 30 hours of work per week. Drivers, moreover, enjoy flexible work schedules, going in when they please and taking as much vacation time off as they want. It is the availability of substantial leisure time, while being able to maintain a middle-income lifestyle, that seems to appeal most to those in the business.

Regulation Through Route Associations

Over the years, the Atlantic City Jitney Association has evolved into a self-regulating organization with its own internal, somewhat rigid, rules of operation. To a large degree, the Atlantic City Jitney Association, a nonprofit cooperative which dates back to the original jitney services of 1915, has assumed the role of service regulator from the city. The Association has become so politically power-ful that the city accedes to its wishes on almost all matters related to jitney opera-tions. Municipal oversight is largely limited to matters of licensing, fare setting, and jitney routing, though even in these areas the Jitney Association wields con-siderable influence. While Atlantic City officials have kept the number of jitney licenses at 190, this has been done with the tacit support of the Association, whose members wish to protect their monopolistic positions and, in particular, their jitney investments. In mid-1995, the market value of a jitney medallion and accompanying vehicle was around $160,000, up considerably from around $100,000 five years earlier. Over the past decade, Atlantic City's medallion values have outpaced inflation and even outperformed the stock market, riding the wave of the city's booming tourism and casino business.[24] However, these are largely monopolistic profits—a sign of an overly restricted jitney industry, one where limits on market entry have remained unchanged in 85 years.

The Atlantic City Jitney Association performs multiple functions. One, it organizes services so as to ensure high efficiency and minimum redundancy while complying with municipal requirements, the main ones being that there be con-tinual services and that at least 10 jitneys operate on Pacific Avenue at all times. Second, the Association advocates and promotes the interests of its membership, particularly in matters related to pricing and service provision.[25] Third, it pro-vides member services, such as a jitney station and garage (where all routes begin, multiride tickets can be purchased, route maps are available, etc.), routine vehicle maintenance, on-site fuel (at a discount), group liability insurance, and a driver's cafeteria. Last, the Association maintains internal rules of conduct, sets operating standards, runs its own traffic court, and serves as the arbiter of driver disputes.

To perform these functions, the Jitney Association has a fairly elaborate inter-nal structure. Its membership consists of all jitney owner-operators in the city, a number that fluctuates between 170 and 190 (the maximum number of licenses allowed). The Association is overseen by a full-time director, who according to the organization's bylaws must be a former driver elected among members. The director meets regularly with the Association's board, comprised of six drivers elected by their peers. Besides setting internal operating policies, the board members also serve as in-field supervisors, each of whom oversees the operations of 30 to 32 independent owner-drivers.

A particularly important function of the Association and its field supervisors is to rotate driving assignments among routes so that everyone gets a fair allocation. This is essential toward preventing overcompetition on the more lucrative Pacific Avenue corridors, mainly Routes 1 and 2, and ensuring at least minimal service provision on the least profitable corridor, Route 3, which mainly serves interior neighborhoods of the city.[26] Each driver has the same schedule on a staggered basis: two days driving Route 1 and then two days off, followed by two days driving Route 2 and then two days off, followed by one day driving Route 3 and then one day off, and then starting the cycle again. Drivers are allotted two shifts per day (e.g., 6:00 to 10:00 A.M. and 12:00 to 4:00 P.M.), and all are assigned several stints of late-night/early-morning services during the course of a month. If drivers decide not to work, supervisors are responsible for mobilizing other drivers to ensure minimal service levels are maintained.

On any given day, 90 jitneys ply along the three routes, with another 90 jitneys potentially in reserve. There are no fixed departing schedules, and when in the field, drivers adjust their own spacing. Supervisors monitor flows along routes they operate on, maintaining contact with their assigned drivers by citizens band radios. If demands are heavy in certain areas and slack in others, supervisors reassign drivers to different routes or directions. This has produced a form of "demand-responsive" paratransit, enabling jitney services to immediately react to shifts and aberrations in ridership.

To discourage overly aggressive driving and promote fairness, the Association has also adopted strictly enforced operating practices and rules of conduct. One is that a driver cannot pass another driver on a route unless the jitney vehicle in front is stopped picking up or dropping off passengers. If a driver infraction is observed by a supervisor or another driver files a complaint, the Association has its own traffic court. A jury of drivers' peers adjudicates these matters, and penalties can be severe for those found guilty (including stiff fines and several days' suspension of driving). The worst punishment is a critical report to City Hall, which is likely to lead to a loss of the offender's mercantile license. The Association also instills a sense of discipline by maintaining a driver's dress code—a blue shirt, a ball cap with the Jitney Association's logo, and khaki pants.

Overall, through a combination of self-policing and self-regulation as well as efficient service practices, the Atlantic City Jitney Association has achieved what no other American city can lay claim to: an almost exclusively privatized intracity urban transit service that requires minimal government oversight and no government subsidies.[27] The Association and its members have been smart enough to recognize that the key to the long-term survival of Atlantic City's jitneys are policies that promote both efficiency and fairness. Thus, the Association has put into place rules and standards that prevent the kinds of problems that have historically plagued the jitney industry—for example, cutthroat competition, overly aggressive driving, cream skimming—from surfacing. Atlantic City's residents, workers, and visitors, in addition to jitney drivers themselves, have been the resulting beneficiaries. While in many ways the Association has evolved into a cartel, or guild—for example, maintaining a ceiling on service supplies, setting internal operating rules, and so on—the Association's responsiveness to market demands and reputation for fairness has won it broad political support.

In sum, Atlantic City demonstrates that successful fixed-route transit is possible if high-quality services are delivered. Part of the success is attributable to Atlantic City's unique history, physical layout, and character. However, a large part is also due to the entrepreneurial drive of jitney owner-operators and the evolution of an internal organizational structure that promotes self-regulation and self-enforcement.

Miami's Jitneys

In contrast to Atlantic City, jitneys in metropolitan Miami compete head-to-head with subsidized public transit services. Sociodemographically, Miami's jitneys have also historically served a more distinct market niche, namely Cubans and others of West Indies heritage, in addition to inner-city blacks. And unlike as in Atlantic City, there is no equivalent to a route association for organizing and internally policing jitneys in greater Miami. This, along with the fact that Miami presents a much larger and more complex urban setting for delivering private jitney services, has at times led to overcompetition and a mass influx of unlicensed, illegal jitney operators. As a result, local government has taken on an increasingly proactive stance in regulating and enforcing jitney policies in greater Miami, certainly much more so than in Atlantic City. For these and other reasons, Miami offers valuable insights into the opportunities and potential problems of expanding private jitney services in large U.S. cities.

This section reviews five phases of jitney evolution in Miami: (1) traditional services (pre-1990); (2) proliferation of unlicensed operators (1990–91); (3) local government crackdown (1991–92); (4) emergency expansion (1992–93); and (5) maturation (post-1993). These phases follow the ebbs and flows of private jitney services in greater Miami, providing insights and lessons into the inner workings of the industry as well as the intended and unintended effects of government policies on service practices. Miami's experiences also highlight the potential volatility of laissez-faire paratransit services in the United States, suggesting when and where they might be best suited.

Traditional Services

Miami has a long history of private jitney services targeted at transit-dependent populations. Their origins can be traced to the early part of this century, when minority entrepreneurs began serving low-income enclaves north of the city that were without streetcar services. By the 1930s and 1940s, several jitney companies had formed, operating sedans between minority neighborhoods and service jobs in downtown Miami and Miami Beach. By 1980, three companies —Liberty City Jitney, King Jitney, and Dade Jitney—were licensed by the city to provide hail services on 28 semifixed routes. All three ran minibuses and sedans between predominantly black neighborhoods in north and northwest Miami, notably Overtown and Liberty City, to downtown. Most company owners leased their permits and vehicles to independent drivers for a flat fee. Drivers kept all fare receipts and covered operating costs.

Applications to operate new jitney routes and expand services outside of Miami's city limits led to the passage of countywide ordinances in 1981 and 1985 that, although regulatory in nature, reconfirmed the area's support for private paratransit services and the reliance on market forces to govern entry into the industry.[28] However, because new applicants proposed routes that duplicated or closely paralleled Miami Metrobus services or preexisting jitney routes, several special studies and task force reports recommended against issuing new permits.[29] Thus, few new permits were issued in the 1980s, save for six temporary permits issued to jitney operators in 1986 to fill in service gaps caused by cuts in Metrobus services. Because of a public outcry at the loss of Metrobus service, Metro Dade Transit Authority (MDTA) later restored services in some areas and revoked the temporary permits of several jitney companies. This caused much bitterness among the affected jitney operators, and to this day is cited by Miami's jitney industry as evidence of the County's duplicity (Urban Mobility Corporation, 1992). Still, by 1988, the number of licensed jitney operators in Dade County stood at 11 (up from just 3 eight years earlier), and some 90 jitney vans and minibuses operated along 20 different routes serving predominantly African-American and Cuban neighborhoods.

Proliferation of Unlicensed Operators

During the 1980s, Miami's continuing influx of immigrants from Cuba and other Caribbean nations, many of whom patronized jitneys in their homelands, combined with local government's tight control of market entry, set the stage for private entrepreneurs to initiate unlicensed minibus services. The discovery of a loophole in a 1981 Florida statute that barred local governments from regulating intercity transportation services opened the floodgates to unlicensed jitneys in early 1990.[30] Privateers took advantage of the loophole to launch unlicensed "intercity" jitney services within metropolitan Miami, running between outlying municipalities, like Hialeah, Coral Gables, and Miami Beach, and downtown Miami. From early 1990 to early 1992, the number of jitneys operating in Dade County jumped from around 90 to an estimated 400, the vast majority of which were unlicensed.[31] Jitneys could be found on nearly every major travel corridor in Dade County, outside of those in well-to-do and predominantly Anglo neighborhoods. Some entrepreneurs concentrated on high-volume corridors, like

Flagler Avenue, Miami's major east-west thoroughfare, competing head-to-head with Metrobus services. Others targeted corridors with large tourist, senior, and service-industry populations, like Miami Beach. Some went after jitneys' "bread-and-butter" markets—low-income Hispanic and black neighborhoods. All charged $1 fares, the same as Metrobus. Along the heaviest trafficked corridors —West Flagler Avenue and N.W. 2nd Avenue—jitneys became so "thick" that average headways during daylight hours were a mere 2 to 3 minutes. Paratransit's 1990–92 "open season" in south Florida proved quite volatile, however. With operators coming and going and companies dividing and merging, jitney routes and services were in a constant state of flux. One study found that around 20 percent of surveyed jitneys stuck to a fixed route. Routes acted as magnets for 40 percent of the jitneys, as they oscillated in and around side streets but always pulled back to main thoroughfares. The other 40 percent favored a particular area, roaming around 50 to 100 city blocks in search of customers (Parsons Brinckerhoff Quade and Douglas, 1993).

The proliferation of unlicensed jitneys brought sharp criticism from Metrobus officials, who charged jitney operators with cream skimming—serving only profitable corridors and leaving low-demand areas, weekend operations, and other high-deficit services to Metrobus. Jitney operators countered that they served a distinct and different submarket—those who value shorter waiting times, faster travel, the ability to flag vehicles at will, and riding with others of a similar cultural background. One study, conducted by the Urban Mobility Corporation (1992), sided largely with the jitney operators. It estimated that Dade County's 400-some jitneys carried 43,000 to 49,000 weekday riders, or around one quarter of Metrobus's weekday ridership. A survey of 570 jitney riders revealed that more than 50 percent "always ride the jitney," and only 31 percent said when deciding between catching a jitney or Metrobus, they use "whichever vehicle arrives first." Over 30 percent of the respondents, moreover, said they would use some other mode other than Metrobus if jitneys were not available. The Urban Mobility Corporation (UMC) study concluded that Metrobus lost around 10,000 daily riders through competition from jitneys and that only around one-fifth of jitney patrons were formerly bus riders. These numbers were derived based on declines in Metrobus ridership on routes with jitney competition over a 30-month period, adjusting for the effects of a fare increase during this time.

A 1994 study by the Center for Urban Transportation Research (CUTR) challenged the UMC findings, concluding that losses in Metrobus ridership corresponded very closely with the influx of unlicensed jitneys in three of four major corridors where jitneys were most common. Part of the reason for the discrepancy lies in how the two studies measured ridership losses. The UMC report looked at ridership in the aggregate while the CUTR study examined changes in rates, specifically riders per revenue hour, thereby controlling for the effects of service changes. While the weight of evidence suggests that most jitney customers were not siphoned away from Metrobus, in some corridors, heavy competition clearly hurt Metrobus in the pocketbook, particularly at a time of sharp cuts in government subsidy support. While one might argue that Metrobus should have responded to lost patronage by curtailing bus services, union clout and public-employee labor protection laws effectively precluded such responses. Notwithstanding the possible negative repercussions of unlicensed jitneys on Metrobus's finances, surveys and data from the 1990–92 expansion period provide a valuable glimpse into the market and performance characteristics of free-enterprise paratransit in a U.S. context. A 1991 survey by Behavioral Science Research, a Miami-based consulting firm, found that south Florida's jitney riders are predominantly low-income workers (78 percent earned below $20,000 per year), and that a large proportion are recent immigrants (53 percent spoke no English).[32] Many came from Jamaica, Puerto Rico, Haiti, and other islands of the West Indies, where private jitneys are common. (In 1990, greater Miami had a larger share of immigrants from the West Indies, 5.5 percent, than any other U.S. metropolitan area.)

In terms of vehicle productivity and cost performance, jitneys generally outperformed subsidized Metrobus services. Such comparisons are problematic in that no single reliable data source on jitney services is available; nor are data across public and private operators exactly equivalent. In the 1992 study, the Urban Mobility Corporation derived ridership, vehicle supply, and operating cost estimates for Miami's jitney (for licensed and unlicensed services combined). Comparing these estimates with Section 15 data compiled for MDTA Metrobus services, Table 2.3 shows that jitneys averaged fewer passengers per vehicle but were far more economical than Metrobus services. Of course, jitneys' lower average vehicle loads reflects the use of smaller vehicles. Still, despite the fact that Metrobuses typically have four to five times the capacity of private minibuses, jitneys averaged just 30 percent fewer passengers per vehicle in 1992. At an average operating expense of $73 per vehicle per day, jitneys cost a fraction of what it took to operate a Metrobus.[33] With each jitney driver averaging 117 daily passengers at a dollar a head, the typical driver cleared around $45 per day, comparable to a minimum wage for an 8-hour workday. This yielded a profit of around 40 cents per rider, compared to a loss of over a dollar per passenger for Metrobus. As with other paratransit services examined in this chapter, Miami's jitneys maintain a cost advantage because their input costs—labor, equipment, overhead, and so forth—are far cheaper. And competition keeps costs low.

One other evaluation from this period compared Miami's jitneys and Metrobus, mainly from a consumer's point of view. After a week of jitney and transit riding, two reporters from the *Miami Herald* found jitneys to be far superior in terms of service frequency, speed, and "friendliness."[34] Metrobus earned higher marks for cleanliness, comfort, and driver vigilance. Services were rated similarly in terms of price value. The reporters gave jitneys a five-star rating for friendliness, noting: "The minibus drivers were courteous and willing to work with passengers, whether it was stopping at a last-minute wave of a hand or giving change for a five-dollar bill. The atmosphere was friendly and folksy." Though highly subjective, this assessment highlights the fact that jitneys and conventional

Table 2.3.
Comparison of Ridership and Operating Cost Statistics Between Private Jitney and MDTA Metrobus Services, 1992

	Jitneys	Metrobus	Jitneys as % of Metrobus
Passengers per vehicle revenue hour[a]	16.3	31.5	51.8%
Annual passengers per vehicle in service[a]	30,900	43,700	70.7%
Daily operating cost per passenger[b]	$0.62	$2.07	30.0%
Daily operating cost per vehicle[b]	$72.00	$507.00	14.2%
Average profit (loss) per passenger[a]	$0.39	($1.03)	—

[a]For jitney services, passenger trips are counted as single revenue-paying journeys. For Metrobus services, passenger trips are counted as unlinked journeys, which means each leg of a multi-leg trip is treated as a single trip. Thus, Metrobus ridership includes trip segments where transfers are used. This tends to inflate the count of passengers on Metrobus relative to that of jitneys.
[b]Cost estimates for jitneys include capital depreciation and debt service payments. Cost estimates for Metrobus services include capital depreciation on equipment, but not debt service.

Sources: Urban Mobility Corporation (1992), Federal Transit Administration (1992).

bus transit are qualitatively different. Despite problems, the 1990–92 period of jitney expansion in greater Miami meant local residents enjoyed far more service-price travel options than most Americans.

Local Government Crackdown

At the urging of Dade County politicians, Florida's state legislature passed an amendment in late 1990 that sought to close the loophole that allowed the proliferation of unlicensed jitneys. The amendment limited statutory exemptions to "intercounty" instead of "intercity" transportation, effectively restoring county control over jitney services. Soon thereafter, Dade County enacted legislation that authorized stricter enforcement, including the impoundment of illegal jitneys.[35] During the first year of the ordinance, illegal jitneys multiplied so rapidly that their sheer numbers overwhelmed enforcement capabilities. In response, Dade County marshaled its resources in mid-1992 and made jitney enforcement a top priority. Working together, the Department of Consumer Services, Metro-Dade police, and regulatory personnel from other county agencies virtually eliminated illegal jitney services by late 1992. During 1992, over 1,200 citations were issued and nearly 700 vehicles were impounded. Early on, the county's crackdown seemed to only force marginal operators out of business. Many others quickly reclaimed impounded vehicles and placed them back into service. However, by mid-1992, stepped-up enforcement took many illegal jitneys out of circulation for good. Growing concerns over public safety made this imperative. A mid-1992 enforcement raid revealed the seriousness of the situation—65 percent of jitney drivers were found to have no chauffeur's licenses, and 48 percent were cited for safety violations.

For Metrobus, stepped-up enforcement yielded immediate benefits. Metrobus ridership for the month of July 1992 was 13 percent higher than in July 1991, while revenue increased by 19 percent (Center for Urban Transportation Research, 1994). Although MDTA had to add bus runs to make up for reduced jitney services, daily farebox revenue was up by around $15,000 as a result of the enforcement campaign.

Emergency Expansion

Hurricane Andrew, which struck south Dade County with devastating force on August 24, 1992, brought new life to Miami's receding jitney industry. The disaster disabled 20,000 cars, dislocated over 200,000 residents, and damaged or destroyed 85,000 businesses. In the wake of this mass destruction, jitneys were quickly enlisted to provide emergency transportation services. A $46 million grant from the Federal Emergency Management Agency (FEMA) enabled MDTA to hire four existing contractors to provide expanded services. A standard turnkey rate of $28 per hour (revenue service plus deadhead hours) was negotiated with the four contractors. The contractors, in turn, recruited around 220 jitney operators, most of whom operated illegally just several months earlier, to provide legitimate services at a guaranteed rate of $15 to $21 per hour. Since most operators were averaging less than half these amounts as independents, many jumped at the opportunity to provide fixed-rate subcontracted services.

Dade County officials worked closely with jitney operators to quickly bring them into compliance with local insurance and safety standards. Vehicle inspections, for example, were conducted seven days a week, and loans were provided to upgrade minibuses. Since many jitney operators already had vehicles ready to go, were familiar with south Dade County, and knew how to operate minibuses efficiently, they were a natural choice for providing supplemental transit services. Enlisting their services effectively solved the illegal jitney problem since more than half of illegal operators became legally employed. Others were able to find more lucrative job opportunities in the massive cleanup and reconstruction efforts.

Within two weeks of the hurricane, jitneys were operating along 12 fixed routes in south Dade County, free of charge. A major trunk route was established along U.S. Route 1 (South Dixie Highway) between Florida City (an area with a large migrant farm-worker population) and the Dadeland South station, MDTA Metrorail's southern terminus, a distance of some 15 miles. Branching out were feeder routes tying residential neighborhoods to makeshift shopping areas and employment sites. Minibuses operated on 5- to 10-minute headways for up to 18 hours a day. Services were adjusted almost daily to respond to shifting travel needs within the hurricane-impacted area. By the spring of 1993, "emergency" jitneys were carrying around 21,000 passengers per day. And by August 1993, one year after Hurricane Andrew, Metrobus ridership was up 35 percent on routes that had previously been plagued by illegal jitney competition.

Maturing of an Industry

County officials hoped to keep the 200 or so south Dade jitney operators legally employed once FEMA support was withdrawn in August 1993, yet the County Board of Commissioners ruled out any subsidy support to jitneys. Having become accustomed to guaranteed pay at up to $21 per hour, few jitney operators showed an interest in providing unsubsidized paratransit services in south Dade County, away from jitney's traditional customer base in north Miami. Services supported by FEMA provided incomes far greater than what most operators were able to eke out prior to the hurricane. Most were not interested in returning to long hours and the hectic pace of prehurricane jitney services. Some operators used their profits from FEMA-supported services to open legal businesses of their own. More lucrative construction-related job opportunities pulled others away from the jitney industry altogether (Center for Urban Transportation Research, 1994). When the county initially requested bids for operating services in south Dade, all bidders sought guaranteed hourly pay of $20 or more and were thus rejected.

The county eventually negotiated with a single company, Red Top Transportation, Inc., to operate jitneys between Florida City/Homestead and the South Dadeland station, mainly along the South Dixie Highway. This route serves mainly farm laborers and non-English-speaking immigrants. Red Top continues to hold the certificate for this intercity route, in most cases leasing vehicles, under the name of Metro Minibus, to a dozen or more independent operators for a fixed fee.[36] Unlike during the period of FEMA-supported jitney services, MDTA today has little involvement with the south Dade County jitney operations. Red Top and MDTA do accept each other's transfers for a 25-cent fee, and Red Top's certificate requires 30-day advance notice of service termination; however, in all other respects the south Dade Metro Minibuses operate as free-enterprise, entrepreneurial jitneys.

Besides the posthurricane jitney route in south Dade, Miami's current jitney services pretty much resemble what they were a decade or more ago, prior to the proliferation of unlicensed operators. Presently, 13 companies are certified to operate along 21 designated routes.[37] By ordinance, no more than 30 percent of any jitney route can duplicate a Metrobus route. Most certificates predate the 1990–92 expansion period of unlicensed jitneys, with routes serving mainly low-income black and Hispanic neighborhoods in north and northwest Miami (Map 2.6). Recent permit holders are required to stick to fixed routes, whereas older operators, like Dade Jitney, King Jitney, and Liberty City Jitney, have been grandfathered to allowed semifixed (e.g., limited route deviation) services. The only other restrictions beyond proper licensing and insurance coverage are that

Map 2.6.
Existing Licensed Jitney Routes in Miami Proper, Exclusive of the Posthurricane
Intercity Route in South Dade County

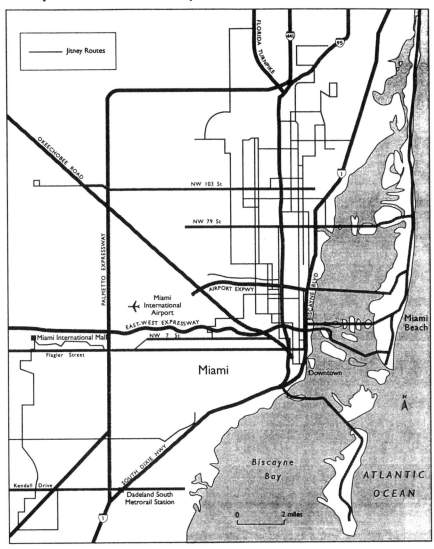

vehicles carry no more than 15 passengers, and operators commit to certain
hours of operation.

Liberty City Jitney has today resumed its role as Miami's largest jitney operator, holding certificates for seven different routes north of downtown. Liberty
City's routes and those of most other operators tie into the Government Center
complex in downtown Miami, an important multimodal transfer point where the

21-mile Metrorail and 1.9-mile downtown people mover (Metromover) come together. Several operators—American Jitney and Transit Express—have sought to carve out new market niches, linking more middle-income neighborhoods in west and south Miami to the Miami International Mall; however, to date these services have been only marginally successful. This has discouraged operators from entering the Miami Beach market, where local officials have sought to replicate Atlantic City's experiences.[38] Unlike in Atlantic City, however, no route association has formed for organizing and advocating the interests of Miami's jitney providers. Overall, Miami's jitney industry remains as fiercely independent as ever.

While some unlicensed operators remain today, in general illegal jitneys pose nowhere near the problems they did in the early 1990s. In addition to the effects of Hurricane Andrew on Miami's jitney industry, the Board of County Commissioners passed an ordinance in 1993 that strengthened the ability of police to seize and impound illegal jitneys given "reasonable cause." Allowable fines were set as high as $1,000 for a first violation, $5,000 for a second violation, and $10,000 for a third or subsequent violation. A third violation within a three-year period also means a vehicle can be seized and forfeited to the county. In recent years, two police motorcycle units have been assigned to jitney enforcement every day. In the continuing battle to circumvent rules and make money in the "informal" transport sector, some local entrepreneurs have begun operating larger and longer vehicles (over 30 feet long and between 15 and 28 seats), using vans that served as airport rental car shuttles in a previous life. Since the county's ordinance does not explicitly refer to this size class of common-carrier vehicle, some enterprising individuals are challenging the system by operating this new, larger form of "jitney." The county has followed suit with a new proposed ordinance that would effectively ban these larger carriers by closing the loophole. In general, the willingness of private entrepreneurs to risk high fines and vehicle impoundment by operating larger minibuses is a sign of overregulation. The struggle to carve out new paratransit niches in greater Miami continues today despite stiff sanctions and intensified enforcement.

Miami's Jitney Experiences in Summary

Overall, Miami's jitney industry has come full circle, returning to its roots after a flurry of episodic events—a statutory loophole that spawned a rash of unlicensed operators, and an act of God that prompted local government to temporarily legitimize formerly illegal operators. Miami's jitney industry today serves mainly transit-dependent populations, just as it historically has. This "settling in" occurred, however, only because of stepped-up enforcement against illegal operations and the withdrawal of hurricane-related subsidy support. It still is not obvious, however, whether Miami's traveling public is better off today as a result. Research suggests that during the heyday of open-market jitney operations, jitneys provided valuable transportation services and carved out a substantially new market niche. Metrobus lost riders and revenues; however, this was largely due to head-to-head competition, even though Metrobus had the advantage of subsidy support. While government's role in regulating jitneys to protect public safety is unimpeachable, the rationale for restricting market entry among prospective operators who meet public safety and fitness standards is hard to defend. In addition to more vigilant enforcement, an appropriate policy response in the wake of increased jitney competition would have been to lift entry restrictions so that operators meeting safety qualifications became legitimate, combined with selective curtailment of Metrobus services. Stiff political resistance—from transit unions, middle-class residents, and other beneficiaries of traditional transit—largely precluded such policy responses. Striking the right balance between government oversight of jitney services and free-market competition remains a significant challenge in greater Miami, just as elsewhere in the United States. Still, Miami's policy makers deserve some credit for allowing private jitneys to continue serving more transit-dependent populations at a time when most American cities have regulated all forms of private paratransit competitors out of existence.

COMMERCIAL VANS

A final form of paratransit reviewed in this chapter is the feeder and commuter vans that ply the streets of New York City, providing both connections to rail stations and express runs to Manhattan. Some are licensed; however, most are not. In many ways, these vans operate like jitneys, following fairly established routes and responding to curbside hails. However, unlike most jitneys, a significant number of vans follow routine schedules, provide long-haul services, are veritable subscription services with the same regular customers, and operate only during peak periods. Compared to jitneys in Miami, Atlantic City, and San Diego, moreover, licensed vans in New York are not held to specific routes and thus are more likely to make slight detours and route adjustments. More generally, New York City's paratransit sector is a hybrid, taking on features of jitneys as well as regularly scheduled subscription vanpools and informal community-based services. Like airport shuttles, some vans provide few-to-one (or few-to-few) services; however, unlike airport shuttles, they rarely carry advanced-reservation fares or are radio-linked to dispatch centers. Overall, commercial feeder and commuter vans form an industry that is unique to New York City—home to the nation's largest population of people of Caribbean ancestry, the nation's most extensive rail network, the nation's densest and most populous urban centers, and one of the most heavily regulated taxicab industries in the country.

While free-roaming commercial vans can also be found in northeast New Jersey,[39] they have become a more prominent fixture of the local transportation scene in New York City than anywhere. Many observers contend that shared-ride vans, equipped with automated communications technologies and which operate like airport shuttles but to multiple destinations, are the model for successful paratransit of the future. The Reason Foundation, an influential libertarian think tank based in Los Angeles, has gone on record in support of automated forms of New York-style commercial vans as the ideal paratransit solution for Southern California (Poole and Griffin, 1994). For these and other reasons, experiences in New York City deserve closer inspection.

Commercial Vans in New York City

Compared to Miami, Atlantic City, and other places with formal jitney services, New York City's paratransit history is fairly short. In the late 1970s, Caribbean immigrants began informally hauling Queens residents to subway stations using passenger sedans. A 1980–81 transit strike triggered an explosion in the city's van population, as entrepreneurs, almost exclusively from the Caribbean, initiated their own transit services. Vans quickly replaced private cars as the vehicle of choice. The heaviest concentration grew around Long Island Railroad stations in the Jamaica section of southeast Queens. Jamaica developed mainly during the postwar auto era, and thus has, by New York standards, fairly low densities and meager subway services. Populated largely by Puerto Ricans, Jamaicans, Haitians, and other Caribbean islanders and, according to locals, historically ignored by city transit officials for this reason, southeast Queens was a natural breeding grounds for commercial paratransit. Throughout the 1980s, van activity spread to Brooklyn and the Bronx, and commuter runs into Manhattan became common. The New York State Department of Transportation (NYSDOT), until 1994 the regulator of intrastate van services, granted legal authority to van operators who could demonstrate a demand for their services and meet fitness and safety standards. Most, however, never bothered to obtain proper licensing, operating with little constraint along the busiest city bus routes and corridors served by private bus carriers, like the Green Bus Company and Jamaica Bus Lines in southeast Queens. Mimicking established bus routes has earned illegal vans the tag, *shadow bus routes.*

One estimate places the number of illegal, unlicensed vans, taxis, buses, and private cars today roaming the streets of New York City at over 75,000, though no one knows how many there are for sure. What is known is that their sheer numbers have overwhelmed enforcement capabilities. A *New York Times* reporter notes: "A police officer gamely ticketing one van after another on Flatbush Avenue on a recent morning said he thought the van traffic was uncontrollable. Two or three sailed by for every one that he ticketed" (Mitchell, 1992, p. A16). For the most part, New York City's vans are still overwhelmingly driven and patronized by blacks from islands of the Caribbean. Like Dade County, New York City has large concentrations of Caribbean immigrants (over 400,000 in 1990, comprising over 5 percent of total population), an important cultural dimension to the proliferation of private van services (Boyle, 1994). Passengers are mostly working people who rely on prompt and dependable paratransit services to reach their jobs. The van industry's customer based has diversified some in recent years, owing mainly to the start-up of commuter van services from Staten Island to Manhattan that cater to a mix of ethnic groups. Research and anecdotes alike reveal that customers prefer vans over subsidized city buses —despite sometimes questionable safety—because they are faster, more comfortable, cheaper, pass by more frequently, make fewer stops, provide guaranteed seats, and take people closer to their destinations.[40] (Much of the vans' speed advantage stems from aggressive driving—making detours to avoid traffic jams, exploiting gaps in traffic flows, staying away from congested areas at particular times of day, etc.). Some patronize vans partly out of loyalty to black-run businesses. The willingness of most drivers to drop passengers off at the front door, accept subway tokens, make change, provide information, and chat with patrons along the way is appreciated by many.

The two main classes of New York City's commercial vans—feeder and commuter services—are discussed below. A third type of commercial paratransit, car services, is also briefly reviewed.

Feeder Vans

Feeder vans operate at the neighborhood level, shuttling residents in outer boroughs to subway stations and community centers. The Metropolitan Transportation Authority (MTA)[41] estimates between 2,500 and 5,000 feeder vans roam the outer boroughs each day, preying off it and private bus firms. Fewer than one in 10 feeder vans have licenses, and even those holding certificates routinely break rules, doing things like loading passengers at bus stops. Areas with the highest concentrations of feeder vans, shown in Map 2.7, are Jamaica Center (along Jamaica, Archer, and Parsons avenues) in Queens and the Flatbush Avenue and Utica Avenue corridors in Brooklyn. Around 500 vans prowl Flatbush Avenue each workday, mirroring one of the city's busiest bus routes, B-41, from the Flatbush Avenue subway station to downtown Brooklyn. The Long Island Railroad station at Jamaica Center attracts as many as 350 vans and 25,000 van patrons each day.[42] Smaller centers of activity have spawned in parts of the Bronx —along Grand Concourse, Westchester, Fordham, and White Plains avenues.

One unflattering account, published in a transit trade magazine, characterized New York's informal feeder services as:

groups of dented vans, some with legal licenses plates, others with stolen ones, that weave around public buses on the same route and careen into bus stops outside the subway exit. There the unkempt, often unlicensed, often illegal alien drivers bleat passengers at a dollar a piece . . . in flagrant violation of state and city laws. (Read, 1991, p. 16)

Feeder vans are indeed notorious for preying on NYCTA's customers, duplicating the paths of established bus routes and illegally soliciting passengers at bus stops. One study estimated that at least 27 percent of bus routes operated by NYCTA and franchised companies face direct competition from feeder vans

Map 2.7.
Parts of Brooklyn, Queens, and the Bronx with High Concentrations of Feeder Van Services

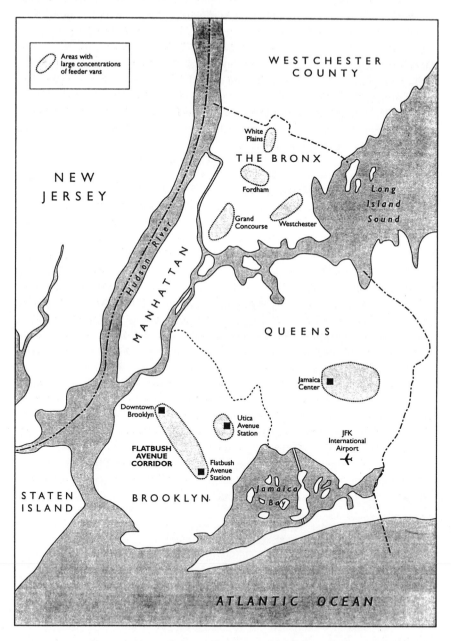

(Trommer and Goldenberg, 1994). It is not uncommon for van drivers to call out public bus route numbers at stops to inform potential passengers of where the van is heading. Feeder vans are so thick in parts of Brooklyn and Queens that average headways are as short as two minutes. Van fares are usually below those of competing public transit services but have historically risen, lagged by a year or two, to match increases in public transit fares (Boyle, 1994). However, some van operators have kept fares at $1, even though local bus fares have risen to $1.25, in order to reduce the need to make and handle change—important to a business that relies on speedy customer transactions. Most vans are owned and operated by the same individual, though some van owners lease their vehicles for a set fee.

Commuter Vans

Commuter vans provide express services from the outer boroughs to lower and midtown Manhattan, making one or two trips per peak period. They usually compete head-to-head with NYCTA or franchised commute bus services. Their popularity lies in providing faster service in better equipment at a lower fare than subsidized competitors. Some of the larger 20-passenger minibus operators provide first-class services—free coffee, on-board televisions, and overhead reading lamps. Passengers usually pay a cheaper fare than for equivalent NYCTA commuter services—$3.50 versus $4 in 1992. Many commuter vans originate in Staten Island, cross the Bayonne bridge into New Jersey, and take the Holland or Lincoln Tunnel into Manhattan.[43] Because they cross state lines, Staten Island–based vans fall under the jurisdiction of the far more permissive Interstate Commerce Commission.

In the mid-1980s, an estimated 700 to 1,100 private commuter vans crossed the bridges into Manhattan each morning, carrying 15,000 to 17,000 passengers (Department of City Planning, 1984; Comsis, 1986; Grava et al., 1989). Most operated without certification or in some improper manner (e.g., underinsured), and over 95 percent of commuter van patrons formerly took public transit. A more recent study found around one-half of vans coming into Manhattan to be licensed (Savas et al., 1991). Presently, 33 New York–based companies and 365 vans are authorized to provide commuter services into Manhattan.

Car Services

Sedans and station wagons that transport low-income patrons to shops, clinics, job sites, airports, and other destinations are the city's fastest growing paratransit sector. This industry is sharply bifurcated between legal and illegal operators. Legal ones, known as "for-hire vehicles," cater to higher income markets, playing a vital role in a city where only half of households own a car and where taxis are scarce outside Manhattan and the airports. City ordinances limit for-hire cars to providing prearranged services. The legal car industry is quite large—some

30,000 licensed vehicles dispatched from 600 base stations serve 170,000 to 300,000 passenger trips per day, 5 to 8 percent of all nonwalk trips made in the city (New York City Taxi and Limousine Commission, 1993). In contrast, up to 20,000 illicit private cars—also called gypsy cabs—operate along main arterials in low-income areas each day, relying on street hail for customers. Like vans, gypsy cabs often raid bus stops, picking up several passengers for $1 each. Gypsy cabs are the least organized and most blatantly illegal form of private paratransit services in the city. Virtually all vehicles are unlicensed, untested, and un- or underinsured. As discussed in Chapter 3, many illegal cars specialize in serving shopping trips. In Brooklyn, hawkers soliciting patrons leaving the Kings Plaza Shopping Center have become a common site; gypsy cab drivers pay hawkers a small commission for each passenger lured in. "Bogus cabs," painted yellow and sporting a rooflight so as to make them hard to distinguish from licensed cabs, thrive in north Manhattan and the Bronx because of a shortage of medallion taxi service.

Public Concerns

The most serious concern with New York's commercial vans is public safety. Because competition is so intense and enforcement is hit-or-miss, vans are all too often operated with reckless abandon. Drivers regularly cut buses off to reach passengers first. Uncoordinated van loading and unloading clogs up busy boulevards. In Manhattan, vans queuing up in midafternoon to haul workers back to the outer boroughs have caused gridlock. In Brooklyn and Queens, vans loitering and cruising around subway stations disrupt the operations of public buses and legitimate operators.

As noted, most van drivers are unlicensed and without insurance. Some have long rap sheets, and too many are engaged in illicit, underground activities, like smuggling drugs. In a few well-publicized cases, overly zealous drivers have caused serious accidents and fatalities.[44] Safety, however, lies in the eyes of the beholder. One study found some customers view vans as safer than public buses because drivers will not pick up drunks, roughnecks, or gang members (Metropolitan Transportation Authority, 1992). For the most part, van operators are hardworking immigrants with few job prospects who believe they can live the American dream by becoming paratransit entrepreneurs. The prospect of being ticketed and paying fines is of little concern, even though the average van driver working busy bus routes earns only $20,000 to $25,000, a meager amount for one of the world's most expensive cities (Fried, 1994). Most have few alternatives.

Another concern is the fiscal impact of illegal services on public transit agencies and licensed bus operators. MTA estimates it has lost as much as 15 percent of revenues to illegal vans on some of its most heavily impacted bus routes. Citywide, the overall loss to the transit authority has been put at $30 million to $50 million annually, or 7 to 10 percent of bus revenues (Metropolitan Transportation Authority, 1992; Fried, 1994). In the Jamaica Center area, MTA estimates that it loses $8,500 in fare revenue per day. Jamaica Bus Lines, the major franchise bus carrier in southeast Queens, saw its monthly patronage cut in half, from 747,000 in 1981 to 366,000 in 1991, because of excess competition from illegal vans, according to company officials (Read, 1991).

On the positive side, even critics acknowledge benefits from commercial van operations. As a homegrown industry, vans provide jobs to tens of thousands of New Yorkers, including ancillary businesses that maintain and service vehicles. They also provide mobility at a time when financially strapped transit systems are unable to expand services. Likewise, they provide valuable backup in case of a transit strike, no idle matter in a city so dependent on transit that a work stoppage can bring near paralysis. And they accomplish all of this without government subsidies.

Van Regulations

Van regulation in New York City is complex, involving multiple layers of bureaucracy and oversight. Today, three different municipal departments are involved in the review of applications for van licenses, and enforcement efforts bring together as many as six local and state offices.[45] With so many illegal vans in such a large, diverse city, regulation and enforcement require tremendous public resources and efforts.

Historically, New York state maintained jurisdiction over intrastate carriers. A Certificate of Convenience and Necessity was used to regulate market entry. Because state regulators routinely approved applications for new van services, local transit officials successfully lobbied to have controls shifted to the municipal level. In 1993, the New York State Senate and Assembly enacted enabling legislation that effectively transferred all regulatory authority over commercial van services to New York City. Soon thereafter, the city passed an ordinance, which took effect in mid-1994, that clamped down on how legalized vans operate. Most stifling has been the provision that vans serve customers on a *prearranged* basis only, thereby barring all street hails. With the exception of lower Manhattan, the municipal regulation also prohibits vans from soliciting, picking up, or discharging passengers at any point along a NYCTA or private bus line.[46] Obtaining a Certificate of Authority to operate a van has also become more difficult, requiring applicants to demonstrate the service will fill an unmet public need and giving NYCTA and private carriers the right to comment upon and protest pending applications; for the past several years, NYCTA has protested all applications and in many cases has wielded virtual veto power.[47] The new law also permits seizure of a vehicle by a police officer or deputized agent of the Taxi and Limousine Commission, the designated enforcer of van regulations, if there is reasonable cause to suspect it is being operated without a license.[48] With the new law in hand, the city's top transportation official is optimistic about the future, contending that "the legislation provides tools to end the urban warfare on the streets of New York between vans and buses" (Fried, 1994, p. 43).

Because of these tough new rules, no new van licenses have been issued since 1994, nor will any likely be issued in the near future. Few van operators seem interested in becoming "legitimate," limited to serving phone-in travel requests and operating on local streets. And few seasoned operators seem fazed by these new rulings. During candid interviews with a *New York Times* reporter, a veteran Jamaican operator vowed "we're still going to work along the bus routes because that's exactly where the people are." Another maintained "even if they don't give us the bus routes, we're going to do it there—we would not be able to make money on the side streets to pay the taxes and the insurance you'll have to have" (Fried, 1994, p. 43).

Van Enforcement

In the early 1990s, local authorities began cracking down on illegal van opera-tors.[49] Periodic enforcement raids continue today, entailing mass field inspec-tions, spot checks by unmarked cars, and foot patrols at subway stations where the vans congregate. Illegal vehicles are towed, passengers are expelled from vehicles, and drivers are fined and sometimes arrested on the spot. The vehicles of repeat offenders and gross violators are routinely seized and forfeited.

In recent years, enforcement efforts have intensified. In 1993, some 4,000 illegal vans and gypsy cabs were seized citywide, a 27 percent increase above prior-year seizures. During an 18-day period in early 1995, city police issued 1,400 summonses, made 40 arrests, and seized 85 vehicles. From a revenue standpoint, enforcement sweeps have proven quite successful. In a concentrated enforcement experiment along Brooklyn's busy Flatbush Avenue corridor in early 1992, ridership rose by 27 percent on affected NYCTA bus routes. Increased fare receipts more than covered enforcement expenses. A year after the experiment, one bus route retained a 20 percent revenue increase compared to preenforcement levels. A subsequent sweep in the Jamaica Center area yielded similar results (Boyle, 1994). At times, van owners have voiced their displeasure over stepped-up enforcement, staging demonstrations and tying up streets in a major show of force.

Overall, enforcement crackdowns have provided only ephemeral relief. The city's illegal van population today remains essentially unchanged. There simply are not enough resources to sustain intensive enforcement efforts, and for New York City's Police Department, ticketing illegal vans is not a high priority. Crackdowns have had the biggest impact on how licensed vans operate. Most legal operators have supported and cooperated with enforcement campaigns targeted at illegals since they stand to gain more riders as a result. Still, legal operators are livid over being barred from bus routes, arguing that detours to side streets greatly inconvenience their customers. Yet heightened enforcement has pressured many into staying off major boulevards. Legal jitneys in Queens now post signs in their windows indicating that they will not stop at bus stops.

Critics charge that enforcement has become an issue only because regulatory standards are too high. Regulators, they contend, set standards for middle-class folks, ignoring the willingness of many lower-income immigrants to sacrifice comfort and a certain threshold of safety in return for a break at the farebox and faster services. First-world standards are being imposed on a population accustomed to third-world-like paratransit services.

Other Policy Responses

Though they openly complain about the poaching practices of commercial vans, New York City transit officials concede that vans are here to stay and thus efforts must be made to integrate them into the region's urban transportation system. One recent initiative, spearheaded by the NYCDOT (regulator of the city's curbspace), has been to erect van stops and create staging zones to facilitate passenger drop-off and pickup in some of the city's most popular van corridors.

Service and Fare Reforms

Another policy response has been to make municipal and franchised buses more competitive with commercial vans. One way of doing this is mimicking their operations.

Along some corridors, NYCTA buses will now stop anywhere along the route, though normally only during "owl" service hours (10:00 P.M. to 5:00 A.M.). Plans are also under way to create more dedicated bus lanes in major van corridors in hopes of giving public and franchised buses a speed advantage.

In 1993, the MTA sought to undercut the competition from vans by offering a $1.50 round-trip fare (known as a Fare Deal) along five Queens bus lines, instead of the normal $2.50. A round trip on a van costs $2.00. During the first two years, revenues from ridership gains offset losses from lower fares according to MTA. The Fare Deal program has since been extended to popular van corridors in Brooklyn and the Bronx as well. In a recent interview of a group of riders at a bus stop outside a subway station in the Bronx, a *New York Times* reporter found few would be won over by a fare break: "more than anything else, the illegal vans's promptness and door-to-door service made them more attractive; most said they would keep taking the illegal vans" (Onishi, 1994). MTA's own analysis has shown enforcement crackdowns to be twice as effective in winning back patrons as reduced round-trip fares (Trommer and Goldenberg, 1994).

Another fare strategy has been to charge a single fare as a way to encourage residents to ride NYCTA buses as feeders to subway stations. Historically, patrons have had to pay separate fares for bus and subway rides. At Jamaica Center, MTA has introduced a 25-cent bus-subway transfer (versus $1.25 for a single fare). Ridership on bus lines feeding into Jamaica Center increased 30 percent during the program's first year, and new-rider proceeds have offset revenue losses from discounts.[50] Also on the horizon is a prepaid, stored-value transit pass, called MetroCard, that can be used anywhere on MTA's bus-subway net-work. Automated fare collection is currently being installed at 69 subway stations throughout the city. One-dollar fares and drivers' willingness to provide change have always given vans a service edge over public buses. The MetroCard should even the field. MetroCard has already spurred innovations in the van industry. After one Queens van owner recently introduced a weekly pass program, several others soon followed suit.

Organizational Responses: Associations

The long-term success of New York's commercial van sector likely also lies in forming cooperatives to advocate the industry's interests and coordinate services, just as jitney operators have done in Atlantic City. In the Jamaica area of Queens, several cooperatives have formed in recent years. One of the first was the Jamaica Association of Van Owners/Operators (JAVO), initiated in 1989 mainly as a lobbying organization devoted to legitimizing neighborhood van services.[51] A JAVO Passenger's *Bill of Rights* was prepared, along with a decal and seal of approval (Figure 2.1). The JAVO service was instrumental in rallying public support for commercial vans at several state hearings held to review the case for licensing vans. JAVO, however, never gained the support of the largest and most influential operator in the area, Queens Van Plan, and as a result was short-lived.[52] Queens Van Plan, however, helped spearhead the formation of JAVO's successor, the Interborough Alliance for Community Transportation, better known as the Alliance. The Alliance has adopted many of the same goals of JAVO, though it has a less visible presence, with its leaders opting to operate more behind the scene. All licensed van operators in southeast Queens—numbering 215 in mid-1995—have joined the Alliance. The organization is perceived by most driver-members as a vehicle for fighting their common nemesis—the MTA. While MTA and the Alliance share one common objective—to rid the streets of illegal van operators—on most other matters, the two organizations are usually poles apart. Like Atlantic City's route association, the Alliance has also begun to police itself, mediating driver disputes and sanctioning those who flagrantly violate operating rules.

TRADITIONAL PARATRANSIT IN SUMMARY

The paratransit modes reviewed in this chapter—shared-ride taxis, jitneys, and commercial vans—are traditional in the sense that they have been the longest-standing shared-ride services available to the general public. In a few areas—the San Ysidro border, north Miami, Atlantic City, and parts of Queens and Brooklyn—they have become the workhorse of the local transit system. Most of these cases share common characteristics. One is serving a specific subpopula-tion, defined partly in terms of income (e.g., poor inner-city residents without cars) but mainly in terms of ethnicity. In south San Diego, Miami, and New York

Figure 2.1.
JAVO Passenger's *Bill of Rights*

JAVO
PASSENGER'S
BILL OF RIGHTS

The JAVO Quality Seal of Approval may be displayed only in Vans owned and driven by individuals who have pledged to adhere to JAVO'S Code of Service and Conduct. Every passenger on a van displaying the JAVO Quality Seal of Approval is entitled to the full protection of the JAVO Passenger's Bill of Rights.

As a JAVO Van Rider, you are entitled to:

1. Safe, reliable and courteous service.

2. A clean, comfortable, well-maintained van that meets New York State safety and vehicle inspection requirements.

3. A van authorized as a common carrier by New York State and displaying proper livery license plates and operator identification on the dashboard.

4. A van carrying public liability insurance equal to or greater than New York State requirements.

5. A licensed, fully trained driver, neatly dressed and well mannered, whose name and photograph are posted on the dashboard.

6. Compliance with all vehicle and traffic laws and regulations.

7. Dependable departures and full schedule information.

8. Safe, orderly procedures for loading and unloading passengers.

9. Fair and reasonable rates.

10. Diligent investigation and timely redress of complaints.

If you have a complaint against a van displaying the JAVO Quality Seal of Approval or would like more information, call JAVO HOTLINE: (718) 712-3421.

City's outer boroughs, an overwhelming majority of paratransit customers are of Hispanic background. The explosion of commercial jitneys and vans in Miami and New York City, many of which are unlicensed, paralleled the surge in immigration from the Caribbean in both places. Predictably, beside foreign foods, dance, and song, these new Americans brought with them other parts of their culture, including an affinity for small-vehicle forms of paratransit. While heavy-handed regulations and stepped-up enforcement have suppressed their numbers in these and other cities, the steady influx of people with Hispanic backgrounds into the United States makes it inevitable that jitneys and vans will continue to proliferate in many large urban centers.

It remains to be seen whether private jitneys and vans can ever gain a market foothold in middle-class America. Atlantic City's jitneys have succeeded in luring middle-class car-owners to mass transit, mainly through providing frequent, reliable services at good value, though this is partly attributable to the uniqueness of the city itself—a compact tourist town with a steady stream of traffic. White-collar professionals also share taxi rides in Washington, D.C., at airport curbsides, and at downtown cabstands where point-to-point trips are common. As reviewed in the next chapter, middle-class Americans have been most attracted to prearranged, subscription services, like vanpools and buspools. Besides the near-ubiquitous airport shuttle vans, other specialized services catering to middle-class clients that have emerged include neighborhood-to-subway shuttle runs and child paratransit.

This chapter demonstrated that jitneys, vans, and shared-ride taxis provide significant performance advantages over conventional bus transit. On a cost-per-passenger basis, where bus operating expenses are typically understated, commercial paratransit were shown to have a decisive edge. Berkeley's racetrack taxipools and Miami's jitneys cost 70 percent less for every passenger carried than comparable public bus services. With San Ysidro's jitney runs, per-passenger costs were 20 percent lower, only because these jitneys compete with one of the most productive bus routes in the country. While Berkeley's shared-ride taxis and Miami's jitneys carried, on average, half as many passengers per hour as their subsidized competitors, they did so with vehicles with 5 to 10 times less capacity. Perhaps most telling are the results of passenger surveys in Miami and New York City. In both places, paratransit customers consistently preferred jitneys and vans over buses for their frequent services, speed advantages, convenience, guaranteed seats, and user-friendliness. One-third of Miami's surveyed jitney riders said they would have walked, driven, or foregone the trip rather than ride Metrobus if jitney services were not available. These are powerful findings, clearly showing that paratransit services in these cities have carved out distinct market niches. While jitneys and vans have taken customers away from public bus systems, they have done so mainly by providing superior services, without subsidies.

To date, restraints on market entry have spawned illegal jitney and van operators in cities like Miami and New York City, and most certainly in other places as well (see the discussions of community-based paratransit in Chapter 3). The chief policy response has been enforcement sweeps and crackdowns. There is clearly a need for safeguarding public safety. Most jitney and van operators acknowledge that their industry is plagued by too many unfit, unlicensed operators. Some argue, however, that one-size-fit-all standards are wrongheaded, ignoring the tremendous diversity of the traveling public. Should everyone be forced to ride in vehicles that are fairly new, meet high liability insurance requirements, and have comfortable, padded seats, paying a premium fare for these provisions? Must van riders in southeast Queens and jitney patrons in San Ysidro, many of whom come from countries where customers give up quality and accept higher risks in return for cheaper fares, be forced to travel in American-style comfort? One can turn the matter of regulatory violations on its head, focussing less on ways of strengthening enforcement and more on ways of loosening or "flexing" regulatory standards.

Overall, shared-ride taxis, jitneys, and commercial vans provide valuable transportation services in areas where they have survived. Legal or otherwise, they have emerged to serve unmet consumer demands, often going into areas poorly served by mass transit systems. Their potential to serve other submarkets, like middle-class customers, is largely unexplored because of regulatory and policy restrictions. Notwithstanding such barriers, a few more specialized forms of commercial paratransit have emerged in recent years that have begun to tap into such markets. It is to the experiences of these alternative services that we now turn.

NOTES

1. Shared-ride taxi demonstrations in small cities like Davenport, Iowa, and El Cajon, California, were particularly successful. The Davenport shared-ride taxis carried over 1,000 persons per day in 1973, nearly 65 percent as many as the local bus system, for an average fare of around $1 (Heathington et al., 1975). El Cajon's shared-ride taxis began in 1972 when the city contracted with Yellow Cab Company of San Diego to provide general-purpose dial-a-ride services to city residents. El Cajon's share-ride taxi demonstration program lasted longer than any other in the nation. In 1992, the city converted the service to a dial-a-ride minibus operation contracted through San Diego County (see Chapter 3). Even after federal demonstration programs ended, shared-ride taxis for the elderly and disabled persons continued to expand in California, Michigan, and Minnesota, all states that dedicate sale tax revenues to public transportation. As in El Cajon, as federal support for mass transit and state dedicated transit funds began to shrink, most subsidized shared-ride taxi services were discontinued in the 1980s because per passenger costs proved to be too exorbitant. These services were generally replaced by specialized dial-a-ride services for the elderly and disabled, sometimes offered through social services agencies. The decline of the nation's unsubsidized shared-ride taxi industry generally predated when subsidized services began to falter. Besides Little Rock, nonsubsidized shared-ride taxi services also existed during periods of the 1960s and early 1970s in Pensacola, Florida, Long Island, New York, Danville, Illinois, Arabi, Louisiana, Westport, Connecticut, and Petersborough, Ontario (Teal, 1978). Today, few shared-ride taxi trips are made in these places. Pensacola has maintained a fare system where the first passenger pays the amount on the fare meter, and the second passenger pays the difference between what the first passenger paid

and the amount on the meter when he or she disembarks. Danville has retained a zone fare system to allow taxi ridesharing, but according to local officials, this is a rare event.

2. There are no comprehensive data sources which provide precise information on taxi travel volumes, and certainly none on taxi ride-sharing. Estimates are based on interviews with staff members of local taxi commissions. In Manhattan, several cabstands north of Central Park will take multiple unrelated passengers to the Wall Street area for $3.50 to $5 per passenger. At the York Avenue–79th Street cabstand, shared-ride taxis have become a ritual. From 5:00 A.M. to 10:00 A.M. each weekday customers queue to catch a ride to Wall Street, four-to-a-cab, at a special fare of $3.50 apiece. Anyone wanting to go elsewhere is out of luck; cabbies refuse to go anywhere but Wall Street, even though they are legally obligated to take all riders where they want to go (Lambert, 1995). In Los Angeles, all taxis can carry up to four passengers within a downtown cordon area for a $4 fare. Chicago's shared-ride taxis operate between cabstands within the Loop district and are thought to be fairly popular. Atlanta's shared-ride taxis charge a flat $5 fee for intra-downtown trips.

3. The flat rate between downtown Los Angeles and the International Airport (LAX) is $24 per trip. Atlanta charges $18 for trips between downtown and Hartsfield International Airport, or $10 per passenger for two or more passengers. San Francisco is unique in charging less, a $24 flat fare, for trips from downtown to airports than for exclusive passenger trips, which are metered fares that can exceed $30. Between Denver International Airport and the city, there are different fares for 21 destination zones.

4. Services became more exclusionary in the sense that, as with many exclusive-ride taxi services across the country, some taxi drivers avoided serving minority neighborhoods in fear for their safety. Little Rock's business community pressured the City Council to introduce exclusive-ride services in part because of a desire for higher quality services to destinations like the airport, though another tacit explanation, according to some, was a desire for class segregation for common-carrier services.

5. Sources: Federal Transit Administration, *1990 National Transit Database: Section 15 Report*. Washington, D.C.: Federal Transit Administration, 1991; U.S. Bureau of the Census, *Summary Tape Files 3A*; interviews with local taxi operators.

6. Sources: Federal Transit Administration, *1990 Section 15 Report*; U.S. Bureau of the Census, *Summary Tape Files 3A*.

7. U.S. Congress, Hearing Before the Subcommittee on Public Utilities, Insurance, and Banking of the House Committee on the District of Columbia, 85th Congress, 1st Session, at 124, 127, 1957.

8. Golden Gate Fields abuts the bay at the western edge of the city of Albany. The race season begins in early February and runs through June. The track is open Wednesdays to Sundays and on holidays. All-day parking is available for $3. The East Bay's major bus operator, Alameda–Contra Costa County (AC) Transit, operates Line 304 between the North Berkeley BART station and the racetrack. The shared-ride taxi operates a slightly more direct route than the Line 304. During the race season, passengers arrive at the North Berkeley BART station around 11:30 A.M. to 2:30 P.M. Racetrack goers return to BART between 3:30 P.M. and 6:30 P.M.

9. Line 304 departs from the North Berkeley BART station every 30 minutes between 11:10 A.M. and 5:40 P.M. No transfers are issued or accepted on Line 304, nor is the monthly pass accepted. Unlike most shared-ride taxi runs, Line 304 stops to receive or drop off passengers between BART and the racetrack.

10. Both the cities of Berkeley and Albany let the market determine the number of cabs operating within their jurisdictions and allow operators to set their own fares up to a ceiling maximum. Shared rides are permitted de jure in Berkeley and de facto in Albany. Neither city reports any problems with shared-ride taxi operators. The regularity of routes, self-regulation among operators, and ease of police enforcement of point-to-point services make illegal operations difficult.

11. Estimated daily operating cost breakdowns are: $16.20 for insurance; $2.05 for maintenance; $3.90 for gasoline and oil; $5.30 for vehicle depreciation and debt financing; and $1.25 for permits. These are amortized costs prorated for the share of time—normally two to three hours per day—of a typical eight-hour shift that taxi drivers concentrate on racetrack services. Most cabbies providing shared-ride services own their own vehicles, typically four- to five-year-old sedans that cost between $4,000 and $5,000 and that are kept for two to three years. A few drivers lease their vehicles from cab companies at around $45 per day, plus gate fees of around $45 per day (which entitles the driver to radio-dispatch calls). Owner-operators normally set aside around $18 per day for insurance and maintenance. Liability insurance costs approximately $5,000 per year. An average weekday of driving is about 70 miles, as much as half of which is for the shared-ride racetrack runs. Sources of data: field interviews with shared-ride taxi drivers; American Automobile Association, *Your Cost of Driving*, Washington, D.C., 1994; and Motor Vehicle Manufacturer's Association, *Motor Vehicle Facts & Figures*, New York, 1994.

12. Net income estimates are based on an average of 4.2 round trips per weekday and 5.5 round trips per Saturday or Sunday, with an average of four passengers per round trip.

13. Los Angeles introduced several jitney experiments over the past two decades. In the 1970s, a strike by the Southern California Rapid Transit District (SCRTD) prompted local officials to authorize La France Transportation Company to operate a jitney along Wilshire Boulevard. The intent was to make taxicabs, which were reaping monopolistic profits from serving office workers along the Wilshire corridor, face greater competition from lower-priced jitneys, which charged a dollar per ride. Once the strike ended, however, competition from public buses, which charged only $0.25 per ride, forced La France out of the jitney business after only a few months of operation (Siracusa, 1990; Lombardo, 1994). Los Angeles's second foray into private jitney services occurred in mid-1982 when California's Public Utilities Commission (PUC) authorized two carriers, Express Transit District (ETD) and Maxi Taxi, to operate along major arterials, including Wilshire Boulevard, in direct competition with SCRTD, which was financially unable to expand services at the time. At the height of the experiment, ETD operated 40 passenger vans on peak-hour headways as short as five minutes. It was estimated that ETD carried around 6 percent of peak-hour transit passengers along routes where they operated (Teal and Nemer, 1986). Surveys showed that a large percentage of ETD's customers were Latinos who liked riding in vehicles driven by other Latinos. The passage of Proposition A in late 1982 that provided dedicated sales tax revenues to SCRTD dealt the death blow to Los Angeles's nascent jitney industry. Lower public transit fares forced Maxi Taxi to fold even before initiating services, and ETD's services lasted only seven months.

14. Mr. Losa began driving a jitney in San Francisco in 1972, soon after immigrating to the United States from the Philippines, a country where jitneys (called "jeepneys" in Manila) are the predominate means of intraurban transportation.

15. Based on interviews, monthly expenses for insurance, gasoline, maintenance, and capital depreciation are estimated to be around $3,800.

16. As a one-man business surviving on a small profit margin, Mr. Losa has learned to be resourceful. He makes most repairs on his vehicle himself. Seated on the dashboard, next to pictures of his first jitney, are cups of screws, washers, and miscellaneous mechanical parts. With older vehicles, he has to be prepared for anything to go wrong.

17. The paratransit ordinance (No. 11) states: "jitneys cannot remain standing on any public street in the city, except to load and unload passengers or when waiting in a holding zone; owners, drivers, or agents cannot solicit passengers on streets, sidewalks, hotels, public resorts, rail stations or airports; and jitney drivers must remain within 12 feet of their jitneys while in service."

18. Evidently some former jitney operators switched from driving jitneys to driving more lucrative airport shuttle vans. These operators let their jitney licenses lapse, replacing them with California Public Utility Commission licenses for common-carrier services. State licenses are less restrictive than local jitney licenses, allowing service providers to operate between cities and giving them the freedom to provide many-to-few services (versus point-to-point fixed route services).

19. Route 932 is a contract service that runs from Centre City in downtown San Diego through the South Bay area and terminates at the San Ysidro border area. Southbound Route 932 terminates west of Interstate 5 and northbound Route 932 begins just south of the jitney boarding zone (see Map 2.3).

20. Some drivers charge seniors $0.75, what they would pay for a public transit ride. Small children sitting on their parents' laps travel for free.

21. Cost data are estimates based on interviews of five San Ysidro jitney drivers. While jitneys run seven days per week, individual operators typically drive six days a week, at their discretion. For the approximately six-mile jitney loop, average weekly costs are as follows: gasoline and oil equals $120; insurance equals $77; maintenance equals $40; capital depreciation equals $27; licenses and fees equals $16; and labor equals $210. Thus, average weekly costs are $490 compared to average revenue intake of $600, yielding a net weekly profit of around $110. Drivers report high average maintenance costs because fairly old bubble-top vans are used and frequent stop-and-go wears down brake linings and tires. Amortized capital cost and debt service estimates are based on a $5,000 purchase price for a used five-year-old vehicle, a seven-year ownership of the used vehicle, 100 percent loans secured at 12 percent interest, and a $1,000 salvage value when sold (usually in Tijuana) at the end of the vehicle's service life. Insurance premiums average $2,000 every six months for the full set of liability coverage mandated by MTDB. Drivers report they often receive citations from police, usually for stopping in red curb zones to pick up fares. Included in the weekly license and fee expense is $6, the prorated share of two $152 traffic citations per year, what drivers say is typical. Only two companies own two jitneys and both hire hourly employees at minimum wage ($4.25 per hour). Thus, most jitneys are independently owned and operated, incurring no significant administrative overhead expenses. Drivers report they take home around 35 percent of gross revenues, or around $210 per week. Combined with the $110 weekly profit, most drivers are earning only around $16,000 per year.

22. Most jitney operators honor senior citizen fares, currently $0.60 per ride for intracity bus services provided by Jersey Transit. Most seniors purchase multiride senior discount coupons at $0.60 per ride. Drivers are reimbursed the value of all coupons returned.

23. Examining the economics of the jitney business is problematic because all information is proprietary. For outsiders, only guestimates are possible. According to inside sources, the cost of owning (including vehicle depreciation and debt repayment), operat-

ing (including insurance, fuel, association dues, and fees), and maintaining an Atlantic City jitney is around $40,000 to $45,000 annually. Assuming an average fare of $1.30 per trip (accounting for $0.60 senior fares) and that the estimated 11 million jitney riders are evenly distributed among 180 jitney owners, this yields an average annual income of $36,900 (using a midpoint $42,500 annual cost figure). Drivers also build equity through appreciation in medallion values. A casual observation of the homes where jitney vehicles are parked throughout Atlantic City further suggests that most owner-drivers are earning more than the typical service worker in the city.

24. Over the years, jitney medallion values in Atlantic City have followed the fortunes and misfortunes of the city itself. In the late 1950s when Atlantic City was a popular tourist destination, the cost of a jitney medallion with a used minibus was around $6,000 (unadjusted). By the mid 1960s, when Atlantic City lost some of its luster and tourist business, the cost of a jitney franchise and minibus had slipped to as low as $2,500. With the legalization of casino gambling in the early 1980s and the subsequent boom in tourism, the fortunes of Atlantic City's jitney owners have risen in parallel.

25. In 1994, for instance, Atlantic City officials proposed a contraflow lane on Pacific Avenue. Fearing that the lane would slow down jitney operations, the Association organized a vocal protest, led by jitney operators and their families, of the proposal. Bowing to political pressure, the contraflow lane proposal was quickly abandoned.

26. Route 1 operates principally along Pacific Avenue and segments of Atlantic Avenue in the southern portion of Atlantic City. Route 2 follows a similar alignment to Route 1, though it does not go as far north on Pacific Avenue, instead doglegging to the interior of the island to serve the Marina area, the newly emerging casino district that is currently the site of Trump Castle and Harrah's. Route 3 is along a much shorter segment of Pacific Avenue than the other two routes, operating principally along secondary roads that connect the Marina area with the Inlet residential area at the northern edge of the city.

27. In coming years, Atlantic City's jitneys may begin to receive external subsidy support. Presently, the Jitney Association has applied for Section 3 capital grants from the Federal Transit Administration to acquire new vehicles that they hope will have some of the charm of San Francisco's famed cable cars and similarly become an icon for the city. The Association has sponsored a competition for designing a new Atlantic City jitney vehicle that it plans to phase in over a five-year period. Casino owners are providing a 20 percent match to Section 3 grants for purchasing future vehicles.

28. Ordinance 81-17, enacted in 1981, formally established Dade County's responsibility for regulating passenger motor carriers, including jitneys. Ordinance 85-20, which remains the current policy of the Dade County Board of County Commissioners, embraced jitneys as a necessary part of the local transportation scene, though it set policies which prohibited expanded jitney services in major Metrobus or established jitney corridors.

29. A 1983 Jitney Policy Report, prepared by the Metro Dade Transportation Administration, recommended restricting new jitney services to areas outside of high-density transit corridors. This effectively precluded any additional jitney services. In 1987, a task force composed of County staff, representatives of the jitney industry, and transit interests was convened to consider ways of further expanding jitney services in keeping with growing Federal interest in privatization. Because of the task force's diverse makeup, little consensus was ever reached on major issues, resulting in a stalemate and inaction.

30. Section 341.102 of the 1981 statute reads: "No county or municipality shall unduly restrict or impose any economic regulation upon the use of nonpublic-sector

buses engaged in intercity transportation, and any existing restrictions shall be invalid. However, a county or municipality may enact necessary safety and traffic ordinances." This meant that localities could not restrict jitney services beyond citing vehicles and operators for safety and traffic violations.

31. A 1992 survey, by Parsons Brinckerhoff Quade and Douglas (1993), found that 18 companies owned and operated some 340 jitneys, and 35 jitneys were owned and operated by individuals. Two of the 18 companies—Metro Jitney and Minibus Owners Association—operated around half of all known jitneys. The Owners Association was a loose confederation of independent owner-operators that coordinated services along six routes. The survey also identified nine primary jitney corridors in Dade County, all serving high-volume thoroughfares in direct competition with Metrobus services.

32. This survey is summarized in the Urban Mobility Corporation's 1992 report.

33. These daily cost estimates are based on information obtained from a survey of jitney drivers, conducted by the Urban Mobility Corporation. The survey found that average daily cost broke down as follows: $15 for insurance, $20 for fuel, $10 for capital depreciation, $16 for maintenance, and $11 for lease fees.

34. The article, Minibuses vs. Metrobuses, published in the April 14, 1991, issue of The *Miami Herald*, is reviewed in the Urban Mobility Corporation (1992) study.

35. The Ordinance, number 91-84, allowed the impounding of vehicles by county officers for such violations of the Motor Vehicle Code as failure to obtain a Certificate of Transportation, an operating permit, a chauffeur's registration, proper insurance, or safety inspection papers.

36. Red Top initially acquired 45 minibuses from Metro Jitney, a prehurricane unlicensed jitney company that was eager to liquidate its assets. During the first year or so of nonsubsidized services in south Dade County, Red Top charged operators $100 per week, allowing operators to keep all fare receipts. Red Top provided vehicles, insurance, and made sure operators were properly licensed. Red Top initially also ran several feeder routes into the South Dixie Highway jitney trunkline, and required each operator to work one or two days per week on these less busy feeders. Today, only trunkline services operate, and some Metro Minibus vans are individually owned and operated. As the sole certificate holder, Red Top's role today is mainly one of leasing permits to owner-operators at a going rate of $25 per day.

37. In late 1995, the following companies were certified to operate jitneys in Dade County: Dade Jitney, King Jitney, Liberty City Jitney, Sun Jitney, Marcello Jitney, Miami Mini Service, Conchita's Transit Express, Excel Transportation, American Jitney, Metro Minibus, Florida Jitney Transportation, Transit Express Jitney, and Meridien Jitney.

38. In early 1995, officials from Miami Beach and MDTA convened a meeting of 10 jitney owners to explore the possibility of running legalized jitneys along interior roads paralleling the beachfront. Because of past failures in serving middle-class markets where Metrobus services compete, no one was interested in the Miami Beach route unless paid on an hourly contract basis.

39. Because of the heavy interstate traffic between New Jersey and the greater New York and Philadelphia metropolitan areas, most New Jersey-based intercity operators are regulated by the Interstate Commerce Commission. The ICC is decidedly procompetition, concerned mainly with willingness, ability, and fitness to provide service. State and local authorities are fairly powerless in controlling market entry. Thus, it is under this unique situation that private van services have emerged in New Jersey. Many operate between northeastern New Jersey and the Port Authority Transit Terminal (PATH) in midtown

Manhattan, duplicating bus runs. Associations have emerged, offering assistance in securing ICC licenses and obtaining insurance. The associations also try to control service practices, though these efforts have been largely ineffective.

40. A late-1988 survey of feeder van customers at the Jamaica Center in Queens revealed the relative importance placed on these factors (Grava et al., 1989). The share of respondents who stated they chose a mode based on six different factors varied as follows for van versus bus riders: convenient pickup—48 percent (vans) vs. 4 percent (buses); close drop-off—46 percent vs. 36 percent; faster service—63 percent vs. 20 percent; fewer stops—15 percent vs. 9 percent; and more comfortable seats—10 percent vs. 5 percent. (Most respondents identified more than one factor.) Overall, 88 percent of surveyed van customers versus 74 percent of surveyed bus patrons said they were satisfied with the service they received.

41. The MTA functions as the region's umbrella transportation organization, overseeing transit operations and policymaking. The operating division of MTA responsible for subway and bus services within New York City is the New York City Transit Authority (NYCTA).

42. Van activity at Jamaica Center has been closely chronicled over the years. A 1988 survey counted 19,100 daily passengers (Grava et al., 1989). The same study found 72 percent of van trips were for work, and 15 percent were for going to school. Other studies estimated between 20,000 to 25,600 daily van patrons converging on Jamaica Center in the late-1980s (Milder, 1988; Clift, 1989). Surveys also showed that around one in five access trips to the Jamaica Center subway station were by van (Milder, 1988).

43. A 1991 study found other areas with significant numbers of Manhattan-bound commuter vans each morning to include: Co-op City and Riverdale in the Bronx; Bath Beach, Bay Ridge, and Coney Island in Brooklyn; and Queens Village, Flushing, Astoria, Howard Beach, and Jewel Avenue in Queens. Around 10 percent of commuter vans heading to Manhattan come from New Jersey (Savas et al., 1991).

44. The incident that caught the most press attention occurred in 1991, when two Brooklyn residents were killed and three others injured after a van jumped a curb. The operator never had a driver's license, had received four summonses for driving illegally, and the van itself was not registered, insured, or inspected (Read, 1991).

45. Presently the New York City Department of Transportation (NYCDOT) acts on all requests for van licenses, with review and comment by the Metropolitan Transportation Authority (MTA), the Taxi and Limousine Commission (whose regulatory jurisdiction lies mainly with taxicabs, limousines, and for-hire cars) as well as private bus companies and individual citizens. Enforcement sweeps have been led by the New York City Police Department, with the assistance of the New York City Police's Surface Crime Unit, NYSDOT Motor Carrier Investigators, the Taxi and Limousine Commission, transit police from multiple rail authorities including the NYCTA and Long Island Railroad, and the NYCDOT.

46. Under Section 9-11 et seq. of Title 35 of the Rules of the City of New York, van operators can technically operate along a NYCTA bus route but cannot pick up or discharge passengers along these routes. This is one of many restrictive conditions van operators must agree to in obtaining a license.

47. All applications are evaluated by NYCDOT in terms of possible negative impacts on existing mass transit services. Applicants must secure "public support statements," an informal written affidavit of support by community backers of the proposed service. An unwritten rule is that 10 public support statements qualifies for the authorization of a

single van. Some have successfully solicited the support of longtime customers. One operator submitted over 1,000 support statements, theoretically allowing authorization for 100 vans. Authorizations are valid for no more than two years. They are subject to mandatory revocation in cases of multiple offenses, like failing to meet insurance and safety inspection requirements, hiring unlicensed drivers, or violating operating rules (e.g., picking up customers at bus stops).

48. A second violation within a five-year period brings a maximum fine of $2,500 and a possible vehicle forfeiture. The city can also place a block (based on the vehicle identification number) on the registration of any vehicle operated in violation of local van regulations.

49. The enforcement campaign involved deputizing participating enforcement personnel to issue Notices of Violation (NOVs). They are issued for violations of laws pertaining to safety inspection, proper licensing, or vehicle operations (e.g., picking up street hails or operating along bus routes). The NOVs carry a penalty of $500, with maximum fines of $5,000.

50. This is according to an internal MTA memorandum cited in the Viewpoints section of *Newsday*, "Speed it Up," July 22, 1994, p. A36.

51. With grant support from the federal Urban Mass Transportation Administration, in 1988 researchers from the City University of New York, Columbia University, and several private firms held a series of meetings that brought together van owner-operators in southeast Queens, leading to the formation of JAVO. Federal funding support reflected an interest in promoting transit privatization at the time.

52. Queens Van Plan (QVP) was the borough's first licensed feeder van service. It initiated services during the subway strike of 1980 and quickly became the largest provider of van services in southeast Queens. The QVP has evolved into a formal corporation, with a president and administrative staff. It currently oversees 53 vans on the street. Drivers own their own vehicles and become members by buying shares in QVP, entitling them to licensing, group liability insurance, and use of the corporate logo. Drivers also pay QVP a monthly fee for radio-dispatch communications, routine maintenance, and use of an off-street parking lot. Radio communications are primarily provided to alert drivers of accumulations of waiting passengers, congestion spots, and police whereabouts. The price of QVP membership is kept secret; in the late-1980s it was estimated to be as high as $5,000 (Grava et al., 1989).

REFERENCES

Belknap, R. 1973. "The San Francisco Jitneys." Berkeley: University of California, Institute of Transportation and Traffic Engineering, unpublished paper.

Boyle, D. 1994. "Jitney Enforcement Strategies in New York City." Paper presented at the 73rd Annual Meeting of the Transportation Research Board, Washington, D.C.

Center for Urban Transportation Research. 1994. *Jitney Enforcement Strategies*. Tampa: Center for Urban Transportation Research, University of South Florida.

Clift, J. 1989. "Analysis of the Impact of Southeast Queens Van Operations on Public Bus Subsidy Requirements." New York: Report presented to the New York State Department of Transportation, June.

Comsis Corporation. 1986. *Public-Private Partnerships in Transportation: A Casebook for Local Elected Officials*. Washington, D.C.: U.S. Department of Transportation, Office of the Secretary of Transportation.

Department of City Planning. 1984. "Inventory and Analysis of Current Van Operations in New York City." New York: Department of City Planning, Technical Report No. 2B, Commuter Van Policy Study.

Federal Transit Administration. 1993. *Transit Profiles: The 1992 National Transit Database, Section 15 Report Year*. Washington, D.C.: Federal Transit Administration, U.S. Department of Transportation.

Fried, J. 1994. "A New Law Escalates the War Against Unlicensed Vans." *The New York Times*. February 13: 43.

Grava, S., J. Gaber, and N. Milder. 1989. *Private Auxiliary Transport at Jamaica Center*. New York: Columbia University, Department of Urban Planning.

Griffin, J. 1986. "San Francisco's Mission Street Jitneys." Los Angeles: University of Southern California, School of Planning and Urban Studies, unpublished paper.

Hall, J. 1978. "Share Ride Taxi in Little Rock: An Operator's Perspective." *Proceedings of the Conference on Taxis as Public Transit*, G. Fielding and R. Teal, eds., Irvine: Institute of Transportation Studies and School of Social Sciences, University of California: 87-91.

Heathington, K., F. Davis, R. Symons, T. Middendorf, and S. Griese. 1975. *An Analysis of Two Privately Owned Shared-Ride Taxi Systems*. Knoxville: University of Tennessee, Transportation Center.

Kitch, E., M. Isaacson, and D. Kasper. 1971. "The Regulation of Taxicabs in Chicago." *Journal of Law and Economics* 14(2): 285-350.

Kuehl, P., and C. Olson. 1974. *Taxicab Industry of Washington, D.C.: Regulatory Perspectives*. College Park: University of Maryland.

Lambert, B. 1995. "Express Service to Wall Street, and Nowhere Else." *New York Times*, April 16: B16.

Lombardo, M. 1994. *The Potential for Jitneys in Los Angeles*. Los Angeles: School of Urban Planning, University of California at Los Angeles, Master's Thesis.

Lyons, D. 1983. *Taxi Regulation in a Free Entry Market: A Case Study of Washington, D.C.* Washington, D.C.: Urban Mass Transportation Administration, U.S. Department of Transportation.

Metropolitan Transportation Authority. 1992. *Van and Car Service Issues Affecting NYCTA Surface Operations*. New York: Metropolitan Transportation Authority, Policy and Planning Division.

Milder, D. 1988. *Van Ridership in Southeast Queens: A Report on a Survey of Area Residents*. New York: DANTH Associates, Private Auxiliary Transport Study.

Mitchell, A. 1992. "Illegal Vans Fight Strong Guerrilla War for New York's Streets." *New York Times*, January 24: A16.

New York City Taxi and Limousine Commission. 1993. *The New York City For-Hire Vehicle Fact Book*. New York: New York City Taxi and Limousine Commission, Office of Policy Development and Evaluation.

Nolte, C. 1988. "The Death Rattle for the Jitney Bus in S.F.: Jitney No. 97 Refuses to Give Up." *San Francisco Chronicle*, July 18: A2.

Onishi, N. 1994. "Neighborhood Report: Parkchester; Bus Fare Dips $1 to Attract Livery Riders." *New York Times*, September 25: Section 13, p. 10.

Parsons Brinckerhoff Quade and Douglas. 1993. *Dade County Transit Corridors Transitional Analysis, Technical Memorandum Task 9, Jitney Survey.* Miami: Dade County Metropolitan Planning Organization.

Read, B. 1991. "Illegal—but Working." *Mass Transit* 18(6): 16-19.

Reinke, D. 1986. "Update on Taxicab and Jitney Reregulation in San Diego." *Transportation Research Record* 1103: 9-11.

Savas, E., S. Grava, and R. Sparrow. 1991. *The Private Sector in Public Transportation in New York City: A Policy Perspective.* Washington, D.C.: U.S. Department of Transportation.

Siracusa, A. 1990. "Jitneys: A Complement to Public Transportation." Los Angeles: City of Los Angeles, City Planning Commission, mimeo.

Suzuki, P. 1995. "Unregulated Taxicabs." *Transportation Quarterly* 49(1): 129-138.

Teal, R. 1978. "Taxis as Public Transit." *Proceedings of the Conference on Taxis as Public Transit,* G. Fielding and R. Teal, eds., Irvine: Institute of Transportation Studies and School of Social Sciences, University of California: 3-27.

Teal, R., and T. Nemer. 1986. "Privatization of Urban Transit: The Los Angeles Jitney Experiment." *Transportation* 13: 5-22.

Trommer, S., and D. Goldenberg. 1994. "New York City Van Legislation." New York: Metropolitan Transportation Authority, Policy and Planning Division, mimeo.

Urban Mobility Corporation. 1992. *The Miami Jitneys.* Washington, D.C.: Federal Transit Administration, U.S. Department of Transportation.

Berkeley's racetrack shared-ride taxi. Passengers exiting shared-ride taxi at the North Berkeley BART station after an afternoon at the Golden Gate Fields racetrack.

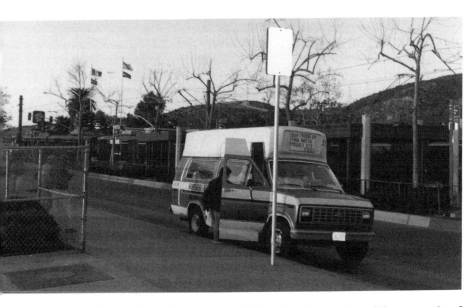

San Diego's Border Express jitney. Connecting the Tiajuana border crossing and the community of San Ysidro, the bubble-top jitney van queues for customers at a holding zone besides the San Diego Trolley station.

San Francisco's downtown jitney. The privately owned and operated jitney service makes efficient use of equipment. During peak hours, a large jitney bus is operated when loads are high (top photo). During the off-peak, when demand is more sporadic, a smaller jitney van is used (bottom photo). Despite fares set by San Francisco's Public Utilities Commission at one dollar to match those of the heavily subsidized Muni bus services, the private jitney service still turns a profit.

Atlantic City's jitneys. The mainstay of Atlantic City's mass transportation system, jitney vans pick up customers at designated jitney stops. Internal rules and regulations prevent jitney owner-operators from overtaking another vehicle unless the vehicle in front is stopped for passengers. The Atlantic City Route Association plans to replace the current jitney fleet with new, side-load vehicles resembling rubber-tire trolleys.

Private jitneys at Miami's South Dadeland Metrorail terminus provide "emergency" transportation services. Hurricane Andrew, which lashed south Dade County in August, 1993, created a huge demand for mass transportation services, prompting county officials to vastly expand the supply of legalized jitneys. A field inspector, standing in front of the vehicle in the photo, records the hours of service and monitors arrivals and departures to ensure only legitimate jitney vans are operating.

Public-Private intermodalism at downtown Miami's Government Center complex.
Jitney vans tie into Metrorail (top photo) and Metromover (bottom photo) systems.

ans queuing for customers at Jamaica Center in southeast Queens. Owned and operated mostly
? men of Caribbean descent to serve clients of Caribbean descent, the commercial vans provide
ainly feeder connections between apartment complexes and subway stations.

legal loading of passengers at a bus stop in Brooklyn. Private operators largely ignore regulations
at prevent vans from loading and discharging customers at bus stops, in part because enforcement is
x and in part because bus stops are the places where potential customers are and want to go.

Airport shuttle vans. By far, the fastest-growing market for private paratransit services has been airport shuttles that operate door-to-door. SuperShuttle has emerged as a leader of airport van services in several large markets by introducing dependable and premium-quality services that limit pickup and delivery stops to no more than three per one-way trip.

Chauffeur van services for children operating in Marin County, California. The growth in two-income, working parents has created a boom business for customized, door-to-door transportation to and from school, after-school activities, and weekend social and sports events.

A Light Rail Shuttle in Santa Clara County, California. The shuttle van connects a light rail station (top photo) to major activity centers like the San Jose International Airport, college campuses, and office parks in the Silicon Valley. Amenities like enclosed plexiglass shelters (bottom photo) promote ridership.

Casual carpooling in the San Francisco Bay Area. Strangers form carpools at designated stops in the East Bay in order to take advantage of the designated carpool lanes that provide time and money savings to three-or-more person carpools that cross the Bay Bridge during the morning peak.

CHAPTER 3

Ridesharing, Shuttles, and Neighborhood-based Services

INTRODUCTION

This chapter complements Chapter 2 by exploring the various service, market, and performance features of commercial paratransit; however, here we look at versions that are more specialized, serving specific clientele or a more definable market niche. The paratransit options discussed in this chapter are defined more in terms of how services are organized—for example, prearranged, advanced reservations, employer-supported, developer-sponsored, community-based—than the kinds of vehicles used or where and how they operate. Indeed, many of these services operate like jitneys, shared-ride taxis, or commuter vans, as discussed in Chapter 2. However, what distinguishes the paratransit offerings reviewed in this chapter is the fact that customers are making related trips for similar purposes, often on a regular basis. It is this relatedness of trip making that allows services, like employer-sponsored vanpools or supermarket shuttles, to be organized and adapted to the special needs of travelers.

SUBSCRIPTION VANS AND BUSES

Subscription van and bus services organized and operated by private carriers gained popularity during the 1970s; however, with time, most of these services have been taken over by government agencies and supported by subsidies. The very nature of subscription services is regularity—both of supply and demand. Subscription services often focus on the commuter market, with "subscribers" paying private operators in advanced for a prearranged, agreed-upon amount and quality of transportation services.

Many early subscription services started in what at the time were remote new towns, like Reston, Virginia, and Columbia, Maryland, well outside the service jurisdictions of public transit authorities. However, as metropolitan areas expanded outward to envelop these new towns and exurbs turned into suburbs, most commercial, commuter-based subscription services came under the wings of regional transit operators, county governments, or third-party brokering agencies (e.g., Commuter Computer in Southern California). Still, several commercial paratransit industries that operate on a subscription basis remain today, catering to fairly unique market niches, notably child paratransit services and residential-based vanpooling. Besides being prearranged, pay-in-advance monthly services, the subscription offerings reviewed in this section differ from the employer-sponsored commuter services discussed later in the chapter in that they are organized by residents, developers, or private carriers rather than employers.

Private Commuter Buses and Vans

In the 1970s and 1980s, successful private bus operations thrived in metropolitan Los Angeles, Washington, D.C., New York-New Jersey, Boston, Houston, and Norfolk-Virginia Beach, where thousands of suburbanites traveled to work centers scattered through each metropolitan area, sometimes in comfortable coaches offering headrests and guaranteed seats (Morlok and Viton , 1980; Multisystems, 1982; Giuliano and Teal, 1985). Many of these earlier services were organized by private bus companies themselves. Since these subscription buses typically made a single round trip per day, companies often redeployed buses in the midday for charter services.

In the Woodlands, north of Houston, and the Meadowlands in Bergen County, New Jersey, two rapidly growing edge cities during the early 1980s, over 25 privately operated commuter buses served their respective residents and employees on an average weekday in the early 1980s (Cervero, 1989). Metropolitan Boston had the largest number of unsubsidized regular-route commuter buses at the time —a fleet of over 300 intercity buses operated by 15 private vendors that carried some 15,000 people to work each day, more than commuter rail services (Giuliano and Teal, 1985). In the Hampton Roads area, some 95 private commuter vans, 150 buspools, and thousands of carpools connected suburban residents to military installations in Norfolk and Newport News in the late 1970s, capturing around 15 percent of work trips to these destinations (Echols, 1985).

The lure of government aid led to the conversion of many earlier subscription van and bus programs to public sponsorship. With public ownership, as much as 80 percent of the cost of purchasing vans and buses was covered by government grants, in addition to shares of operating costs. To subscribers, going public meant economizing on commuting. Many regional transit agencies that entered the subscription bus business smartly contracted out their services to private companies, thus keeping wage levels comparable to what they were under private ownership. Effectively, then, the transfer of subscription bus and vanpool services to public ownership meant gaining access to capital subsidies, a transfer payment that benefitted local authorities and suburban commuters alike.

Among the U.S. transit agencies currently involved in the commuter bus business in a big way are Pace Transit (suburban Chicago), Houston Metro, and Golden Gate Transit (GGT) and San Mateo Transit (SamTrans) in the San Francisco Bay Area. In 1992, GGT contracted out for long-haul services on 22 commuter routes, most tying Marin and Sonoma County residents to jobs in downtown San Francisco's Financial District. Some services are effectively quasi-public, as in New York City. There, six private bus lines operate over 20 express routes, carrying some 60,000 workers to Manhattan jobs each day (or around half of bus trips into Manhattan).[1] The city helps underwrite the cost of these services and, by granting firms exclusive franchises for specific routes, shields express operators from direct competition (other than from the illegal operators discussed in Chapter 2). Notwithstanding these subsidies and protections, private express bus operators are relatively cost-effective—in 1990, their average operating cost per vehicle mile was around 30 percent lower than that of the New York City Transit Authority's express bus and cross-town services (Savas and Cantarella, 1992). Supplementing these express bus franchises are the 600 or so private commuter vans, half of which are unlicensed, that descend on Manhattan each morning (see Chapter 2)

Even states have gotten into the commuter bus business. Because of the growth in intercity and cross-state commuting, Maryland's Mass Transit Administration today contracts with private carriers to provide express bus runs, called Flyer Services, that feed either into Washington Metrorail stations (e.g., Shady Grove, Silver Spring) or major employment centers in the Baltimore region. Over 7,000 Maryland commuters patronize these express services each day, paying fares that cover 60 to 80 percent of operating costs.

Washington state dominated in the provision of transit agency–sponsored vanpool services in 1993, with Seattle Metro comprising over 40 percent of the national total (Table 3.1). In all, 15 percent of vanpool services provided by public transit agencies in the United States were privately contracted (Federal Transit Administration, 1994). The average publicly supported vanpool recovered an estimated 60 percent of fully allocated costs (including depreciation and debt service) through fares, a high recovery rate by public transit standards though still a far cry from two decades earlier when private subscription services generated profits.

While subsidized vanpools are now the industry norm, privately initiated, organized, and financed vanpools can still be found today. Many serve long-haul commutes that extend beyond the service jurisdictions of public transit agencies. An example is a reverse-commute vanpool that operates between the Oakland-Berkeley area of the East Bay and the University of California at Davis, a distance of around 80 miles each way. Organized by 14 employees of the university who got together on their own by communicating through fliers and word of mouth, the vanpool operates each weekday as a one-to-few service, collecting participants at the El Cerrito BART station parking lot and reverse commuting along Interstate 80 to several parts of the Davis campus. Participants lease their van

Table 3.1.
Largest Vanpool Programs Sponsored by United States Public Transit Agencies, 1993[a]

	Total Vans in Operation	Percent Contracted	Passengers per Vehicle Mile	Annual Passengers (1,000s)	% of Agency Total by Vanpools Passengers	Vehicle Miles
Seattle (Metro), WA	509	0.0	8.9	2,161.5	2.6	7.6
Chicago (Pace Transit), IL	116	12.1	9.5	522.3	1.4	6.1
Snohomish County, WA	70	0.0	9.4	230.3	4.5	10.6
Brevard County (SCAT), FL	69	100.0	4.0	258.0	34.2	42.5
Richland-Ben Franklin, WA	62	0.0	8.4	315.9	4.2	26.2
Tacoma (Pierce Transit), WA	61	0.0	10.5	219.8	2.1	7.8
Bremerton County, WA	45	0.0	6.8	119.3	3.7	11.9
Winston-Salem, NC	35	0.0	122.7	151.1	4.1	22.5
Phoenix (RPTA), AZ	33	100.0	9.4	148.9	9.8	26.8
Orlando (LYNX), FL	29	100.0	7.5	100.5	0.9	7.1
Spokane, WA	25	0.0	11.6	73.1	0.9	2.7
Olympia, WA	19	0.0	4.4	94.9	2.8	12.0
Charlotte, NC	18	0.0	11.0	127.5	1.1	5.4
Birmingham, AL	16	0.0	7.5	114.9	1.9	7.8
Nashville, TN	16	0.0	7.0	68.1	1.0	7.0
Norfolk (TRT), VA	16	0.0	11.3	74.6	0.9	3.7
St. Louis (MCT), MO	15	100.0	11.0	77.3	7.2	9.8
Orange County (OCTA), CA	12	0.0	11.5	27.6	0.1	0.4

[a]Agencies operating or contracting at least 10 vanpools.

Source: Federal Transit Administration, *1993 National Transit Database, Section 15 Report Year, Data Tables.* Washington, D.C.: Federal Transit Administration, U.S. Department of Transportation.

from VPSI, Inc., a national van leasing company, and split monthly fees (including a $70 tab for one of the participants to schedule drivers and weekend usage) evenly, coming to $10 per day in 1995. Because California state law allows a 40 percent tax credit—up to $480 per year—for vanpooling expenses, the true cost to participants is closer to $7 to $8 per day.[2] Driving duties are rotated. Members have access to the van on weekends by scheduling use in advance. Overall, most vanpools serving Bay Area residents—approximately 700 according to RIDES for Bay Area Commuters, the regional rideshare brokering agency—are owned or leased by private individuals; there are comparatively few vanpool programs sponsored by employers or transit agencies, in part because state law provides tax breaks that make it economical for vanpoolers to foot their own bills.

Child Paratransit Services

Chauffeuring children and teenagers to school and weekend events has become a boom business in the 1990s, fueled by the growth in two-income, working parents. Child van services provide individually customized door-to-door transportation to and from school, after-school activities, orthodontist appointments, music lessons, and weekend social and sports events. Currently, around 250 firms across 43 states operate specialized van services for children on a contract, subscription basis, with over two-thirds located in the northeast (New Jersey, Maryland, Virginia), midwest (Michigan, Illinois, Indiana), California, and Florida.[3] Some are mom-and-pop operations that use one or two vans, many times run by husband and wife teams, one spouse driving the van and the other soliciting business and answering telephone calls out of their home. More typical are firms that run two to three vans, operated by two salaried (nonunionized) drivers who maintain contact via cellular phone with the owner/manager who operates out of his or her house. A handful of companies in greater Los Angeles, Denver, Washington, D.C., San Francisco, Detroit, Ft. Lauderdale, and other cities are much more substantial operations, with anywhere from 10 to 32 vehicles, an administrative office, a maintenance garage, and centralized radio-dispatching facilities.

The two industry leaders, Kids Kab (based in Oakland County, Michigan) and Kanga Kab (headquartered in New Jersey), initiated services in the early 1990s. Kids Kab was started when Pamela Henderson, a working mother of three children in Birmingham, Michigan, distributed 200 fliers in the spring of 1991, offering to transport neighborhood children to and from school and special activities. In the first three days she received over 600 responses (Orski, 1993b). At first, all trips were scheduled by hand, and three vans carried about 50 kids per day. By 1993, Kids Kabs expanded into a far-flung network of 27 franchises in 12 states that collectively carried 50,000 riders per month. Kids Kabs soon spawned numerous imitators. Some franchisees overcapitalized too quickly and in the face of increased competition within a year's time went out of business. Today, Kids Kabs has 18 franchises across seven states, averaging around 38,000 riders per month, down some 25 percent from two years earlier.[4] The largest Kids Kabs franchise, run by the founder-owner in Michigan, operates 17 12-passenger Ford Econoline vans and maintains a fully automated routing and billing system.

Service practices across the industry are fairly similar. Because safety and security are uppermost in parents' minds, children are usually issued photo identification cards that become their van admission ticket. Children are not left unattended unless greeted at the door by a parent or other preapproved person. To allay parents' fears of turning their children over to strangers, drivers are carefully screened, including extensive background checks, driving exams, and personal interviews. Often, mothers, retirees, and school bus drivers are hired at modest hourly wages. The largest child transportation carrier in the country, VanGo out of Encino, California (with 32 vans and over 9,000 monthly trips), reports that only 15 percent of driver applicants are hired. In terms of eligibility, companies normally set no age limit, though few carry children younger than three years old or who are not toilet trained. VanGo will serve infants and toddlers as long as they are accompanied by a licensed nanny.

A standard industry practice is to charge a fixed fee based on a minimum number of rides per month. According to the National Child Transportation Association, fees range from $4.50 per trip in small rural areas to $8 per trip charged by large operators in big cities.[5] For large firms like Kids Kab, parents normally pay around $2,500 to $3,000 per child for the school year and extracurricular activities (as late as 7:00 P.M.). VanGo averaged monthly revenues of around $80,000 in 1995, like most carriers, catering to predominantly upper-middle-income suburban households. In most cases, parents first pay a registration fee and then arrange their child's travel itinerary in advance. Services are normally prepaid the first of each month, eliminating the need for children to carry and drivers to collect cash and providing operators a cash flow advantage.

The bread-and-butter market for child transportation services is school trips, making up over half of all contracted trips. During midday, some operators provide charter services to day-care centers, senior citizens, and airport travelers or engage in package delivery.[6] After-school hours are usually dedicated to extracurricular activities, like gymnastic classes and tennis lessons. On weekends and when school is out of session, operators focus on other markets: birthday parties, summer camps, shopping malls, recreational theme parks, and sports events. VanGo has set up its own summer program, Summers on Wheels, that for $300 per week takes children and teenagers on daily excursions to the beach, Disneyland, and other Southern California attractions. In Florida, one enterprising operator convinced a local orthodontist to schedule children in groups so that van trips could be efficiently consolidated. Overall, the industry has shifted away from providing telephone-requested services on short notice to prearranged contract services with parents, schools, day-care centers, sports camps, YMCAs, and other groups.

As intercity carriers, child transportation services are normally regulated by states. Because they limit services to a specific clientele (children) and operate on a contract basis, they are typically licensed as charter services, a designation that imposes few regulatory constraints other than meeting minimum liability insurance coverage and driver fitness standards. All businesses operate vans that carry 15 or fewer passengers, thereby avoiding more stringent insurance requirements. No state has yet enacted regulations that are specific to the child paratransit industry; however, California is presently exploring this possibility. Because children are our most cherished and precious resource, it is just a matter of time before tighter controls over this industry can be expected. Like airport shuttle vans, however, the market demand for specialized child transportation services is too entrenched and powerful for heavy-handed regulations, as in most other commercial paratransit sectors, to survive politically. Overall, after a period of market shake-out, the child transportation industry is now reaching maturity, providing a highly specialized paratransit service that has become a permanent fixture on the urban mobility scene.

Residential-based Commuter Services

Another unique example of subscription services is vanpools and club buses initiated by either residential developers or residents themselves. Thus, unlike most ridesharing programs that are organized at the destination end (i.e., workplace), these programs organize trips at the origin, or residential end. Two of the most significant initiatives to date were both based out of planned communities on the fringes of large metropolitan areas—the Reston Commuter Bus for residents of Reston, Virginia, and the Homeowner Vanpool set up for residents of the Antelope Valley in north Los Angeles County.[7] Because residents of these suburban communities often worked at different offices in the same general vicinity—that is, federal offices in the nation's capital in the case of many Restonians, and downtown or west Los Angeles's aerospace complex for many Antelope Valley residents—community-based subscription van services were cost-effective.

Vanpools and buspools with many-to-one routing are only attractive for long commutes, typically 20 miles or longer, because only then is the time spent picking up other passengers en route a small share of total door-to-door travel time. Reston and the Antelope Valley met this criterion. While Reston's subscription service was organized by residents, in the Antelope Valley, the residential developer, Kaufman & Broad Corporation, initiated and marketed vanpools. The Woodlands, a new town 27 miles north of Houston, operated similar residential-based subscription van services in the 1980s. Around one in seven commuters reached their jobs by commuter buses or vanpools at the height of the program, an impressive achievement for a middle-income suburban community. None of these residential-based subscription services exist today, all having been taken over by public entities; however, their experiences provide glimpses into the working of alternative models of commuter transportation services.

Reston Commuter Bus

The Reston Commuter Bus (RCB) was organized in 1968 by a group of Reston residents who were looking for a commuting alternative for the 22-mile trip into Washington, D.C. No express public bus service was available at the time. The residents formed a cooperative and contracted with a private company to provide high-quality commute runs using spacious, temperature-controlled coaches with tinted glass and comfortable seats. The cooperative managed RCB's buspools to ensure that revenues covered contract costs and produced a small profit to pay administrative expenses. Additional runs were not contracted until a waiting list of prospective subscribers was of sufficient size to cover costs. The RCB monthly ridership catapulted from just over 1,000 passengers in 1968 when services began to 57,000 in 1977. This outpaced Reston's population growth—3,000 to 30,000—over the same period. By the late 1970s, around one-third of Reston residents who worked in downtown Washington, D.C. were RCB subscribers. Coaches averaged nearly 30 passengers per revenue hour of service, an impressive level of vehicle productivity, even by today's standards (Multi-systems, 1982).

A combination of bad business decisions by the RCB contractor and an expansion of the service jurisdiction of the Washington Metropolitan Area Transit Authority (WMATA) led to RCB's demise in 1979. The RCB per-passenger-trip cost had risen from just over a dollar in 1974 to $1.50 in 1979, so public takeover of service was welcomed by many subscribers. During most of the 1980s, WMATA used eight large-size vans to make some 75 express runs per day between Reston and Washington, D.C., with rides booked on a month-to-month basis. Today, Fairfax County has taken over express bus services, now called the Reston Express, which provide commute-hour runs for some 2,500 passengers per month to the District and employment centers along the Dulles corridor. This is considerably below what RCB was serving nearly two decades earlier, despite the growth of Reston's population to 58,000 and its employment base to 30,000 in the mid-1990s. Overall, job decentralization, expanded employer-sponsored vanpools, and the opening of private toll facilities like the Dulles Greenway have cut into the market base of residential-based commuter services in metropolitan Washington, D.C.

Residential-based Subscription Vanpools

In early 1992, Kaufman and Broad Corporation, one of the largest single-family homebuilders in Southern California, launched an experimental subscription vanpool program. Called Homeowner Vanpools, at its height the program operated seven vans (12 to 15 passengers) that carried around 100 Antelope Valley residents to jobs in downtown Los Angeles, west Los Angeles, Edmund Air Force Base, and employment hubs in the San Fernando Valley. Vans were leased from VPSI, Inc.; subscribers paid between $69 and $205 monthly, depending on the size of vehicle and distance traveled, and also split gasoline costs. Van drivers commuted for free and got unlimited use of vehicles during noncommute periods. By managing the program and placing the company's name and logo on the vehicles, Kaufman and Broad felt it enhanced its corporate image and marketability of its properties. In 1994, however, the program was taken over by Commuter Transportation Services (CTS), Inc., Southern California's regional ridesharing agency, in part because being run through CTS or sponsored by employers meant participants could receive rebates as high as $100 per month from the Los Angeles County Metropolitan Transportation Authority. Also, a downturn in the regional economy and sluggish home sales prompted Kaufman and Broad to stop participating in the program and refocus its efforts. Still, by all accounts, the Homeowners Vanpool program was a successful, if short-lived, experiment with residential-based ridesharing.

The story in The Woodlands was quite similar. In the mid-1980s, The Woodlands Corporation, developer of the new town north of Houston, sponsored The Woodlands Commuter Services vanpool program because public transit did not serve the area. Vanpools were provided on a monthly subscription basis and priced to recover full costs. By 1990, however, subscription vanpools to and from The Woodlands were taken over by Brazos County, replaced by publicly subsidized express bus services.

One place where residential-based subscription services remain today is in fast-growing Montgomery County, Maryland, in large part because of the county's 20-year-old Adequate Public Facilities Ordinance (APFO). The ordinance stipulates that developers must commit to trip reduction measures before building or occupancy permits are issued. The Robey Road Commuters Association, for instance, was formed by a single-family homebuilder to provide free minivans to groups of homeowners and renters who rideshare. In this instance, vanpools functioned as a congestion mitigation measure that satisfied the APFO requirements and allowed the developer to continue building homes.

EMPLOYER-SPONSORED RIDESHARING

Empty automobile seats are probably the most wasted resource in the urban transportation sector. By far, the most successful initiatives to fill these seats to date have been organized and funded, in total or in part, by large employers. In a nationwide study of 160 employer-sponsored carpool and vanpool programs, Wegman (1989) found average ridesharing rates of 17 percent and benefit/cost ratios of 2.2 to 21.2. Although employer vanpools are not pure commercial paratransit services, in the sense that many companies help underwrite costs, nonetheless they represent examples of paratransit provided by the private sector absent of government subsidies.[8] And in most cases, the majority of costs are covered by beneficiaries, the workers themselves.

Ridesharing Successes

In the 1970s and 1980s, ridesharing programs launched by Rockwell International in Golden (Colorado), Lawrence Livermore Laboratory in Alameda County (California), and the Tennessee Valley Authority in Knoxville attracted 60 percent or more of all employees to carpools and vanpools (Dingle Associates, 1982; Multisystems, 1982). Other corporate-sponsored programs with employee participation rates exceeding 40 percent during the 1980s were found at Fluor Corporation in central Orange County (California), Tektronix, Inc., of Beaverton (Oregon), the 3-M Company of St. Paul (Minnesota), Transnational Motor, Inc., of Grand Rapids (Michigan), and Puget Power and U.S. West of Bellevue (Washington).[9] Motivated by factors as diverse as deferring parking expansion costs, conserving energy, and being good corporate citizens, these firms also offered incentives like preferential parking, free lunches, travel allowances, raffle gifts, and subsidized group auto insurance to lure workers into carpools and vanpools.

The most successful employers-sponsored vanpool programs in recent times have been sponsored by TransAmerica in San Francisco (19 percent vanpool modal split), Arco Oil Company in Los Angeles (14 percent), Allergan, Inc., in Orange County (9 percent), and tenants of the Bishop Ranch Office Park in San Ramon, California (9 percent). Presently, around 70 vanpools serve Bishop Ranch employees; part of the cost for these services are written into the long-term leases signed by the 195 business tenants who reside in Bishop Ranch, a condition the city of San Ramon placed on the project's developer as a traffic mitigation measure. In Bellevue, U.S. West wins top honors for the highest non-drive-alone modal splits for a company outside a central business district (CBD) —74 percent, consisting primarily of carpoolers (Comsis, 1994). This is a remarkable achievement for a suburban employer and is mainly the product of no-nonsense parking polices: namely, limiting supplies (one space per three workers) and charging commercial rates for single-occupant parkers (and making parking free for vehicles with three or more occupants). In contrast, another nearby office building in downtown Bellevue provides more than one space per worker at no charge. Commuting habits in this building are strikingly different —85 percent of workers drive alone and only 8 percent carpool or vanpool (Cervero, 1993). In a recent nationwide assessment, Reid Ewing (1993) concluded that aggressive employer-based ridesharing incentives can reduce daily vehicle commute trips to worksites by 5 to 15 percent; if substantial parking charges are levied as well, this number climbs to 20 to 25 percent or more.

Along some corridors, HOV lanes have been equally valuable in attracting commuters to vanpools and carpools.[10] The 11-mile-long Shirley Highway HOV in northern Virginia saves vanpoolers an average of 20 minutes per trip relative to general traffic lanes; as a result, carpools and vanpools comprise 57 percent of person trips and 92 percent of vehicles on the HOV lanes, with remaining travel by bus transit (Kain et al., 1992). Other major vanpool carriers are HOV lanes on the San Bernardino Freeway, San Francisco Bay Bridge, the Lincoln Tunnel and Gowanus Expressway connecting to New York City, Seattle Interstate 5 North, and Dallas's Interstate 305 (Table 3.2). The high passenger throughput relative to the number of vehicles on the Shirley Highway HOV lanes testifies to that facility's popularity with vanpoolers, a significant number coming from affordable housing enclaves in the fast-growing exurban counties of Prince William and Fauquier in northern Virginia.

TMAs and Ridesharing

In the late 1980s, Transportation Management Associations gained popularity as forums for advocating the mobility interests of firms in edge cities and large-scale office parks. At the time, many companies began handing over to TMAs such functions as ride matching, rideshare marketing, and occasional sponsorship of carpools and vanpools (Cervero, 1986; Orski, 1988). Some TMAs, like those representing the Hacienda Business Park and Bishop Ranch east of Oakland,

Table 3.2.
Major Vanpool and Carpool HOV Facilities in the United States, 1992

	No. of Directional Lanes		Length (miles)	A.M. Peak Hour HOV No. of Van & Carpool		Description
	HOV	Free-way		Vehicles	Passen-gers	
Washington, D.C.:						
I-395 (Shirley)	2R	4	11.0	2,573	11,276	Exclusive lanes, Freeway ROW
Seattle, WA						
I-5 North	1E	4	4.6	7,691	9,476	Concurrent flow lanes
I-90	1W	3	6.2NB/ 7.7SB	6,070	6,798	Concurrent flow lanes
San Francisco, CA						
I-80 (Bay Bridge)	4W	5	2.3	2,325	8,273	Concurrent flow lanes, Toll plaza bypass
Dallas, TX						
I-30E	1E	4	5.2WB/ 3.3EB	7,000	7,600	Contraflow lanes
New Jersey/ New York						
SR 495 (Lincoln Tunnel)	1I	3	2.8	4,475	7,380	Contraflow lanes
Gowanus Freeway	1I	4	2.0	3,794	7,569	Contraflow lanes
Los Angeles CA I-10 (San						
Bernardino Freeway)	1E	4	12.0	1,374	4,352	Exclusive lanes, Freeway ROW

Notes: R=reversible   W=westbound only   NB=northbound   WB=westbound
        E=each direction   I = inbound only   SB=southbound   EB=eastbound

Sources: Turnbull (1992), Kain et al. (1992).

El Segundo in west Los Angeles, and Tysons Corner in northern Virginia, focused much of their efforts on providing companies ridesharing services, mainly in response to mandatory trip reduction ordinances enacted by local governments. A 1992 survey found that 63 percent of 150 nationwide TMAs provided some level of programmatic support for vanpools, and 38 percent did likewise for buspools (with services usually brokered through the TMA to a third-party contractor); the same survey showed that 33 to 40 percent of TMAs provided carpool/vanpool subsidies and around 20 percent arranged for free or discount parking for ride-sharers (Ferguson et al., 1992).

Increased employer and TMA involvement in promoting ridesharing failed to stem the tide of rising solo commuting, however. Between 1980 and 1990, ridesharing lost almost 4 million commuters across the U.S., from about 19 million to about 15 million, reducing its market share of work trips by one-third, from almost 20 percent to just over 13 percent (Pisarski, 1992). Average vehicle occupancy for commute trips dropped from 1.15 to 1.09. Even Houston, which embarked on developing the nation's largest HOV network in 1984, saw around 70,000 ridesharers switch to solo commuting during the 1980s. Research suggests that a combination of cheaper gasoline prices, rising labor force participation among women, and increasing suburbanization were largely responsible for commuters giving up ridesharing in favor of solo commuting during the eighties (Federal Highway Administration, 1994).

Ridesharing and Regulations

With the passage of the Clean Air Act Amendments of 1990, the driving force behind rideshare programs in more recent years has been government regulation, specifically requirements that nonattainment areas introduce Transportation Control Measures (TCM). In California, the South Coast Air Quality Management District enacted its own requirement, Regulation XV, mandating that large employers reduce drive-alone commutes to their work sites and prepare annual trip reduction plans identifying TCMs they plan to implement. Several years after Regulation XV's 1988 enactment, fewer than a third of large employers in greater Los Angeles subsidized employee vanpools and carpools; more common were "low-cost, low-impact" activities like rideshare marketing programs and preferential parking for carpoolers and vanpoolers (Giuliano et al., 1993; Orski, 1993a). There were exceptions, however. The TMA for Warner Center, an edge city in the western San Fernando Valley, formed one of the largest vanpool networks in the country in the wake of Regulation XV. By 1992, the Warner Center TMA featured a fleet of 75 15-passenger vans (with VPSI as the contractor), supported by such incentives as guaranteed ride home (in case subscribers have midday emergencies or end up working late), preferential parking, and transportation vouchers. Throughout Southern California, Commuter Transportation Services, the regional ridesharing broker, reported that over 2,000 vanpools existed in 1994, and some 50 firms helped underwrite their workers' ridesharing expenses.

Despite the good intentions behind Regulation XV, drive-alone rates in the Los Angeles basin rose from 77.2 percent in 1992 to 80.6 percent in 1994. Even the Northridge earthquake of January 1994 that brought down major freeway stretches in Los Angeles failed to change commuting behavior very much—in the aftermath, only around 4 percent of Los Angeles County commuters switched to carpools and vanpools (Commuter Transportation Services, Inc., 1994). Partly because of these disappointments, the California Legislature terminated the state's eight-year experiment with trip reduction mandates in late 1995, opting instead for voluntary initiatives that allow employers to substitute "emissions equivalency" programs, like remote sensing (to determine if any employees' cars are gross emitters) and vehicle scrappage programs.

CASUAL CARPOOLS

Not all ridesharing programs in the United States have been formally organized. Perhaps the most laissez-faire form of transportation "privatization" in the U.S. are casual carpools, wherein commuters spontaneously organize themselves to ride to work with strangers. Causal carpooling, popular in greater San Francisco–Oakland and Washington, D.C., with some activity also in Denver and Pittsburgh, differs from hitchhiking in that dozens of individuals gather at transit stops to catch rides from motorists looking to fill vacant seats. Carpools form because there is a direct incentive—usually both time and monetary savings. In the Bay Area, around 8,000 commuters form three-person, one-way casual carpools each weekday in order to shave 20 minutes off the morning commute and avoid $1 bridge tolls by using the HOV bypass lane leading to the Bay Bridge toll plaza (Beroldo, 1990; Brock, 1993). There, casual carpools have evolved as a many-to-few form of commercial paratransit—people residing in "many" locations all over the East Bay gather at transit stops and freeway entrances to catch rides to a "few" locations in downtown San Francisco, like the Transbay bus terminal and BART stations along Market Street.[11] Recent surveys show that around 55 percent of Bay Area casual carpool drivers and 90 percent of casual carpool riders used to commute by some other non-drive-alone means—either in formal carpools or vanpools, or by mass transit (Brook, 1993). Most prefer casual carpools because the ride is free and they have a guaranteed, and often more comfortable, seat. They also usually get to work faster than by transit and definitely faster than commuting alone. Perhaps the most important lesson from the casual carpool experience is the importance of providing incentives—like HOV lanes—in enticing Americans to share rides.

Mostly well-dressed professionals of all races, male and female alike, the Bay Area's casual carpoolers line up at well-known spots leading to the Bay Bridge, and catch the first car—be it a subcompact or luxury model—that pulls up. Some staging zones are near transit stops, giving people the option of riding a bus or train in case, on the rare occasion, no driver comes by. At the busiest pickup points, a steady stream of cars and passengers hook up during most morning hours. Two passengers at the head of the "people queue" get in the first car in the "vehicle queue" and, usually after a brief greeting, the carpool dashes off to the city. No money changes hands between the driver and passengers. Because strangers are co-occupying the vehicle and many value some privacy in the morning, there is an unwritten code of conduct—little conversation, no radio music, and no smoking.

In that the average Transbay BART commuter incurs operating deficits of $1.30 per trip (ignoring capital costs) and deficit levels are even higher on AC Transit's Transbay routes, casual carpools function both as "load shedders" (relieving public transit operators of having to expand costly peak-hour services) and "deficit skimmers." While taxpayers should be grateful for the casual carpool phenomenon, public transit agencies in the Bay Area have long tried to eliminate spontaneous ridesharing on the grounds that these services are robbing them of revenues. This is certainly borne out by surveys—in 1985 and 1987, between 76 and 85 percent of casual carpool passengers formerly got to work by transit (Beroldo, 1990). Since large transit operators like BART and AC Transit typically exhibit diseconomies of scale, or no better than constant returns, the only thing casual carpools are guilty of is succeeding in an imperfect marketplace (i.e., one where both public transit riders and single-occupant motorists accumulate substantial subsidies).[12] Nonetheless, AC Transit has restructured its fare policy so that Transbay express bus commuters pay a double fare for east-bound afternoon services. This has dampened but by no means eliminated the incentive for casual carpooling. Hundreds of East Bay commuters are willing to pay two-way bus fares for one-way service given the opportunity to receive what many perceive to be a superior carpool ride in the morning. One might argue that an efficiency-minded organization would have responded to a reduction in peak-hour service by curtailing operations and perhaps redeploying equipment and personnel to other corridors. Unfortunately, such responses are rare among transit agencies that operate as public monopolies and that rely on subsidies to shield them from the burden of rising operating costs. And as discussed in Chapter 8, public transit employees are represented by powerful labor unions that fight efforts to curtail services in fear of workers losing jobs.

FEEDER SHUTTLES AND CIRCULATORS

Another increasingly popular form of paratransit supported by the private sector has been shuttle vans that either feed into transportation terminuses, typically rail stations, or circulate within neighborhoods or activity centers. Today, most feeder runs, like the Reston Internal Bus System (RIBS) and Orange County's minibus connections to Metrolink commuter rail stations, are government supported.[13] On rare occasions, unsubsidized privateers have made a living operating regular-route shuttles.[14] Where service gaps remain, however, employers, developers, and others have shown a willingness to step in and sponsor shuttles for their workers and tenants. These private shuttles, of course, are not philanthrophic gestures. Businesses have some financial stake in introducing them. An employer who has relocated offices to a suburb may initiate a shuttle run from a transit stop to the new location as an incentive for retaining existing workers (e.g., Princeton shuttle, discussed below). To remain competitive in attracting the best workforce, employers in remote campus-style office parks may sponsor a noontime shuttle to nearby shopping centers (e.g., Bishop Ranch shuttle). Shoppers' shuttles may be funded by downtown businesses (e.g., Tampa, Florida; Portland, Oregon), suburban merchants (Walnut Creek, California), or transportation management associations (e.g., Tysons Corner, northern Virginia). And property developers may be required to provide shuttle connections to transit stops as a traffic mitigation measure (e.g., White Flint shuttle outside Washington, D.C.)

Table 3.3 summarizes the various types of feeder shuttle services that are financed, at least in part, by private interests that are currently operating in the United States. Experiences with these services are discussed below.

Developer and Employer Shuttles

Two of the first rail shuttle services in the U.S. were sponsored by developers and tenants of Bishop Ranch and Hacienda Business Park, both large-scale

Table 3.3.
Types of Feeder Shuttle Services Involving Private Sector Support
Operating in the United States

	Description
Employer-Sponsored	
Stamford, CT: Pitney Bowes, First Stamford Place Shuttles	Short shuttles between offices and Metro North commuter rail stations, free to employees.
Princeton, NJ: Forrestal Center shuttles	Connects the office park to the Princeton Amtrak station, sponsored by four corporations on a cost-sharing basis.
Developer-Sponsored	
Montgomery County, MD: White Flint Shuttles	Two circulators that link offices and shopping centers to the White Flint Metrorail station, free to anyone.
Friendship Heights Shuttles	Shuttle links condominium project to Metrorail and shopping mall, financed by condominium association fees.
Fairfax County, VA: Tysons Corner Shuttles:	Minibus feeders to transit stops and shopping malls, operated by two high-rise residential developments.
Public-Private Partnerships	
San Mateo County, CA: Consolidated shuttles	Combined six private employer-sponsored shuttles that serve BART and CalTrain commuter rail with more productive series of feeders co-financed by employers and joint-powers agreement.
Santa Clara County, CA: LRT shuttles	Eight jointly funded fixed-route and demand-responsive shuttles carrying over 1,000 passengers per day between LRT stops and work sites, free to anyone.
Tampa, FL: Downtown shuttle	Co-sponsored by Hillsborough Area Regional Transit and the private sector, shuttles connect downtown Tampa and the Westshore business park with the city's historic district, port, hotels, and retail district.

employment centers 35 miles east of San Francisco. In the mid-1980s, Bishop Ranch contracted for two 41-passenger buses to connect employees of companies leasing office space to the Walnut Creek BART station (and during lunchtime to a nearby shopping center); around 4 percent of Bishop Ranch's eligible work force took advantage of the free shuttle connections. Two of Bishop Ranch's tenants, Pacific Bell Telephone Company and Chevron Corporation, operated their own shuttles. By the early 1990s, both of these services were canceled because of escalating costs, though Bishop Ranch itself has retained an on-site midday circulator.[15] At its height, Hacienda's shuttle was even bigger—five buses tied the Park to the nearest BART station, 12 miles away, for a dollar one-way fare; in the wake of an economic recession, this service was eliminated in the early 1990s as well.

Two examples of unsubsidized employer shuttles presently operating are rail feeders in Connecticut and a bus interliner in Memphis. Pitney Bowes Corporation of Stamford, Connecticut, contracts for a shuttle that carries 140 workers per direction per day between the Metro North commuter rail station and the firm's international headquarters. Nearby, First Stamford Place operates a similar service as part of a development agreement. In Memphis, the owner of a care facility for the elderly operates a shuttle that picks up employees dropped of at the terminus of a Memphis Area Transit bus stop and carries them to the worksite some four miles away.

Property developers and consortiums of employers have also gotten into the shuttle business. In fast-growing Montgomery County, Maryland, the developer of the Nuclear Regulatory Commission (NRC) near the White Flint Metrorail station introduced two shuttle runs in response to the County's Adequate Public Facilities Ordinance. Even though NRC itself is right across from the Metrorail station, by introducing the shuttle service the developer was able to secure development permits by enabling employees of offices beyond walking distance of the station to more conveniently access Metrorail. Currently, four 22-passenger vans ply the one-mile White Flint loop and two-mile Executive Boulevard loop every 10 minutes in the peak and 15 minutes off-peak. The fare-free service is 100 percent developer financed and available to anyone. Presently, around 1,000 customers ride the shuttles each workday. Vehicles are packed during the peak. During noontime, many areawide employees hop on the shuttles to access the White Flint Mall and White Flint Plaza. According to the shuttle coordinator, at least one employer in the White Flint area bought an office building on the shuttle route because of the shuttle's presence.

Residential developers have also backed shuttle services in recent years. The Rotunda and Montebello, two high-rise residential complexes in Tysons Corner in northern Virginia, operate minibuses for the half-mile trip to major bus and subway lines and shopping malls. At Friendship Heights, near downtown Washington, D.C., a small bus shuttles apartment dwellers to a nearby Metrorail station and neighborhood shopping center. In each case, residents financed the shuttle services through annual condominium fees (Orski, 1993c).

Presently, the largest multiemployer feeder shuttle service is sponsored and funded by four corporate tenants of the Princeton Forrestal Center, a 1,600-acre research and office park in central New Jersey. These companies relocated to Forrestal Center from Manhattan in the 1980s. To ensure that their New York City employees could conveniently get to work, they contracted with a private company to operate minibuses between the Center and Princeton's Amtrak station, seven miles away. These peak-hour feeders operate on 25-minute headways that are designed to meet incoming and outgoing trains. Employees ride free. The feeder buses serve around 160 trips per day at an average contract cost of around $2.50 per trip. This compares to an average operating cost of $2.83 per passenger trip for public bus services operated throughout New Jersey by New Jersey Transit Corporation in 1993.[16] Since contract costs include capital expenses while the cited costs for New Jersey Transit do not, the privately supported feeder buses average at least a 30 percent cost savings relative to publicly operated services. To further increase productivity, the Princeton shuttle's private contractor redeploys minibuses during off-peak hours and on weekends to provide feeder connections between Amtrak and a regional shopping center in nearby Plainsboro township.

Public-Private Partnerships

In the San Francisco Bay Area, a number of innovative partnerships between the private sector (e.g., employers, business park developers) and rail transit operators have formed in recent years to provide feeder shuttle services.[17] These groups have coalesced primarily because there is a direct financial incentive— AB 434, a state law that allocates proceeds from a vehicle registration surcharge specifically to programs like feeder shuttles.[18] In all, over 150 public-private shuttles (excluding those related to airport access or ADA activities) operate in the region (Cervero et al., 1995). Seventy percent provide peak-hour connections to rail stations; the remainder feed into park-and-ride lots, interconnect campuses (of high-technology firms, hospitals, and universities), or circulate within activity centers, like suburban downtowns (e.g., Walnut Creek). All cosponsored shuttles are privately contracted.

San Mateo County Shuttles

A public-private partnership success story is the consolidation of six private shuttles into a system of three shuttles sponsored by the Multi-City Transportation System Management Agency (MTSMA), a joint powers authority created by eight cities in northern San Mateo County. The six earlier employer shuttles fed into BART and CalTrain commuter rail stations. Their schedules overlapped and runs were unproductive, averaging fewer than six passengers per hour at a cost of around $4 per passenger trip. For example, Genentech, a biomedical firm with 2,000 employees, ran a single shuttle van to the San Mateo CalTrain station.

Homart, a nearby property management firm with 2,500 workers housed in a large office building, ran a single minibus to BART and CalTrain stations. Between the two companies, just three trips to CalTrain and one to BART were possible during the commute period. With the formation of MTSMA, the two shuttles were replaced by two midsize coaches providing eight runs operating on 20-minute headways to BART and six runs on half-hour headways to CalTrain. Average monthly ridership on the consolidated runs has shot up to 5,100 passengers on the BART shuttle and 2,200 passengers on the CalTrain shuttle (Murray et al., 1995).

Santa Clara County's Light Rail Shuttles

The most extensive network of rail-feeder shuttles in the Bay Area operates in Santa Clara County. Presently, eight shuttles tie into the county's light rail transit (LRT) system—an 18-mile at-grade line that links downtown San Jose to the Silicon Valley to the north and residential neighborhoods to the south. Services are cosponsored by employers and the local transit operator, the Santa Clara County Transportation Authority (SCCTA), with funding assistance from the regional air quality district.[19] The shuttles were conceived as feeders for residents and workers who are beyond walking distance of LRT stops, such as in the Silicon Valley where low-density, master-planned office parks dot the landscape.

The eight existing LRT shuttles operate as both fixed-route and demand-responsive services, depending on the hour of day (Table 3.4). Most shuttles follow prescribed routes, with set stops and timetables (with headways varying from 5 to 30 minutes during peak hours) (Map 3.1). Three of the shuttles—Metro/Airport, IBM, and Kaiser/Santa Teresa—provide off-peak services on a dial-a-ride basis (requiring 10- to 15-minute lead times). All shuttles are free. Collectively, Santa Clara's LRT feeders transport over 1,000 workers per day, most of whom are well-salaried professional workers.[20] This accounts for around 8 percent of access trips to and from LRT stops, a very high market share by national standards. The benefits of high shuttle-rail access are counted not only in lower public outlays for park-and-ride lots but also reduced tailpipe emissions.

Santa Clara County's privately contracted shuttles have been fairly cost-effective—the average contract cost was $2.64 per passenger trip in 1993. This is considerably below the operating cost (ignoring debt service) of $4.15 per passenger for several SCCTA fixed-route bus services that connect Silicon Valley office parks with LRT and CalTrain stations.[21] On a cost-efficiency basis, the shuttles also enjoy a substantial edge: they cost $41.15 per revenue vehicle hour to operate in 1993, compared to $106.82 per revenue vehicle hour for the comparison bus routes. Most of the LRT shuttles' cost advantage comes from lower compensation and wage rates; while SCCTA's bus drivers and LRT attendants are unionized, most shuttle operators are not. Overall, it has been their role in attracting motorists to LRT commuting that makes Santa Clara County's LRT shuttles most noteworthy. Silicon Valley's auto-oriented built environment—

Table 3.4.
Santa Clara County LRT Shuttles: Levels of Service, 1994

LRT Shuttle	Year Service Initiated	Peak Service Type	Peak Headways	Non-peak Service Type	Average Daily Ridership (one-way trips)
Metro/Airport	1988	F	10 min. & 20 min. - A.M. 5 min. & 10 min. - P.M.	F/DR	235
Great American	1988	F	15 min	n/a	345
Lockheed	1994	F	30 min	n/a	30
River Oaks	1993	F	20 min	n/a	45
Intel	1993	F	25 min	n/a	30
IBM	1994	F	15 min	DR	190
Kaiser	1994	F/DR	on request	F/DR	85
Creekside	1993	DR	30 min	n/a	40

Notes: F = Fixed route   DR = Demand Response   n/a = no service available

typified by sprawling, campus-style office parks, acres of parking asphalt surrounding worksites, and stand-alone buildings—has meant most origins and destinations are well beyond walking distances of LRT stops. Good-quality feeder connections have thus become necessary for the long-term survival of LRT. Unless convenient shuttle connections between LRT stops and worksites are available, most of Silicon Valley's well-paid workforce will forego the hassle of LRT commuting and drive instead, particularly given that nearly all have a free parking spot waiting for them. The LRT shuttles, then, play a small but important and growing role in inducing rail travel. Their value, then, lies every bit as much in reducing traffic congestion and improving air quality as it does in attaining some financial productivity target.

Tampa's Downtown Shuttles

The San Francisco Bay Area is not alone in crafting public-private partnerships that sponsor efficient shuttle connections. Together with the private sector, Hillsborough Area Regional Transit (HARTline) in Tampa has recently initiated several services using creative financing approaches. One shuttle, launched in late 1994, provides noontime service between the Westshore business park and downtown Tampa, with its historic district, restaurants, and entertainment attractions. Because of Westshore's campuslike setting, nearly all workers previously drove to reach off-site restaurants. Now, over half of lunchtime access trips to downtown restaurants are by shuttle. In early 1995, an all-day shuttle running from the Port of Tampa, where cruise lines and the aquarium are located, to downtown hotels and restaurants was also initiated. Funding has come from an

Map 3.1.
Fixed Routes of the Santa Clara County LRT Shuttles

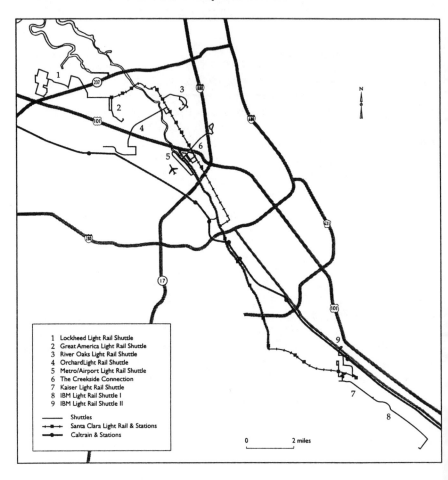

1 Lockheed Light Rail Shuttle
2 Great America Light Rail Shuttle
3 River Oaks Light Rail Shuttle
4 OrchardLight Rail Shuttle
5 Metro/Airport Light Rail Shuttle
6 The Creekside Connection
7 Kaiser Light Rail Shuttle
8 IBM Light Rail Shuttle I
9 IBM Light Rail Shuttle II

——— Shuttles
——■— Santa Clara Light Rail & Stations
——●— Caltrain & Stations

0   2 miles

assessment district formed by the Downtown Partnership, service contracts with thirty restaurants, and development income from the Port Authority. Because of sensitivity to environmental conservation, shuttle buses in downtown Tampa operate using both compressed natural gas and electric batteries.

DIAL-A-RIDE SERVICES

The distinguishing feature of dial-a-ride (DAR) paratransit is its demand responsiveness—whenever a trip request is made by telephone, a vehicle (typically a van) is dispatched within a relatively short period of time to serve the trip. A DAR is usually a door-to-door service. As such, DAR operates like a phone-in shared-ride taxi. Today, nearly all DAR services are subsidized and targeted at special groups, like senior citizens. The only commercial DAR services open to the general public of any magnitude are airport shuttles. These are discussed in Chapter 7 in the context of recent state regulatory reforms aimed at promoting head-to-head competition in this sector.

In the 1970s, several privately contracted DAR services open to the general public were initiated as demonstration projects, subsidized with both local and federal dollars. Three of the largest programs were launched in El Cajon, California, Danville, Illinois, and Davenport, Iowa, with dial-in shared-ride taxis providing curb-to-curb services in each place. While in the early years, transit's officialdom had high hopes for DAR, with time the cost of underwriting these services proved prohibitive. Few general-public DARs survived beyond the 1980s. Figure 3.1, which compares the performance of DAR versus fixed-route bus services, underscores the uphill struggle facing demand-responsive, curb-to-curb paratransit services.[22] In 1993, the operating cost per passenger trip of DAR was more than five times that of bus transit—$10.38 versus $1.79. While DAR costs less to operate each mile, because of its much lower average loads, its cost per passenger mile was nearly four times as high—$1.39 versus $0.36. On any service-effective criteria, DAR fares poorly against bus transit; in 1993, for instance, U.S. bus transit averaged 14 times as many passengers per vehicle revenue mile as did DAR—2.94 versus 0.21. It is because of numbers like these that, In the midst of continuing government cuts to transit, many localities have lim-

Figure 3.1.
Comparison of Performance and Productivity Between Dial-a-Ride and Bus Transit Services Operated by United States Public Transit Agencies, 1993

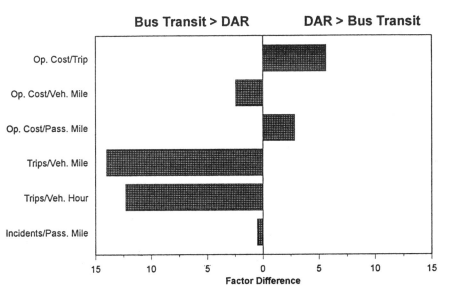

ited their DAR activities to special services for the elderly and disabled populations that comply with ADA requirements.

Notwithstanding DAR paratransit's high costs, general-public DAR services remain prominent in parts of Southern California—Orange County, Riverside County, and San Diego County—as well as a handful of other areas, like Dallas –Ft. Worth, Chicago, Rochester (New York), Norfolk–Virginia Beach, and Hamilton (Ohio). Hamilton, a city of 61,000 some 25 miles north of Cincinnati, has replaced nearly all of its fixed-route service with DAR minibuses and vans that circulate within designated "wedges" of the city, providing door-to-door service. Travel between wedges occurs via several mainline routes and a downtown "pulse-point" where customers transfer to another van or minibus. Orange County has a similar zoned DAR system, with minibuses and vans responding to ride requests within designated 10 to 12-square-mile areas; those wishing to travel outside the zone of origin must transfer to another vehicle at a zone boundary.[23] The Norfolk–Virginia Beach region has a variety of fare options for the general public to patronize the Maxi-Ride DAR system, including one-zone monthly Fare Cutter Cards of $20 plus $1.35 per trip and All-Zone Cards (good for traversing any of the 10 zones) for $38 plus $0.80 per trip. In several U.S. cities, notably Portland (Oregon), Danville (Connecticut), and Contra Costa County (California) general-public DAR is more specialized, functioning as feeders into rail stations. Although some general-public DARs are quite punctual, requiring only one-hour advanced reservations (e.g., Portland, Ft. Worth), in most cases one-day advanced notice is necessary.

No area of the country has accumulated a longer history of experience with general-public DAR services than metropolitan San Diego. In 1973, officials from El Cajon, a suburb 15 miles east of downtown San Diego, contracted with San Diego Yellow Cabs, Inc., to provide a "turnkey" DAR service, called the El Cajon Express. Yellow Cabs was the chief architect, designing, operating, and refining the service subject only to minimum service criteria. As designed, the El Cajon Express operated 7 days a week, 24 hours a day anywhere within the city; for trips to destinations outside El Cajon, vehicles operated like exclusive-ride, metered taxis (Urban Mass Transportation Administration, 1976). By 1980, ridership on the El Cajon Express grew to around 600 trips per day, and at a dollar fare per trip, the service covered around 30 percent of its cost, comparable to fixed-route bus services in the area. The same year, the El Cajon Express was averaging over eight passengers per vehicle hour, a very high rate of productivity for a suburban, community-based service. Other suburban communities, like La Mesa, Coronado, and Lemon Grove, soon followed suit, contracting for their own general-public DAR services. In all cases, contractors were reimbursed on a per passenger-mile basis.

As San Diego's trolley line extended into the eastern suburbs in the mid-1980s, thus providing another mobility option for the region, and the cost of curb-to-curb contract services continually rose, the financial performance of general-public DAR services began to falter. Figure 3.2 shows that the subsidy per passenger

Figure 3.2.
Trends in Subsidies per Passenger, General Public Dial-A-Ride Services in Metropolitan San Diego, 1974–1994, in Unadjusted Dollars

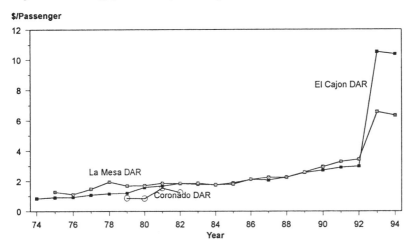

$/Passenger

trip climbed steadily during the 1980s. By 1990, each passenger trip on the El Cajon and La Mesa DARs incurred around a $3 deficit. Feeling the fiscal strain, both cities decided to replace their per passenger-mile subsidies with a fixed monthly contract amount set according to an agreed-upon miles of service. Yellow Cab opted not to rebid on these less lucrative services. Instead, DAR was contracted to the county transit operator, the San Diego County Transit System (CTS), in 1992. With an increase in fare to $4 per trip (from one-third to half this amount in previous years), ridership on El Cajon's DAR plummeted to only 60 per day, a tenth of what it was a decade earlier. Today, the deficit per rider exceeds $10. La Mesa's DAR has fared only slightly better. Given such poor performance, it is unlikely that the San Diego region's general-public DARs will survive much longer. Presently, both El Cajon and La Mesa are considering replacing them with fixed-route shuttles that feed into San Diego Trolley stations.

Overall, the future of general-public DAR in the United States is not very promising, outside special niche services, like commercial airport van services or ADA-sponsored services. What could save DAR, however, is technology. The advent of low-cost, high-performance computer hardware, moderately priced scheduling and dispatching software, off-the-shelf automatic vehicle location technology, and electronic mapping software could eventually give rise to a far more efficient and cost-effective form of DAR services than is known today. Orange County, California, uses advanced automated technologies to promptly and efficiently serve nearly 2 million annual DAR trips, mostly targeted at seniors and disabled persons, though services are also available to the general public on a 24-hour advanced reservation (Teal, 1993). The prospects for growing a smart DAR paratransit industry in the United States are explored further in Chapter 9.

COMMUNITY-BASED PARATRANSIT

A final form of paratransit is the informal network of private cars and vans that provide transportation to major destinations in and around residential neighborhoods. Community-based forms of paratransit thrive in many poor, minority, inner-city neighborhoods where vehicle ownership levels are low and licensed taxicabs rarely come by. With such a large captive market, thousands of enterprising inner-city residents who own cars and vans have sought to fill this market void, providing prompt, reliable transportation to supermarkets, health clinics, shopping centers, sports venues, and other destinations for a fee. Nearly all are illegal, and most vehicles are un- or underinsured. Yet public officials tacitly allow what has varyingly been called "hacks," "black cabs," "gypsies," and "bandits " to operate since the middle-class and upper-crust establishment are largely oblivious to and unthreatened by their existence.

Several researchers have gone to great lengths to covertly study this illicit phenomenon, applying what social scientists call participant-observation techniques—namely, they or their assistants became illegal neighborhood-based paratransit operators. Peter Suzuki, a professor from the University of Nebraska, quickly became an expert on the subject after driving what he calls a "vernacular" cab in a predominantly black neighborhood of Omaha for over a year. In Omaha, underground cabs work from storefronts known as "delivery stands" and respond to call-ins handled by telephone dispatchers (often the owners) and a few walk-ins. Omaha's storefront cabs operate with little interference from local law enforcement and regulatory agencies, resulting in "a quasi-dual cab system: vernaculars for the black community and the other four regulated cab companies for the rest of Omaha" (Suzuki, 1995, p. 133). More informal are drivers working from telephone booths or roaming the streets without a fixed center, estimated to number as high as 1,500 in Philadelphia.

Every large city seems to have its own version of neighborhood-based paratransit that caters to the poor (Suzuki, 1985, 1995; Farkas and De Rouville, 1988). Boston's illegal shared-ride cabs serve the working-class and black communities of Roxbury and Dorchester and focus primarily on shopping trips. There, a group of longtime drivers working out of a Roxbury mall have formed their own association. More formalized is the network of some 400 hacks that wait for customers outside supermarkets and shopping malls in inner-city Baltimore. Some 25 social clubs in Baltimore are also served by these hacks. Chicago's unlicensed jitneys have similarly grown into a full-fledged, internally organized industry. Between 200 and 300 jitneys operate in the poorest neighborhoods of west and southside Chicago, working out of grocery stores, bars, and other businesses, employing as many as 5,000 drivers (Kitch et al., 1972; Suzuki, 1995). A network of citizen-band radios and even cellular phones are used to dispatch drivers in the field to waiting customers, usually for short-haul trips. Operators openly advertise their services by means of business cards distributed throughout local neighborhoods. Recently, Chicago officials have sought to legalize jitneys by removing entry restrictions and allowing unregulated pricing as a way of improving service quality and safety in the south and west sides, though these initiatives have been politically stalled. In Los Angeles and New York City, illegal cabs and jitneys compete with licensed taxi cabs for everything from the lucrative airport market to short downtown trips, often flagrantly violating rules (e.g., queue hopping, soliciting at bus stops). Nearly all of Los Angeles's bandit cabs are driven by Latinos. No one really knows how many "gypsy cabs" and illegal jitneys operate in New York, with numbers ranging from 8,000 to 45,000 (Suzuki, 1995). As noted in Chapter 2, most of New York's illegal car-operators come from the Caribbean, loiter around bus stops and shopping centers for customers, and have established "turf."

The most in-depth and illuminating study to date on illegal neighborhood-based paratransit services was conducted in Pittsburgh by Otto Davis and Norman Johnson (1984). Hiring student research assistants to be illegal jitney drivers, Davis and Johnson were able to gain insights into both the culture and mobility roles of this underground industry. They found that station house jitneys—operating out of apartments, gasoline stations, grocery stores, or garages—were the most prevalent form of illegal paratransit. In the early 1980s, Pittsburgh had around 45 station houses in predominantly black neighborhoods. The second most common service concentrated on picking up customers at supermarkets. In total, around 500 illegal operators plied the streets of Pittsburgh in the early 1980s, twice as large as the number of legal taxi operators. The researchers found that prospective jitney riders used sign language and codes to communicate with drivers, thus avoiding authorities. They also found that illegal drivers were no more likely to have an automobile collision than licensed cab drivers, and almost regardless of distance, jitney operators undercut cab fares by around 15 percent. In Pittsburgh and elsewhere, unlicensed services have managed to survive the authorities because they serve the very neighborhoods that many licensed cab drivers refuse to enter.

Not all community-based paratransit is illegal or unsanctioned. In many parts of the country, special neighborhood mobility programs have been mounted in hopes of improving the accessibility of inner-city poor residents to job opportunities. The Nickerson Gardens Resident Management Corporation (NGRMC), for instance, is a nonprofit organization managing a 5,000-unit public housing project in South Central Los Angeles. In the late 1980s, the NGRMC launched a government-assisted program of vocational training, job placement, child care, and small business creation for residents of Nickerson Gardens. The Corporation soon discovered that inadequate transportation was a serious obstacle to many residents finding and retaining jobs. Poor bus services and excessive transferring caused some residents to be late for training classes and job interviews. With local assistance in 1993, the NGRMC received a $1.3 million federal grant to organize a neighborhood mobility program that uses vans to connect residents to job sites and child-care centers. The van system employs Nickerson Gardens residents as drivers, dispatchers, mechanics, and supervisors, thus expanding job opportunities within the neighborhood. In recent years, similar community-based mobility programs, initiated through government assistance, have surfaced in poor neighborhoods of Chicago (ACCEL program), Little Rock (JOBLINKS), and at least a dozen other U.S. cities. Although the jury is still out on whether these programs will reduce joblessness and improve skill levels, they nonetheless demonstrate that community-based van services are effective means of linking inner-city residents to suburban jobs.

Last, another version of neighborhood-based transportation services that has gained recent attention is car co-ops. Neighborhood car sharing has caught on in several German cities. Called Stattauto (car alternative), Germany's car co-ops have around 3,000 members who share cars on an advanced reservation basis.[24] Since there are far more subscribers than cars, nearly all trips involve ridesharing. A small group in Eugene, Oregon, has recently formed a neighborhood car co-op modeled after the German experience (LaFond, 1994).

SPECIALIZED PARATRANSIT IN SUMMARY

In sum, an assortment of special "niche market" paratransit services can be found across the United States today. Although regulations and market distortions have no doubt suppressed these specialized services below what they might otherwise be, there is now enough of an accumulated history of these services to provide glimpses into their promise as players on America's future urban mobility scene. Private commuter buses and vans proliferated throughout the United States in the 1970s, but over the past two decades these services have increasingly been taken over by local authorities or employers. A handful of residential-based commuter van services continue today, both formal and informal. More unique have been child paratransit services and what arguably is the most free-enterprise form of commuting, casual carpools. Feeder shuttles have also gained popularity. On the other hand, dial-a-ride vans, offering perhaps the highest quality services of any paratransit option, have been relegated to very limited market niches, like airport transport and curb-to-curb access for the physically disabled, because of their high costs.

Some of the comparisons presented in this chapter between specialized paratransit and conventional fixed-route bus transit underscore the inherent cost-effectiveness advantages of commercial transportation services. The contract costs of running Princeton's corporate-sponsored shuttles, for instance, are around 12 percent less per passenger than the unit costs for public bus services in the same area, even when public capital outlays are not counted. In Santa Clara County, LRT shuttles enjoy an even greater cost advantage—around 36 percent less per rider than public buses that also function as feeders. While some of the cost savings are a result of low wages paid to paratransit operators, the adaptation of service levels to match consumer demand and the use of vehicles in off-peak hours for activities like charter services have also raised productivity.

While progress has been made in opening the market to commercial paratransit operators over the past several decades, America's offerings remain fairly modest by international standards. Only by looking abroad can one gain a full appreciation for the untapped potential of commercial paratransit in the United States. For this, we turn to the next chapter.

NOTES

1. Private operators providing express bus services to and within New York City include Green Bus Lines, Jamaica Buses, Triboro Coach Corporation, Command Bus Company, Queens Transit Corporation, Steinway Transit Corporation, Liberty Bus Company, and New York Bus Company.

2. In addition, employer-provided ridesharing benefits, like free parking, are fully exempt under California tax law and exempt up to $75 per month under federal tax law.

3. Some of the information in this section was obtained from an interview with the Director of the National Child Transportation Association, which maintains a national inventory on many, though not all, service providers.

4. The first franchise was awarded in July 1991, and since that time Kids Kabs has received several thousand franchise applications. Today, a franchise goes for $28,000. Franchisees must be located in areas that have 7,000 to 10,000 children between the ages of 3 and 17 within a seven-mile radius.

5. Most carriers charge flat fares per trip. In large metropolitan areas, a distance surcharge is normally added. VanGo of Southern California adds distance surcharges based on increments of four miles per trip. To avoid excessive deadheading, VanGo limits its services to a 50-mile radius of the San Fernando Valley.

6. Kids Kab, for instance, changes its distinct red and blue vehicle identification signs to accommodate other markets. Sometimes a "white-out" magnetic sign is used when transporting teenagers who are embarrassed to be identified as "kids." When transporting seniors, a sign that says "Big" is often added so that the logo reads "Big Kids Kab" (Orski, 1993b).

7. In the early 1960s, commuter groups in Marin, Sonoma, and Napa counties in northern California contracted with private bus companies to operate services north of the Golden Gate Bridge; however, these services were soon taken over by the Golden Gate Bridge, Highway, and Transportation District (GGBHT). Similar events occurred in metropolitan New York–New Jersey and greater Boston in the 1960s.

8. Financially, vanpool and carpool participants gain both directly and indirectly from employer assistance. Both direct and in-kind contributions from employers—like free parking, cost sharing for van leases, and insurance underwriting—are exempt from Federal income taxes up to a value of $75 per month.

9. Not all of these high ridesharing rates were sustained over the long term. In the late 1980s, for instance, fewer than 10 percent of 3M employees were ridesharing, about the same share found for most other St. Paul area employers, despite the company's continuing support—hiring a full-time coordinator, ride-matching assistance, vanpool subsidies, preferential parking for vans, and subsidized transit passes. The drop in vanpooling has been attributed to some employee turnovers and relocation, as well as the expansion of flexible work hours (thus complicating ridematching) (KT Analytics, 1989). Experiences in California likewise reveal that high rates of employee participation in commute

option programs are difficult to sustain indefinitely (Orski, 1993b). Three of five suburban employment centers in the San Francisco Bay Area saw a slow but steady attrition in the rate of ridesharing and transit usage during the first five years of trip reduction efforts.

10. A study of the opening of HOV lanes on State Route 55 in Orange County, California, in the mid-1980s, for instance, found that 57 percent of the carpools and vanpools did not exist previously when there were no HOV lanes (Weseman et al., 1989).

11. More casual carpooling takes place in the Bay Area than anywhere else. However, as is not the case in other sites around the country, casual carpooling in the Bay Area is decidedly a unidirectional phenomenon—to downtown San Francisco in the morning. Casual carpooling does not work well in the evening for several reasons. One, there are no time savings because, except for one freeway on-ramp, there are no HOV lanes in the eastbound direction. Neither are there any eastbound tolls. Also, East Bay destinations are scattered all over.

12. Perhaps the most perverse effect of casual carpools is that many fill up suburban park-and-ride lots at BART stations in the morning. A 1986 survey by BART counted 570 commuters parking in the Orinda station lots (which collectively hold 1,380 cars) and joining casual carpools. Of course, casual carpoolers are behaving rationally in taking advantage of free parking spaces, just as BART commuters. The appropriate policy response to this problem is to charge for parking, not just at BART stations but everywhere, under the simple logic that parking spaces have some resource scarcity value (in the form of occupied land, materials, and maintenance). That is, the problem does not lie with casual carpooler parking free, but rather with nearly *all* commuters parking free.

13. RIBS, funded by Fairfax County using proceeds from development proffers, features five buses that make a bidirectional 8-mile loop between six village centers and the Town Center of Reston, taking 40 minutes. The 22-passenger shuttle vans stop for hail requests anywhere along the route and charge a quarter per ride. Ridership has jumped from 5,200 per month in 1990 to around 18,000 per month in 1995. In early 1994, OCTA contracted for over 200 small buses and vans to provide feeder connections to the six Metrolink stops in Orange County. Within the first year of service, the feeder vans and minibuses were handling over 3,000 passengers per day, well above what was projected. Free-of-charge, the feeder buses serve around 10 percent of access trips to Orange County Metrolink stations. Other publicly funded shuttle programs operate in Memphis, Chicago (Pace Transit), San Mateo, Marin, San Diego, Contra Costa counties in California, and in Tampa, Boston, Dallas, and Danbury, Connecticut.

14. The only known example of this at present is an airport shuttle serving residents of Poway in San Diego County. Poway is an upscale, suburban community with the highest median income of any incorporated city in the county. In 1983, the county began an airport shuttle run. Peerless, Inc., operated the service under contract from 1988 to 1993 and gained popularity among many well-to-do residents who could have afforded a taxi but preferred the shuttle. In late 1993, the county awarded the shuttle contract to a new provider. Peerless decided to continue operating the airport shuttle on its own, dropping its fare $0.50 below what the city-funded shuttle charged in hopes of profiting from a loyal customer following. Many Poway residents continue to ride the unsubsidized Peerless shuttle to the airport.

15. These abandoned shuttle services were subsequently picked up by BART and Contra Costa County. The BART Express, contracted by BART, and County Connection, contracted by the county, provide regular services to the Walnut Creek and Bay Fair BART stations for $1.15 to $1.30 per trip. The Hacienda Park Owners Association offers

free BART Express passes to all workers in the Park as a mitigation measure in compliance with a local trip reduction ordinance (enacted by the city of Pleasanton). Likewise, Bishop Ranch's developers cover full costs for all workers in the complex who ride the County Connector feeder bus to and from the Walnut Creek BART station.

16. Source: Federal Transit Administration, *Transit Profiles of the Thirty Largest Agencies, for the 1993 National Transit Database, Section 15 Report Year,* 1994.

17. Most Bay Area shuttles are cofunded by employers. Currently, the Emery Go-Round Shuttle that ties employment centers and residential projects to BART and an Amtrak station in Emeryville, a booming enclave of high-end job growth north of Oakland, receives the most developer contributions. The Emeryville Developer Group has funded over half the expenses for the free shuttle service as conditions of approval of development permits.

18. AB 434 allows air quality management districts to impose a surcharge of up to $4 on motor vehicle registrations to fund transportation projects that help achieve air quality targets. The Transportation Fund for Clean Air is only available to public agencies, and funds are restricted to seven types of transportation projects, including "feeder shuttle service to rail and ferries" and "rail-bus integration."

19. In fiscal year 1993-94, SCCTA's light rail shuttle program received $380,000 in AB 434 funding from the Bay Area Air Quality Management District. It has principally been because of this funding that public-private partnerships of shuttle services have expanded in the Bay Area.

20. While most services are targeted at Silicon Valley employees, the shuttles are often used by others, such as Mission College students, airport passengers, and patrons of the Great America Theme Park. Although employers help underwrite the services, since public monies are also involved, anyone is allowed onboard.

21. This is the average unit cost for SCCTA bus routes 40, 41, 43, and 44. The cost estimates are based on SCCTA's in-house cost allocation equation that imputes costs on the basis of $40.40 per revenue vehicle hour and $1.29 per revenue vehicle mile of service. While capital depreciation and administrative overhead costs are imbedded in these unit costs estimates, debt service expenses are not.

22. Data are for services operated by U.S. public transit agencies only (i.e., excluding services contracted by social services agencies) in 1993. DAR services operated by public transit agencies include those that are restricted to the elderly and handicapped and other special clientele, in addition to general-public services. Source: Federal Transit Administration, *National Transit Summaries and Trends,* Washington, D.C., 1995.

23. The Orange County Transportation Authority (OCTA) has one of the largest DAR services available to the general public, featuring 238 19-passenger minibuses and vans that served 1.8 million passenger trips in 1993. This OCTA DAR service is restricted to seniors and the disabled except during peak hours, when a subscription service is available to the general public. A party of five or more passengers travelling to a single destination, referred to as a group load, can travel through up to four zones without changing vehicles. Group load trips must be arranged at least one week in advance. OCTA's DAR services are expensive—around $40 per vehicle revenue hour and $7.50 per passenger trip—in part because the fleet is 100 percent wheelchair accessible.

24. Members of Stattauto who wish to use a car simply phone into a reservation center. Schedulers try to consolidate car usage to the extent possible. In Berlin, where the first German car co-op was formed in 1988, a variety of automobiles are distributed around 14 parking lots. Car keys and travel logs are kept in safe-deposit boxes at lots, to which

members have magnetic card-keys. Members fill out travel reports for record keeping and accounting. Stattauto bills monthly for kilometers travelled, hours of use, and any taxi rides that are charged to members' cards. Becoming a Stattauto member requires a $600–$1,000 subscription fee, modest monthly dues, and on-time payment of monthly car-lease expenses.

REFERENCES

Beroldo, S. 1990. "Casual Carpooling in the San Francisco Bay Area." *Transportation Quarterly* 44(1): 133-150.

Brock, V. 1993. "Casual Carpooling: An Update." San Francisco: RIDES for Bay Area Commuters.

Cervero, R. 1986. *Suburban Gridlock.* New Brunswick: Center for Urban Policy Research.

———. 1989. *America's Suburban Centers: The Land Use–Transportation Link.* Boston: Unwin Hyman.

———. 1993. *Transit-supportive Development in the United States: Experiences and Prospects.* Washington, D.C.: Federal Transit Administration, U.S. Department of Transportation.

Cervero, R., T. Kirk, F. Mount, and C. Reed. 1995. *Paratransit in the San Francisco Bay Area: Providing Feeder Connections to Rail.* Berkeley: Institute of Urban and Regional Development, University of California, Berkeley, Working Paper No. 637.

Commuter Transportation Services, Inc. 1994. *State of the Commute Report, 1994.* Los Angeles: Commuter Transportation Services, Inc.

Comsis Corporation. 1994. *Overview of Travel Demand Management Measures.* Washington, D.C.: Federal Highway Administration, U.S. Department of Transportation.

Davis, O., and N. Johnson. 1984. "The Jitneys: A Study of Grassroots Capitalism." *Journal of Contemporary Studies* 4(1): 81-102.

Dingle Associates, Inc. 1982. *Ridesharing Programs in Business and Industry.* Washington, D.C.: Federal Highway Administration, U.S. Department of Transportation.

Echols, J. 1985. "Use of Private Companies to Provide Public Transportation Services in Tidewater Virginia." *Urban Transit: The Private Challenge to Public Transportation,* C. Lave, ed., Cambridge, Massachusetts: Ballinger.

Ewing, R. 1993. "TDM, Growth Management and the Other Four Out of Five Trips." *Transportation Quarterly* 47(3): 343-366.

Farkas, A., and M. De Rouville. 1988. "The Potential of the Jitney: A Case Study of the Baltimore Metropolitan Area." *Transportation Quarterly* 42(1): 89-105.

Federal Highway Administration. 1994. *NPTS: Travel Mode Special Report.* Washington, D.C.: Federal Highway Administration, U.S. Department of Transportation.

Federal Transit Administration. 1994. *Data Tables: For the 1993 National Transit Database, Section 15 Report Year.* Washington, D.C.: Federal Transit Administration, U.S. Department of Transportation.

Ferguson, E., C. Ross, and M. Meyer. 1992. *Transportation Management Associations in the United States.* Washington, D.C.: Federal Transit Administration, U.S. Department of Transportation.

Giuliano, G., and R. Teal. 1985. "Privately Provided Commuter Bus Services: Experiences, Problems, and Prospects." *Urban Transit: The Private Challenge to Public Transportation*, C. Lave, ed., Cambridge, Massachusetts: Ballinger.

Giuliano, G., K. Hwang, and M. Wachs. 1993. "Employee Trip Reduction in Southern California: First Year Results." *Transportation Research* 27A(2): 125-137.

Kain, J., R. Gittell, A. Daniere, S. Daniel, T. Somerville, and L. Zhi. 1992. *Increasing the Productivity of the Nation's Urban Transportation Infrastructure: Measures to Increase Transit Use and Carpooling*. Washington, D.C.: Federal Transit Administration, U.S. Department of Transportation.

Kitch, E., M. Isaacson, and D. Kasper. 1972. "The Regulation of Taxicabs in Chicago." *Journal of Law and Economics* 14(2): 285-350.

KT Analytics. 1989. *An Assessment of Travel Demand Approaches at Suburban Activity Centers*. Cambridge, Massachusetts: Transportation Systems Center, U.S. Department of Transportation.

LaFond, M. 1994. "Cooperative Transport: Berlin's Stattauto (Instead of Cars)." *Rain* 14(4): 2-6.

Morlok, E., and P. Viton. 1980. "Self-sustaining Public Transportation Services." *Transport Policy and Decision-Making* 1: 169-194.

Multisystems, Inc. 1982. *Paratransit for the Work Trip: Commuter Ridesharing*. Washington, D.C.: Urban Mass Transportation Administration, U.S. Department of Transportation.

Murray, G., C. Chambers, D. Koffman, and A. Winn. 1995. *Strategies to Assist Local Transportation Agencies in Becoming Mobility Managers*. Menlo Park: Crain & Associates.

Orski, C. 1988. "Traffic Mitigation and Developers." *Urban Land* 47(3): 16-19.

———. 1993a. "Employee Trip Reduction Programs: An Evaluation." *Transportation Quarterly* 47(3): 327-341.

———. 1993b. "Kids Kab." *Private Sector Briefs* 4(11): 1.

———. 1993c. "Residential-based Transportation Services." *Private Sector Briefs* 4(11): 2.

Pisarski, A. 1992. *New Perspectives in Commuting*. Washington, D.C.: Federal Highway Administration, U.S. Department of Transportation.

Savas, E., and A. Cantarella. 1992. *A Comparative Study of Public and Private Bus Operations in New York City*. Washington, D.C.: Federal Transit Administration, U.S. Department of Transportation.

Suzuki, P. 1985. "Vernacular Cabs: Jitneys and Gypsies in Five Cities." *Transportation Research* 19A: 337-347.

———. 1995. "Unregulated Taxicabs." *Transportation Quarterly* 49(1): 129-138.

Teal, R. 1993. "Implications of Technological Developments for Demand Responsive Transit." *Transportation Research Record* 1390: 33-42.

Turnbull, K. 1992. *High-Occupancy Vehicle Project Case Studies*. Austin: Texas Department of Transportation.

Urban Mass Transportation Administration. 1976. *Small City Transit: El Cajon, California—City-Wide Shared-Ride Taxi Service*. Washington, D.C.: Urban Mass Transportation Administration, U.S. Department of Transportation.

Wegman, F. 1989. "Cost-Effectiveness of Private Employer Ridesharing Programs: Employer's Assessment." *Transportation Research Record* 1212: 88-100.

CHAPTER 4

International Experiences with Paratransit

PARATRANSIT ABROAD

Internationally, the paratransit sector is quite diverse. It ranges from one-person rickshaws to 25-passenger minibuses and almost everything in between in terms of speed, comfort, and carrying capacity. In the developing world, paratransit's market share spans from a low of about 5 percent of motorized trips in Dakar, Taipei, and Tel Aviv, to some 40 percent in Caracas, Bogotá, Istanbul, and Kinshasa, and as high as 65 percent in Manila and other cities of Southeast Asia (Takyi, 1990; Allen, 1993).

Paratransit's most common global trait is private ownership. Presently, the private sector serves more than 75 percent of bus transit trips in the third world, and virtually all trips made by paratransit (Armstrong-Wright, 1993). Private firms have proliferated mainly because of their proven ability to contain the kinds of runaway costs that have historically afflicted subsidized public transit. One-man jitney and minibus businesses help reduce overhead expenses and waste. Driven by the profit motive, paratransit entrepreneurs aggressively seek out new and expanding markets, innovating when and where necessary. Where market entry is unrestricted, paratransit is fiercely competitive, especially in low-income, developing countries (Roth and Wynne, 1982). In many instances, route associations, similar to those in Atlantic City (see Chapter 2), have formed to coordinate and rationalize services. Levels of public control vary considerably among nations, though the general pattern has been that as countries modernize and industrialize, the paratransit sector is more tightly controlled. This is mainly because of a desire to accommodate the explosive growth in faster, higher-performing private automobiles. Restricting paratransit as a way of enhancing the automobility of the middle-class minority has predictably raised questions about the social equity of such policies in many areas.

Most paratransit systems in developing countries closely approximate what have been called jitneys in this book. The archetypical paratransit service in the Third World consists of a constellation of loosely regulated owner-operated collective vehicles that follow more or less fixed routes with some deviations as custom, traffic, and hour permit. They respond to hail calls pretty much anywhere along a route. However, every system—whether the 2,000 matatus of Nairobi, the 15,000 *carros por puesto* minibuses in Caracas, or 30,000-plus jeepneys of Manila—has some kind of unique twist. Some regularly make route detours and others don't; some load customers in the rear of the vehicles and others on the side; some are governed by federations of jitney owners while others engage in daily head-to-head competition; some have comfortable padded seats and others have hard wooden benches. In a comprehensive evaluation of jitneys in different countries, Isaac Takyi (1990) rated them high in terms of frequency, speed, load factors, and relative costs but gave them low marks for service regularity and reliability (except for peak periods), comfort, and safety records.

The variety of paratransit offerings abroad are reflected below:

- *Damascus's minibuses.* As part of Syria's newfound enthusiasm for private investment, over 10,000 minibuses, known affectionately as *mice*, today dominate the thoroughfares of Damascus, having relegated state-run buses to largely shuttling government workers from ministry to ministry (Jehl, 1995). Instead of waiting half an hour for a bus, residents can now count on a minibus passing by every few minutes. At about 10 cents, the standard fare is about what buses used to cost, and riders can count on a seat being available. Many former public bus drivers have become minibus entrepreneurs, in most cases tripling their monthly take-home pay.

- *Buenos Aires's colectivos.* In Argentina's capital, some 30,000 privately owned, brightly colored 21-seat minibuses, called colectivos, and 50-seat private coaches have totally taken over city bus operations, earning profits on routes previously monopolized by deficit-riddled public bus services. Over half of total travel in Buenos Aires is by colectivos, more than twice the share of the private car (Allen, 1993). Most residents live within several blocks of a colectivo route, and where services have been extended into new parts of the city, property values have invariably increased (Schodolski, 1985; Ferrarazzo, 1990). While colectivos generally follow fixed routes, they deviate as necessary to avoid congestion. Some 500 colectivo companies have banned together to build the city's minibuses using imported truck chassis, do body work, manufacture batteries, and run insurance companies that write policies to cover their fleets.

- *Belfast's black cabs.* In Belfast, some 400 *black taxis* provide perhaps the most successful shared-ride taxi services in the developed world, carrying some 40,000 passengers daily, or around 15 percent of all public transport trips (Nutley, 1990). Born of necessity in the wake of Northern Ireland's social upheavals, Belfast's black cabs (named for the distinctive Austin FX4 taxicabs purchased on London's secondhand market) carry six passengers per vehicle and deviate from main routes to provide door-to-door services (Lavery, 1986). Two associations with elected governing bodies oversee shared taxi services in Belfast today, coordinating operations and purchasing, insuring, and maintaining their members' vehicles. Association membership, as well as service areas and clientele, are predictably segregated along the sectarian lines that characterize life in Northern Ireland.

• *Hong Kong's Public Light Buses.* Hong Kong has two distinct types of private paratransit—2,800 unregulated, red minibuses (RMB) which follow no prescribed routes, and 1,600 green minibuses (GMB) which operate under nonexclusive route franchises granted by the government, with fixed routes, fares, and timetables. Also called Public Light Buses, Hong Kong's minibuses carry 1.7 million passengers per day, or 16 percent of all motorized trips (Hong Kong Transport Department, 1994). Since legalized in 1969, minibuses have filled the gaps in the transport network, including quality gaps, typically operating perpendicular to mainline bus and rail services (Lee, 1989; Meakin, 1993). Minibus fares are completely unregulated and, as a result, adjust up and down according to market conditions, with some drivers doubling their prices during torrential downpours.[1] Overall, minibuses have become a critical link in perhaps the most transit-oriented advanced, industrialized city in the world, one where 90 percent of the 10.5 million daily motorized trips are made by mass transit.

Only a few studies have examined the economics of paratransit services abroad. Research consistently shows that jitneys and minibuses confer substantial economic benefits, both to the public sector and private operators. Alan Walters (1979) found each minibus in Kuala Lumpur averaged around $12,800 (in 1978 dollars) in total public benefits (i.e., consumer surplus) each year. Studies of minibuses in Hong Kong and jitney services in Manila found annual rates of return on capital to range from 100 to 130 percent (Roth and Wynne, 1982; Lee, 1989). As passenger volumes rise above a certain threshold (usually 5,000 or more per direction per hour), however, the economic advantages of paratransit begin to plummet, reflecting the limitations of smaller vehicles in carrying large line-haul loads. In the developing and developed worlds alike, paratransit best operates in a supporting and supplemental, rather than substituting, role.

Three case studies of paratransit services outside of the continental United States are presented in this chapter: Puerto Rico's públicos, Mexico City's peseros and colectivos, and Southeast Asia's vast spectrum of motorized scooters, jitneys, microbuses, and minibuses. Policy lessons that might be transferred to the United States and elsewhere are emphasized in each case.

PUERTO RICO'S PÚBLICOS

Perhaps more than anywhere else, Puerto Rico occupies the middle ground between the United States and the developing world on a socioeconomic, politicocultural, and urban transportation scale. Officially a commonwealth without statehood status but under U.S. political jurisdiction, Puerto Rico's economy is closely tied to Washington; culturally, however, the island has more in common with the Dominican Republic, Jamaica, and other parts of the Caribbean. Puerto Rico's experiences with free-enterprise paratransit arguably offer more insights into the challenges and prospects for stimulating the commercial paratransit sector in the United States than anywhere else.

Crowded cities, congestion, and modest incomes have given rise to an extensive paratransit network by U.S. standards. With 3.8 million residents inhabiting an island of 3,459 square miles, Puerto Rico's population densities are among the world's highest. San Juan, the island's capital and largest municipality with 430,000 inhabitants (and a metropolitan population of over 1.3 million), has three times more vehicles per lane-mile of road than any city on the U.S. mainland. In 1990, half of all inbound directional lane miles on San Juan's major arteries were classified as congested (Puerto Rico Department of Transportation and Public Works, 1995). While Puerto Ricans average the highest per-capita income in Latin America ($3,600 in 1990), they make do with half the per capita income of the poorest American state, Mississippi, and the island is classified no higher than an upper-middle-income developing country by World Bank standards.

The Público System

Puerto Rico's público system consists of some 12,000 automobiles, vans, and minibuses distributed over around 900 routes throughout the island. The prevalence of licensed públicos is partly a product of history—in the absence of direct government sponsorship of transit, since 1907 the private sector always has been the dominant provider of mass transportation services. Though similar to jitneys, públicos actually provide a much wider array of services, including jitneylike intraurban transport along fixed routes, door-to-door services within neighborhoods, line-haul intercity travel, and even taxipooling. In many ways, *público* defines an organizational approach to paratransit more than a particular type of service. Felipe Luyanda and Podaru Gandhi (1989, p. 110) note: "the fundamental characteristic of the 'públicos' is the institutional arrangement that includes the government incentives and regulations, the route associations, and the high percentage of owner-operators with significant flexibility in the way they operate their businesses." By Puerto Rican law, públicos are considered common carrier vehicles with passenger capacities of 17 or less; larger vehicles are classified as buses.

There are three types of público routes: local (intracity), intercity, and line service. Local públicos operate on fixed routes but with variable schedules, connecting main town centers with surrounding residential and commercial areas, and stopping anywhere for curbside hails. Intercity públicos provide unscheduled, fixed-route connections between cities and towns, picking up passengers along the way. Line services operate mainly between San Juan and other island municipalities according to published schedules. Drivers are allowed to deviate from routes to provide door-to-door service for a negotiated surcharge. Most line services operate from terminals; currently, 24 are listed in San Juan's Yellow Pages.

San Juan's público network is the island's most elaborate. Currently, 2,200 vans and minibuses operate over 2,700 route miles of service on 121 designated routes, serving around 120,000 passenger trips per day within the metropolitan area.[2] This is 50 percent more than the number of passengers on the 41-route subsidized municipal bus system, Metropolitan Bus Authority (MBA). Still, públicos accommodated only 3.7 percent of all motorized trips in greater San Juan in 1990, down from 7.7 percent in 1976 and 9.2 percent in 1964. MBA's relative standing has fallen even more, serving only 2.4 percent of all passenger trips in 1990, down from 19.6 percent in 1964 (Puerto Rico Department of Transportation and Public Works, 1995). Públicos are more popular than MBA buses even though they cost patrons two to four times as much—$0.50–$1 versus $0.25—per trip. Their greater frequency and higher average speeds largely explain why. Still, San Juan's paratransit sector has suffered a fate similar to its U.S. mainland counterpart—declining market share in the face of growing competition from the private automobile. Only in the case of work trips have públicos maintained a fairly high market share by U.S. standards—around 12 percent nationwide and as high as 70 percent along some of the island's densest corridors (Luyanda et al., 1986; Puerto Rico Department of Transportation and Public Works, 1995).

Públicos are most common in Bayamón and Rio Piedras, two dense urban communities south of downtown San Juan (each with around 200,000 residents) that together comprise 64 percent of all intrametropolitan routes and 74 percent of all ridership.[3] In both communities, públicos make up over half of all motorized trips to and from their respective town centers. Central Bayamón's públicos average the shortest headways (18 seconds), heaviest loads (13.4 riders per vehicle), and highest revenue intake ($66 per vehicle per day, in 1982 currency) in all of Puerto Rico and rank among the most productively used vehicles anywhere (Luyanda and Gandhi, 1989). These phenomenally short headways reflect the tremendous density of públicos on Bayamón's central routes—on average, 30 vehicles per route (Puerto Rico Department of Transportation and Public Works, 1995).

Surveys show that as with many public transportation users on the U.S. mainland, público patrons tend to be captive—over 40 percent are from households with incomes below the island's average and 30 percent are from households without cars (Luyanda and Rodríguez, 1995). Around a third of customers live in homes without telephones. It is because of riders' low incomes that públicos operate at relatively low profit margins. It would be a mistake to characterize públicos' customer base as exclusively captive users, however. Islandwide, around 5 percent of all users are professional workers (Luyanda and Rodriguez, 1995), and in parts of San Juan (such as the Miracle Mile office corridor in the Hato Rey district), most riders are from middle-class households.

Regulation and Policy

Públicos are one of the most tightly regulated paratransit industries outside the U.S. mainland. Puerto Rico's Public Service Commission (PSC) controls market entry, fares, and routes. The only real discretion operators enjoy is when to work; they are not held to any set schedules. By most accounts, PSC is very protective and rules with an iron fist.[4] The PSC carefully scrutinizes applications for market entry based on "needs and convenience" assessments and inputs from existing operators. It tends to favor the status quo, especially when incumbent operators feel threatened by new entrants. From 1985 to 1995, the number of público permits islandwide hovered around 11,700 to 11,900 even though Puerto Rico's population grew by around 10 percent (de Cuba, 1995; World Bank, 1995). The PSC grants five-year renewable authorizations and imposes stiff sanctions for such violations as invading another route, operating unsafe vehicles, or unruly behavior. Also involved in the regulation of públicos is the Department of Transportation and Public Works, which oversees licensing, vehicle registration, and the construction of terminals and público stops on state roads. Local governments regulate the siting of curbside and off-street terminals and stops on municipal roads.

While authorities can be faulted for overregulating fares and services, most observers agree that some degree of government oversight and control is essential. Problems like oversupply of vehicles on popular routes, limited services during periods of low demand, poor transfer connections, absence of scheduling information, and underinsured vehicles continue to plague Puerto Rico's paratransit sector. It does not follow, however, that tight regulation of routing and pricing is the best way to mitigate these problems. In a more competitive marketplace, critics argue, entrepreneurs could be expected to choose routes and design fare systems (e.g., time-of-day differentials) to maximize ridership and profits.

To promote owner-drivers' interests, Puerto Rico's públicos are loosely organized into associations, or what locals call "unions." Unions attempt to rationalize services within a defined territory. They share a common place at terminals (mainly to coordinate vehicles departures), rotate services between vehicles, and sometimes buy tires and parts wholesale. More formal arrangements are cooperatives which pool resources to create operator benefit programs, pay wages to night shift drivers, and coordinate operations.

While the commonwealth maintains tight controls over the paratransit industry, where government policy most differs from that of the United States is with regard to policy incentives. In that públicos are the island's dominant form of public transportation and have substantially relieved governments of the kinds of heavy subsidy outlays found in the mainland United States, public policies have sought to reward paratransit entrepreneurs with lower registration fees, excise tax exemptions on vehicle purchases, and low interest loans. Automobiles in Puerto Rico are much more expensive than on the mainland, with excise taxes adding 20 to 50 percent to the base cost of a vehicle, depending on engine size, weight, and accessories. Operators solely dependent on their público proceeds for income are exempted from excise taxes. Given that San Juan's drivers eke out a modest existence, earning only $150 to $250 per week after expenses (de Cuba, 1995), such benefits are crucial to the fiscal viability of público services.[5] With público "medallions" worth as much as $8,000 (by law), operators use them to secure low-interest loans through the Commercial Development Corporation at participating local banks.

Perhaps the most important form of government aid has been the provision of multistory terminals near town plazas. Partly funded by grants from the U.S. Department of Transportation,[6] terminals offer vehicle staging areas (first in–first out), facilitate transfers between routes, provide protection from weather, and enhance security and public safety. Equally important, they function as holding pens during slack hours—a safe haven where públicos queue in an enclosed, centralized location rather cluttering the narrow and crowded streets of San Juan and other cities. Vehicles are released from terminals at a slow, steady rate during the off-peak—when a van at the head of the line is three-quarters full, it proceeds to its designated route and the next in line fills its slot. A terminal supervisor orchestrates all movements. During peak hours, demand is so high that vehicles need not stack up in terminals. Rather, minibuses pull into staging areas, quickly fill up, and proceed along. The biggest terminals are in greater San Juan's two largest suburban centers—Bayamón (681 parking spaces) and Rio Piedras (311 spaces). Bayamón's terminal is one of the largest anywhere, an imposing five-story structure near the town center that dominates the area's skyline.

Some top Puerto Rican transportation officials charge that públicos are an endangered species, victims of rising automobile ownership and traffic congestion, and that building terminals and providing fiscal incentives are not enough to save them from extinction. Reformists call for more automobile disincentive —e.g., higher vehicle ownership fees and fuel taxes—to reinforce paratransit incentives like excise tax exemptions and provision of terminals. While paid parking is more common and more expensive in San Juan than in its mainland U.S. counterparts, high parking and excise charges have not stemmed the tide of vehicle ownership—up 35 percent from 1980 to 1990.

In San Juan, a significant challenge in coming years will be to successfully integrate públicos into the city's 19.4-mile, double track, grade-separated rail transit system, Tren Urbano, scheduled to open in 1999. By restructuring routes to allow públicos to function like rail feeders, the hope is that eliminating main-line operations along congested arterials will increase average operating speeds and thus ridership productivity of vans and minibuses. Through good planning and careful route design, the inherent complementarity of small-vehicle feeders and high-capacity line-haul services should help bring about more efficient travel patterns in greater San Juan.

Paratransit in Puerto Rico in Summary

Overall, Puerto Rico's experiences with público services provide useful lessons to America's paratransit policy makers. Because of públicos' sheer dominance as a mass transport carrier throughout the island, government protections to ensure minimum travel needs and public safety standards are met has become even more imperative than in the mainland United States. However, as regulators have amassed greater power and controls, they have at times overstepped their mandates, tightly controlling supplies, routing, and pricing. In these respects, Puerto Rico's paratransit regulatory environment is even more restrictive than in mainland cities like Miami and Atlantic City, and more recently, Houston and Indianapolis. However, where the commonwealth deserves credit is in providing fiscal incentives and infrastructure specifically targeted at paratransit entrepreneurs. Consequently, its policies have made público riding a bargain relative to the cost of owning and using a car. And by providing convenient terminals and staging areas, públicos operate efficiently without drawing the consternation of and political backlash from middle-class motorists who might otherwise be paralyzed by swarming vans and minibuses. It has been through striking this balance between government oversight and promotion that públicos remain an important part of the local transportation scene. While paratransit in Puerto Rico has lost market shares to the private automobile, worsening traffic conditions and the emergence of mainline rail services in San Juan promise that it will continue to serve a healthy market niche. Importantly, Puerto Rico's públicos provide living proof that small-vehicle paratransit can serve as the mainstay of mass transportation, without direct government subsidies, in a land under U.S. jurisdiction.

MEXICO CITY'S PESEROS AND COLECTIVOS

As the world's largest metropolis, with an estimated population as high as 22 million, Mexico City poses mobility challenges that are unparalleled. The Federal District, the 500-square-mile administrative area that makes up the national capital and economic and cultural hub of the country, claims a more manageable 8.5 million inhabitants. However, with population having nearly doubled every decade since 1930, urban growth has in recent decades spilled well beyond the Federal District into the surrounding state of Mexico. It is the Federal District and its adjoining suburbs that make up the megalopolis of Mexico City, with an official 1990 population of 15.1 million and an unofficial one of well over 20 million. Today, about one-quarter of Mexico's population resides in greater Mexico City, which covers just 1 percent of the country's surface area (Cushman and Wakefield, 1994). With urban development of such magnitude has come strains on public infrastructure and services—from water supply to sewage treatment to transportation—that are unprecedented.

Presently, over 37 million motorized trips are made each day within metropolitan Mexico City, 70 percent occurring within the Federal District (CGT, 1994). Nearly 3 million private automobiles are registered in the metropolis, and vehicle ownership has risen at least twice as fast as the region's 2.5 percent annual population growth rate. During peak hours, traffic within the District crawls at an average speed of 9 kilometers per hour. The crush of automobiles has produced some of the worst smog conditions anywhere, exacerbated by mountains that ring the valley and contain pollutants. Conditions are further aggravated by the large population of old, poor-running cars that have no catalytic converters and Mexico City's high altitude, which reduces engine efficiency (Armstrong-Wright, 1993). The Federal District has imposed a Days off the Road scheme which restricts private and government vehicles from operating at least one day a week, on a rotating basis, according to the last digit of license plates.[7] While conditions are very severe, congestion and pollution would be much worse were it not for the dynamic and wide-ranging metropolitan transportation system that has evolved over the years in response to explosive growth. Notably, a hierarchy of transportation services—both public and private—has emerged, providing a rich mix of travel options in terms of geographic coverage, vehicle carrying capacities, and levels of integration. At the top of the hierarchy and forming the backbone of the network is Metro, a rubber-tired high-speed subway system, built by the French in the 1960s and modeled after the Parisian subway. Metro's nine lines crisscross the District, totaling 158 kilometers of guideway and 135 stations. With average peak-hour headways of around a minute and daily ridership nearing 5 million, Matro is one of the most extensive and highly patronized rail transit systems in the world (larger in size and claiming more riders than all others metros in Latin America—São Paulo, Rio de Janeiro, Buenos Aires, Caracas, Santiago —put together). Around one in five daily trips made within the District use the Metro for at least one leg (Benitez and Gomez, 1990). Without Metro, the high densities and urban agglomerations found throughout the core of the District would be unattainable. To the degree the nation has prospered from having governmental, financial, and cultural affairs in a compact urban arrangement, Metro has yielded benefits that go well beyond improved mobility.

With Metro forming the main arteries of the region's transit network, equally vital to the lifeblood of the metropolis have been the network's capillaries—the extensive system of paratransit feeder services, known locally as *peseros* and *colectivos*. In the 1950s, taxi drivers operating along the city's busiest boulevards began augmenting income by picking up multiple unrelated passengers, charging them a flat fee—one peso. The mode quickly grew in popularity and became known as a pesero. As peseros increasingly became the public transportation mode of choice, taxi sedans were gradually replaced by Volkswagen vans, also known as *combis*, during the sixties and seventies. Today, combis are being replaced by 23-seat minibuses which burn unleaded fuel. The name *colectivos* generally refers to these larger minibuses.

Paratransit in Mexico City: The Supply Side

Peseros and colectivos grew and adapted throughout the 1970s and 1980s in response to the rapid expansion of the Metro system. What has evolved is a hub-and-spoke transport network that closely mimics predominant travel patterns and facilitates transfers. Institutionally, the arrangement has clear lines of responsibility—government is the provider of mainline services and the private sector takes care of branch connections. However, supplementing the private paratransit sector, though more in the background, have been several publicly supported surface transportation modes—notably, the Ruta-100 bus network, 19 trolley buslines, and the 30-kilometer Tren Ligero light rail system (Montoyo, 1992). Hierarchically, these public surface routes function more as distributors, filling in mainline service gaps of the Metro and serving more intermediate-distance trips.[8]

The hierarchy of paratransit services in greater Mexico City is further revealed by Table 4.1. Taxis provide on-call, curb-to-curb services whereas other paratransit modes ply principal routes. Pesero sedans tend to serve the lowest-volume corridors and make slight route detours at riders' requests. Combis normally carry two to three times as many riders as sedans and concentrate mainly on intermediate-volume markets in the suburbs. Minibuses seat up to 25 passengers with room for an equal number to stand. Table 4.1 also shows that vehicles have segmented themselves out geographically, with smaller vehicles serving shorter-haul customers (more often in the suburban-exurban fringes of the state of Mexico) and larger vehicles traversing longer distances (more often within the Federal District). Overall, market segmentation by vehicle capacity and corridor has helped to rationalize the use of scarce road space.

Presently, there are around 100 paratransit routes in Mexico City, and each route averages around 15 deviation branches. Thus, there are some 1,500 variations among the 100 or so main paratransit routes. Central Mexico City is virtually saturated with peseros and colectivos during peak periods. Middle-class suburbs are also well served. Many barrios and slum areas on the periphery receive thinner services, not only because their residents are less able to pay market-rate fares but also because roads leading to these areas are often in poor condition and too steep to negotiate. The routes of nearly all peseros and colectivos in the surrounding state of Mexico end at the terminal station of a Metro line.

Peseros and colectivos normally begin service at around 6:00 A.M. and continue until as late as 10:00 to 11:00 P.M. Some high-demand routes provide 24-hour service. Headways vary by demand. During peak hours, a steady stream

Table 4.1.
Mexico City's Hierarchy of Paratransit Services, 1994

	Seating Capacities (No. of Passengers)	Typical Route Operating Ranges (One way Kilometers)	1994 Vehicle Inventory		
			Federal District	State of Mexico	Total
Taxis	2-3	3-6	56,059	8,456	64,515
Peseros: Sedans	5-6	2-4	763	2,626	3,389
Peseros: VW Vans	10-14	5-10	22,690	13,860	36,550
Colectivos: Minibuses	22-25	10-20	20,493	9,527	30,020
TOTAL	—	—	100,005	34,469	134,474

Source: Comision General de Transporte (1994), field surveys (November 1994).

of jam-packed vehicles funnel into and out of Metro stations. During the off-peak, vehicles queue outside of stations and normally leave only when they are at least half full.

Most peseros and colectivos are individually owned and operated under the direction of a route association. Many owner-operators drive during an 8:00 to 9:00 morning shift and lease their vehicles for the evening shift.[9] Colectivo mini-buses cost an estimated $0.71 per kilometer to operate in November 1994 (just prior to the devaluation of Mexican currency), yielding around $0.22 in driver earnings per kilometer. Each workday, colectivo owner-operators average around $50 in net daily income, whereas lease-operators clear around $28.[10] Overall, colectivo drivers earn a comparable salary to public bus drivers, though they receive no benefits and have less job security.

Where Mexico City's paratransit vehicles fall short is in vehicle quality, victims of constant, heavy usage. Fleets are often minimally maintained and breakdowns are common. Outside of oversubscribed peak hours, however, peseros and colectivos usually provide a comfortable ride. Moreover, drivers are generally no more aggressive than other motorists, unlike in most other developing countries with thriving paratransit sectors. This is mainly because Mexico City's paratransit routes are controlled by associations, thus easing some of the competition for customers. In fact, there is a fair amount of camaraderie among paratransit operators belonging to the same route association.

Paratransit in Mexico City: The Demand Side

Paratransit reigns supreme among all forms of travel in greater Mexico City. Table 4.2 shows that colectivos, peseros, and taxis combined to handle around 40 percent of motorized trips in the Federal District and 37 percent of trips in the state of Mexico in 1994. Paratransit was more heavily patronized than all public transit combined in the Federal District and carried comparable loads as motor buses in the state of Mexico. Combining demand and supply figures (i.e., from Tables 4.1 and 4.2) reveals that the average daily passenger load of a colectivo operating in metropolitan Mexico City is around 280. Average daily peseros ridership is 120 passengers per Volkswagen van and 65 passengers per sedan. Mexico City's paratransit sector also plays a dominant role in getting patrons to and from Metro. According to preliminary origin and destination survey data compiled by the Comision General de Transporte (CGT), the region's transportation planning organization, approximately 10 times as many people access the Metro via paratransit as do by walking. A significant number of those reaching Metro stations via vans and minibuses are middle-class professionals and government workers.

Together, Metro and its paratransit feeders have dramatically increased accessibility to the urban edge, home to millions of rural immigrants and poor households. (Only 10 percent of Metro users have the option of driving instead of using Metro.) Metro's fares have been kept low—on average, only 1.1 percent of a day's

Table 4.2.
Daily Motorized Trips in Greater Mexico City, 1994

	Federal District		State of Mexico		Metropolitan Area	
	Total	Percent	Total	Percent	Total	Percent
Public Transportation						
Metro	4,488,000	17.6	0	0.0	4,488,000	12.2
Light rail	15,000	0.1	0	0.0	15,000	0.1
Ruta-100 (surface						
diesel bus)	3,208,000	12.6	0	0.0	3,208,000	8.7
Electric trolleybus	330,000	1.3	0	0.0	330,000	0.8
Other bus (autobus)	0	0.0	4,385,000	38.2	4,385,000	11.9
Paratransit						
Colectivos (minibuses)	5,738,000	22.5	2,287,000	19.9	8,025,000	21.7
Peseros (combis						
& sedans)	2,772,000	10.9	1,831,000	16.0	4,603,000	12.5
Taxis	1,615,000	6.3	102,000	0.9	1,717,000	4.6
Private Automobile	7,316,000	28.7	2,864,000	25.0	10,180,000	27.5
TOTAL	25,482,000	100.0	11,469,000	100.0	36,951,000	100.0

Source: Comision General de Transporte (1994)

minimum wage during the 1980s.[11] Since they are unsubsidized, however, paratransit's fares have generally been far higher—around U.S.$0.18 in late 1994, or around 5 percent of the average daily wage of an unskilled worker.[12] Because many of the poor living on the periphery make as many as five connections per day, urban transport costs consume as much as a quarter of a day's minimum salary.

Besides increasing accessibility, Mexico City's Metro-paratransit combination has indelibly shaped urban form. Prior to 1970, the radial bus-based transit network served to reinforce the region's monocentric structure. With nearly all buses running to the core of the metropolis, congestion on radiating boulevards became increasingly intolerable. The opening of Metro and its feeder network served to redistribute growth outward, leading to a more polycentric settlement pattern. Gross densities for the metropolitan area, for instance, stood at 150 inhabitants per hectare in 1987, identical to what they were in 1940, despite the region's population having rocketed from 1.76 million to 18.64 million over this period (Benitez and Gomez, 1990). Peseros and colectivos, in particular, served as the "tentacles" that allowed those living on the periphery to reach the core, thus adapting to, and in so doing, reinforcing, the region's dispersed settlement pattern. At many Metro stations, especially terminals, commercial centers (e.g., department stores, food kiosks, service outlets) have evolved around paratransit-bus staging areas, in sharp contrast to the sprawling park-and-ride lots that surround most suburban rail stations in the United States.

Regulation

As a mostly free-enterprise, unrestricted paratransit sector emerged following Metro's 1969 opening, it quickly became clear that laissez-faire transport in such a large, complex metropolis was leading to chaos. Prior to this time, although peseros and colectivos were technically illegal, they were tolerated by local officials as a necessary evil in the absence of suitable alternative public transportation (Roschlau, 1981). Over time, government regulations that have both legitimized and controlled peseros and colectivos have evolved, in recognition of both their vital importance yet potential threat to mobility within the metropolis.

The Comision General de Transporte oversees paratransit within the Federal District, and a counterpart authority has jurisdiction over the seven municipalities and unincorporated areas in the outlying suburbs. These organizations control entry by issuing permits and licenses. They also determine permitted routes of operation, set tariffs, and maintain performance standards.[13] Within these limitations, however, private operators are free to operate as they choose, including the hours they work and schedules they maintain. Because of a purported oversupply of minibuses, the Federal District has not issued new paratransit permits for many years. On Route 2, one of the busiest and longest-standing routes in the District, no new permits have been granted since 1968. The presence of a bustling black market for counterfeit colectivo licenses and permits (costing around U.S.$100), however, raises some doubt as to whether present-day minibus supplies excessively outstrip demand.

In controlling routes, regulators deserve credit for rationalizing services and reducing inefficiencies on the urban transit network. Once Metro opened, the CGT began issuing paratransit licenses only for routes that fed into Metro stations. Cross-town and long-haul radial services were largely eliminated. Most likely, even without government's guiding hand, pesero and colectivo operators would have adapted services quite similarly in order to maximize efficiency and profits. Regulators have also prohibited suburban buses and colectivos from the surrounding states of Mexico and Morelos from entering the District core, restricting them to peripheral Metro stations instead.

Other government offices oversee other aspects of paratransit affairs in greater Mexico City. Federal involvement is largely limited to regulating vehicle exhaust, a responsibility of the secretary of transport and communications. More problematic has been enforcement of regulations. Over the years, these responsibilities have vacillated between the city's police department and the Direccion General de Autotransporte Urbano, the District authority in charge of public transportation services. Shifting roles have mainly been an outcome of internal power struggles as different political groups have gone after what is often viewed as a potentially lucrative business—collecting fines for actual and alleged violations of government rules. However, no District authorities have the resources to enforce rules among some 100,000 licensed paratransit operators in the city, much less the tens of thousands of unlicensed ones. Currently, only around 200 officers in the District enforce paratransit regulations. Despite the presence of a thick handbook of rules and regulations for peseros and colectivos, requirements are largely unenforceable.

Role of Route Associations

In light of these enforcement difficulties and given the enormity of Mexico City's paratransit sector, the emergence of proactive route associations was inevitable. Each of the 100-plus pesero and colectivo routes in the Federal District is today represented by a route association.[14] Additionally, there are 15 umbrella organizations that actively lobby for the interests of the paratransit industry in general and their constituent route associations specifically. Overall, then, a hierarchical organizational structure has evolved to administer and promote the city's hierarchy of paratransit services.

Among the functions carried out by route associations have been: secure authorizations for branch routes and organize the allocation of vehicles on these routes; assist owner-members in obtaining vehicle loans from banks and the government; settle claims stemming from accidents; and represent members in dealings with government officials. The city's largest route associations elect a full-time president and governing board and maintain administrative offices, central dispatchers (for vehicles equipped with shortwave radios), and service garages. In addition to routine maintenance and repairs, associations' garages stockpile vehicle parts, like tires and oil filters, that are available to members at a discount.

Over the years, many route associations have evolved more or less into cartels, successfully lobbying to set limits on licensing and route expansions. The amount of power wielded by associations is by all appearances directly proportional to size. For the largest and most established associations, such as the Route 2 association that oversees 2,500 minibuses and VW vans in central Mexico City, the degree of control is considerable—besides chasing away illegal operators from their members' routes, they hire field attendants to direct passenger boardings at busy terminal, keep the police at bay through solicited and unsolicited "payments," and maintain records of drivers' log-in and log-out times.

Paratransit in Mexico City in Summary

Mexico City's multitier, hierarchical network of Metro-paratransit-bus transit has been absolutely indispensable in restraining the use of the private car and supporting a megalopolis the size and complexity of the Federal District and its suburbs. Colectivos and peseros handle over a third of motorized trips within the region, more than either the private automobile or all public transit services combined. Overall, the network of radial rail lines and branching paratransit feeder services has allowed a spread-out, polycentric metropolis to take shape, relieving development pressure on, yet maintaining the preeminence of, the central core.

Mexico City's transit network is as noteworthy for its institutional configurations as it is for its physical ones. Public operators provide mainly trunkline rail and bus services which are complemented by private paratransit feeders. Straddling this public-private spectrum are route associations. In an unbridled marketplace, Mexico City's route associations have become absolutely indispensable organizations for coordinating and rationalizing paratransit service delivery, while at the same time protecting and promoting the interests of their members.

Despite the overwhelming popularity of peseros and colectivos, there have been rumblings at the central level in recent years to replace vans and minibuses in the District with standard bus coaches. Paratransit would be limited to serving less-travelled suburban markets. Some high-level officials believe bigger vehicles will ultimately reduce congestion and air pollution. Because route associations have become a strong political force in their own right, however, most observers doubt that commercial paratransit can be completely regulated out of existence as it has been in most of North America.

PARATRANSIT IN SOUTHEAST ASIA

Traffic congestion is as severe in the large cities of Southeast Asia as anywhere in the world. It is also a major cause of fatalities and the chief source of air pollution (Rimmer, 1986; Faiz et al., 1992). In cities like Jakarta, Bangkok, and Manila, where rush-hour speeds have slowed to 6 to 8 kilometers per hour in core areas, congestion is largely a product of growth in the motorized vehicle population far outpacing road expansion (Midgley, 1993; Wanisubut, 1995). In all three cities, vehicle registrations grew at an annual rate of between 10 and 15 percent throughout the 1980s and early 1990s, whereas only a few kilometers of roads were typically added in these cities each year over the same period (Spencer and Madhavan, 1989; Armstrong-Wright, 1993). Less than 10 percent of total urban space in Jakarta, Bangkok, and Manila, moreover, is devoted to roadways. By comparison, road space makes up 22 percent of the land area in London and 24 percent in New York City (Sinsap et al., 1988; Poboon et al., 1994). The problem is not just a lack of capacity, but also a lack of a functional road hierarchy. Just as rivers rely on good tributaries, there must be a well-functioning network of local streets that interconnect with collectors and arterials for traffic to circulate efficiently. In many Southeast Asian cities, few good distributor roads are available. What would be considered local streets in the developed world are forced to function as collectors in the third world. In Bangkok, the net result of rapid motorization[15] and limited road capacity has been near-paralysis—3 million person-hours are lost each day in the metropolitan region because of average traffic delays of two or three hours (Sussman and Bonsignore, 1993). One study estimated that Bangkok loses about a third of its potential gross city product through congestion-induced delays (Midgley, 1993).

Paratransit takes many names, shapes, and forms in Southeast Asia, generally characterized by three-wheelers, jitneys, collective taxis, and minibuses that cruise the streets for customers, providing both door-to-door and fixed-route, mainline services. Ranging from human-powered three-wheel bikes (becaks, rikishas) and motor scooters (bajajs, tuk-tuks, mobeks) to small buses (bemos, opelets, mikrolets), Southeast Asia's paratransit sector offers a spectrum of services in terms of seating capacity, speeds, geographic coverage, levels of comfort, and fares (Roth, 1988; Chujoh, 1989). Some vehicles cater to short trips of two to three blocks, others serve more intermediate-distance travel, while still others cover entire regions. Because many roads and alleys are so narrow and poorly maintained, paratransit also penetrates areas that buses cannot. Rides are not always comfortable, but fares are usually cheap. Additionally, the informal paratransit sector in Southeast Asia, as in most other developing regions, has become an important source of urban employment, particularly for young males who have temporarily migrated from the rural countryside, providing as much as 15 percent of total employment in some cities (Walters, 1979; Silcock, 1981; Kartodirdjo, 1981). Most drivers rent vehicles from small companies and syndicates. The shares of microvehicle drivers estimated to own their own vehicles is only 15 percent in Jakarta and Bandung, 9 percent in Manila, and 1 percent in Bangkok (Shimazaki and Rahman, 1995). Paratransit drivers work hard and long hours to make ends meet, on average around 13 hours per day in Bangkok (Agad, 1990).

Laissez-faire or Regulation?

Many Southeast Asian cities find themselves in a heated debate over whether to dismantle their free-market paratransit services, replacing them with metros and large buses operated by the public sector. In more industrialized and modern cities like Kuala Lumpur and Singapore, private paratransit has largely given way to public operators. Rapidly growing megacities like Jakarta and Bangkok are poised to follow suit.

Southeast Asia's informal paratransit sector expanded during the post–World War II era when few people owned cars and governments were too cash-strapped to mount credible transit services. By the early 1970s, there were an estimated 140,000 paratransit vehicles (bajajs, helicaks, bemos, and becaks) in Jakarta and 90,000 in Surabaya, Indonesia (Jacobs and Fouracre, 1974). Today, Manila's 12- to 15-passenger jeepneys, which are converted surplus U.S. army jeeps, are the city's dominant public transport mode; three-fourths of Metro Manila residents patronize public transit each day, and of them, 77 percent take jeepneys. Jeepneys cover 610 kilometers of Metro Manila roads compared with 310 kilometers covered by the city's 14 bus companies.

Since some paratransit vehicles are human-powered and most others have low power-to-weight ratios, Southeast Asia's paratransit fleets are universally slow. Motorists, trucks, and public buses have thus found it difficult to coexist with them. Paratransit drivers are also frequently criticized for reckless and overly aggressive driving in Manila, Jakarta, and other large cities in the region. Also, foreign advisors often argue that paratransit modes have hampered the development of more modern transportation systems and technologies in this part of the world (Rimmer and Dick, 1980; Mogridge, 1983). For these and other reasons, human-powered paratransit has been largely eliminated from large Southeast Asian cities, and most slow-moving modes have been restricted to specific zones.[16] Some critics warn, however, that the handwriting is on the wall and that the paratransit sector's days in Southeast Asia are numbered (Rimmer and Dick, 1980; Roth, 1988; Roschlau, 1989; Dimitriou, 1995). Among the reasons given for the backlash against paratransit are foreign consultants and other hired guns, many of whom take only taxis in these cities and don't appreciate how important paratransit is to the urban poor, are culturally predisposed against paratransit; foreign lenders are seeking to export modern transport technologies to developing regions, a form of technological imperialism; and in the drive toward modernization, particularly in image-conscious national capitals, paratransit is viewed as an inferior, obsolete mode suitable for more backward countries (Thomson, 1977; White, 1981; Rimmer, 1986; Cervero, 1991). Usually unmentioned is the fact that paratransit has consistently shown itself to be an economic asset, providing services at a lower cost per seat mile without government subsidies, in addition to providing badly needed services for and jobs in poor neighborhoods (Roth and Wynne, 1982). Some find it puzzling that paratransit is being primed for regulation and retrenchment at a time when privatization and self-reliance are being actively promoted in other sectors (e.g., toll roads, solid waste, water supplies) of Southeast Asian economies (Roschlau, 1989).

Paratransit Diversity: A Market Response to Poor Roads

While paratransit provides low-performance services, an overlooked benefit is that it compensates for the inadequacies of urban road systems in Southeast Asia. The adaption of free-enterprise paratransit services to the poorly developed hierarchy of roads is demonstrated by experiences in eight large Southeast Asian cities, shown in Map 4.1: the Indonesian cities of Jakarta, Surabaya, Medan, and Bandung; and elsewhere, Bangkok (Thailand), Manila (the Philippines), Kuala Lumpur (Malaysia), and Singapore. Each of these cities has over 1.5 million inhabitants and is either a national capital or regional center of the largest and most rapidly industrializing, free-market nations of the region. Table 4.3 summarizes population, density, and basic transportation characteristics of the eight cities. Jakarta is the most populated city in Southeast Asia, and its neighbor to the south, Bandung, with over 1.8 million inhabitants living in an 81-square-kilometer area, is one of the densest. With the exception of the more modern and affluent city-state of Singapore, most Southeast Asian cities have few kilometers of roads relative to their populations. This makes them natural breeding grounds for spawning a diversity of commercial paratransit services.

Despite the explosive growth in car population, paratransit ridership remains strong in most of these eight cities. In Manila and Jakarta, over 60 percent of all mass transportation trips recorded in the 1980s were served by medium- and

small-sized privately owned vehicles (Chujoh, 1989; Halcrow and Fox Associates, 1982). In Medan, the largest city on the island of Sumatra, over three-quarters of all motorized trips in the 1980s were by microbuses, minibuses, scooters, and hired motorcycles (Renee-Park, 1989). Minibuses handle an estimated 40 percent of mass transportation trips even in relatively prosperous cities like Kuala Lumpur (Shimazaki and Rahman, 1995). In greater Bangkok, where around one in five of the 10.5 million daily mass transportation trips are by paratransit, surveys show many users are working class residents making shopping and personal business trips (Tanaboriboon et al., 1993).

Classes of Service

Overall, there are five classes of mass transport vehicles among these eight cities, summarized in Table 4.4. Starting with those vehicles with the highest seating capacities, Class I is made up of both standard stage coaches and double-decker buses, operated by public and private enterprises. Class II vehicles consist of minibuses, designed to carry intermediate loads of 12 to 24 riders. Included here are Manila's jeepneys, Jakarta's mikrolets, and Bandung's Daihatsu kolts. The third class is made up mainly of microbuses—four-wheeled van-size vehicles that accommodate 6 to 11 passengers (e.g., Jakarta's opelets and Medan's bemos). Class IV vehicles are motorized three-wheelers, each serving 2 to 4 passengers, such as Bangkok's colorful tuk-tuks, named for their loud two-stroke engine noise, Manila's motorized tricycles, and Jakarta's bajajs, as well as what is the fastest-growing paratransit mode in Southeast Asia, for-hire motorcycles (called ojeks in Indonesia). A final class consists of human-powered three-wheel and horse-powered four-wheel vehicles—for example, Medan's becaks, Manila's horse carts (calesa), and Singapore's rikishas (now banned except for tourist zones). Vehicles in the last two classes normally provide individual, door-to-door services, whereas other vehicle classes provide collective-ride, fixed-route services (with occasional deviations). Also, fares are normally negotiated for door-to-door services in smaller-class vehicles but are fixed (sometimes on a distance basis, as with Manila's jeepneys) for larger vehicles operating along prescribed routes.

The inventories of motorized paratransit and mass transit vehicles in these eight cities are summarized in Table 4.5, for different years. In Jakarta, Manila, and Medan, over half of mass transportation seating capacity is provided by motorized paratransit vehicles. If human-powered and horse-drawn vehicles were counted, paratransit's relative capacity in these cities would be even higher.

Perhaps more than anywhere, Jakarta has an unusually rich variety of passenger transport modes—from double-decker city buses to (illegal) human-pedaled becaks and most everything in between. With its large population (11.5 million in 1995) and concentrations of poor residents, loosely regulated paratransit market, and steady stream of unemployed rural in-migrants, metropolitan Jakarta's paratransit sector today counts well over 80,000 privately operated mini- and micro-vehicles—becaks,[17] low-powered for-hire motorcycles (ojeks), bemos, micro-

Table 4.4.
Classes of Mass Transport Vehicles in Southeast Asian Cities

Class	Capacity Range	Cities	Types of Vehicles
I.	25–88 passengers	Jakarta, Singapore	Stage buses (55), Double-deckers (88)
		Manila, Bandung,	Stage buses (50)
		Medan, Surabaya	Stage buses (50)
		Kuala Lumpur	Stage buses (50),
		Bangkok	Stage buses (50), Public buses (34)
II.	12–24 passengers	Jakarta	Minibus (24), Large opelet (17)
		Manila	Minibus (24), Jeepney (16)
		Bangkok	Minibus (18), Pickup (14)
		Kuala Lumpur	Minibus (24)
		Bandung	Kolt/sudak (14)
		Surabaya, Medan	Mikrolet (12)
III.	6–11 passengers	Jakarta	4-wheel bemo (10), Mikrolet (8), 3-wheel bemo (7), Mebea/mobet (7)
		Surabaya, Medan	Bemo (7)
		Bandung	Bemo (8), Kijang (6)
		Bangkok	Silor (7)
IV.	1–5 passengers	Surabaya	Angguna vans (5), Ojek (1)
		Jakarta	Bajaj (3), Helicak (3), Ojek (1)
		Bangkok	Tuk-tuk/samlor (3), Motorcycle (1)
		Medan	Motor becak (3), Ojek (1)
		Manila	Motor tricycle (2)
V.	1–3 passengers (non-motorized)	Manila	Calesa (3), Tricycle (2)
		Bandung, Medan	Becak (2), Dokar (2)
		Jakarta, Surabaya	Becak (2)
		Singapore	Rikisha (2)
		Kuala Lumpur	Rikisha (2)

Note: Values in brackets indicate carrying capacity of modes, exclusive of driver.

Sources: Cervero (1991), Gunawan (1992), Shimazaki and Rahman (1995)

buses (mikrolets), and minibuses. In contrast, the paratransit sectors of Singapore and Kuala Lumpur have been reined in through a combination of regulations, public takeovers, and increased car ownership.[18]

Besides carrying capacities, other operating features of the paratransit services listed in Tables 4.4 and 4.5 differ markedly. One general rule is that the smaller the vehicle, the more limited the geographic coverage. In Metro Manila, for

Table 4.5.
Transit and Motorized Paratransit Vehicle Stocks and Capacities,
Eight Southeast Asian Cities

	Number of Vehicles	Total Capacity	
		No. Seats	Percent
Bandung (1988)			
Stage bus	2,500	125,000	47.3
Minibus	2,700	64,800	24.6
Opelet, sudako, kolt	3,300	46,200	17.5
Bemo, kijang	4,000	28,000	10.6
Total	*12,500*	*264,000*	*100.0*
Bangkok (1994)			
Public bus	5,250	210,000	51.0
Private bus	1,450	72,500	17.6
Minibus	2,400	43,200	10.5
Silor	7,900	47,400	11.5
Samlor/tuk-tuk	7,400	22,200	5.4
Hired motorcycles	16,600	16,600	4.0
Total	*41,000*	*411,900*	*100.0*
Jakarta (1990)			
Double-decker bus	160	13,440	2.1
Stage bus	5,100	280,500	43.7
Minibus, mikrolet, opelet	10,850	195,300	30.4
Opelet, bemo	9,400	84,600	13.2
Bajaj, helicak	16,300	32,600	5.1
Ojek	35,000	35,000	5.5
Total	*76,810*	*641,440*	*100.0*
Kuala Lumpur (1985)			
Stage bus	1,920	96,000	89.1
Minibus	490	11,760	10.9
Total	*2,410*	*107,760*	*100.0*
Manila (1989)			
Stage bus	4,200	210,000	29.0
Minibus	850	20,400	2.8
Jeepney	30,800	492,800	68.1
Total	*35,850*	*723,200*	*100.0*
Medan (1988)			
Stage bus	2,200	110,000	49.6
Microbus	6,000	72,000	32.4
Bemo	4,000	28,000	12.6
Motor becak	4,000	12,000	5.4
Total	*16,200*	*222,000*	*100.0*
Singapore (1988)			
Double-decker bus	450	39,600	8.0
Stage bus	8,150	456,400	91.1
Minibus	20	320	0.1
Total	*8,620*	*496,320*	*100.0*

(continued)

Table 4.5 (continued).
Transit and Motorized Paratransit Vehicle Stocks and Capacities,
Eight Southeast Asian Cities

	Number of Vehicles	Total Capacity No. Seats	Percent
Surabaya (1994)			
Stage bus	1,900	95,000	71.7
Minibus, mikrolet	840	10,080	7.6
Bemo, opelet	3,600	14,400	10.9
Angguna van	1,000	5,000	3.8
Ojek	8,000	8,000	6.0
Total	*15,540*	*132,480*	*100.0*

Note: Statistics for registered motorized forms of paratransit only, exclusive of human and horsed powered vehicles. Statistics on for-hire motorcycle services (e.g., ojek) are only presented for Bangkok, Jakarta, and Surabaya, although these services exist in other cities as well.

Sources: Cervero (1991), Renee-Park (1989), Kusbiantoro (1988), Tanaboriboon (1994), DKI Jakarta (1990), Rimmer (1986), JICA (1985, 1986), Galvante (1988), Been and Chen (1989), Colin Buchanan and Partners (1994).

example, around 65 percent of bus trips are over 7.5 kilometers in length while an equal share of jeepney trips are under 5 kilometers (JICA, 1985). There are also sharp contrasts in rates of passenger throughputs. In Jakarta, the average number of passengers per kilometer of service is 1.5 for human-powered becaks, 4 for three-wheel bajas, and 7 for bemo microbuses (Shimazaki and Rahman, 1995). On a daily basis, passenger loads per day in Bangkok vary from 35 on hired motorcycles, 58 to 60 on silors (small Daihatsu or Suzuki pickups) and tuk-tuks, 520 on minibuses, and 1,300 on stage coaches (JICA, 1990).

In these eight cities, past consulting reports (Wilbur Smith and Associates, 1974; Kocks, 1975; JICA, 1985, 1987, 1990) have specifically mentioned the conflicts between paratransit modes and other motorized traffic as a major source of congestion. Other factors that have been blamed for worsening congestion, besides rapid motorization rates, include narrow, poorly maintained roads; piecemeal road development; lack of road connectivity and excessive deadends, like the fishbone road patterns (soi roads) of Bangkok; spillover of pedestrians and street vendors into roads; insufficient off-street parking; the absence of land use controls, resulting in the poor siting of major traffic generators (e.g., open-air markets); and minimal enforcement of traffic laws (Jacobs and Fouracre, 1974; Kirby et al., 1986).

Hierarchical Paratransit for Non-hierarchical Roads

For these eight Southeast Asian cities, strong associations were found between levels of diversity in paratransit services and various indicators of road capacities and hierarchies. Specifically, the greatest variety of paratransit modes, both in terms of types and seating capacities, generally exists in Southeast Asian cities with the least amount of road capacity per capita and a poor road hierarchy. For example, the simple correlation between an index of "variation in types of paratransit modes" and "kilometers of paved roads per capita" for these eight cities was -0.52.[19] Medan, for instance, has a diverse paratransit system (1-passenger for-hire motorcycles, 2-passenger becaks, 3-passenger motorized becaks, 7-seat bemos, 9-seat jitneys, 12-seat microbuses, 24-seat minibuses, and 50-seat coaches) but minimal road capacity (27.4 kilometers of paved roads per 100,000 residents in 1989) and a poor road hierarchy (in particular, few main arteries and distributors). In Medan and many other Southeast Asian cities unencumbered by heavy-handed regulations, the mix of paratransit fleets and services has evolved so as to adapt to the low-capacity, poorly interconnected road systems. Harry Dimitriou (1995) has also recently shown that the assortment of paratransit services in five Javanese cities adapt nicely to the mix of footpaths, village roads, distributors, and main arteries that exist. These findings are consistent with theories advanced by Gabriel Bouladon and Y. Sasaki, cited in Dimitriou (1995), that hold that the absence of a hierarchy of transport technologies (in terms of speeds and spatial coverage), especially between the pedestrian and motor car, is a root cause of transportation-related overconsumption—of road space and clean air resources —in many advanced societies.

Statistics aside, one can find anecdotal situations where these propositions are borne out. Take Jakarta, for instance. Because rivers originating in the southern mountain range flow north toward the city, Jakarta's north-south streets are well-developed, paralleling the rivers on firm soil beds. Most east-west streets, on the other hand, have an undulating profile, are narrow, and generally lack continuity. Bottlenecks are common at east-west bridge crossings. Over the years, a number of paratransit modes, like bajajs, bemos, and mikrolets, have plied their trade over Jakarta's east-west passageways. Most north-south roads, on the other hand, have been banned to all but private motorists and public buses. Thus, in Jakarta, paratransit operations have been leaned upon to increase the passenger through-puts of deficient east-west thoroughfares. Ostensibly, they have evolved in number and composition to serve these under-capacity, poorly connected corridors —that is, they have functioned as a modal response to the inadequacies of Jakarta's road system.

The complementarity of paratransit is also highlighted in Surabaya, capital of West Java. While 48-54-passenger buses operate along north-south axes to and through the city center, 8-10-passenger bemos and 5-seater Angguna vans operate mainly in an east-west direction, from outlying areas to intermediate terminals at the boundary of the old city. Human-powered becaks and hired motorcycles (ojeks) are found throughout the city; however, they predominate in remote villages on the metropolitan periphery and in a few old neighborhoods that ring the city center. Being both legally and physically restricted from crossing main roads and bottlenecks, becaks function mainly to transport passengers from remote areas and hard-to-access neighborhoods to bemo stops for further travel.

Overall, paratransit has a fairly narrowly defined role to play in the mobility scene of Southeast Asian cities, functioning mainly to provide feeder and collector services. Equally alarming in most cities is the absence of high-capacity mainline services. Jakarta plans to open a north-south metro rail system and a series of orbital tollroads as build-operate-transfer schemes. Also, three concessionaire expressway projects and three rail transit projects are in the final design stages or are currently being built in Bangkok. Over $1 billion in new distributor roads in greater Bangkok are also now under construction (Wanisubut, 1995). Where Southeast Asia has made the most impressive strides, however, has been through demand-side as opposed to supply-side strategies. Specifically, high import duties, registration fees, excise taxes, and road user charges have been used to restrain automobile ownership and usage. Singapore's area licensing scheme that charges motorists for entry into downtown areas during peak periods has also effectively contained traffic congestion; motorized traffic in Singapore's core has dropped by an estimated 50 percent below pre-road-pricing levels (Richards, 1990). Many traffic officials from Southeast Asia similarly view curbing three-wheelers, jitneys, and minibuses as a potentially effective traffic management approach under the presumption that paratransit is an inefficient user of road space.[20]

Regulatory and Institutional Environments

As average incomes and vehicle ownership rates have risen, regulatory controls over the paratransit sector have stiffened in Southeast Asian cities. In the case of Singapore and Kuala Lumpur, paratransit has largely been banned except for private bus and minibus services on designated routes and rikishas in tourist areas. In most other cities, limits have recently been placed on the number of licensed paratransit carriers, and most slower-moving vehicles (classes IV and V in Table 4.4) have been restricted to operating in low-income neighborhoods and outlying commercial districts. In Bangkok, the numbers of licensed tuk-tuk and silor vehicles have been held at 7,500 and 8,000, respectively, for years. Authorities in both Bangkok and Jakarta have banned human-powered carriers altogether, and Manila's regulators have barred tricycles from main roads. All Southeast Asian cities prohibit anything smaller than a minibus from using expressways. Tight controls have generally spawned a highly visible underground paratransit sector everywhere except Singapore and Kuala Lumpur; as long as illegal operators stay away from busy roads and middle-class neighborhoods, however, government officials have generally ignored them. Even without lids on market entry, loose federations of minibuses and microbus operators in Manila, Jakarta, Surabaya, and Medan have kept supply and demand in balance through self-regulation.

With regard to most other areas of paratransit operations, authorities in Southeast Asia have been fairly permissive by first-world standards. Fares, schedules, and hours of operation are rarely if ever regulated. Paratransit vehicles are also usually allowed to stop at any curbside and operate in any lane (except on expressways or major thoroughfares). Paratransit, and indeed all transportation services, have been burdened by fragmented bureaucracies in many Southeast Asian cities. Bangkok's bureaucracy is perhaps the most notorious. There, the Bangkok Mass Transit Authority (BMTA), the state-owned operator of public buses, also oversees the supplies and routing of privately owned buses and minibuses. The three-wheel tuk-tuks, silors, and taxis are regulated by the department of land transport, which controls market entry, areas of operation, licensing of drivers, and the setting of standards for vehicle fitness and insurance coverage. The fastest growing "informal" service, the 40,000-plus for-hire motorcycles that ply the sois and back alleys of Bangkok, are unregulated (though hired motorcycles are restricted to sois by "informal" agreement).[21] Metropolitan police, along with special units from several government agencies, enforce paratransit regulations; however, oversight is lax because managing traffic flows and responding to accidents are assigned much higher priority. Overall, more than 30 government agencies are involved in urban transportation planning, operations, and policy making in greater Bangkok. Moreover, there are three statutory committees and four ad hoc interagency committees to oversee and coordinate the actions of these bureaus. Overlapping mandates have caused great confusion and unavoidably impeded progress in the transportation arena. Indeed, Bangkok's thriving free-enterprise paratransit sector has emerged partly in response to institutional inertia and the void in public-sector transportation services.

Paratransit in Southeast Asia in Summary

The meteoric growth in automobile ownership is often blamed for the horrendous traffic congestion found in most large Southeast Asian cities. Many cities, originally built for foot and hoof travel, are unable to handle the explosion in automobile and truck traffic. Without commercial paratransit services, however, conditions would be much worse in many cases.

Paratransit has historically been the backbone of Southeast Asia's urban transportation systems. Over the years it has shown a remarkable adaptability and resiliency. Most modes have carved out unique and distinct market niches. Pedicabs and three-wheelers link narrow residential alleys to mainline bus routes. Microbuses provide access to nearby markets, and minibuses and medium-sized fleets connect cross-town neighborhoods and major urban centers. In terms of seating capacities, operating speeds, and geographic coverage, Southeast Asia's paratransit sector is well adapted to the physical road plant. Modally, it has compensated for road capacity and network deficiencies so as to provide relatively high levels of passenger throughput. Although bajajs, bemos, jeepneys, minibuses, and their brethren provide extensive coverage, high frequency, and almost door-to-door service which is affordable to the masses, many policy makers in Southeast Asia still view them as inefficient users of road space.

Any retrenchment in paratransit services in Southeast Asia should be guided by market conditions, rather than heavy-handed government fiat. As traffic flows improve and more people opt for private automobility on toll roads (as in Jakarta and Bangkok), the paratransit market itself can be expected to respond over time by appropriate service cuts and consolidation. Experiences in Southeast Asia provide compelling evidence that market entry and exit, service levels, and pricing are best left largely to competitive market forces.

LESSONS FROM PARATRANSIT IN THE DEVELOPING WORLD

Paratransit in the developing and developed worlds take on subtle but important differences. In the United States and other industrialized nations, there are many more instances of demand-responsive services, like dial-a-ride vans, and institutional sponsorship, such as subscription vans underwritten by employers. In many third-world cities, paratransit is virtually demand-responsive not because of dial-up, dispatch services but because micro- and minibuses come by so frequently. Institutionally, private individuals, as opposed to employers or government, organize and operate paratransit in the megacities of Latin America and Asia, sometimes under the umbrella of a route association. The most notable distinction, however, is the bewildering array of services that bridge the gap between public buses and private automobiles—in terms of capacities, operating ranges, comfort levels, and routing flexibility—in the developing world.

Unlike in the United States, paratransit services are universally cheaper than public transit services in Latin America and Asia owing mainly to the existence of competitive marketplaces, high labor productivity, and compact cities that shorten travel distances and produce frequent seat turnovers. The affordability of paratransit services has meant that most segments of society have comparable levels of accessibility, in sharp contrast to much of the developed world where only those at the right age, with enough income, and the physical ability to drive can easily get around. While free-enterprise paratransit has been faulted for causing traffic jams, in reality it has mostly played a complementary as well as compensatory role in the urban transportation sectors of most third-world cities. Most notably, Southeast Asia's commercial paratransit sector appears to have evolved, in part, as a modal response to poor roads, compensating for the lack of network hierarchies and limited throughput capacities.

Overall, governments have been more receptive to paratransit in developing countries partly because of their inabilities to mount adequate public transit alternatives. High charges and taxes for motoring and automobile ownership have also bolstered paratransit in cities like Jakarta and San Juan. However, the hands-off policies of some governments have also created institutional gaps related to service planning and integration. In many cases, route associations have stepped in to help fill this gap, functioning as institutional forums for rationalizing services. While most associations perform a coordinating role, some, such as in Buenos Aires, select and employ operators and set schedules. Not all experiences with route associations, however, have been positive. Following the deregulation of urban transportation services in Santiago, Chile, in 1980, an oligopoly of route associations colluded to significantly raise transit fares without any commensurate expansion or improvements in services (Drabéra, 1993).[22] In recent years, however, Santiago officials have begun competitively bidding for the right to serve downtown corridors, and fares (in inflation-adjusted terms) are today close to what they were in pre-deregulation days (Rivasplata, 1993). In Belfast, associations governing shared-ride taxi services have created an oligopoly by jealously guarding and restricting membership (Nutley, 1990). Even Mexico City's route associations have stifled competition by effectively lobbying government to freeze the issuance of new permits. Experiences with deregulation in Colombo, Sri Lanka, however, have been markedly different than in Santiago and other places. There, the local government allowed privateers to offer bus and minibus services free of fare and route regulation, but maintained a publicly owned bus system, Central Transport Board (CTB). Tariffs did not rise significantly in Colombo, nor did cartels form as in Santiago, because of CTB's policy of keeping very low fares to help the poor, forcing private operators to do likewise in order to compete. Overall, the lesson abroad as well as in the United States is that transit privatization without competition provides few service or pricing benefits to customers. Clearly, the best offense against collusion and anticompetitive behavior is to maintain fairly open market entry, complemented by enforcement of fitness and performance standards, as appropriate. The lack of governmental resources to monitor and enforce standards, however, has instead prompted some rapidly developing countries to close the gates to paratransit market entry altogether.

Notwithstanding efforts to ban minibuses and microvehicles in some cities, it is a safe bet that paratransit and private carriers will continue to dominate the urban transportation scene in a lot of foreign cities, from Manila to Damascus, in the foreseeable future. However, as countries continue to industrialize and modernize, and road systems are upgraded, it is an equally safe bet that paratransit services will evolve and redefine themselves, focusing on specific niche markets where they enjoy competitive advantages—rail feeders, low-income neighborhoods, and business district circulators. This has already occurred in Mexico City, and with the scheduled opening of the Tren Urbano rail system, many público routes in San Juan are being reconfigured to function mainly as rail feeders. It would be a mistake for countries with thriving paratransit sectors in place to dismantle them, wholesale, in the drive toward economic prosperity and modernization. This is one area where public policy makers are best advised to avoid the mistakes of many first world countries. Clearly, there is a regulatory role for government in protecting public safety and ensuring efficient road travel in developing and developed countries alike. Just as the United States and Europe can learn from the experiences with free-enterprise transport in Asia, Latin America, Africa, and the Middle East, developing countries can gain from the experiences with effective traffic management (e.g., HOV lanes), licensing of drivers, and maintaining vehicle fitness standards. However, the prevalence of competitive, privately owned, and diverse mass transportation services in many parts of the world represents a tremendous economic asset that should be retained. It is ironic that at the same time many cities in the developing world are cutting back on the paratransit sector and substituting large public buses for small private vehicles, many first world cities are contemplating opening up markets to the private sector to foster greater competition and service innovations. Apparently, third-world cities want their transport sectors to look more like those of first-world cities, and first-world cities want to mimic features of successful small-vehicle transit systems in the developing world. Finding the right balance between government control and free-enterprise transportation services remains a significantly public policy challenge in the first and third worlds alike. As to America's experiences in this regard, we turn to the next four chapters, Part 2 of this book.

NOTES

1. In the 1970s and early 1980s, the policy toward Public Light Buses was mainly prohibition and restriction. In the late 1980s, a more receptive stance was taken in Hong Kong toward minibuses in recognition of their complementary role (Meakin, 1993). Still, problems persisted, such as RMB drivers cruising congested corridors for fares. With over 85 percent of minibuses individually owned and operated, government regulation proved difficult. In 1990, a policy of "containment" was introduced, denying RMBs access to new housing estates and expressways and imposing stopping restrictions. Government also aimed to convert more RMBs to GMBs that served as rail and ferry feeders. Studies showed, however, that once RMBs converted to GMBs, operators became more complacent and unresponsive to shifts in market demand. Vehicles also became older and service levels declined (Lee, 1989).

2. Over 30,000 external público trips, with one end outside the San Juan region, are also made each day. Thus, total daily público trips within metropolitan San Juan exceeds 150,000.

3. In 1995, over 122,000 trips per day were made on públicos terminating in these two urban centers (counting both intrametropolitan and intercity trips). This averages to nearly 180 público trips per capita each year.

4. PSC was established in 1917 to regulate all forms of for-hire transportation; however, it was only in 1962 that legislation was passed that gave the authority substantial powers to regulate entry and in 1974 to regulate routing and pricing (Luyanda and Rodríguez, 1995).

5. Most público operations are a family enterprise. Families may own more than one vehicle, but drivers are generally either members of the family or relatives. Around 40 percent of público operators own their own vehicles, and the rest are hired drivers (Takyi, 1990).

6. The Urban Mass Transportation Administration, predecessor to today's Federal Transit Administration, provided over $22 million in capital grants during the 1980s to help finance público terminals across Puerto Rico, with the largest outlays going for terminals in Bayamón ($7 million) and Rio Piedras ($6 million).

7. Vehicle travel bans, also implemented in Santiago, Chile, and Athens, Greece, have encouraged some people to take mass transit and share rides; however, they have faced compliance problems. One problem has been the creation of a market for cheap, second-hand vehicles that are generally more polluting and less efficient than newer models. Motorists purchase these vehicles for use on days when they are prohibited from driving their primary vehicle, thus subverting the intent of the ban.

8. Ruta-100 was organized in 1981 after the Federal District brought all of the region's private bus operators under a single public authority. After acquiring private concessions, the government rationalized routes, modernized and refurbished buses, and improved maintenance standards. In 1990, however, the Federal District returned Ruta-100 services to the very independent cooperatives that originally ran bus services. The District has retained some controls over routing and service policies of the former Ruta-100 bus network; however, in recent years service has been in a state of flux, with some indications that they may soon be totally privatized.

9. From field surveys, it was found that the typical owner drives his vehicle from 6:00 A.M. to around 2:30 P.M. The driver then washes the vehicle and fills it up with gasoline. The vehicle is then leased for a set fee (an average of U.S.$15 per day in late 1994) from 3:00 P.M. until around 10:30 P.M. Upon completing his shift, the lessee washes the vehicle and fills it with gasoline so the owner can begin his shift promptly the next morning.

10. These estimates are based on field interviews with colectivo owners, drivers, and route association officials for Route 2, one of the busiest and most established routes in the city. They are based on November 1994 cost figures when the Mexican New Peso (NP) was worth approximately one-third of a U.S. dollar and rely on the following input assumptions. Minibuses are assumed to be driven an average of 80,000 kilometers per year. A new minibus costs U.S.$32,000 and is resold after seven years for 20 percent of the original price (i.e., for U.S.$6,400). New equipment purchases are paid over a three-year loan period at a 21 percent interest rate (i.e., U.S.$43,300 in total payments). The fixed costs per 100 kilometers of service (expressed in U.S. dollars) are: $4.65—depreciation; $7.70—interest payment; and $1.10—license, insurance, and fees. Variable costs per 100 kilometers of service are: $22.00—fuel and oil; $2.50—maintenance and tires; and $22.10—driver wages. Thus, total operating costs are around $60 per 100 kilometers. With an average farebox income of $92 per shift or $71.50 per 100 kilometers, the profit margin to vehicle owners for the first three years is 19 percent. Once the vehicle is paid off after three years, the rate of return increases to 36 percent (i.e., for years four through seven).

11. The subsidized Metro is one means by which the Mexican government has maintained low wages without too much social pressure, but at a high cost. In 1987, total operating expenditures for Metro was in the neighborhood of U.S.$700 million, almost 70 percent of which was covered by local and federal subsidies (Benitez and Gomez, 1990).

12. In late 1994, a distance-based fare structure was in place, with officially regulated fares ranging from 0.55 New Pesos (18 cents) for trips up to 5 kilometers and 1.1 New Pesos (36 cents) for trips over 17 kilometers. In practice, however, colectivo operators collected 1.5 New Pesos (50 cents) for long-haul trips within the metropolitan area.

13. Among the performance standards, minibus and van drivers are required to attend a training school, must have four years of driving experience, and must be over 23 years of age. Driver's licenses can be suspended or revoked in the case of accidents. Regulations also prevent owner-operators from holding the permits to more than three vehicles. The only significant vehicle fitness standard is that microbuses and vans must be replaced

after seven years of service. Normally, vehicle owners sell their fleets to operators in other states of Mexico after their seventh year of service life.

14. Despite their strong presence in the Federal District, there are no route associations in the surrounding state of Mexico. Instead, the state itself plans, administers, and organizes all local colectivo and pesero services.

15. Bangkok's rapid motorization has been attributed, in part, to proautomobile government taxation policies. In 1992, according to one source (Poboon et al., 1994), there were around 200 automobiles per 1,000 inhabitants, by far the highest rate among Asian cities, including richer cities like Singapore (101 per 1,000 in 1990) and Hong Kong (43 per 1,000 in 1990). In 1991, the Thai government lifted the ban on importing fully assembled small-engine cars and dramatically reduced the import duties on small cars from around 300 percent down to 20 to 30 percent as a means of improving quality of the nation's automobile manufacturing industry through increased foreign competition.

16. In 1962, Bangkok abolished all pedicabs and a decade later merged 25 private bus franchises into a regional bus authority. Jakarta stopped issuing licenses for human-powered becaks in 1972 and banned them from the city limits altogether in 1990. Manila has restricted jeepneys to specific streets and cut back on licenses to the point where illegal operations are thought to outnumber legal ones. Singapore has eliminated its pirate taxis and over the past several decades consolidated 11 private Chinese bus companies into a single state-controlled enterprise (Rimmer and Dick, 1980; Krynetr, 1988).

17. While human-powered transport has been officially banned in Jakarta, the number of illegal becaks operating in the capital has in fact increased, today exceeding 30,000 (Dimitriou, 1995).

18. In Kuala Lumpur, some 40 privately owned and operated minibuses are the sole paratransit survivor. Except for tourist areas, Singapore's rickshaws and minibuses have been replaced by stage and double-decker buses as well as a metro network.

19. The correlation was estimated for different time points among these eight cities, thus providing 16 pooled cross-sectional/time series data points. "Mode type diversity" represents the coefficient of variation (standard deviation divided by mean) based on the number of vehicles in each vehicle class. Indexes are also weighted for the average seating capacity of vehicles in each class. High values indicate high variation in basic types of passenger vehicles. "Road hierarchy" indexes represent the coefficient of variation measured from the lineal kilometers of roads within each class of road (e.g., expressway, arterial, collector, and local). The correlation between "mode diversity" and "road hierarchy" index was -0.36. For more details on this analysis, see Cervero (1991).

20. Few studies have actually substantiated this. Vukan Vuchic (1981) estimates that on a passenger per road space basis, microbuses in Jakarta are 4 to 5 times less efficient than a conventional bus and 2 to 3 times less than a minibus. Bajajs and bemos are said to be 10 to 13 times less efficient in the use of road space than a bus. These are static calculations, however, ignoring the fact that minibuses and microbuses come by far more frequently than standard buses. In Metro Manila, for instance, 38 jeepneys pass by each hour, on average, over a typical one-kilometer stretch, compared to 11 public buses (JICA, 1985).

21. Increasingly, hired motorcycles deliver passengers to their destinations on main streets. Their rising popularity partly lies in their ability to maneuver around stalled traffic and squeeze into vacant road space. While regulations require motorcycles to operate only in curb lanes, lack of enforcement has resulted in aggressive driving behavior (Tanaboriboon et al., 1993).

22. Deregulation in Santiago did attract more private paratransit providers. The number of minibuses, known locally as *liebres*, increased from 1,558 in 1978, just before deregulation, to 2,700 in 1985. The fastest growth was in shared-ride taxis, increasing from 600 in 1978 to 4,200 in 1985. Minibuses have generally charged riders only around half as much as conventional buses, though their fares rose 93 percent between 1978 and 1985 (Allen, 1993).

REFERENCES

Agad, V. 1990. *Paratransit: Taxis and Tuk-Tuks in Bangkok.* Bangkok: Asian Institute of Technology, Master's Thesis.

Allen, J. 1993. "Transport Organization and the Latin American Megacity." *CODATU VI: Urban Transport in Developing Countries.* Paris: Graphi Imprimeur, pp. IV-1–IV-10.

Armstrong-Wright, A. 1993. *Public Transport in Third World Cities.* London: HMSO Publications.

Been, C., and Y. Chin. 1989. *Public Transportation Systems in Singapore.* Manila: University of the Philippines, Transport Training Center.

Benitez, N., and G. Gomez. 1990. "The Mexican Experience." *Rail Mass Transit for Developing Countries.* London: Thomas Telford.

Cervero, R. 1991. "Paratransit in Southeast Asia: A Market Response to Poor Roads?" *Review of Urban and Regional Development Studies* 3: 3-27.

CGT—Comision General de Transporte. 1994. *Viajes Pasajero en Dia Habil en la Ciudad del Mexico y su Area Metropolitana.* Mexico City: Comision General de Transporte.

Chujoh, U. 1989. "Learning from Medium-and-Small-Sized Bus Services in Developing Countries: Is Regulation Necessary?" *Transportation Research* 23A(1): 19-28.

Colin Buchanan and Partners. 1994. *Bus Management and Operations Improvement Implementation Project: Existing Public Transport Movement in Surabaya.* Jakarta: Ministry of Communications, Directorate General Land Transport.

Cushman and Wakefield, Inc. 1994. "Mexico City Metropolitan Area." *ULI Market Profiles: 1994.* Washington, D.C.: The Urban Land Institute, pp. 75-79.

de Cuba, N. 1995. "Still Going." *Smart Living* 3 (March 30): 10-11.

Dimitriou, H. 1995. *A Developmental Approach to Urban Transport Planning: An Indonesian Illustration.* Aldershot, England: Avebury.

DKI Jakarta. 1990. *Data Lalu Lintas Dan Angkutan.* Jakarta: Dinas Lalu Lintas Dan Angkutan Jalan Raya.

Drabéra, R. 1993. "Deregulation of Urban Transport in Chile: What Have We Learned in the Decade 1979-1989?" *Transport Reviews* 13(1): 45-59.

Faiz, A., C. Weaver, K. Sinha, M. Walsh, and J. Carbajo. 1992. *Air Pollution from Motor Vehicles: Issues and Options for Developing Countries.* Washington, D.C.: The World Bank.

Ferrarazzo, A. 1990. "Mass Transit in Buenos Aires." *Mass Transit* 12(4): 20-21.

Galvante, E. 1988. *Urban Transport Problems in the Philippines: Prospects for Solutions.* Manila: University of the Philippines, Transport Training Center.

Gunawan, W. 1992. *Assessment of Transportation Growth in Asia and Its Effects on Energy Use, the Environment, and Traffic Congestion: Case Study of Surabaya,*

Indonesia. Washington, D.C.: The International Institute for Energy Conservation.

Halcrow and Fox Associates. 1982. *Capital Investment Folio Project.* Manila: Metropolitan Manila Commission, Office of the Commissioner for Planning.

Hong Kong Transport Department. 1994. *Traffic and Transport Digest.* Hong Kong: Transport Department.

Jacobs, G., and P. Fouracre. 1974. "Urban Transport in Developing Countries." *Traffic Engineering and Control* 15(2): 80-84.

Jehl, D. 1995. "Let Loose on Streets, 10,000 Mice Route Buses." *The New York Times International.* October 23, p. A8.

JICA, Japan International Cooperation Agency. 1985. *The Metro Manila Transportation Planning Study.* Manila: Ministry of Transportation and Communications.

JICA, Japan International Cooperation Agency. 1986. *Klang Valley Transportation Study.* Kuala Lumpur: Ministry of Transportation and Communications.

JICA, Japan International Cooperation Agency. 1987. *Arterial Road System Development Study in Jakarta Metropolitan Area.* Jakarta: Ministry of Public Works.

JICA, Japan International Cooperation Agency. 1990. *The Study of Medium to Long Term Improvement/Management Plan of Road and Transport in Bangkok.* Bangkok: Ministry of Transportation.

Kartodirdjo, S. 1981. *The Pedicabs in Yogjakarta.* Yogjakarta, Indonesia: Gadjah Mada University Press.

Kirby, R., M. Tagell, and K. Ogden. 1986. "Traffic Management in Metro Manila: Formulating Traffic Policies." *Traffic Engineering and Control* 27(5): 262-269.

Kocks, F. H. 1975. *Bangkok Transportation Study.* Dusseldorf: F. H. Kocks KG/Rhein-Ruhr Eng.-Gmbh.

Krynetr, P. 1988. "Bangkok Mass Transit Authority: A Case of Monopoly Versus Competition." *Urban Transport in Developing Countries: Which Policies for Our Towns? CODATU IV: Urban Transport in Developing Countries.* Paris: Graphi Imprimeur.

Kusbiantoro, B. 1988. "Effectiveness of Bus and Bemo in Bandung." Jakarta: Paper presented at the CODATU IV Conference, Jakarta, Indonesia.

Lavery, H. 1986. "Black Taxis: The Shared Taxi Service in Belfast." *Omnibus Magazine* 375: 39-43.

Lee, E. 1989. "Planning and Control of Paratransit Services in Hong Kong." *Transport Reviews* 9(4): 279-303.

Luyanda, F., and P. Gandhi. 1989. "Characterization of the Público System of Puerto Rico." *Transportation Research Record* 1212: 107-115.

Luyanda, F., P. Gandhi, and S. González. 1986. *Evaluation of the Transferability of the Público System of Puerto Rico to Other Areas.* Washington, D.C.: Urban Mass Transportation Administration, U.S. Department of Transportation.

Luyanda, F., and J. Rodríguez. 1995. "Public/Private Partnership in the Operation of the Público System of Puerto Rico." *Proceedings: Encuento UPR/MIT Sobre el Tren Urbano.* San Juan: University of Puerto Rico.

Meakin, R. 1993. "Management of Taxi and Minibus Services." *Keep a City Moving: Urban Transport Management in Hong Kong,* L. Wang and A. Yeh, eds., Hong Kong: University of Hong Kong.

Midgley, P. 1993. *Urban Transport in Asia: An Operational Agenda for the 1990s.* Washington, D.C.: The World Bank, Technical Paper Number 224.

Mogridge, M. 1983. "The Jakarta Traffic Management Study: Impact of High Paratransit Flows." *Transportation Engineering and Control* 24(9): 441-448.

Montoyo, E. 1992. "Transportation in the Metropolitan Area of Mexico City." *Public Transport International* 2(2): 40-49.

Nutley, S. 1990. *Unconventional and Community Transport in the United Kingdom.* New York: Gordon and Breach Science Publishers.

Poboon, C., J. Kenworthy, P. Newman, and P. Barter. 1994. "Bangkok: Anatomy of a Traffic Disaster." Perth, Australia: Paper presented at the Asian Studies Association of Australia Conference 1994, Asia Research Centre, Perth, July.

Puerto Rico Department of Transportation and Public Works. 1995. *Tren Urbano: Draft Environmental Impact Statement.* San Juan: Department of Transportation and Public Works, Highway and Transportation Authority, Government of Puerto Rico.

Renee-Park, Gmbh. 1989. *Central Area Action Plan, Kotamadya Medan.* Medan: IBRD Medan Urban Transport Project.

Richards, B. 1990. *Transport in Cities.* London: The Bath.

Rimmer, P. 1986. *Rikisha to Rapid Transit.* Sydney: Pergamon Press.

Rimmer, P., and H. Dick. 1980. "Improving Urban Public Transport in Southeast Asian Cities: Some Reflections on the Conventional and Unconventional Wisdom." *Transport Policy and Decision Making* 1: 97-120.

Rivasplata, C. 1993. "Transit Coordination in a Multi-Operator Market: The Cases of Santiago and San Francisco." *CODATU VI: Urban Transport in Developing Countries.* Paris: Graphi Imprimeur, pp. IV-31-IV-42.

Roschlau, M. 1981. *Urban Transport in Developing Countries: The Peseros of Mexico City.* Vancouver: University of British Columbia, Centre for Transportation Studies, Masters' Thesis.

————. 1989. "Nationalisation or Privatisation: Policy and Prospects for Public Transport in Southeast Asia." *Transportation Research* 23A(6): 413-424.

Roth, G. 1988. "Private Sector Roles in Urban Public Transport." *Private Innovations in Public Transit,* J. Weicher, ed. Washington, D.C.: American Enterprise Institute.

Roth, G., and G. Wynne. 1982. *Learning from Abroad: Free Enterprise Urban Transportation.* New Brunswick, New Jersey: Transaction Books.

Schodolski, V. 1985. "The Little Bus System That Can: Argentina's Colorful 'Colectivos.'" *San Francisco Examiner* (September 8):, p. T-16.

Shimazaki, T., and M. Rahman. 1995. "Operational Characteristics of Paratransit in Developing Countries of Asia." Washington, D.C.: Paper presented at the 74th Annual Meeting of the Transportation Research Board.

Silcock, D. 1981. "Urban Paratransit in the Developing World." *Transport Reviews* 1(2): 151-168.

Sinsap, G., S. Limcharoenchat, and C. Athivongthanavat. 1988. *Urban Transportation Problems in Bangkok: Prospects for Solution.* Manila: University of the Philippines, Transport Training Center.

Spencer, A., and S. Madhavan. 1989. "The Car in Southeast Asia." *Transportation Research* 32A(6): 425-437.

Sussman, J., and R. Bonsignore. 1993. *Urban Congestion in Bangkok: A Framework for Immediate Action and for a Strategic Plan.* Bangkok: Asian Institute of Technology.

Takyi, I. 1990. "An Evaluation of Jitney Systems in Developing Countries." *Transportation Planning and Technology* 44(1): 163-177.

Tanaboriboon, Y., V. Sapkota, and L. Madrona. 1993. "Roles of the Paratransit Systems in the Developing Countries. Bangkok Case Study." *CODATU VI: Urban Transport in Developing Countries.* Paris: Graphi Imprimeur, pp. IV-43–IV-53.

Thomson, J. 1977. *Great Cities and Their Traffic.* London: Gollancz.

Vuchic, V. 1981. *Urban Public Transportation Systems and Technology.* Englewood, New Jersey: Prentice-Hall.

Walters, A. 1979. "The Benefits of Minibuses." *Journal of Transport Economics and Policy* 13: 320-334.

Wanisubut, S. 1995. "Bangkok Transport: A Way Forward." *The Wheel Extended* 87: 18-24.

White, P. 1981. "The Benefits of Minibuses: A Comment." *Journal of Transport Economics and Policy* 15: 77-79.

Wilbur Smith and Associates. 1974. *Urban Transport Policy and Planning Study for Metropolitan Kuala Lumpur.* New Haven: Wilbur Smith and Associates.

World Bank. 1995. *Social Indicators of Development.* Baltimore: The Johns Hopkins University Press.

Hong Kong's Public Light Buses. Free-ranging, privately owned and operated red-striped minibuses ply the streets of Victoria Island, Hong Kong. Fares are adjusted according to market demand and operating conditions, with drivers sometimes doubling and tripling prices during periods of heavy rainfall. Studies show the unsubsidized and largely unregulated red-striped minibuses are more market-responsive and cost-effective than the subsidized and more tightly regulated green-striped minibuses.

Papeete's Le Truk paratransit services. In Tahiti's capital, privately operated flatbed trucks converted into sideseat passenger carriers are the workhorse of the city's mass transportation system, serving the majority of motorized passenger trips within the central city. Even tourists heavily patronize Le Truk services.

Mexico City's Colectivos. Some 30,000 22-seater private minibuses provide both mainline and feeder services in one of the world's largest megalopolises. A colectivo "collects" passengers along one of Mexico City's grand boulevards, Paseo de la Reforma (right photo). Most minibuses, however, function as feeders to Metrorail stations, such as the Pantitlan station, terminus of four Metrorail lines (bottom photo).

Mexico City's Route Associations. Members of the Route 2 association, one of Mexico City's largest paratransit cooperatives, fraternize in Chapultapec Park during off-peak hours.

San Juan's Pùblicos. During off-peak hours, pùblico vans are stacked in a 5-story terminal at Bayamón, a suburban community south of San Juan. Terminals provide vehicle staging areas, weather protection, and a security presence, in addition to facilitating transfers.

Bangkok's Tuk-Tuk. The 3-passenger tuk-tuk, or samlor, is seemingly ubiquitous throughout Bangkok one of the world's most crowded and congested cities. Bangkok's paratransit modes operate along so streets and narrow alleys that most larger vehicles cannot penetrate.

Saigon's Six-Seater Selam. Virtually all mass transportation trips in Ho Chi Minh City are via privately owned and operated selams that seat six but often carry twice as many passengers. Fares are only around four U.S. cents for a ride of two to three kilometers.

The Manila Jeepney. Decoration of the flamboyant, baroque-style jeepneys has evolved into a true folk art. Basic body colors (red, blue, yellow, green, and lilac) are embellished and adorned with exuberant designs and slogans, chrome plated accessories, and cassette players pumping out the latest music. Jeepneys have been described as a "celebration on wheels."

Jakarta's rich hierarchy of paratransit services. The market has given rise to a wealth of paratransit offerings that operate at different speeds over different geographic ranges, provide varying seating capacities and levels of comfort, and pass on different per kilometer charges. Top, human-powered and motorized becaks, officially banned but still found on the urban periphery. Bottom, the ever-present, 2-3 passenger, bright orange-colored bajajs. Facing page, top, an 8-passenger Mikrolet cruising for customers near Jakarta's Kota train station. Facing page, bottom, a 24-passenger Metro Mini bus with a fare collector/hawker soliciting passengers at the rotary near the Kota station.

Paratransit obstructing traffic. The three-wheeler bajaj, a mode often maligned for tying up traffic because of slow speeds and aggressive driving, noses into an automobile stream along a busy artery in Jakarta. Pressure continues to mount to reduce paratransit services in Jakarta, in spite of the crucial role paratransit plays in providing affordable, door-to-door transportation services to carless households.

Bas Mini services in Kuala Lumpur. The private minibus, called Bas Mini in Malay, has for years generated profits against huge losses sustained by larger publicly owned buses. Pressures to "modernize" mass transportation in Malaysia's capital city has lead to recent cuts in Bas Mini services.

Diversity of paratransit in Medan. Outside of the large national capitals of southeast Asia, paratransit canvasses the cityscape, and is indeed an indispensible form of crosstown travel. In Medan, North Sumatra, a wide array of privately owned and operated three-wheelers, jitney sedans, microbuses, minibuses, and full-size coaches haul residents throughout the city of two million inhabitants.

PART II

REGULATORY AND POLICY ENVIRONMENTS

CHAPTER 5

Paratransit's Regulatory Environment

URBAN TRANSPORTATION REGULATION

Government regulations are pervasive throughout America's urban transportation sector. In the United States, urban transportation regulations have traditionally embraced principles of public welfare economics. Taxis, jitneys, and private bus-pools have fallen under government control in the belief that their ascendancy would undermine common-carrier public transit services and public safety. Regulations govern other areas of urban transportation as well, such as minimum parking supplies, street design standards for new residential subdivisions, fleet-average fuel economy requirements for new cars, and federal mandates for barrier-free accessibility and off-peak fare discounts for the elderly and handicapped (regardless of their household incomes). Scott Reznick and Paul Bardack (1994, p .2) remark:

Urban transportation is a "regulated industry." Since the late nineteenth century, the pro-vision of urban transportation services has been suffused with the public interest and, therefore, subject to extraordinary "economic regulation." The urban transportation industry is created by law, not by market forces.

Government's interest in promoting urban transportation is rooted in the belief that, like education, urban transportation is a "merit good"—society as a whole is better off as a result of economic and social benefits conferred by enhanced mobility. In the urban transit arena, governments have historically sought to pro-tect franchise carriers or public providers from competition in the belief that mass transit, like water and electric utilities, is fundamentally a natural monopoly.

Natural monopolies have three principal attributes: economies of scale (where average costs decline as supply expands), peak-load demands, and storable resources. Urban mass transit clearly has the latter two traits: high diurnal (morning and evening) peak demands and the ability to store idle equipment (buses, trains) in reserve during off-peak hours and low seasons. It is less clear whether urban transit enjoys economies of scale. Most recent research indicates that at most urban transit engenders constant returns to scale.[1] Only in the case of very capital-intensive rail transit systems do any significant economies appear from expanding services. Since commercial paratransit do not compete with rail services, any economic justification for restricting these services on natural monopoly grounds would appear to have little foundation.[2] Nonetheless, it has been under the natural monopoly banner that a thicket of regulatory controls has been erected over the years, introduced through a steady stream of local, state, and federal laws, that control urban transportation service delivery, the entry and exit of new service-providers, fare rates and structures, operating standards, and vehicle and driver fitness levels.

In addition to the natural monopoly argument, another rationale given for maintaining a single transit-service provider is to ensure all segments of an area's population receive adequate services. A single transit company, the argument goes, will best serve the public interest by operating in sparsely populated areas and using the proceeds from money-making services to help cover the losses— that is, will cross-subsidize services. With numerous firms, competitors will actively vie for customers in more built-up, high-volume areas in order to maximize profits, leaving other areas unserved. To guarantee that every neighborhood receives services, regulators argue that the public has an obligation to protect carriers from excessive and ruinous competition and ensure that they receive a fair rate of return. However, this does not imply that a single, protected transit company is best able to serve a low-density area at the lowest cost. Economists would argue it is preferable to serve low-demand areas with lower-cost, competitively bid paratransit runs than high-cost public bus routes. While there might be a role for public sponsorship of services, it does not follow that public operators with high labor costs should always deliver the service themselves.

Another reason given for regulating private transit providers is to avoid anticompetitive or oligopolistic behavior, such as price-fixing among a cartel of operators. However, price-fixing and collusion would likely only be problems if restrictions were placed on market entry. An open market should ensure the emergence of a rich mix of products of a similar nature (i.e., substitutes). For example, if shared-ride taxis are a close substitute for shuttle vans, the vans must price competitively with taxis, as well as other companies in the industry, or lose market share. Indeed, it is the prospect of unrestricted paratransit entry producing a full spectrum of service options that benefit consumers with wider travel choices that both holds high commercial promise for paratransit and reduces the chances of anticompetitive cartels from emerging.

Overall, there have been few significant regulatory reforms to date that have responded to changing market conditions, transportation options, and public policy concerns. From a review of urban transportation regulations in Pennsylvania, Reznick and Bardack (1994, p. 5) remarked: "Many of today's state and local regulatory frameworks carry forward legal and economic premises first devised roughly seventy-five years ago." While mandates affecting urban transportation, such as trip reduction ordinances, air quality control plans, and full-accessibility requirements, have proliferated in recent years, the overall governmental regulatory framework has remained rigid and largely unchanged during much of this century. The time seems ripe for seriously revisiting urban transportation regulations and scrutinizing their purposes, effects, and relevancy to today's policy environment.

LEGACY OF PARATRANSIT REGULATION

The first regulation of urban transportation in the United States involved the granting of franchises to electric utility companies to operate streetcar and trolley lines around the turn of the century. In most cities, only one streetcar franchise was awarded.[3] Because of the high capital costs for rail investments, sole franchisers enjoyed a protected natural monopoly status.[4]

Treating streetcars as natural monopolies promoted the interests of local governments, which were anxious to see their tax bases expand into the streetcar-served suburbs,[5] the franchisee, who might not have to built streetcar lines if not protected from competition, and riders, who benefitted from low fares written into franchise agreements. Franchises often stipulated a nickel fare, which traction companies were more than willing to accept, given the opportunity to bring transit under the monopoly of the electric utility industry (Warner, 1962; Crump, 1970). Even at this time, most streetcar lines were being subsidized, as transit was often part of an overall real estate development package (Fogelson, 1967; Fishman, 1987). The principle of cross-subsidization was being fully exploited —electric utilities and real estate magnates would willfully sustain losses operating streetcar services as long as they could extend routes into the suburbs to reap the rewards of land speculation.

Cross-subsidies were also occurring among transit riders and creating the conditions for a serious competitor to streetcar services to emerge. The flat nickel fare and free transfer privileges stipulated by most streetcar franchises meant that short-distance travelers were cross-subsidizing those making long-haul trips (i.e., they paid more per mile travelled). Franchises thus had the misallocative effect of preventing operators from introducing more efficient, marginal-cost pricing, and penalizing those making short-hop trips. This paved the way for urbanites with cars to start offering faster, more direct, and more comfortable alternatives to the streetcar for about the same nickel fare. With the jitney, which at the time was the nickname for a nickel, came the first serious threat to electric streetcar services.

Jitneys first appeared in Los Angeles in 1914 during a period of high unemployment when hundreds of car owners almost simultaneously began offering rides for a nickel. Jitneys quickly spread to hundreds of other U.S. cities. By the summer of 1915, over 62,000 privately owned and operated jitneys were plying their trade in U.S. cities (Eckert and Hilton, 1972). Many jitney operators were unemployed, newly arrived immigrants to the United States, and quite a number were black. Few had the political connections or economic clout to match streetcar companies. Shortly after entering the scene, jitneys were noticeably cutting into streetcar operators' incomes. They were also notorious for speeding ahead of streetcars and picking up passengers at streetcar stops. By 1920, nearly all jitneys were regulated out of existence by public authorities at the insistence of streetcar and trolley line owners who sought to reestablish their protected monopoly positions.[6]

Taxis, which exploded in numbers during the Great Depression years when thousands of Americans were out of work, came under similar attack. In the absence of entry controls, seemingly anyone who could obtain an automobile by loan, lease, hook, or crook, became a cab driver.[7] Streetcar operators and later bus companies sought to restrict the entry of taxis in most U.S. cities to lessen their competition. Protestations that free competition would lead to violent taxi wars, predatory behavior, and unscrupulous practices were common. Large taxi companies generally welcomed regulation in hopes of limiting the number of independent, part-time drivers and of increasing fares.

Today, all U.S. cities regulate taxis to some degree. Restrictions on taxi market entry is almost universal. Until recently, the number of permitted cabs was limited in every major U.S. city except Washington, D.C., and Honolulu. Most cities restrict entry by fixing the number of licenses, or medallions,[8] but a handful of cities, notably Los Angeles and Boston, grant exclusive franchises to one or a few companies, who then decide how many cabs they will operate. Because of restrictive practices, large taxi fleets offering services of fairly uniform quality have become the norm in most big cities.

Restricted entry has meant that taxi supplies have not always kept pace with demand. In some cities, it is difficult to catch a cab during rush hours. Another consequence has been high fares, made possible by monopolistic profits. Table 5.1 presents taxicab licensing and fare statistics for 10 selected large U.S. cities. Cities with franchises or restricted entry average markedly higher fares than cities that allow virtually open entry into the taxicab market. The correlation between 1995 cab licenses per capita and average fares for a three-mile trip was -.82. High levels of supply are thus strongly associated with cheaper fares in these 10 cities. In Washington, D.C., an unrestricted city that boasts over 10 cabs for every 1,000 residents (by far the highest ratio in the country), the fare for a typical three-mile trip is around half what one would pay in Los Angeles, where notoriously restrictive entry regulations hold the ratio to around 0.4 cabs per 1,000 residents. New York has maintained a lid of 11,787 cabs for decades, even though one is hard pressed to find an empty cab during the 5-o'clock rush hour.[9]

Table 5.1.

Comparison of Taxicab Licensing, Tariffs, and Shared-Ride Policies for Ten Selected United States Cities: Listed in Order of Highest 1995 Fares

	Licensing Policy	No. of Vehicle Licenses	Licenses/ 1,000 popu- lation	1995 Tariff Structure	Fare for 3-Mile Trip, 1 Person	Shared-Ride Allowed?	1995 Medallion Value
Los Angeles							
1995	N-F	1500	0.43	FD- $1.90,	$6.70	Yes—only at cabstands	None—License
1983	N-F	1500	0.51	M- $1.60	$5.90	within downtown and	($600/yr.)
1970	N-F	1025	0.45		-	to/from airports	
Indianapolis							
1995	N	460	0.63	FD- $0.95,	$6.35	Yes—rarely used since	None—License
1983	N	326	0.52	M- $1.80	$3.10	no flat/zone fares	($102/yr.)
1970	N	326	0.61		-		
San Diego							
1995	N	916	0.78	FD- $1.30,	$6.25	Shared-ride services	None—License
1983	N	900	1.10	M- $1.65	$4.60	provided by jitneys	($200/yr.)
1970	N	280	0.40		-		
New York City							
1995	N	11787	1.61	FD- $1.50,	$6.00	Yes—within Manhattan	$162,000-
1983	N	11787	1.70	M- $1.50	$3.70	zones and to/from	$220,000
1970	N	11755	1.52		-	airports	
Boston							
1995	N-F	1565	2.72	FQ- $1.50,	$5.90	Yes—rarely used since	$95,000
1983	N-F	1525	2.69	M- $1.60	$4.75	no flat/zone fares	
1970	N-F	1575	2.53		-		
Atlanta							
1995	N	1582	4.02	FD- $1.50,	$5.70	Yes—within downtown	$7,000
1983	N	1450	3.38	M- $1.40	$3.80	and to/from airport	
1970	O	1880	3.82		-		
Denver							
1995	F	1157	2.47	FD- $1.40,	$5.60	Yes—fare rules and	None—License
1983	F	507	1.02	M- $1.40	$4.05	flat-fares to/from	($20/yr.)
1970	F	310	0.60		-	airport	
Seattle							
1995	N	665	1.29	FD- $1.20,	$5.40	Yes—rarely used since	None—License
1983	N	570	1.20	M- $1.40	$4.40	no flat/zone fares	($240/yr.)
1970	N	320	0.60		-		
Chicago							
1995	N	5600	2.01	FQ- $1.50,	$4.80	Yes—within downtown	$33,000
1983	N	4600	1.50	M- $1.20	$3.60	and to/from airports	
1970	N	4600	1.42		-		
Washington, D.C.							
1995	O	6700	11.04	Zone Fares	$3.20	Yes—citywide zones	None—Licenses
1983	O	8600	13.50		$2.45	and flat fares to/from	($26/yr.)
1970	O	9800	14.70		-		

Key:
N = Number of vehicles restricted
F = Franchise requirement, with restriction on total number of vehicles
O = Open entry policy
FD = Flag Drop
FQ = Flag Drop plus first quarter-mile of travel
M = Mileage rate

(continued)

Table 5.1 (continued).
Comparison of Taxicab Licensing, Tariffs, and Shared-Ride Policies for Ten Selected United States Cities: Listed in Order of Highest 1995 Fares

Notes:
a = 1995 licenses to 1990 population; 1983 license to 1980 population; 1970 license to 1970 population.
b = Average fares. Fare structures vary among taxi cab companies in some cities (e.g., San Diego, Seattle) and by destination in others (e.g., Atlanta). Often fares to and from airports are higher. Most cities also add a per-hour surcharge to reflect costs associated with traffic congestion.
c = Fare based on flag-drop and mileage charges only.
d = In September 1995, Indianapolis deregulated taxicab services, removing ceilings on market entry and limiting fares to a cap. An estimated 50 more taxicab permits were issued in the last quarter of 1995.
e = San Diego removed entry restrictions on taxicabs in 1979 and reinstated a ceiling in 1984.
f = Atlanta lifted restrictions on taxi licenses in 1965 because of civil rights violations. In 1981, controls on entry were reintroduced.
g = Washington's zone fares for a single or shared-riding passenger is $2.80 for traveling within a zone, $3.20 for crossing one zone, and a $1.10 surcharge for each additional zone crossed. A $1.00 per trip surcharge is added for evening (4:-6:30 P.M.) rush hour trips. A $1.50 surcharge is also added for phone reservations. For a typical 3-mile trip, the $3.20 charged is assumed to be for crossing one zone during off-peak hours.

Sources: Telephone surveys of taxicab agency supervisors; Frankena and Paulter (1984); Kirby et al. (1974); Foster (1979).

Another consequence of restricted taxicab supplies is inflated medallion prices, currently moving toward $200,000 apiece in New York City, and exceeding that amount for franchises. Some cities, like San Francisco and Los Angeles, have deflated medallion prices by passing ordinances that prohibit the private sale of taxicab permits, making them nontransferrable.

With jitneys regulated out of existence and taxi supplies tightly restricted in most cities following the Great Depression, coupled with the pro-automobile policies that followed the Second World War (like federally funded highway programs), the fate of the paratransit industry was largely sealed. A steady stream of regulations governing market entry, service practices, fares, and insurance premiums have limited mass transit to the handful of options found in most U.S. cities today—public bus transit, exclusive-ride taxis, airport shuttles, and specialized dial-a-ride vans.

LEGAL FOUNDATIONS FOR PARATRANSIT REGULATIONS

The legal foundations for contemporary laws and regulations governing paratransit and other common-carrier modes of transportation are found in the U.S. Constitution and subsequent court rulings. Governed by the due process requirements of the Fourteenth Amendment, local transportation regulators during the first part of this century had to make sure that their prohibition of jitneys and other competitors on natural monopoly grounds was legally defensible (Resnick and Bardack, 1994). The 1879 Supreme Court decision in the case of *Munn* v. *Illinois* provided the necessary legal precedent for localities to regulate streetcar companies for purposes of protecting the "public interest."[10]

It was the Supreme Court ruling on the *Smyth* v. *Ames* case that set the constitutional standard that remains today for local and state regulation of natural monopolies and in particular the setting of rates.[11] The Court ruled that regulators can simulate a competitive rate of return in a protected, noncompetitive industry through valuing assets, determining a fair rate of return, and establishing rate structures. Cities and states interpreted this to mean, without any threat of retribution, that they were constitutionally empowered to craft permanent protections for the electric streetcar industry. Their first real opportunities to flex their newfound regulatory muscles was in reaction to the onslaught of jitney competitors. Only a handful of jitney operators in Atlantic City and San Francisco survived the stiff regulations that ensued. Note Reznick and Bardack (1994, p. 17), "a young regulatory framework intended to secure the disparate interests of streetcar operators, riders, and municipal officials had prevailed."

CURRENT PARATRANSIT REGULATORY ENVIRONMENT

Building upon these legal precedents, local and state governments have today enacted a variety of statutes, ordinances, and regulatory rulings that govern almost every aspect of commercial paratransit services in the United States. The next chapter examines contemporary local regulations policies, while Chapters 7 and 8 do likewise for the state and federal levels of government. Before turning to these chapters, it is instructive to review the provisions of two federal statutes, the Motor Carrier Act of 1935 and the Transportation Act of 1940, that set the stage for most government regulations pertaining to market entry and exit.

Common Carrier and Contract Carrier

The Motor Carrier Act and Transportation Act established two categories of interstate carrier, *common* and *contract*, that fall under the jurisdiction of the Interstate Commerce Commission (ICC). Most localities and states have adopted the same concepts and terminology in establishing regulations that govern urban transportation services. A common carrier provides transportation services to the general public in return for compensation. Its services are compulsory, meaning it must serve everyone who is able to pay. Among common carriers are fixed-route, regularly scheduled services (e.g., subscription buses, rail lines) and flexible, irregular operations (e.g., shuttle vans, taxis, jitneys, tour buses, and chauffeur services). Most commercial paratransit providers, then, are common carrier operators.

Designation as a common carrier operator subjects the designee to the highest level of scrutiny when services are being proposed, and the most stringent regulation and oversight after operations begin. For instance, since common carriers are normally liable for loss or injury to passengers, they typically are held to high insurance and indemnity standards. In return for these more stringent controls, common carriers are normally afforded some protection from outside competition through a special certification requirement.

Contract carriers, in contrast, provide specialized services to meet the needs of one or more contract clients. Thus, bus services under contract to transit agencies or employers are contract carriers, as are dial-a-ride vans operating under an

ADA contract. Contract carriers generally face less stringent scrutiny and restrictions. For example, entry and exit restrictions are rarely placed on contract carriers; rather, rules and regulations typically govern vehicle and driver fitness, minimum insurance levels, and hours of permissible operation.

Certificates of Entry

For most state and some local jurisdictions, the burden of proof for demonstrating that a new proposed service will promote the public interest lies with the applicant. Often, an applicant petitioner must receive a "certificate of public convenience and necessity" before operations can begin. Some jurisdictions apply more lenient regulatory standards that allow certification if the new service is, broadly defined, within the "public interest." Existing operators usually are allowed to review the service application and can in many cases file a grievance to block market entry. Although the exact certification process varies across jurisdictions, the essence of the "public convenience and necessity" requirement is, according to Reznick and Bardack (1994), best reflected in the very first bus case decided under the Federal Motor Carrier Act in 1939, *Pan American Bus Lines Operation*:

The question, in substance, is whether the new operation or service will serve a useful public purpose, responsive to a public demand or need; whether this purpose can and will be served as well by existing lines or carriers; and whether it can be served by applicant of the new operation or service proposed without endangering or impairing the operations of existing carriers contrary to the public interest.

In reality, the number of definitions of "public convenience and necessity" equal the number of jurisdictions which apply this standard. States like Texas and Illinois now consider the mere application for an intercity common-carrier permit demonstrates that the applicant's proposed service fulfills a public need. In contrast, Hillsborough County, Florida, has set a series of strict "public convenience and necessity" criteria in judging whether to issue new taxicab permits to applicants: proof of inadequate current services, proof of ability to provide the requested service, assurances of no adverse effects on existing permit holders, economically sound methods for providing the services, and submittal of a cost-effective management plan. In general, local and state laws place the burden of proving inadequacy of existing services squarely on the shoulders of the applicant, and typically give existing service providers a "first chance" of providing the needed service before certifying the applicant.

Other Common Carrier Regulatory Requirements

Common carriers must also receive regulatory approval to discontinue services. Normally, exit is permitted if a petitioner can demonstrate that the full cost of running a service exceeds revenue intake. Other carriers, however, can attempt to block an exit request if they believe they will be unfairly burdened from having to pick up their competitor's service. Pricing, both in terms of fare rates and structures, of common carrier services is also normally regulated. Economic studies, conducted periodically by regulators and their staffs, are used to set whatever tariff structure will ensure full cost recovery and provide usually anywhere from an 8 to 15 percent return on investment. In principle, tariff structures should also promote equity, clarity, ease of administration, and revenue buoyancy. Rarely in practice, however, do tariffs and rates rise in close step with escalating service costs. Additionally, restrictions on when and where common carriers can operate, maximum passenger loads per vehicle, and nonpassenger activity (e.g., freight, package delivery), effectively limit the markets that are served. And since common carriers have virtually unlimited liability, minimum insurance requirements can be substantial. Many localities and states have adopted the minimum liability coverages stipulated under Section 18 of the Bus Regulatory Reform Act of 1982: $5,000,000 for for-hire vehicles that seat 16 or more passengers and $1,500,000 for vehicles that seat 15 or fewer (e.g., jitneys and shuttle vans).

Administering and Enforcing Regulations

A Byzantine network of local, regional, and state authorities has evolved for administering and enforcing these regulations. In the case of taxis, dial-a-ride services, and (in the few cities where they exist) jitneys, while local authorities (e.g., taxi commissions, paratransit bureaus) exercise control over entry, exit, pricing, and service features, safety matters typically remain vested in the state (for example, the licensing of drivers). Enforcement of certification requirements, vehicle fitness, and driver qualifications sometimes lies with local police departments, sometimes with paratransit authorities, and sometimes with state regulators. Whenever illegal operators are caught, the enforcement agency often issues a citation, sometimes impounds the vehicle, and with repeat offenders, may take the interloper to court, seeking a cease-and-desist or sometimes civil penalties.

In many cases regional transit authorities also exert control and virtual veto power over the routing of taxis and dial-a-ride services within their district boundaries. In most metropolitan areas, a state regulatory commission has authority to oversee private subscription buses and vanpools. Where services cross state boundaries, the Interstate Commerce Commission has jurisdiction. All in all, many overlapping layers of government are involved administering and enforcing the complex web of regulations that today govern commercial paratransit operations.

Regulation and Politics

The very subjective nature of market entry rulings and fare regulations invariably means that some degree of politics and brokering seeps into the decision-making process. Regulatory agencies have generally developed a reputation for being conservative and favoring the status quo. The charge of regulatory commissions has often been interpreted as protecting the monopolistic rights of public transit systems and taxi franchises, and most authorities tend to rigidly enforce existing laws in this pursuit. In most instances, existing services prevail in unfair competition suits. Regulatory agencies are sometimes identified as enforcers rather than advocates of change, as are most policing authorities. This posture, critics charge, has impeded innovation and inhibited the emergence of a dynamic and robust urban transportation marketplace. Of course, these are generalizations and exceptions do occur. As to specific regulations and policies governing commercial paratransit at each level of our federalist system, and their effects on the industry, we now turn to the next three chapters.

NOTES

1. As discussed in Chapter 1, several early studies suggested tendencies toward transit scale economies by demonstrating that larger transit systems exhibited lower unit costs than smaller ones (Wells et al., 1972; Lee and Steedman, 1970). More recent studies, however, cast some doubt on these earlier findings. Wabe and Coles (1975), for example, found that the average cost per kilometer rose with fleet size for a number of British transit systems studied. Since larger bus systems tend to operate under conditions of greater surface street congestion and stronger union pressures on wages, incidences of diseconomies of scale have been found within the industry. These findings have since been corroborated by other researchers (Williams, 1979; Viton, 1981; Cervero, 1988).

2. One recent study found a decreasing return to scale in the airport shuttle van industry. Using 1990 data for 23 California shuttle van operations, this study found that total miles of service increased by 7.8 percent for every 10 percent increase in the number of vans owned by firms. The analysis suggests that van services provided by multiple small-independent operators can lower industry costs (Strauss et al., 1992).

3. The two notable exceptions were Washington, D.C., and New York, which granted multiple streetcar franchises—the former because local officials could not resolve a dispute between competing requests for franchises, the latter because its large geographic area could support more than one system.

4. At the time, streetcars were viewed as the wave of the future. They required huge investments in a citywide grid of right-of-way, tracks, bridges, tunnels, electrical wiring, powerhouses, and substations. Protecting this expensive financial investment from competition was deemed appropriate. Officials reasoned that the cost of expanding services by attracting new streetcar operators would exceed the cost of existing franchisees extending their lines. Consumers, they argued, would ultimately bear the costs of competition in the form of higher fares and higher suburban housing costs.

5. Some local elected officials benefitted directly in financial terms by granting exclusive franchises. In return for such favors as invoking eminent domain rights to acquire occupied land, streetcar operators sometimes were in cahoots with local politicians, giving them cash payoffs and sharing some of their real estate profits.

6. Streetcar operators went to great lengths to ensure that laws were passed that would soon drive the jitneys out of business. For example, jitney owners were typically required to obtain franchises, pay onerous license fees, and post liability bonds (which were expensive because many jitneys had terrible accident records). In many cases, jitneys were for-

bidden to operate on streets with trolley lines. Some regulations limited jitneys to speeds of 10 miles per hour or less. Still others required jitneys to operate a minimum number of hours each day or to specify their routes and schedules in advance, thus reducing jitneys' competitive advantage in adapting services to market demand and concentrating on peak periods (Black, 1995).

7. In addition to unemployment, the vast inventory of unsold automobiles at the height of the Depression helped spur the taxi industry. Many automobile manufacturers and dealers leased unsold cars to men out of work in return for a share of their daily income. Although fewer people could afford to ride in taxis during the Depression years, the supply of taxis skyrocketed. There were 20,000 taxicabs in New York City alone (versus around 11,800 today), and an estimated 150,000 taxicabs nationwide (Shaw et al., 1983). Only 84,000 of these taxicabs belonged to pre-Depression operators. Oversupply quickly led to fare wars, cutthroat competition, extortion, and unsafe driving practices.

8. A medallion is a metal plate signifying proper taxi licensing that is bolted onto the car body where it can be easily seen (sometimes on the hood, sometimes on the trunk).

9. A limit on the supply of cabs in New York City was first set at 13,595 by the Haas Act in 1937. About 2,000 medallions were surrendered during the end of the Great Depression when business was poor and were never reissued. A lid on supply has made a medallion a valuable commodity. Currently, the going price for a medallion owned by an independent operator is around $165,000. For medallions owned by cab companies, the street value is closer to $220,000. New York City officials are quick to note that the city's supply of licensed paratransit vehicles is much higher—4.3 vehicles per 1,000—when other for-hire vehicles, like limousines, vans, and service cars are tallied (New York City Taxi and Limousine Commission, 1993). For-hire vehicles have proliferated precisely because of the city's shortage of medallion cabs in north Manhattan and the outer boroughs. Current plans call for an increase in the number of medallions in the city to 12,187 by auctioning off 400 new ones, in expectation of raising over $80 million for the city's treasury.

10. This case held that a state statute fixing the maximum rates that owners of grain elevators in the Chicago area could charge customers was in the public interest. The grain operator enjoyed a virtual monopoly of grain traffic in the Great Lakes region. The courts ruled that the grain operations had become imbued with a broader public interest and that restricting prices was not a deprivation of property without due process of law.

11. In the case, Union Pacific shareholders sued a number of railroad companies that had challenged the power of Nebraska state regulators to classify freights, fix rates, and impose penalties for violations. The court ruled that the failure to ensure a "fair return" would amount to unconstitutional confiscation.

REFERENCES

Black, A. 1995. *Urban Mass Transportation Planning*. New York: McGraw-Hill.

Cervero, R. 1988. *Transit Service Contracting: Cream-Skimming or Deficit-Skimming?* Washington, D.C.: Urban Mass Transportation Administration, U.S. Department of Transportation.

Crump, S. 1970. *Ride the Big Red Cars: How Trolleys Helped Build Southern California.* Corona del Mar, California: Trans-Anglo Books.

Eckert, R., and G. Hilton. 1972. "The Jitneys." *Journal of Law and Economics* 15(2): 293-389.

Fishman, R. 1987. *Bourgeois Utopia: The Rise and Fall of Suburbia.* New York: Basic Books.

Fogelson, R. 1967. *The Fragmented Metropolis: Los Angeles, 1850–1930.* Cambridge, Massachusetts: Harvard University Press.

Foster, H. 1979. *Telephone Survey of Taxicab Supervisory Agencies.* Washington, D.C.: Urban Mass Transportation Administration, U.S. Department of Transportation.

Frankena, M., and P. Paulter. 1984. *An Economic Analysis of Taxicab Regulation.* Washington, D.C.: Bureau of Economics, Federal Trade Commission.

Kirby, R., K. Bhatt, M. Kemp, R. McGillivray, and M. Wohl. 1974. *Paratransit: Neglected Options for Urban Mobility.* Washington, D.C.: The Urban Institute.

Lee, N., and I. Steedman. 1970. "Economies of Scale in Bus Transportation." *Journal of Transport Economics and Policy* 4: 15-28.

New York City Taxi and Limousine Commission. 1993. *The New York City For-Hire Vehicle Fact Book.* New York: New York City Taxi and Limousine Commission, Office of Policy Development and Evaluation.

Reznick, S., and P. Bardack. 1994. "Reinventing Urban Transportation: A New Regulatory Vision." Philadelphia: Commonwealth Development Associates, consulting report.

Shaw, L., G. Gilbert, C. Bishop, and E. Pruitt. 1983. *Taxicab Regulation in U.S. Cities.* Washington, D.C.: Urban Mass Transportation Administration, U.S. Department of Transportation.

Strauss, R., T. Cherkas, F. Patterson, C. Texeira, and E. Velez. 1992. *The California Airport Shuttle Van Industry.* San Francisco: California Public Utilities Commission, Transportation Division.

Viton, P. 1981. "A Translog Cost Function for Urban Bus Transit." *Journal of Industrial Economics* 29(3): 287-304.

Wabe, S., and O. Coles. 1975. "The Short and Long Run Cost of Bus Transport in Urban Areas." *Journal of Transport Economics and Policy* 1: 127-140.

Wells, J., N. Asher, M. Flowers, and M. Kamran. 1972. *Economic Characteristics of the Urban Public Transportation Industry.* Washington, D.C.: Institute of the Defense.

Williams, M. 1979. "Firm Size and Operating Cost in Urban Bus Transportation." *Journal of Industrial Economics* 28(2): 209-218.

Warner, S. 1962. *Streetcar Suburbs.* Cambridge: Harvard University Press.

CHAPTER 6

Local Regulations and Policies Governing Commercial Paratransit

LOCAL TAXI AND PARATRANSIT REGULATIONS

Nearly all U.S. cities and most urbanized counties have passed ordinances which regulate and license taxis and any other permitted common-carrier forms of paratransit that operate within their jurisdictions.[1] Municipal control and oversight of paratransit encompasses the domain of intracity services—normally taxis, and where they exist, jitneys, neighborhood dial-a-ride vans, and any other (typically short-haul) shared-ride services. Counties normally have jurisdiction over similar services in unincorporated areas and smaller communities.

In local settings, regulations governing commercial paratransit are almost always part of the same ordinances regulating taxicabs. Municipal rules and regulations usually pertain to five main areas: (1) market entry and exit; (2) insurance and indemnity; (3) vehicle and driver fitness; (4) pricing; and (5) service practices.

Market Entry and Exit

Entry controls restrict the number of taxi and paratransit companies and vehicles allowed to operate within a jurisdiction. Limits are usually set by ordinance, are determined according to principles of "public necessity and convenience," and in most large cities are adjusted fairly infrequently (sometimes only once every decade or more). Types and levels of entry control vary significantly, however (Shaw et al., 1983). On the "most controlled" end of the spectrum are predetermined ceilings—such as Atlanta's limit of 1,582 taxicab medallions in 1995. Least controlled is open entry, currently found only in a handful of large U.S. cities, notably Washington, D.C., Indianapolis, Houston, and Honolulu.[2] In between is a mix of entry regimens: population rations, "public convenience and necessity" criteria, franchise systems, and minimum standards.

Population ratios fix the number of medallions or licenses to changes in population—such as 2.0 cabs per 1,000, Chicago's current rate. Some localities, typically smaller ones, allow market entry when an individual or firm petitions on the grounds of "public convenience and necessity" (an entry standard more often applied at the state level). Decisions are sometimes made case by case and other times based on satisfying predetermined criteria specified in an ordinance. In many cases, protests lodged by incumbent taxi operators or public transit agencies effectively block market entry. In Dade County, Florida, however, the burden of proof that new jitney services fail to meet convenience and necessity standards lies with the protester, not the applicant. Protesters, including Miami's Metrobus, must prove the proposed service is duplicative or potentially harmful to public safety interests. To ensure a high level of compatibility, Dade County does not allow any single carrier to cover more than 30 percent of jitney route miles in the county unless there are no alternatives.

Some jurisdictions, like Madison, Wisconsin, and Little Rock, Arkansas, operate a franchise system, which grants licenses to one or more taxicab companies and then usually allows these companies to determine the number of taxicabs they will operate. Franchises are normally awarded on a competitive basis every three to five years. Since franchises create an oligopoly of sorts, granting franchisees the freedom to set supply levels does not always translate into more plentiful services. The city of Los Angeles, for instance, limits the supply of taxis by granting exclusive five-year franchises to five different cab companies.[3] Still, the city's ratio of around 0.45 cabs per 1,000 residents is one of the lowest in the country. Minimum standards and open entry impose the least controls on taxi and paratransit supplies. However, minimum standards can be more restrictive than other forms of entry control, depending on just how low the minimum floor is set and whether existing operators collude to block new entrants. In Charlotte, N.C., and Sacramento, minimum standards include providing 24-hour radio dispatch service and maintaining a minimum number of operating taxicabs on hand.

Compared to state jurisdictions, market exit tends to be fairly straightforward for local taxi and commercial paratransit services. In nonfranchise cities, exit effectively occurs, by default, when independent owner-operators decide not to renew permits. Some localities only reissue vacated permits periodically (e.g., once every three years), depending on market trends and factors like incidences of formal complaints (e.g., over cab long waits at cabstands and unserved telephone requests).

Other Local Regulatory Provisions

Most cities and counties set performance standards for drivers and vehicles. Insurance requirements are universal. Typical driver fitness standards include possessing a state chauffeur's license, being at least 21 years of age, and having no prior criminal convictions or arrest warrants. In some cities with large immigrant populations, like New York, Miami, and Los Angeles, drivers must also pass an English-language exam and a local geography test (demonstrating a knowledge of major streets and destinations in the area). Many ordinances authorize the police department to review applicants and give the chief of police the latitude to deny a taxi driver's permit when the moral character of an applicant is in doubt. In terms of vehicle fitness, taxicabs and jitneys are typically required to adopt a characteristic color scheme and have the name of the company or owner painted on the side of the vehicle. Taxicabs and jitneys are normally inspected by the police department to ensure that they are in proper working order. Some ordinances set a limit on the age of operating vehicles, usually with a maximum of five to eight years. A motor vehicle liability policy is always required, as is an insurance indemnity binder that covers the city or county from any liability. Insurance standards do not usually vary much across localities.

Local taxi and paratransit ordinances also regulate fares, both rates (e.g., flag drop charges, cost per mile) and structures (e.g., distance metered fares, zonal fares, late-night surcharges, package delivery charges). In some cities, tariff policies are set by the transportation commission or its equivalent, and no deviation is allowed. Some index tariffs to rates of return—Chicago has long applied a standard of increasing tariffs when the ratio of operating expense to revenues moves above 86 percent. In other cities, like San Diego and Indianapolis, maximum and minimum tariffs are set. The most laissez-faire policy is to allow the industry to set its own fares. However, even with industry fare-setting, some degree of accountability to the municipality or county is typically required; the most common requirement is for companies to register fares with the local police department. With fare decontrol, operators are also often required to display their fare rates on placards visible from both the rear passenger seats and from the outside (such as on rear side windows).

Last, most local ordinances govern some aspect of service delivery—geographic extent and hours of operations, shared-ride policies, driver dress codes, prohibitions on smoking, and so on. Normally, services are limited to the geographic boundaries of a jurisdiction; drivers usually can drop off a customer outside the service area, but must return to the jurisdiction to pick up a new fare.[4] Taxi ridesharing is permitted in most large cities (see Table 5.1 in Chapter 5), though group-riding tends to be limited to point-to-point services (e.g., from downtown cabstands). In smaller cities, most ordinances explicitly prohibit shared-ride services, including dial-a-ride (common-carrier) vans and jitneys, involving the pickup and drop-off of unrelated parties who have different origins and destinations. Where allowed, ridesharing requires the consent of the initial passenger. Some ordinances do not speak to the matter of ridesharing at all, which technically would mean it is permitted de facto, though in practice ridesharing does not occur unless explicitly allowed. Shared-ride provisions, moreover, usually stipulate fare structures, such as flat or zonal fares, or a single flag drop charge for multiple parties. In Denver, fares are prorated. If two people share a cab, the first customer dropped off pays 80 percent of the initial meter reading, while the second customer pays 80 percent of the final meter reading. If the two shared-ride passengers are going to the same destination, they split the fare in half and pay only an additional $0.50 each.

Service Coordination and Fragmentation

Within some large metropolitan areas, a Byzantine network of overlapping, and sometimes conflicting, local taxi and paratransit regulations exists. The sheer number and complexity of local regulations can frustrate attempts by taxicab and paratransit operators to provide coordinated, multicity services. All 88 cities in Los Angeles County, for instance, have their own separate taxi regulations, and thus a costly, fragmented system ill-suited to cross-county services. Many cities, like Los Angeles, limit the territories of operations. Any taxi operator wishing to ply his or her trade across multiple localities faces a mountain of red tape and add-on charges. Shared-ride taxi services are illegal throughout Southern California, except in downtown Los Angeles and Burbank. Jitneys and flexible-route paratransit are flatly outlawed (except for dial-a-ride vans, which are licensed by the state), and most cities require that all fares be distance metered, rather than permitting flat-rate fares for certain routes (as used by airport van companies).

Perhaps no metropolitan area poses such a fragmented regulatory environment as greater New York City. The city itself has jurisdiction over private bus lines that operate entirely within the five boroughs except where they form part of interstate service. The New York City Charter gives the Board of Estimates responsibility for granting franchises for bus services within the city. The City Department of Planning oversees the Uniform Land Use Review Procedure relative to proposed private bus routes. The Taxi and Limousine Commission maintains jurisdiction over the licensing of all for-hire vehicles except vans. The New York City Department of Transportation acts on all requests to initiate van services. Local transit authorities and bus franchises review all van licensing applications. Enforcement is coordinated by all of these entities, as well as city police and the Port Authority of New York and New Jersey. An entirely different bureaucratic apparatus exists west of the Hudson River in New Jersey. Carriers operating across state lines are licensed by the Interstate Commerce Commission. Methods of regulation range from routinely approving completed application forms (ICC) to elaborate public conferences and necessity reviews with multiagency evaluation (New York City). The time needed to get an answer varies from several months (ICC) to several years (New York City). Indeed, the business of regulating and overseeing commercial paratransit in the nation's largest metropolis is an enormous institutional undertaking.

While bureaucratic fragmentation no doubt inhibits service coordination and drives up costs, it also protects the livelihood of taxi and paratransit companies within a jurisdiction. Differences in regulations and their enforcement may serve as a barrier to entry by operators from surrounding communities and new start-ups. Thus, while on the one hand local regulations frustrate attempts by operators to provide multijurisdictional services, on the other hand they may protect existing companies by shielding them from unwanted competition.

CASE REVIEW: LOCAL REGULATIONS IN THE SAN FRANCISCO BAY AREA

This section presents a case summary of the existing local regulatory environment governing taxi and commercial paratransit services in the San Francisco Bay Area. I surveyed existing taxicab and paratransit regulations for the region's three largest cities—Oakland, San Francisco, and San Jose—and a sample of 10 medium-sized cities with 50,000 to 200,000 inhabitants. Smaller cities (with less than 50,000 residents) were also surveyed; however, none of these cities had taxicabs based in their cities and, consequently, had no taxicab ordinances.

Table 6.1 summarizes the results of the survey. The table compares existing regulations across cities in terms of their restrictiveness over entry control, fares, and shared-ride privileges.

Table 6.1
Taxi and Paratransit Regulations in the San Francisco Bay Area—1994

	Entry Control				Fare Regulation			
Cities	Predetermined Ceiling	Convenience and Necessity	Franchise System (w/no limit on # of vehicles)	Minimum Standards and/or Open Entry	Governmental Fare Setting	Maximum and/or Minimum Fares	Industry Fare Setting	Shared Ride Permitted?
Large, 200,000+								
Oakland	✓				✓			No
San Francisco	✓					✓		w/ Consent
San Jose				✓	✓			w/ Consent
Medium, 50,000-200,000								
Berkeley				✓	✓			Yes
Fremont				✓		✓		Yes[1]
Hayward	✓				✓			No
Livermore	✓				✓			No
Mountain View	✓						✓	w/ Consent
Palo Alto	✓						✓	Yes[1]
Pleasanton	✓				✓			No
Richmond			✓				✓	Yes
Sunnyvale			✓		✓			w/ Consent
Walnut Creek			✓		✓			w/ Consent

✓ = Condition Exists

[1] Not addressed in ordinance, permitted de facto.

Entry Control

As Mark Frankena and Paul Paulter (1984) found in a nationwide survey, local taxi and paratransit regulatory coverage in the Bay Area increases with city size. Oakland and San Francisco both set a ceiling on the number of taxi medallions or permits granted. Oakland capped the total at 310 permits in 1989, what the police department believed to be the maximum number of operators that the city could effectively regulate. While the demand for permits remains high, the city plans to maintain this ceiling for the foreseeable future given the proliferation of smaller companies and current enforcement difficulties. (The largest company in Oakland holds 27 permits; remaining permits go mostly to independent owner-operators and small companies.[5])

In San Francisco, medallions are licensed to individuals.[6] Annual public hearings are held to issue new licenses to prospective operators who are on the waiting list. Every three or four years, the San Francisco Policy Department, the city's paratransit regulator, increases the number of medallions by 50. In 1984 there were 76 medallions; in 1987, 811; and in 1992, 866. Thus, rather than setting standards of public convenience and necessity, San Francisco has opted instead to expand taxi supplies at a gradual, steady rate. Among large Bay Area cities, San Jose has the least restricted entry. New permits are issued as long as applicants meet minimum standards (related to insurance and hours and territory of coverage). More stringent standards are imposed on cabbies who serve the airport and operate wholly within the city limits.

The Bay Area's medium-size cities exhibit a broader mix of taxi regulations, generally occupying the middle ground in terms of restrictiveness. Most medium-sized cities require taxi applicants to prove that the new service meets some public convenience and necessity standard. In Livermore and Hayward, their respective city councils and police departments weigh the following when reviewing applications: the financial responsibility of the applicant; whether existing taxi operators are providing sufficient service to the public; and whether existing firms are making a reasonable return on investment. In most cases, applicants must submit documentation demonstrating that the new service will meet public convenience and necessity "requirements." These requirements typically amount to a financial statement listing assets and liabilities as well as demonstrating that the "minimum requirements" found in other jurisdictions, such as liability insurance standards, are met.[7] In all cities that hold "convenience and necessity" public hearings, existing operators normally lodge protests against the petitions. Protesters often complain that they are barely eking out a living and that more taxicabs will only reduce their incomes. However, such testimony appears to have little impact in that, officials report from all cities surveyed, companies that meet minimum requirements are routinely issued permits. Those interviewed in the Bay Area's medium-sized cities report that their city councils have not limited nor displayed interest in limiting the supply of taxis in their jurisdictions. Generally, a laissez-faire attitude prevails in those jurisdictions which control entry through public convenience and necessity requirements.

Franchise operations are fairly uncommon in the Bay Area. Among cities surveyed, only the Silicon Valley community of Sunnyvale operates a franchise system; there, franchises are competitively bid and firms are permitted to operate as many cabs as the market will bear. Among Bay Area cities, the city of Richmond is by far the most permissive—there have never been entry restrictions, nor are there plans to introduce them in the future.

The demand for taxicab permits in medium-size cities vacillates from jurisdiction to jurisdiction and from year to year. In Fremont, there were six applications in 1994 and none the prior year. There, six companies have dominated the taxi market for years. In Walnut Creek, the city used to cap the number of taxicabs that could operate. In 1992, the City Council opted to allow free entry as long as minimum requirements are met. Prior to 1992, five operators served Walnut Creek; soon after deregulation, this number doubled.

Fare Regulations

In the Bay Area's three largest municipalities, local ordinances govern taxi and paratransit fare policies. In Oakland and San Jose, flag-drop charges and fare rates are preset (e.g., $2/mile in Oakland). San Francisco, on the other hand, has established a fare ceiling. San Francisco cabbies can charge no more than $3 per mile and can set fares as low as they please. In San Francisco and other places with fare ceilings, drivers almost always collect the maximum fare allowed.

Six of the 10 medium-size Bay Area cities surveyed regulated fares: two specified fare rates and structures by ordinance, and four set fare ceilings. Four medium-size cities, however, imposed no limits on taxi tariffs, allowing the local taxi industry itself to charge what the market will bear. In most of these cases, local taxi firms must file their fare rates and structures with the municipal police department. The city of Richmond does not regulate taxi fares at all.

Shared-Ride Taxi and Jitney Services

Compared to most U.S. metropolitan areas, the Bay Area is fairly permissive when it comes to shared-ride taxi and jitney services. Provisions for sharing rides are typically a one-paragraph section of the city code. In Livermore, a fast-growing suburb on the eastern fringes of the region known best for the Lawrence Livermore Labs, shared rides are not permitted by ordinance: "When a taxicab or automobile for hire is engaged, the occupants shall have the exclusive right to the full and free use of the passenger compartment, and it is unlawful for the owner or driver of such vehicle to solicit or carry passengers contrary to such right" [section 4.40.130]. In Mountain View in the heart of the Silicon Valley, shared rides are permitted by consent: "No driver shall permit any other person to occupy or ride in such taxicab, unless the person or persons first employing the taxicab shall consent to the acceptance of the additional passenger or passengers" [section 30.26.A]. All nine of the 13 medium-to-large Bay Area cities surveyed permitted some form of shared-ride taxi service, either at the discretion of drivers, with the consent of the first passenger, or de facto (by the absence of any reference to ridesharing in ordinances).

The region's two largest cities, San Jose and San Francisco, both allow taxi ridesharing with the consent of the passenger and, as discussed in Chapter 2, San Francisco has had laws on the books permitting jitney services since 1914. While San Francisco's population densities are high enough to support profitable shared-ride taxi and jitney services, the presence of numerous alternative, and heavily subsidized, public transit modes (trolleys, light rail, buses, cable cars) has limited demand. Moreover, few taxi riders opt for ridesharing as a way to save money because most are probably unaware of this possibility. And few drivers, save for Berkeley's racetrack shared-ride taxis (see Chapter 2), have sought to go after this potential niche market, preferring exclusive-ride fares instead. As a one-to-one fixed-route loop service, the racetrack shared-taxi charges a flat $2 one-way fare. While other Bay Area cities theoretically allow shared-ride services, the absence of any demonstrable market has made this a nonissue in the minds of most. In fact, most municipal ordinances allowing shared-ride services, either through consent or driver discretion, do not directly address how fares would be brokered and collected, a potentially important consideration since nearly all Bay Area cabbies charge distance-metered fares. Where no passenger consent for ridesharing is required, drivers are presumably given the latitude to decide how shared-ride charges are most fairly apportioned. Where passenger consent is required and in the few instances where taxi ridesharing occurs, the normal practice appears to be that passengers split the flag drop charge and the costs for any detours or circuitous trips are deducted from the tab.

Bay Area Local Regulations in Summary

A wide array of local policies govern taxicab and paratransit market entry, pricing, and service practices in the San Francisco Bay Area. While multiple jurisdictional authority over local services has unavoidably caused fragmentation and increased costs, overall, the region's taxi and paratransit regulatory environment is fairly permissive. One city, Richmond, imposes no constraints on market entry, pricing, or ridesharing. In general, an open-door, free-enterprise philosophy prevails over much of the region. Even where taxi applicants must demonstrate that a "public convenience and necessity" will be served and existing firms try to block market entry, local regulators almost always side with applicants.

Yet despite the region's permissive regulatory environment, there are few exemplary commercial paratransit services to be found. While San Francisco had as many as 80 jitneys operating up and down Mission Street in the early 1970s, all of the Mission Street jitneys have gone out of business, and today only a downtown transit-feeder jitney remains, despite an ordinance on the books that still permits jitneys to operate.[8] And while many Bay Area localities allow taxi ridesharing, in practice little occurs.

The suppression of commercial paratransit in the Bay Area would appear to be less a result of overregulation than some other factors. One factor could be availability of a rich assortment of subsidized public transit alternatives. By national standards, Bay Area residents rely on public transit services to a relatively high degree—in 1990, 9.3 percent of the region's employed residents commuted by public transit, the sixth highest rate in the country (behind metropolitan New York City, Chicago, Philadelphia, Boston, and Washington, D.C.). Other pricing distortions, like free employee parking (enjoyed by an estimated 80 percent of the region's workforce) and fuel taxes that do not reflect the true cost of externalities, no doubt have placed commercial paratransit operators at a competitive disadvantage and inhibited jitney and shared-ride taxi patronage. The existence of a somewhat fragmented regulatory structure might have also stymied the region's commercial paratransit industry, although most local sources we interviewed did not perceive this as a very serious problem. It is to the experiences of two other U.S. cities that recently lifted regulatory controls over jitneys and shared-ride services, Indianapolis and Houston, that we now turn to further probe these questions.

RECENT EXPERIENCES WITH LOCAL PARATRANSIT DECONTROLS IN THE UNITED STATES: INDIANAPOLIS AND HOUSTON

During 1994 and 1995, the cities of Indianapolis and Houston both lifted market-entry restrictions on jitneys, shared-ride taxis, and most other forms of locally controlled commercial paratransit services. Thus, their experiences provide an update to the carefully researched findings on the effects of taxi and paratransit regulatory reforms of the late 1970s and early 1980s, reviewed in Chapter 1. Since many of the cities that deregulated taxi (and, less frequently, jitney services) one to two decades ago have subsequently reintroduced new controls (e.g., San Diego, Seattle), looking at recent experiences from Indianapolis and Houston is useful in a contemporary policy context.

Indianapolis's Jitney and Paratransit Deregulation

Several years ago, Indianapolis's beleaguered public transit system, METRO, was in danger of going out of business, a victim of steadily declining ridership —from 15.5 million annual passengers in 1984 to 9.5 million in 1992—and escalating costs. Mayor Steven Goldsmith, who was elected on a platform of ridding local government of waste and inefficiencies through competitive contracting, embarked on a program of injecting competition into the city's urban transport sector. Besides bidding out public transit services to private firms, among the sweeping changes introduced by the Goldsmith administration was the lifting of all barriers to market entry and service practices for taxis, jitneys, and limousine services, effective July 1, 1994. The *New York Times* called Goldsmith's policies "the nation's most daring experiment in transforming local government into a business-like enterprise."[9]

A jitney van plied along one of Indianapolis's busiest thoroughfares in the early 1980s, a time when the city first experimented with relaxing paratransit regulations. This service developed a bad reputation for unreliable and poor services, however, and was subsequently shut down. With the 1994 deregulation package, jitneys have again been embraced by city officials. The ordinance places no restrictions on the supply of jitneys, defined as a common carrier that accommodates no more than 15 passengers. Jitney operators are free to set whatever fares they choose, as long as they submit a fee schedule to the city and conspicuously display their tariffs on side windows.[10] The only service restrictions are that jitney operators define route origin and destination points, times of operation, and a corridor where they plan to operate. The only other requirements pertain to meeting insurance, vehicle safety, and driver fitness standards (having a chauffeur's license and passing an exam on the geography of the city). Within these minimal confines, jitney operators can fashion services however they see fit, whether as fixed route or deviated route services. Among all existing jitney ordinances in the United States, Indianapolis's is by far the least restrictive.

Despite the city's open-door policy to jitneys, in late 1995, more than one year after the ordinance was passed, there were no takers. Local officials attribute this in part to poor reputation of the prior jitney service.[11] A bigger reason, however, is that Indianapolis is unabashedly an auto-oriented city—it has an excellent freeway and arterial network, no downtown or suburban congestion to speak of, a high auto ownership rate (1.6 vehicles per household), and cheap, ample, and convenient downtown parking. These factors, coupled with the city's low average densities (2,000 persons per square mile) and the suburbanization of jobs, have cut deeply into mass transportation usage. Surveys show that nearly 98 percent of all regional trips are by car, as are 85 percent of work trips to downtown. Additionally, jitney operators must compete with a heavily subsidized public bus system—passenger fares covered just 25 percent of METRO's operating costs in 1994 (ignoring capital costs and debt service).

More significant have been the effects of decontrols over taxi services. The 1994 reforms removed ceilings on taxi permits as well as the burden of proof that new entrants satisfy a public convenience and necessity requirement.[12] Cab fares were also replaced by price caps and operators were authorized to carry up to six unrelated passengers, to make package deliveries, and serve ADA clients using wheelchair-accessible cabs. The supply of taxis increased sharply within the first year of the reforms, to over 500 cabs, or more than 25 percent above pre-deregulation levels. While average cab fares have remained largely unchanged, average waiting times have gone down and incidences of nonresponse to phone requests have remained infrequent.[13] The biggest increase in cabs has been at the airport (where cabs must enter a queue) and downtown, where a popular and successful indoor mall recently opened. So far, relatively little taxi ridesharing has been reported.

Another recent event that could stimulate Indianapolis's fledgling commercial paratransit sector was the redirection of dedicated state sales tax funding for transit from the transit operator to city government. Indiana dedicates 0.73 of 1 percent of state sale tax proceeds to a Public Mass Transportation Fund. Historically, Indianapolis's share of the proceeds have gone directly to METRO. After lobbying by Indianapolis's mayor and others, Indiana's General Assembly passed a law in 1995 that distributes dedicated transit funds for counties containing a consolidated city to the consolidated city rather than regional transit authority. With these funds in hand, the city has recently issued a number of Requests For Proposals to convert express buses to entrepreneurial jitney services. This action stands to benefit commercial paratransit as well as the city treasury by replacing heavily subsidized public bus services with less subsidized jitney vans. Perhaps equally important, the city will be in a position to competitively contract out transit services without fear of running afoul of federal labor protection requirements, notably the 13(c) provision. Since the city itself is not a transit operator and does not receive federal transit operating support, transit unions would have no basis in trying to block city efforts to competitively bid out jitney van services under the guise of 13(c) violations.

Houston's Jitney Ordinance

In 1924, Houstonians voted to ban jitneys from their streets in a referendum when local streetcar companies threatened to raise fares. Some 60 years later, an enterprising taxicab driver, Alfredo Santos, decided to reintroduce jitneys to Houston based on his firsthand experience as a jitney patron in Mexico City. The *Houston Press* described Mr. Santos's foray into the jitney business:

Wearing a cowboy hat so potential passengers could easily spot him, he would drive East End streets holding out fingers for the number of places available in his cab. Yellow Cab (which controls about 60 percent of Houston's 2,000 licensed cabs) found out about the practice and threatened him with the loss of his cabby's lease if he didn't go back to running his meter as required by law.[14]

Santos was unfazed, comforted by the fact that he was making considerably more operating an illegal jitney than a legal taxicab. He offered this advice to aspiring jitney operators:

The secret to operating a jitney is to run the route religiously, make lots of quick trips, and develop new customers. Perhaps a driver will occasionally deviate to take a passenger home in a pouring rain or help someone get their groceries to the doorstep. But the driver will need to return quickly to the route to maintain the quality of service.[15]

Santos charged a flat rate of $1 for trips up to five miles and openly advertised his service by flyer and over Spanish-speaking radio.

Santos ran his jitney from mid-1983 until mid-1984 when, in response to complaints filed by Yellow Cab Company, the city cracked down and forced him to stop. Undaunted, Mr. Santos filed a lawsuit against the city in 1989 alleging that Houston's 65-year-old no-jitney ordinance violated both the Sherman Antitrust Act and his constitutional Fourteenth Amendment rights.[16] In 1994, the U.S. District Court ruled in favor of Mr. Santos, permanently enjoining the city from enforcing an ordinance banning "shared-ride taxi services" from city streets, saying it was arbitrary, outdated, and served no purpose.

The first draft of the revised ordinance presented to Houston's city council in early 1995 proposed allowing as many operators into the jitney business "as the market will bear" based on a resolution prepared by the Citizens for Jitneys. The draft ordinance proposed virtually no restrictions on jitneys other than meeting safety and legal liability standards similar to taxis and displaying fares on the exterior of vehicles; besides no constraints on fares, routing, or vehicle age, size, or color, jitney drivers would not be required to speak or read English, could stop anywhere along a route, and would not have to disclose financial records to the city. Seeing the handwriting on the wall, Metro, the Houston area's public transit authority, decided to get a step on jitney entrepreneurs by contracting out supplemental private jitney services for a five-mile-long segment of the Westheimer Boulevard corridor. For two months in the spring of 1995, privately owned and operated white sedans marked FasTrak plied these routes, carrying around 1,400 customers per week.[17] Metro reimbursed operators $25 per day for these services, on the rationale that load shedding some customers on high-demand routes would save them at least this much (relative to expanding their own services). Two months into the experiment, FasTrak operators concluded they could not earn enough at $1.25 per ride (the most they could charge since Metro bus fares were just $1) and ceased operations. Observers faulted the program for three other reasons: the private operator was overenthusiastic in buying a fleet of new cars and renting office space for a fledgling, untried business; the sedans had too few seats; and some of the corridors had too few transit-dependent residents.[18]

Conceding to pressures from local taxi companies, Houston's city council unanimously approved a new jitney ordinance in September 1995 that temporarily limits the number of jitney licenses issued to 50. The city will evaluate jitney performance over a nine-month pilot period and, because of the court ruling, most observers agree, will likely remove all restrictions to market entry. The ordinance imposes no restrictions on fares (other than filing a fee proposal) or service (other than prohibiting jitneys from stopping at Metro bus stops and requiring that a route plan be filed). Besides meeting insurance and fitness standards, all jitney vehicles must be painted white (supposedly to help monitor operations), seat no more than 15 passengers, and be less than five years of age.

Six months into Houston's jitney pilot program, no legal jitneys were plying their trade on the streets of Houston. Two individuals had filed a jitney application and paid a $100 license fee; however, no one had gone so far as putting legalized vehicles on the streets. Even Alfredo Santos, who waged a five-year legal battle to reinstate jitneys and won, but subsequently went into another business, has shied away from becoming a legal jitney operator. The consensus is that jitney operators, who would need to charge at least $2 per ride to financially survive, cannot compete with $1 subsidized Metro bus fares or make a go of it in a heavily auto-oriented city like Houston, not even in Hispanic and transit-dependent neighborhoods. The money-losing experiment with the subsidized FasTrak jitneys in early 1995 cast skepticism in the minds of many prospective entrepreneurs. Skeptics also charged that requiring vehicles to be fairly new made the service too costly for residents of poor neighborhoods. Thus, while an estimated 20 or so illegal jitneys continue to serve Houston's low-income neighborhoods, using older vehicles and minimal (or no) insurance coverage to keep fares down, after finally winning approval for publicly sanctioned jitneys, so far there have been no takers.

Lessons from Indianapolis and Houston

Recent experiences in Indianapolis and Houston make clear that the real barriers to commercial jitney services are not simply regulatory in nature. Even with a permissive local regulatory environment, virtually no one has stepped forward to operate legalized jitney services in these two cities. While recent reforms have legalized jitneys in a handful of large, mainly East-Coast, metropolitan areas with large Latin American immigrant populations, for many medium-size and less dense U.S. cities, local deregulation does not seem to be enough. The reality seems to be that market economics, regardless of how salutary and open-ended local regulations are, dictate whether entrepreneurs will test the waters and introduce shared-ride jitney services in most areas of the country. Presently, the market economics—comparatively cheap public bus fares, an abundance of free parking, low motoring charges—are clearly working against jitneys and other commercial paratransit options. In the case of Houston, the insistence that jitney vehicles be relatively new, which runs counter to the very notion of jitneys as no-frills, inexpensive transit options, has similarly suppressed the industry. Clearly, the challenge in stimulating the commercial paratransit sector goes well beyond simply lifting market entry, pricing, and vehicle routing constraints.

LOCAL POLICY AND REGULATORY REFORMS

Perhaps the most far-reaching and effective action local governments could take to stimulate commercial paratransit would be to remove or reduce subsidies to their competitors, including public transit. In 1993, 29 percent of all operating revenues provided to U.S. public transit agencies came from local governments, mainly in the form of dedicated sales and property taxes (American Public Transit Association, 1995). Of course, assistance from higher levels of government has historically been used to keep public transit systems afloat and when capital costs are counted, their subsidies make up an even higher share of government aid—37 percent in 1993 versus 26 percent from local treasuries. Thus, efforts to maintain a "level 'financial' playing field" between commercial paratransit and conventional public transit will require a trilateral effort. However, to the degree that the federal share of aid to transit continues to erode (from 29.5 percent of operating assistance in 1980 to 6.1 percent in 1993) and local governments make up the difference, they will increasingly be in a position to fashion fiscal programs that treat private paratransit operators fairly. This might take the form of limiting public transit services to high-demand corridors with economies of scale, competitive contracting of selected services, and opening up the marketplace for all remaining common-carrier services. The poor and other needy groups could be provided vouchers and user-side subsidies to ensure they receive high levels of transit services; commercial paratransit operators could then compete for this market which, over time, would improve service quality and contain costs.

Perhaps the one area where local governments could do the most to stimulate commercial paratransit would be to revise zoning ordinances to eliminate free parking. An estimated 95 percent of Americans currently park free at their workplaces (Shoup, 1995). Case studies in Los Angeles, Ottawa, and Washington, D.C., reveal that on average when employers pay for parking, 67 percent of workers drive alone, compared with only 42 percent driving alone if employees have to pay for parking themselves (Shoup and Willson, 1992). Municipal zoning laws also tend to encourage an oversupply of parking—typically the setting of a minimum floor and no ceiling on parking leads to inflated supplies as developers try to gain a marketing edge over their competitors (Willson, 1995). While this means customers can easily find a space to park, all too often it also means that roads leading to such establishments are jammed from everyone driving their cars to get there. Portland, Oregon, capped downtown parking supplies at 43,000 spaces in 1972, even though some 30,000 new jobs have since been added to downtown and retail shopping has risen dramatically. Mandatory parking charges were also introduced. These measures have paid off in the form of comparatively high transit modal splits among downtown employees—around 40 percent in 1990, compared to a metropolitan average of 6 percent (Parsons Brinckerhoff Quade & Douglas, 1995).

Of course, to the degree that market distortions are removed in the local transportation sector, it will still be necessary for more municipalities and counties to liberalize their taxi and paratransit ordinances. First and foremost, market entry and exit restrictions should be removed. Likewise, there is no compelling reason to maintain controls over tariffs or service practices (in particular, taxi ridesharing) as long as operators openly reveal their price structures to prospective customers and follow standard driver safety rules. Localities should resist requiring licensed operators to use new vans and sedans; as has been the case in Houston, this drives up the cost of paratransit and defeats the very purpose of providing customers more travel choices. In general, the marketplace is better at regulating supply, prices, and service mixes than government fiat. Instead, ordinances should focus solely on issues of driver and vehicle fitness, minimum liability insurance requirements, and other matters which bear on public safety. It is unlikely that in the case of Los Angeles County, for instance, all 88 municipalities would repeal regulations governing entry, pricing, and service in a timely and coordinated fashion. One possibility would be for councils of government to create model paratransit ordinances that open local markets to jitney-type services and urge member governments to enact such ordinances (Cervero, 1992; Poole and Griffin, 1994). A consolidated ordinance would promote service coordination, reduce administrative and enforcement costs, and set consistent service and safety standards. Another way to promote greater coordination would be to have counties rather than municipalities license and oversee commercial paratransit services, as currently practiced in Florida's Dade County (Miami area) and Broward County (Ft. Lauderdale area). Of course, consolidated government is no guarantee of stimulating commercial paratransit even with a permissive regulatory environment. The city of Indianapolis, whose 362 square miles encompasses much of Marion County, has enacted what amounts to a unitary taxi and paratransit ordinance that lifts all barriers to market entry; yet no private, common-carrier shared-ride services have emerged to date.

Last, local governments might be forced to deal with several logistical matters in their pursuit of free-enterprise paratransit services. For one, most taxis charge distance-metered fares. Shared-ride taxi services, however, would require a more flexible tariff structure, such as zonal or flat fares. Consideration might be given to distance metering of fares for exclusive-ride services and zonal fares for shared ride services (with some driver discretion, such as price adjustments for relatively short trips that cross a zone). Additionally, initiatives to deregulate paratransit would clearly spark a political backlash among taxi drivers who have paid over $100,000 for medallions in cities like New York and Boston. One might argue that those who benefitted from regulation have no implicit right to special protection and must bear the risks of deregulation—no one promised them protection in perpetuity. Still, some compensation would likely be needed for those who paid the prevailing medallion prices under the regime of limited entry; otherwise a spate of lawsuits would be filed by those seeking to recoup their losses. Whether reimbursement funding came from proceeds aimed at removing urban transportation market distortions—for example, congestion charges, parking income—or other sources would be a political decision. Other actions that local governments might consider to promote commercial paratransit include preferential operating treatment (e.g., allowing vans and jitneys to enter auto-restrictive zones) and developing smart paratransit systems, topics addressed later in this book.

NOTES

1. Only three states completely regulate taxis—Maryland, Pennsylvania, and Nevada. Florida, on the other hand, has devolved all responsibilities for common-carrier transportation regulations to county governments.

2. Open entry simply means no limits are placed on the number of licenses and permits issued. Applicants still must meet insurance and fitness standards and abide by rules governing pricing and service levels.

3. Franchises are granted to operate mainly in different areas of the city. Individual franchises are competitively bid out every five years on a staggered basis. Each franchisee is initially allowed a set number of medallions, or licenses, that can be adjusted upward or downward within a franchise period. In Los Angeles, the number of cabs rarely increases markedly because most drivers and owner-operators want to limit competition.

4. Los Angeles has enacted strict rules governing operators' service territories. The city has four zones. A taxicab driver licensed for one zone cannot pick up a passenger from another zone, even if the trip ends in that cabby's zone. The only place where a cab driver can pick up a passenger outside his or her zone is at the Los Angeles International Airport.

5. According to city officials, small companies have made the enforcement of insurance regulations particularly difficult. Smaller operators apparently face more difficulties in maintaining minimum insurance standards. The city is considering limiting future permit transfers to operators belonging to medium-size or large firms. By ordinance, permits are nontransferable. However, in the case of a death or retirement, permits can be traded on the open market. In recent years, the going rate for a permit, radio, and company name has been $6,000. While operators have traditionally belonged to larger firms, new entrants in Oakland's market tend to form smaller companies.

6. Medallions are nontransferable. They can be returned to the police department; however, this has never occurred. They can also be leased and subcontracted to others, including companies or cooperatives, but the owner of the medallion is required to drive a minimum percentage of time. Many of San Francisco's taxi firms are actually cooperatives. Medallion owners pool their medallions and share a common color scheme and logo.

7. The most significant difference between those jurisdictions that use public convenience and necessity standards and those that use minimum requirements to control entry is time delays. In Livermore, the process can take six months before an application is approved. In Hayward, the police department pools applicants until there are at least three so that a public hearing can be held.

8. In general, the same rules governing taxi operations govern San Francisco's jitney services. As a common carrier, jitneys are expected to meet the same insurance requirements set for all common carriers in the state. The only serious restriction placed on jitneys is that their fares cannot fall below the conventional bus fares charged by the San Francisco Municipal Railway (Muni).

9. Quoted in D. Cady, "Goldsmith's Plan to Alter Bus Routes Ignores the Rider Who Use Them Most," *Indianapolis Star*, section B, p. 1, August 6, 1995.

10. Fares can change at any time. The only restriction is that jitneys cannot charge on a per-mile basis and that the text of fare schedules displayed on the outside must be at least three inches high and schedules inside the vehicle must be "in plain view of passengers."

11. As a reminder of the earlier problems with jitneys and in response to the Goldsmith administration's efforts to privatize city bus services, the head of the local transit union has on numerous occasions parked a rusted-out station wagon outside the Statehouse in downtown Indianapolis, with a sign warning local citizens that this is the future of public transportation in Indianapolis. Source: K. Morgan, "Metro Proposal May Put Mayor in Driver's Seat," *Indianapolis Star*, p. 1, March 6, 1995.

12. Prior to the ordinance, the city had a ceiling of 600 taxicab licenses, although no more than 392 licenses had ever been issued. Every time an applicant petitioned for a permit, a coalition of taxi interests brought suit against the city on the grounds there was no demonstrable public convenience and necessity being served, so the ceiling effectively stood at 392 permits—or around 0.53 cabs per 1,000 residents, one of the lowest rates for a city of its size in the United States.

13. Long-time drivers have complained in media coverage and organized protests, claiming that taxi deregulation has attracted an influx of foreign cab drivers who are willing to undercut their fares and who will eventually force many out of business.

14. M. Berryhill, "Jitney Jihad: Yellow Cab Goes to War to Keep Jitneys off Houston Streets." *Houston Press*, February 2–8, 1995.

15. Ibid.

16. The actual suit was filed by the Institute for Justice, a libertarian legal foundation based in Washington, D.C. The foundation has successfully helped promote the deregulation of taxicabs in Denver, Indianapolis, Cincinnati, and Boston. All of these suits have alleged that peremptory regulations deny citizens the right to earn a livelihood serving a public need, and is thus a "taking" that violates the Fourteenth Amendment (Bill of Rights).

17. FasTrak vehicles, owned and operated by private entrepreneurs, shuttled alongside Metro's regular bus routes. People could flag FasTrak vehicles anywhere along the route and be dropped off at destinations up to one-quarter mile off the assigned routes. Prearranged trips were prohibited to avoid head-to-head competition with private taxicabs.

18. Metro's current plans are to resume the FasTrak services with a new jitney operator sometime in the future.

REFERENCES

American Public Transit Association. 1995. *1994–1995 Transit Fact Book*. Washington, D.C.: American Public Transit Association.

Cervero, R. 1992. "Transportation Alternatives in a Congestion-pricing Environment. Searching for Solutions." Washington, D.C.: Federal Highway Administration and Federal Transit Administration, Addendum to Publication No. 6, pp. 8-1— 8-19.

Frankena, M., and P. Paulter. 1984. *An Economic Analysis of Taxicab Regulation*. Washington, D.C.: Bureau of Economics, Federal Trade Commission.

Parsons Brinckerhoff Quade & Douglas. 1995. "Topic 2 Report: Station Area Development." Washington, D.C.: Transit Cooperative Research Program, Transportation Research Board, H-1 Project.

Poole, R., and M. Griffin. 1994. "Shuttle Vans: The Overlooked Transit Alternative." Los Angeles: Reason Foundation.

Shaw, L., G. Gilbert, C. Bishop, and E. Pruitt. 1983. *Taxicab Regulation in U.S. Cities.* Washington, D.C.: Urban Mass Transportation Administration, U.S. Department of Transportation.

Shoup, D. 1995. " An Opportunity to Reduce Minimum Parking Requirements." *Journal of the American Planning Association* 61(1): 14-28.

Shoup, D., and R. Willson. 1992. "Employer-paid Parking: The Problem and Proposed Solutions." *Transportation Quarterly* 46(2): 169-192.

Willson, R. 1995. "Suburban Parking Requirements: A Tacit Policy for Automobile Use and Sprawl." *Journal of the American Planning Association* 61 (1): 29-42.

CHAPTER 7

State Regulations and Policies Governing Commercial Paratransit

THE STATE REGULATORY ENVIRONMENT

Whereas intracity paratransit services fall under the purview of local governments, states almost universally maintain jurisdiction over intercity operations—that is, private subscription buses, airport ground transportation carriers, for-profit vanpools, and cross-town dial-a-ride van services. Thus, across the United States, most longer-distance, interjurisdictional common-carrier services, and virtually all contract carrier services (e.g., charter buses), are controlled by state regulators. Any generalizations about state regulations of paratransit, however, end about here. In most other respects—their geographical jurisdictions, control over market entry and exit, insurance requirements, and so on—state policies vary, sometimes markedly. Some states, like Florida and Texas, grant nearly all intrastate transportation regulatory powers to cities and counties. Other states jealously protect all regulatory powers subsidiary to the federal government, limiting municipal control largely to taxi services.

Overall, state regulations have not formed insurmountable barriers to free-market paratransit services, at least not to the degree of many local regulations. In recent years, many states have accommodated requests to initiate private commuter buspools, employer-sponsored vanpools, specialized dial-a-ride vans, and airport shuttle services. Where many have drawn the line, however, is in allowing many-to-many shuttle van services to nonairport destinations. Usually new entrants bear the burden of proof that they will serve an unmet market demand before a certificate of public convenience and necessity is issued. Many states have an unwritten rule that, for nonairport van services in particular, existing

carriers should be shielded from additional competition. In cases where operators have ventured to provide intercity van services, protests lodged by taxi franchises and charter bus companies have often effectively blocked market entry.

This chapter complements the previous one by further probing the existing
regulatory and policy environment affecting commercial paratransit in the United
States, with the focus here on states. The next section summarizes findings from
a recent survey of paratransit regulations in 12 fairly urbanized states. Rules and
requirements related to market entry and exit, pricing, service policies, and liability insurance are reviewed in an effort to assess and generalize about the restrictiveness of state paratransit regulations. This is followed by a case summary of
the effects of state regulatory reforms to stimulate the airport van industry in
California and the prospects for expanding intercity van services to nonairport
destinations. The chapter concludes with discussions of ways to further stimulate
commercial paratransit services through changes in state regulations and policies.

STATE REGULATIONS OF COMMERCIAL PARATRANSIT SERVICES

I conducted a survey in early 1995 of state regulations governing for-profit,
passenger carrier services. The survey was targeted at large, urbanized states
with at least one metropolitan area over 1 million population (since commercial
paratransit likely has the greatest market potential in large urban areas). Fairly
complete information was compiled for twelve states: California, Colorado,
Florida, Illinois, Indiana, Massachusetts, Minnesota, New Jersey, New York,
Oregon, Texas, and Virginia. These 12 states comprised a little over one-half of
the nation's 1990 population. Questionnaires were initially sent to a professional,
typically management-level, staff member of each state agency, followed by an
in-depth informant interview conducted over the telephone. Various reports and
documents prepared by the regulatory agencies of these 12 states also helped
inform the analysis.

State Regulatory Agencies and Their Jurisdictional Authorities

Many state regulatory agencies maintain vestiges of their original role as regulators of electrical streetcar lines. Early streetcars were propelled by electricity
generated from large powerhouses and distributed along citywide grids. As
designated public monopolies, they were granted exclusive franchises and operating rights and thus protected from outside competition. Because powerhouses
also provided electricity to the general public, regulation of streetcars often fell
under a state Public Utilities Commission (PUC). In 15 states, including California, Colorado, Georgia, Oregon, Massachusetts and Texas, intercity transportation is still regulated by a PUC. The most common state regulatory title today,
however, is Public Service Commission (24 states). A few states (Illinois, Okla-
homa, Virginia) regulate common carriers through a commerce commission, and

a handful have recently transferred regulatory authority to their state departments of transportation (Michigan, Minnesota, New Jersey, and New York). Florida has relinquished all state authority over transportation to county governments, and Arizona, Illinois, and Texas have largely lifted state oversight over intercity services altogether.

States generally define their jurisdiction over for-profit, inter-city passenger services along two dimensions: geography and type of service. Table 7.1 summarizes existing standards used among the 12 surveyed states (including Florida's two most urbanized counties, Dade and Broward, whose ordinances are representative of extraterritorial regulations in the state). Most states limit their regulatory authority to passenger transportation that crosses municipal boundaries. For example, in California, all carriers which operate more than 2 percent of their revenue miles outside any single municipality (or municipality and unincorporated part of a county) fall under the state's jurisdiction. Most states, however, apply a more simple rule that transfers control over intracity services to municipalities, leaving all remaining authority to the state. Oregon grants municipalities modest extraterritorial powers, allowing cities to regulate services that operate as much as three miles outside their boundaries. Texas allows large cities, like Houston and Dallas, to regulate services that operate in suburban communities within their respective metropolitan areas.

In terms of service type, states almost universally regulate contract services (e.g. charter buses) and common carriers, including both fixed-route and irregular route services, that are open to the general public for a fee (and which cross city or county boundaries). Included here are for-hire limousines and vans, for-profit carpools and vanpools, intercity taxis, subscription buses, and other commercial interurban services. Normally exempt from state regulations are employer-sponsored carpools and vanpools (which carry 15 or fewer passengers), emergency vehicles, and school buses.[1] For a period, however, vanpool cooperatives formed by community groups, like the original Reston Commuter Bus program in northern Virginia, were technically considered illegal in many states, although today most states permit these services as long as liability insurance coverage is met (Davis and Burkhatten, 1978). In Colorado, state regulators even control municipal taxi services, using a system of "regulated competition" in municipalities of 60,000 residents or more and "regulated monopoly" elsewhere. Connecticut, Rhode Island, Delaware, Montana, and Nebraska likewise control taxicabs, treating them as common carriers just like intercity bus and trucking companies.[2]

Several states have narrowly defined their jurisdictions over common-carrier services. Illinois only regulates for-profit passenger vehicles which seat 10 or more passengers and which go to airports. In Indiana, regular fixed-route services, like commuter buses, are not regulated. However, irregular route services, like limousines, airport vans, and nonemergency medical carriers, are.[3]

In most states, contract services, like for-hire limousines and charter services, face less stringent regulatory requirements than common carriers. In some places, this has prompted limousine operators to register as contract operators and ille-

Table 7.1.

Criteria for Defining Jurisdiction over Common-carrier Transportation Services

	Regulations	
	By Geography	*By Type*
California	Intracity regulated by munici-pality (98% of service must be within city boundaries, or city and unincorporated county, to be exempt from state authority).	Common carriers: certificate of convenience & necessity Limousines: certificate of convenience & necessity Taxi: exempt from state
Colorado	Cities with 60,000 inhabitants or more have different rules for taxis, but all areas are regulated at the state level.	Common carriers: certificate of convenience & necessity Taxi: certificate of convenience & necessity Charter/contract: permit only
Florida	No regulations at state level.	No regulations at state level
Dade Cy.	Inter- & intracounty transporta-tion is regulated by the county.	Common carriers: certificate of convenience & necessity (including jitneys) Taxis: certificate of convenience & necessity
Broward Cy.	Inter- & intracounty transporta-tion is regulated by the county (taxis & limousines).	Taxis & limousines (all vehicles for hire with 8 passengers or less) must win lottery to obtain permit. Cap on taxi & limousine permits set on population-based formula Vehicles larger than 8 passengers: need only occupational license & meet safety requirements
Illinois	Only carriers which go to airports are regulated by the state.	Common carriers to airports & with seating capacity for 10 or more passengers: certificate of convenience & necessity All others: exempt from state
Indiana	Inter- & intracity transportation is not regulated by the state. The state only regulates service which goes from city to unin-corporated area.	Limousines, special & charter services, & non-emergency medical: certificate of convenience & necessity Taxi: exempt from state Common carrier (regular route): not regulated
Massachusetts	Taxis fall under municipal jurisdiction.	Common carriers: certificate of convenience & necessity (regulators not concerned with the adequacy of other service providers in awarding certificate)
Michigan[a]	Taxis (metered vehicles from 3 to 9 passengers) fall under municipal jurisdiction.	Common carriers (all private for-hire carriers with seating capacity of 15 passengers or less are called "limou-sines"): "Fit, willing, & able" standard
Minnesota	Taxis are regulated at the municipal level.	Common carriers (regular route & "Special transportation service"): certificate of convenience & necessity Limousines, special passenger services (Limousines which are not in luxury vehicles): Permit Charter: Permit

Table 7.1 (continued).
Criteria for Defining Jurisdiction over Common-carrier Transportation Services

	Regulations	
	By Geography	By Type
New Jersey	Taxis & jitneys fall under municipal jurisdiction.	Common carriers less than 25 passengers: certificate of convenience Charter: certificate of convenience & necessity Limousines: permit only Taxis: exempt from state
New York	Taxis regulated at municipal level. State regulates rest of New York except New York City.	Common carriers: certificate of convenience & necessity Limousines & taxis: exempt from state
Oregon	Taxis regulated at municipal level. Any transportation which remains within any municipality or a three-mile buffer outside any municipality, is exempt from state regulations.	Common carriers (fixed route): certificate of convenience & necessity Charter: Certificate of convenience & necessity Taxi: exempt from state
Texas	Taxis regulated at municipal level. No common carrier regulations at state level.	No regulations at state level
Virginia	All transportation within municipal boundaries exempt from state regulation.	Common carriers: certificate of convenience & necessity Charter: certificate of convenience & necessity Taxis: exempt from state

Definitions:
Common carriers (irregular or regular route): services which may be used by the general public, for a fee which is paid by individual passengers by distance or by trip, on a pre-arranged basis if irregular route (dial-up services, such as airport shuttles), and not pre-arranged if regular route (fixed or semi-fixed route, and sometimes fixed schedule). This usually excludes limousines, charter services, services which cater to specific populations (ambulances, non-emergency medical, schoolbuses), and services not provided for profit (carpools).
Charter: usually not fixed route, operates with a set customer list, and fee is a lump sum payment for all passengers.
Limousine: Not fixed route, usually luxury vehicle, 8 passengers or less, operates on a pre-arranged basis only (cannot take hails).
Taxi: Not fixed route, takes hails, operates with meter, with or without shared rides, 8 passengers or less.

[a]The State of Michigan passed its Limousine Transportation Act in 1990. This act, however, has been neither rescinded nor implemented. Thus, information presented for Michigan should be considered tentative.

gally provide common-carrier services (such as taking curbside hails, operating a fixed route) on the side. The rationale for treating common carriers and contract services differently is rarely expressed in state statutes. The chief reason is that common-carrier services are more closely scrutinized in return for greater monopoly protection. In a free-market, loosely regulated environment, however, there would be no grounds for treating common-carrier and contract services differently.

It is because charter services are treated more leniently that the state of California is presently trying to reclassify child paratransit services as common carriers (or what the state's PUC calls Passenger Stage Corporations). Because of increased competition in this industry (see Chapter 3), there is growing concern that service quality could decline, thereby jeopardizing the safety of children.

New proposed regulations would impose restrictions on time of day and durations of operations and set limits on ages of children who could be carried. While it is unlikely the PUC will try to inhibit the growth of this industry, one can expect California and other states to begin setting service quality and safety standards out of growing concern for children's welfare, even if operators remain licensed as charter carriers.

Market Entry and Exit

For intercity common carriers to receive an operating permit, they must first initiate an application and, in most cases, demonstrate the proposed service meets a public convenience and necessity standard. If a state regulatory body finds that the applicant has proven this, the applicant must then meet various financial, vehicle, and operator fitness standards.

Applications for Market Entry

Applying for a state permit is often a lengthy and sometimes a costly process, enough to dissuade some would-be start-ups from even going forward. Table 7.2 summarizes the application process in the 12 surveyed states, including how the public is notified of the application and the conditions under which a public hearing is held. In 1995, application fees ranged from a low of $25 in Texas (which subsequently has eliminated all fees) to $500 or more in California, Michigan, and Florida's urban counties. The public is notified of all applications, usually through a newspaper or the regulatory agency's bulletin. The length of time it takes to act on an application depends on whether any formal protests are lodged. Existing operators often file protests, claiming either that the new service will create ruinous competition or fails to meet industry standards. Public transit agencies often protest when private commuter bus routes are proposed within their service areas. The New York City Transit Authority, for example, has filed a protest against every common-carrier application proposed for the metropolitan area over the past decade. Formal protests can extend the length of time it takes to issue a permit to as much as nine months in some states, like Colorado and California.

Public Convenience and Necessity

Normally, the litmus test of whether state regulators side with applicants or protesters is the public convenience and necessity standard, discussed in Chapter 5. In principle, this means demonstrating convincingly that the service will satisfy an unmet need of the travelling public and make a profit without harming existing carriers. Most states allow applicants to submit written petitions, affidavits, or letters in arguing their case for public convenience and necessity, though some, like Minnesota, require that applicants appear before the regulatory board,

Table 7.2.
State Transportation Application Fees and Processes, 1995

State	Application Fee	Application turn-around time	*Notification:* Responsible party Notificants or notification method	Application Public Hearing: Necessary Conditions Most Likely Protesters
California	High	Med.-High	Applicant Public Transit, all common carriers	Upon Protest Common carriers, public transit agencies
Colorado	Med.	Med.-High	Agency Other carriers	Upon Protest Existing Carriers
Florida				
Dade County	n/a	Med.-High	Agency Municipalities, all other carriers	Upon Protest Existing carriers, public transit
Broward County	High	High	none	none
Illinois	High	Med.	Applicant Newspaper	Mandatory Other carriers
Indiana	Low	Med.	Agency Newspaper	Upon Protest Other carriers (but rare)
Massachusetts	Med.	Low	Agency Carrier	Mandatory None are successful
Michigan	High	n/a	none	none
Minnesota	High	Low-Med.	Agency Subscription bulletin, public transit authority if within jurisdiction	Upon Protest Other carriers
New Jersey	Low	Low-High	Applicant Other carriers, newspaper	Upon Protest Other carriers, NJ Transit, Municipalities
New York	Med.	Med.	Agency Subscription bulletin	Upon "Valid" Protest Other carriers (but rare, and only for fitness), public transit only protests applications in NYC

(continued)

Table 7.2 (continued).
State Transportation Application Fees and Processes, 1995

State	Application Fee	Application turn-around time	Notification: Responsible party Notificants or notification method	Application Public Hearing: Necessary Conditions Most Likely Protesters
Oregon	Med.	Low-Med.	Agency Newsletter to all carriers	Upon Protest Other carriers (but rare)
Texas	Low	n/a	none	none
Virginia	Low	Med.	Applicant Other like carriers	Mandatory Other carriers

Fee Ranges:
Low: $25 - 99
Med.: $100-299
High: $300-550

Time Ranges:
Low: <2 mos.
Med.: 2-6 mos.
High: 6-12 mos.

give an oral testimony, and be cross-examined. Formal market studies are rarely required.

Some states are quite lenient in their interpretations of convenience and necessity. In Massachusetts, the very application for a permit is interpreted to mean that the proposed service can make a profit and serve a bona fide market demand. There, no protests against new intercity carriers have won since the mid-1980s. Similarly, protests against airport shuttle applications are fruitless in California, though the state's PUC is far more sensitive to allegations of unfair competition for other intercity services. Other states are highly protective of existing operators, requiring proof that existing carriers are providing inadequate services. Colorado's "regulated monopoly" policy virtually eliminates competition for intercity services within large metropolitan areas, like Denver-Boulder.

Some states have adopted a narrow definition of "public convenience." In Minnesota, for example, public convenience is interpreted to mean service to public areas only. Under this definition, airport shuttles cannot go door-to-door (but rather only to transportation terminals)—many-to-one vans, like limousines, are viewed as luxury services and thus outside the sphere of the general public's interest.

Public convenience and necessity standards have also been used to block market exit. Some state regulators insist that carriers continue serving sparsely populated areas in return for the right to expand services into more lucrative markets. Illinois's Commerce Commission historically denied requests to drop services, even those that were clearly money losers. Because of a decline in intercity bus and van ridership (outside the airport market), a number of operators in the

Chicago area applied for federal interstate licenses to operate services across the Indiana and Wisconsin state lines, thus preempting state regulations. As a result, Illinois abandoned its constraints on market exit.

Service, Pricing, and Fitness Requirements

Once convenience and necessity is demonstrated, intercity carriers typically must file a service and tariff plan and meet fitness standards—minimum insurance coverage, vehicle safety, and driver qualifications (e.g., chauffeur license, good driving record)—before permits are issued and services can commence. For commuter buses and other regular services, route and schedule restrictions are normally defined in the initial application and in certificates of public convenience and necessity. Any proposed routing or scheduling change often opens up the service again to public hearings and protests, something most carriers want to avoid. Routes and schedules are regulated to varying degrees among states, though the general trend has been toward permissiveness. In Oregon, fixed-route regulations govern only the line-haul, typically freeway, portions of trips; Oregon regulators place no restrictions on other route segments (e.g., within neighborhoods, downtowns, etc.).

State regulators are perhaps the most lenient when it comes to tariffs. The normal practice is to let market forces determine fares and rate structures. Most states allow fares to be changed at any time as long the new tariff proposals are filed 10 to 30 days in advance of the change. Most states also require applicants to file basic financial reports (e.g., a proposed balance sheet) and have anywhere from 30 to 50 days working capital available.

Minimum insurance liability coverage also varies noticeably among states (Table 7.3). Those states that have adopted federal standards for interstate carriers, like Indiana and Massachusetts, have the highest liability requirements. Insurance premiums for common carrier services have risen sharply in many urbanized states in recent years.[4] In New Jersey and New York, the cost of liability insurance has increased so much that many operators are reported to be cutting back on maintenance and holding onto their fleets longer. Yet vehicle safety and driver qualifications are tightly regulated in both states. New York state requires all applicants to have some prior experience in the passenger transportation industry. Some states require common carrier operators to check the driving histories of job applicants or sub-contractors before offering employment. California requires companies to enroll in the "Pull Notice Program" of the Department of Motor Vehicles, which provides computerized accounts of drivers' records. It is the fear that deregulation and more open competition would compromise public safety that prompts many state authorities to maintain a tight rein over all inter-city common carrier services.

Table 7.3.
Insurance Coverage Requirements, 1995

State	Rating for insurance liability for carrier with seating capacity of ≤15*	Vehicle seating capacity	Liability levels** ($1000)
California	High	≤8	750
		9-16	1,500
		≥17	5,000
Colorado	Med.	≤17	500
		8-15	1,000
		16-31	1,500
		≥32	5,000
Florida Dade County	Low	≤15	50/100/50
		>15	1,500
Illinois*	Med.	≤15	150
		>15	300
Indiana	High	≤15	1,500
		>15	5,000
Massachusetts	High	≤15	1,500
		>15	5,000
Michigan	High	≤9	1,000
		10-15	2,000
Minnesota	Med.	≤12	100/300/50
		13-20	100/350/50
		21-32	100/400/50
		≥33	100/450/50
New Jersey	Low	≤13	25/100/min:25 max:50
		13-31	25/200/min:25 max:50
		≥32	25/100/min:25 max:50
New York	Med.	≤13	100/300/50
		>13	100/400/50
Oregon	Med	(by vehicle weight) <26,000 lbs	standard insurance for personal pssgr. vehicles
		>26,000 lbs	750

Table 7.3 (continued).
Insurance Coverage Requirements, 1995

State	Rating for insurance liability for carrier with seating capacity of ≤15*	Vehicle seating capacity	Liability levels** ($1000)
Texas	Med.	<5	No requirements
		5-25	500
		>25	5,000
Virginia	Med.	≤13	250
		≥13	500

*Insurance requirement ratings: ($1,000) Low: 100 to 200 Med.: 201 to 550 High: 1 million or more	**Single entries are maximum liability requirements for single occurrences. Three-slashed entries are for: per person/ per occurrence/property damage

Regulatory and Policy Reforms

Despite concerns over safety, many states have adopted a more conciliatory and permissive attitude toward intercity paratransit services in recent times. In the past five years, Rhode Island, Delaware, Texas, and New York have all sought to relax or eliminate market entry requirements, with varying degrees of success. In New Hampshire, the state constitution has opened the way to unrestricted market entry by holding that "free and fair competition in the trades and industries is an inherent right of the people." Idaho has taken the stance that anyone with a satisfactory safety record and who is financially fit can operate intercity vans and buses.

The state that has done the most to open the intercity passenger market to free competition is Arizona. In 1982, Arizona's state legislature completely deregulated common-carrier services, permitting freedom of entry, exit, pricing, and service levels. To obtain an operating license in Arizona, an applicant only needs to meet fitness standards, including financial responsibility for insurance. Arizona's deregulation package also affected intraurban services provided by taxis, private buses, and airport limousines. Immediately following deregulation, increased competition led to a surge in new taxi businesses, especially small, independents serving the Phoenix and Tucson airports (Teal et al., 1984). Limousines and van services also expanded into airport markets. More competition and less concentration (i.e., reduced market domination by a few firms) failed to lower fares, however. Elsewhere, the affects of statewide deregulation have gone unfelt. Beyond shuttle vans to airports, no new jitney or commercial transit-like services have been initiated in Phoenix or Tucson, for the same reasons that local deregulation failed to spur new services in Indianapolis and Houston. Driving and parking remain cheap in Phoenix and Tucson, and for those inclined to share rides, subsidized public transit fares are too low for privateers to compete and make a profit. As spread-out cities (each with around 2,500 persons per square mile), the private automobile reigns supreme in Phoenix and Tucson—in 1990, around 90 percent of workers commuted by car in both places. Overall, transportation deregulation affected too small a share of Arizona's urban travelers, the vast majority of whom drive or take subsidized public transit, to have much impact.

Beyond deregulation, some states have sought to stimulate the commercial intercity paratransit sector by providing direct financial assistance. New York state has established a dedicated fund that allows counties to contract for private common carrier services that feed into public transit terminals. New Jersey's Department of Transportation now requires New Jersey Transit, the largest public transit operator in the state, to contract out some intercity services to private operators. In Massachusetts, employer shuttle vans pay lower state vehicle registration fees.

CALIFORNIA'S DEREGULATION OF AIRPORT SHUTTLE VANS

In 1980, California Public Utilities Commission relaxed its standards for newcomers to have to prove the need for new airport van services.[5] Since the expansion of airport-type shuttle vans into other markets, some have argued (see Poole and Griffin, 1994), represents one of the most promising hopes for commercial paratransit, California's experiences with deregulating airport vans deserve closer inspection.

Although historically a protectionist agency, California's PUC decided to open intercity airport access services to limited competition because, it believed, the natural monopoly argument for safeguarding established carriers had lost credibility.[6] At the urging of staff economists, the commission adopted a policy that if applicants can charge "reasonable and compensatory" rates, then the proposed service is "necessary and convenient" for the public. Today, the Commission only denies an application because of safety concerns or past illegal activity. While before it typically took companies around eight months to obtain a license to serve airports (assuming they could meet the burden of proof of an unmet need), now most applicants can secure a permit within one month without any public hearing.

The PUC's laissez-faire attitude ignited a boom in the airport ground transportation business, as taxis, limousines, shuttle vans, chartered buses, and airport coaches vied for the premium fares many airport customers are willing to pay. Within the state's two major metropolises, greater Los Angeles and the San Francisco Bay Area, the airport van industry grew from nil in 1976, when airport shuttles were first allowed, to 26 companies in 1987, and to over 60 companies in 1994. California's shuttle van industry has successfully carved out an untapped niche of the airport access market: a service quality and price mix that falls between those of taxicabs/limousines and scheduled buses.

Pioneering California's airport shuttle van industry was a single carrier, Super-Shuttle International. SuperShuttle initially entered the Los Angeles and Bay Area markets in the early 1980s with some 100 vans and more than doubled its fleet size by 1989. SuperShuttle quickly gained a reputation for prompt, dependable, and premium-quality service (limiting pickup and delivery stops to no more than three per one-way trip). As required by both the Los Angeles International and San Francisco International (SFO) airports, SuperShuttle serves all inbound airport trips through advanced telephone reservations; outbound trips may be either prescheduled or on demand. Today, SuperShuttle remains the dominant airport shuttle operator in both areas, capturing an estimated 35 to 45 percent of market revenue in LAX and SFO. (This is down from the late-1980s, when SuperShuttle had cornered over three-quarters of the airport market.) Overall, studies showed that the airport van industry became less concentrated following deregulation, with the four largest firms capturing around 70 percent of the market in 1990, down from 88 percent two years earlier (Strauss et al., 1992).

By the early 1990s, California's shuttle van industry was carrying over 8 million passengers a year and generating over $100 million in revenues. Shuttle vans handled 5 percent of ground access trips to LAX and 10 percent of trips to SFO in 1993 (from zero in 1978). Robert Poole and Michael Griffin (1994, p. 6) note: "It is in auto-oriented Los Angeles that the success of airport shuttle vans in 'getting people out of their cars' has been most dramatic. The decline in auto mode share from 76.3 percent of all airport trips in 1978 to 69.9 percent in 1993. . . . is primarily due to the growth of shuttle vans." They calculate that the 974,000 annual shuttle van trips to LAX, each averaging 3.5 customers and travelling 25 miles, has reduced tailpipe emissions in the South Coast Basin by some 65 tons annually.

Increased competition cut into California's airport shuttle industry's profits. Figure 7.1 reveals that as more firms entered the LAX and SFO markets in the late 1980s, profit margins tumbled, from 7 to 8 percent in 1988 to virtually nothing two years latter.[7] About 45 percent of firms reported net income losses in 1990. SuperShuttle's profit margin had shrunk to only around 2 percent in 1990, though its return on equity remained at 10 percent or more. Today, the airport market shakeout continues, with some companies exiting followed by newcomers taking their place. Overall, having some profitable and some unprofitable firms and a steady stream of new entrants and exiters are signs of a healthy industry. Stiff competition also seems to be giving rise to innovations, in particular the emergence of paratransit brokerage firms that contract out dispatching, routing, marketing, and maintenance services to independent driver-owners.

While the supply and mix of airport vans increased at both LAX and SFO, so did the number of complaints by airport authorities (about battles over curb space and congestion), by large firms and incumbents (over alleged cream skimming and unfair competition),[8] and by some customers (about nonpickups and overcharging). A 1991 survey revealed that 39 percent of frequent airport shuttle customers from Southern California thought service quality had declined, and 20

Figure 7.1.
Changes in Number of Firms and Profit Margins for Airport Shuttle Vans
Operating to LAX and SFO, 1988–1990

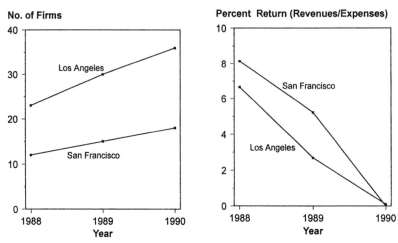

percent thought it had improved (Strauss et al., 1992). (Still, 93 percent of surveyed shuttle customers rated the service they received "acceptable" or better.) Because of increased complaints, airport authorities have instituted strict on-premises rules for operating shuttle vans and have stepped-up enforcement,[9] and California's PUC has placed several six-month moratoria on new airport entrants. Overall, however, California's airport access industry remains very competitive today.

EXPANSION INTO NONAIRPORT SERVICES

While California's PUC has embraced competition within the airport access industry, it has been far more reticent in extending these privileges to other types of intercity markets, such as commercial van services to downtowns, suburban employment centers, shopping malls, college campuses, recreational theme parks, sports stadia, and other major trip generators. Currently, scheduled, flexible-route, intercity van services do not exist in the United States, except for some of the illegal jitney vans operating in New York, Miami, and other large cities. In studying the possibility of such services in Southern California, Poole and Griffin (1994, p. 21) argue that: "If the PUC recognized them. . . . and created relatively open licensing, this new industry would essentially bypass the local taxicab regulations (as has occurred with airport van services)."

Experiences in California suggest that a combination of regulatory and economical barriers have constrained commercial van operators from branching out. California's PUC continues to apply a strictly interpreted public convenience and necessity standard in reviewing proposals for nonairport shuttles. Vocal opposition by taxi owners or local transit authorities is usually enough to deny an entry request. In California's Coachella Valley (the Palm Springs–Palm Desert part of Riverside County), an applicant recently proposed an innovative many-to-many van service between several jurisdictions within Riverside County. Vehicles would be used for a mix of runs to downtown areas, airports, and enclaves with large senior populations. Local public transit authorities united to oppose the application, contending that it would result in overcompetition and impose economic hardships. At the public hearing, several taxi companies protested that the applicant was simply trying to circumvent fare restrictions and medallion caps set by municipalities by operating between cities. Giving in to political pressure, the PUC rejected the application.

Even when the PUC allows an airport van operator to venture into other markets, this is no guarantee for success. In 1991, PrimeTime Incorporated, the second largest airport shuttle service in Southern California, decided to test the commuter market waters by running unsubsidized vans between Pasadena and downtown Los Angeles for a six month period. As with airport shuttles, this was a few-to-one operation, with the one being downtown Los Angeles rather than LAX. The daily commuter vans lost money because they had to keep their fares low to compete with the subsidized bus routes operating along the same Pasadena –downtown Los Angeles corridor. After six months, the service folded. According to company officials, the service was very close to breaking even and, they believed, it would have only taken one other condition, like the elimination of free parking in downtown Los Angeles, to make the service profitable.[10]

It is clear that, besides PUC deregulation, a number of accompanying policy reforms would be necessary if regionwide commercial van services are to become a reality. Most effective would be policies that reduce hidden subsidies to motorists and parkers as well as direct subsidies to public transit operators. Break-even fares for airport shuttle van services have been calculated at around 50 cents per passenger mile (at occupancies of 3 to 4 passengers per vehicle); according to Michael Cameron (1991), fares set at this level in combination with congestion tolls of 10 cents per vehicle mile could make peak-period commercial van services profitable in Southern California. Another study estimated that for a typical 12.5 mile one-way trip in the greater Los Angeles region, shuttle vans carrying six passengers cost around $2 more per passenger than solo driving.[11] If, however, average employee parking charges were $4.29 per day, shuttle vans would cost around $2.25 less per passenger. Adding a freeway congestion toll of 15 cents per mile to these parking fees would give shuttle vans an edge of around $5 per passenger for each 12.5 mile trip. Even more advantageous would be adding a system of High Occupancy/Toll (HOT) express lanes (which would charge solo commuters 25 cents per mile and allow vans to run free); in combination with parking charges, this would save each shuttle van passenger around $7 per trip (Poole and Griffin, 1994).

Several factors, summarized in Table 7.4, could impede efforts to expand intercity commercial van services, even with road pricing. For one, as a many-

Table 7.4.
Differences in Commercial Van Services to Airports
versus Major Employment Centers

Characteristic	Airport	Other Urban Centers	Policy Strategies to Make Commercial Vans Competitive at other Urban Centers
Service configuration	Many-to-one	Many-to-many	Introduce automated vehicle location systems (AVL) and other advanced transit technologies
Parking	Market rates	Free or subsidized	Introduce parking charges; cash out free parking
Peaking	Flatter; more even daily and weekly spread of demand	Sharper peaks; costlier services	Introduce flextime and modified work schedules; promote mixed-use development
Customer base	Business travelers; more "captive" markets	Residents making regular trips; more "choice" travellers	Market-based pricing of roads; higher charges would hurt captive commuter markets the most; reduce inequities through user-side subsidies and paratransit deregulation

to-many service, commercial van transportation is fundamentally different from many-to-one airport shuttle runs. The need to operate ubiquitously, with myriad origins and destinations, imposes large extra costs related to vehicle dispatching and routing. The founder and president of SuperShuttle International expressed skepticism when interviewed: "It's an incredibly large leap to go from many-to-one to many-to-many services. Many-to-many services for the transportation disadvantaged under ADA costs three and one-half times as much per passenger as many-to-one airport shuttle services. I can't see many-to-many SuperShuttle vans in any universe I can imagine."

The universe that might begin to make many-to-many van services economical is Automated Vehicle Location, or AVL, technologies. Through technologies as simple as signposts or as advanced as satellite-based locating and guidance system, it is now possible to geographically monitor the real-time movement of vehicles, dynamically route and dispatch vehicles, track on-time performance, and inform customers when vans and buses will arrive. These possibilities are explored in Chapter 9.

Another impediment to expanding commercial van services is the large differential in parking charges between airports and most other destinations. Most airports and nearby vendors charge market rates for parking, as high as $20 per day at major airports, thus removing a huge hidden subsidy to motorists. If downtowns and other activity centers charged commercial parking rates similar to those of airports, private van services to these destinations would more likely be remunerative as well. Airport van operators might also be reluctant to enlarge their markets because the peak demands for airport access trips and commute trips often coincide. Since the peaks for work trips are more pronounced than for airport business, the marginal costs of adding commuter vans would be especially high.[12] Last, common carriers view airport markets as lucrative and risk free. Airport travellers represent captive markets, in part because they face potentially high fees if they park for extended periods of time.[13] The large volume of business travelers on expense accounts and tourists willing to splurge also make airport markets attractive. Overall, if California's PUC extended free-market standards to commercial vans and other intercity services, the stage would be set for an entirely new form of urban transportation. However, deregulation, in and of itself, would clearly not be enough. Experiences in Southern California underscore the importance of linking regulatory reforms to market-based pricing and other corrective measures.

STATE POLICY AND REGULATORY REFORMS

Many of the same suggestions made in Chapter 6 for local policy reforms hold for state governments as well. Foremost is the need to reduce market distortions. At the state level, some modest inroads have been made in reforming parking policies. In 1992, California's legislature passed a bill, AB 2109, that attempts to cash out free parking—giving employers who provide free parking as a paid fringe benefit the option of offering workers the cash value instead (and thus the option of saving money through ridesharing). AB 2109 applies only to firms in air quality nonattainment areas, with 50 or more employees, and which lease parking spaces from a third party.[14] Still, one study showed that 58 percent of large companies in high-density office centers in Southern California leased parking spaces for their employees; in downtown Los Angeles, the share was 71 percent (Shoup, 1995).

States, which in 1993 provided 38 percent of all operating subsidies to U.S. public transit systems, could also revise their transit assistance programs to reward productivity (e.g., apportioning dedicated transit funds based on ridership performance), thus creating an incentive for public authorities to contract some services to efficiency-minded commercial paratransit operators. States could also stimulate competition by redirecting operating assistance from public transit authorities to more impartial regional bodies, such as councils of government or metropolitan planning organizations. As discussed in Chapter 6, Indiana now transfers dedicated state sales tax revenues to consolidated cities rather than public transit operators in hopes of stimulating private sector competition.

On the regulatory side, there appears to be no compelling reason for imposing market entry and exit, price, service, and vehicle-occupancy restrictions on intercity carriers. However, experiences with airport van deregulation suggest that states do have an important regulatory role to play in setting and enforcing operating and safety standards. If not, in a highly competitive environment, those carriers who follow the rules are likely to lose out to those who routinely break them. One standard might be that certain classes of intercity carriers be affiliated with some kind of radio dispatching service that enables them to provide real-time service to all forms of passenger demand (e.g., inbound and outbound services). This would both safeguard public safety and allow for some degree of equity among competitors. While state control over vehicle quality, insurance coverage, driver qualifications, and vehicle fitness is generally accepted as necessary, government requirements should pretty much stop here.

It is in the area of market entry and exit that state regulatory revisions would do the most good. Some states have liberated intercity services by replacing public convenience and necessity requirements with a public interest standard. This approach asks whether new entrants will benefit the public rather than whether they will potentially harm existing carriers. If convenience and necessity criteria and public hearings are retained, states should statutorily shift the burden of proof from applicants to protesters, as currently is the case for interstate common-carrier services. Under this logic, it is assumed anyone attempting to bear the costs and absorb the risks of initiating new services believes an unserved market demand exists; it is up to incumbent operators to prove otherwise. Likewise, "first chance requirements" that give existing operators the first right to serve an unmet need are anticompetitive and should be repealed. And while non-profit, employer-sponsored vanpools are exempt from certification requirements, most states either ban or apply restrictive entry standards to commercial vanpools. Any enterprising employee who takes the initiative to provide van service for his or her co-workers is entitled to a fair profit, and should be treated no differently than other commercial operators.

In some urbanized states, like New York, New Jersey, and California, existing statutes governing minimum liability coverage, worker's compensation insurance, and driver qualifications are viewed by many operators as onerous and too expensive. Although always a contentious issue, whether states with large numbers of low-income individuals making inter-city trips can afford very high margins of safety needs to be more openly debated. In response to federal deregulation of inter-city bus services in 1982, Tennessee lowered its standards for vehicle quality. There, church buses, school buses, family passenger vans, and other privately owned vehicles were called into service in rural areas which lost inter-city bus services. These vehicles provided low-priced services for those who did not mind sacrificing comfort. These were temporary measures to cushion the blow from inter-city service cuts that over time were removed by the Tennessee legislature.

Last, states are in a position to pass legislation that eases the ability of municipalities and counties to promote free-enterprise paratransit services within their jurisdictions. Enabling localities to create consolidated, countywide taxi and jitney ordinances, for instance, might improve service coordination. "One stop shopping" for obtaining necessary local and state licenses would likely lower administration costs. And where antitrust laws inhibit the formation of route associations, paratransit co-ops, and brokerage firms, such restrictions should be repealed.

NOTES

1. If a type of intercity service is excluded from state regulations, it almost is never regulated by another tier of government, like a county. For example, charter carriers have been regulated by the state of Illinois and are not regulated by any other government entity.

2. Kentucky controls market entry for taxicab services by issuing certificates of public convenience and necessity, but delegates control over tariffs to localities.

3. This curious twist came about when Indiana adopted federal insurance standards for common carriers. The political trade-off was that fixed-route common carriers became exempt from state oversight.

4. Other significant overhead expenses incurred by many intercity common carriers are worker's compensation insurance and employer and social security taxes. Many operators question whether the industry can afford such a high margin of safety. One Southern California airport shuttle van operator reports that worker's compensation accounts for around 20 percent of its payroll expenses. Besides physical disabilities, numerous claims in the transportation field are paid out to stress-related illnesses (which, many believe, have a high incidence of fraud). In some states, like California, firms pay no worker's compensation if they subcontract services rather than hire employees. This has prompted most airport shuttle owner-operators to hire independent contractors rather than directly hire drivers. Still, a 1991 investigation found that six of the seven largest carriers serving the Los Angeles International Airport were in violation of worker's compensation rules, failing to adequately cover their employees (even though they claimed to be using some combination of contractors and employees). Another reason airport shuttle firms have shifted increasingly to subcontracting is that they can reduce fraud. Shuttle van operations, like taxi operations, are cash businesses with little or no employer control over driver cash collection. One study reports that employee shuttle van drivers in California may steal over 10 percent of all passenger revenues. Independent contractors, on the other hand, pay a fee to the service-operator so there is no risk of employee theft (Strauss et al., 1992).

5. The PUC took a procompetition stance in reaction to existing airport shuttle operators who were pressing hard to limit competition, continually appealing to the PUC to issue new certificates only if existing operators failed to provide satisfactory service. A "certificate of public convenience and necessity" remains the mechanism for a business to provide common carrier services, along with three other stipulations: a nonrefundable application fee of $500 ($300 to transfer a permit from one carrier to another); a public notification of the application, including a letter of intent sent to all public transit authorities and taxi companies which operate in the same jurisdictions; and a public hearing if requested by transit authorities, taxi lobbies, or any other interests that oppose the application.

6. Technically, licensed operators are not just restricted to airports, but to other transportation terminals as well. In Southern California, for instance, some airport van operators also serve the downtown Amtrak terminal and the Catalina Ferry terminal in Long Beach.

7. Profit margins were calculated from data compiled by California's Public Utilities Commission on total annual revenues and expenses (including annualized expenses for capital depreciation and debt service) of private firms.

8. Large airport shuttle operators argue that California's PUC has gone too far in loosening the regulatory noose and has placed the industry in a perilous situation, both financially and in terms of safety. Their biggest complaint is that small, independent operators concentrate only on the lucrative outbound services from airports, leaving the large carriers with the more expensive advanced-reservation, inbound services. (Most small operators do not haul people to the airport because of the high overhead costs of maintaining reservations, dispatching, and router systems.) Rather, the newcomers often aggressively vie for the curbside and loop the airport repeatedly in search of outbound customers. Large operators view this as a nonlevel playing field. As long as they are required to serve inbound customers and incur the associated infrastructure expenses, over the long run they will be unable to compete with small independents. All services, they argue, will eventually fall to the lowest common denominator—a single operator who services outbound customers. During an interview, the founder-owner of one of Southern California's largest airport van services predicted that, unless new regulations are introduced, the airport van industry will become a tragedy of the commons—"an over-fished pond where only a few companies contribute fish to the pond and most others are taking fish out of it." According to California's PUC, some of the problems faced by large, longtime airport van operators are related less to unfair competition and more to bad business decisions—mainly, expanding operations and overcapitalizing during the early 1990s when the state's economy took a downturn.

9. In Southern California, LAX introduced a policy that all vans and limousines entering the premises must bring a party to the airport or have an outbound reservation; however, enforcement of this rule has proven difficult. Both LAX and SFO limit the amount of dwell time that shuttle operators can maintain at curbside.

10. PrimeTime also negotiated with the downtown Los Angeles Transportation Management Association (TMA) to operate a for-profit subscription van service from the San Fernando Valley to downtown Los Angeles on a contract basis, but this plan was aborted by the dissolution of the TMA in 1992. PrimeTime and other operators also entered into discussions with TMAs in Warner Center and the Burbank Media District, two of Los Angeles's largest edge cities, about providing similar commercial van services; however, the failed experiment with the Pasadena shuttle van service dissuaded them from moving forward (Cervero, 1992).

11. These calculations assume a 1991 intermediate-size car that costs 13.7 cents per mile to operate. Because drivers typically ignore the sunk costs of vehicle ownership and weigh only marginal operating costs when making a mode choice decision, these calculations ignore the full costs of motoring, like capital depreciation, insurance, and financing charges.

12. There is also normally a rise in airport traffic in the midday as well as on weekends and holidays, allowing vans and drivers to be more fully employed throughout the year. One way that operators could make more productive use of extra vans purchased for commuter markets is to assign them to charter and ADA-type services during the midday, and to shopping malls, theme parks, and sports events on weekends.

13. Studies show the break-even point in the cost of taking a shuttle or driving and parking at an airport ranges from four to 26 days of airport parking (depending on parking costs and access mileage); for California's largest airports, it is always less expensive to take a car if the parking duration is less than four days (Strauss et al., 1992).

14. Enforcement of AB 2109 has been stalled pending the outcome of federal tax reforms regarding parking cash-out (see Chapter 8).

REFERENCES

Cameron, M. 1991. *Transportation Efficiency: Tackling Southern California's Air Pollution and Congestion.* Oakland: Environmental Defense Fund.

Cervero, R. 1992. *Fostering Commercial Transit Alternatives in Greater Los Angeles.* Los Angeles: The Reason Foundation, Policy Study No. 146.

Davis, F., and D. Burkhatten. 1978. *Vanpooling Institutional Barriers.* Washington, D.C.: U.S. Department of Energy, Transportation Programs Office.

Poole, R., and M. Griffin. 1994. *Shuttle Vans: The Overlooked Transit Alternative.* Los Angeles: The Reason Foundation, Policy Study No. 176.

Shoup, D. 1995. "An Opportunity to Reduce Minimum Parking Requirements." *Journal of the American Planning Association* 61(1): 14-28.

Strauss, R., T. Cherkas, F. Patterson, C. Texeira, and E. Velez. 1992. *The California Airport Shuttle Van Industry.* San Francisco: California Public Utilities Commission, Transportation Division.

Teal, R., M. Bergland, and T. Nemer. 1984. *Urban Transportation Deregulation in Arizona.* Washington, D.C.: Urban Mass Transportation Administration, U.S. Department of Transportation.

CHAPTER 8

Federal Regulations and Policies Affecting Privatization and Commercialization of Paratransit

INTRODUCTION

In the United States, the federal government has been both a *promoter* and a *regulator* of private transit services. As a promoter, its policies have sought mainly to transfer the provision of selected public bus services from public providers to private providers. To a large degree, the privatization policies of the Federal Transit Administration have been aimed at making the production of public transit more efficient: that is, substituting lower-cost private sector inputs (e.g., labor, equipment) to produce public bus services more efficiently (e.g., more miles of service per vehicle). Outside the Americans with Disabilities Act, however, federal policies have done little to promote, and a fair amount to inhibit, the emergence of commercial—free-enterprise, for-profit—paratransit services.

This chapter examines the roles and consequences of federal policies and regulations as they relate to these two aspects of transit service delivery: first, privatization and second, commercialization. Again, it is important to stress the differences. Privatization is fundamentally about transferring some service delivery responsibilities to private operators, with oversight and control of services still residing with public transit authorities. Commercialization is centrally about promoting a competitive marketplace in the urban transit and paratransit sectors, what this book largely focuses on. The chapter closes with recommendations on how federal policy might be revised not only to bring about more privatization, but more importantly, the commercialization of urban transit and paratransit services.

PRIVATIZATION: OPPORTUNITIES AND BARRIERS

Over time, a series of rules and policies have been adopted by various federal agencies, but mainly the Federal Transit Administration, that both promote and inhibit the privatization of mass transit. This section reviews these initiatives and summarizes what we know about their impacts.

Antecedents

Historically, U.S. transit services have been the province of the private sector. From the horse-drawn omnibuses of the 1850s, to the turn-of-the-century electric trolley lines, to the bus companies of the postwar era, public transit was largely owned and operated by private businesses. By *public transit,* I mean mass transit that serves the public at large, not necessarily mass transit that is operated by a government agency.

Public transit ridership reached a peak in the U.S. of nearly 24 billion passenger trips in 1945, at the end of the Second World War. Ten years later, ridership had plummeted to 11 billion trips annually. Rising incomes, the shift from military to domestic production, and pent-up consumer demand after years of wartime rationing led to a postwar boom in the sale of automobiles and single-family homes. Federally subsidized mortgages, cheap land in the suburbs, and the U.S. Congress's passage of the 1956 interstate highway program, the most expensive public works project ever, further encouraged suburbanization, making it increasingly difficult for conventional bus services to compete with the private automobile. By the late 1950s and early 1960s, America's mass transit industry—which was still largely privately owned and operated—was on the verge of collapse. Transit was caught in a vicious cycle of plummeting ridership inducing service cuts that chased more riders away and forced even deeper cuts.

At the insistence of big-city majors who were too cash-strapped to buy failing transit companies and who feared absolute pandemonium if their transit services ceased, Washington first entered the transit picture in the 1960s. In 1961, a special study group on Transportation Policies in the United States found some grounds for federal involvement in transit affairs:

The Federal Government has a vital interest in the free flow of commerce in all parts of the United States, in the preservation and propagation of national wealth and tax production, in the provision of the best living and working conditions for the majority of its citizens, and in establishing the facilities and conditions necessary for the national security. To the extent that inadequate urban transportation facilities and the decline of public transport increase the total cost of daily economic activities, there is cause for immediate attention. (U.S. Senate, 1961: 594)

Referred to as the Doyle Report, this was perhaps the first official document acknowledging a federal responsibility for the welfare of America's struggling transit industry.

In April of the same year, a comprehensive report was released by the Advisory Commission on Intergovernmental Relations outlining possible local, state, and federal roles and responsibilities for the nation's mass transportation services. The report, prepared under Public Law 86-380, suggested a number of reasons that the federal government should promote public transportation, including: (1) the need to protect interstate commerce and defense traffic from urban congestion; (2) the need to offset some of the "pro-highway biases" of federal transportation policies; (3) the need to protect the federal investment in other fields, such as housing and air-pollution abatement; (4) the unique ability of the federal government, with its vast fiscal and managerial resources, to play a lead role in the construction and operation of transit facilities and services; and (5) the need to establish agreements for interstate metropolitan transit services.

These early reports became the driving force behind congressional approval of a small transit demonstration program under the Housing Act of 1961. However, it was the passage of the Urban Mass Transportation Act of 1964 under the Lyndon Johnson administration that provided the first-ever sustained source of capital assistance to transit. This landmark legislation would disburse $3.3 billion in federal grants over 10 years to help municipalities purchase transit systems, replace aging fleets, and build and equip new rapid transit systems.[1] In 1950, only 28 percent of mass transit services in the United States were provided by publicly owned and operated firms; by 1970, this figure exceeded 70 percent.

Washington's protransit shift was not welcomed on all fronts. Critics argued that mass transit is strictly a local concern—since local residents are the primary beneficiaries, they should bear full costs. Some also feared that federal involvement would impose new bureaucratic rules on the transit industry, compromise principles of separation of powers, and ultimately discourage efficient management packages (Smerk, 1964; Ott and Ott, 1969). Economists argued that capital grants would distort investment decisions, resulting in overcapitalization and the premature retirement of buses and rail cars (Hilton, 1974; Tye, 1976). Such concerns were particularly prevalent among local business interests. In a 1963 survey of over 1,000 members of the U.S. Chamber of Commerce, 73 percent felt that Washington should refrain from any financial grants-in-aid to local bus companies.

By the early 1970s, urban riots had called national attention to the plight of the urban poor, the Organization of Petroleum Extracting Countries (OPEC) oil embargo exposed American vulnerability to foreign control of petroleum supplies, and defining events like Earth Day had brought environmental concerns to the forefront of the national policy agenda. Republicans and Democrats alike rallied behind transit. The Richard Nixon administration proved to be one of transit's staunchest advocates, spearheading the passage of the Urban Mass Transportation Assistance Act of 1970, which provided $10 billion over 12 years for new system construction. Even the American Road Builder Association and Secretary of Transportation John A. Volpe, formerly a highway builder, testified before

Congress in support of the legislation. Alan Altshuler (1980, p. 36) credits transit's popularity of the time to the perception that it was good for America's cities:

Though its direct constituency was relatively small, its ideological appeal proved to be extremely broad. Whether one's concern was the economic vitality of cities, protecting the environment, stopping highways, energy conservation, assisting the elderly and handicapped and poor, or simply getting other people off the road so as to be able to drive faster, transit was a policy that could be embraced. This is not to say that transit was an effective way of serving all these objectives, simply that it was widely believed to be so. . . . Transit turned out, in short, to be an ideal centerpiece for urban policy of a conservative administration.

By 1970, transit's annual operating deficit had reached the $300 million mark, a sizable sum considering that the industry had been largely self-supporting just four years earlier. Many local treasuries were beginning to feel the weight of this new financial burden, so for protransit interests, the creation of a federal transit operating assistance program was the next logical step. A confluence of events led to Washington's eventual capitulation to subsidize local transit operations. The Arab oil embargo of 1973–1974, the Watergate scandal and resignation of a president in 1974, New York City's financial crisis, and growing signs of defeat in Vietnam provided a context where newly inaugurated President Gerald Ford sought to mount domestic programs that demonstrated his administration's leadership in difficult times. Barely a week after Ford's confirmation, a delegation of 14 big-city mayors met with the president and, after hard-fought negotiations, won his support for transit operating aid, culminating in the passage of the 1974 National Mass Transportation Assistance Act that provided $11.8 billion in both transit capital and operating assistance through 1980. Throughout the remainder of the 1970s, the transit industry generally found a receptive and supportive political climate in Washington.

As the decade came to a close, federal dollars seemed to be providing very little in the way of tangible dividends, however. Though operating assistance had almost doubled from $3.45 billion to $6.32 billion between 1975 and 1980, ridership (ignoring transfers) was moving at a snail's pace, increasing just 12 percent—from 5.65 billion to 6.36 billion—during the same period. Most of the aid, research showed, was dissipated by inflation, rising wage levels, and diminishing productivity (Sale and Green, 1978; Barnum and Gleason, 1979; Cervero, 1984). Between 1960 and 1980, transit operating expense per seat mile went up 55 percent in constant (inflation-adjusted) dollars; higher wages accounted for three quarters of this increase, and higher factor prices (e.g., for fuel) and lower productivity accounted for much of the remainder (Pickrell, 1985). As critics had feared, operating assistance was not spurring ridership increases, but instead was shielding local operators from escalating costs and productivity declines.

The Ronald Reagan administration entered office in 1980 partly on a mandate to slash federal spending and divest Washington's involvement in local affairs. Mass transit support was one of the first federal programs targeted for elimination. When it became evident that a full withdrawal of federal support would be politically infeasible, the administration's interests shifted to encouraging greater private-sector participation in delivering transit services. It was under the Reagan administration, then, that federal interest in privatization of public transit swung into full force.

Federal Policies and Programs That Promote Privatization

Several sections of the amended 1964 Urban Mass Transportation (UMT) Act first introduced federal rules and guidelines for promoting private sector participation in the planning and delivery of public transit services: Section 8, Section 3, and Section 9. Until the Reagan and Bush administrations, however, the effects of these rules on industry practice were fairly nominal.

Section 8(b)1 stipulates that a comprehensive urban transportation planning process be carried out through metropolitan planning organizations (MPOs). MPOs, through their constituent members, develop plans and programs. *Section 8(o)* directs grantees (MPOs and local public transit authorities) to encourage the maximum feasible participation of private enterprise in the plans and programs funded under the Act.

Section 3(e) of the Act prohibits the use of Federal aid for acquiring or competing with private mass transportation companies, with some exceptions: when the project or program is vital to local interests; when the local program provides for the maximum feasible participation of private transit companies; and when just and adequate compensation is paid to companies for the acquisition of their franchises or property, to the extent required by applicable state or local laws.[2]

Section 9(f) sets out procedures for developing programs and projects funded under the Section 9 formula grant program (the basic transit program which cities rely upon for their transportation needs). Section 9(f) requires that in developing projects and programs, grantees must consult with "interested parties, including private transportation providers" and that they consider the "comments and views. . . . of private transportation providers."[3]

It was not until the Reagan administration that these rules and stipulations of the 1964 act were taken very seriously. Using these three sections as a foundation, in October 1984 the administration adopted and published its policy on "Private Enterprise Participation in the Urban Mass Transportation Program" in the *Federal Register*. The stated intent of this new policy was to provide clear guidelines to "grantees and private sector providers on specified private sector provisions of the UMT Act"—namely, how to execute the Sections 8(o), 3(e), and 9(f) provisions. The implicit agenda, however, was to encourage the competitive contracting of public transit services to private providers. Note Eliot Sclar et al. (1989, p. 9), the policy "charged localities with the responsibility of demonstrating that they were actively encouraging private firms to participate in the provision of new and restructured local services. Unless UMTA was satisfied on this score, localities would not be able to obtain or retain matching funds for these services."

Under this new policy, private operators had to be afforded an opportunity to participate in the development of an MPO's Transportation Improvement Program (TIP), notified of proposed transit service expansions and new opportunities, and consulted on the planning and implementation of new transit programs and projects. The policy also required local transit authorities to periodically (at least every three years) submit documentation of their privatization efforts, including assessments of whether private operators could more efficiently provide existing services. Last, the policy tried to level the bidding "playing field" by specifying a fully allocated cost accounting method to ensure that *all* public agency costs (including overhead) were weighed against the costs of competing private contractors. To make sure these policies were being adhered to and to promote the interests of private firms, an Office of Private Sector Initiatives was established within the Urban Mass Transportation Administration, FTA's predecessor, in 1984.

Prior to the 1984 privatization initiative, a conflict inherent in the UMT Act resided between Section 2(b), that called for transit service "to be operated by public or private mass transportation companies determined by *local needs*," and other sections promoting private participation in transit. Section 2(b) made it possible for localities to claim that labor protection concerns created a "local need" to minimize private involvement. The Reagan administration's privatization policies tipped the scales decidedly in favor of private-sector involvement regardless of local priorities:

UMTA does not consider it acceptable for localities to foreclose opportunities for private enterprise by simply pointing to local barriers. . . . In general, a simple reference in the public record to public agency labor agreements or local policy that calls for direct operation of all mass transportation providers, would not satisfy the private enterprise requirements of the Act" (Urban Mass Transportation Administration, 1984).

Federal Rules and Policies That Inhibit Privatization

Labor Protection Legislation

The chief federal barrier to private-sector provision of transit services is *Section 13(c)* of the UMT Act.[4] This labor protection clause guarantees that public transit employees will not be adversely affected by any program involving federal transit grants.[5] Over time, 13(c) has been interpreted to mean that workers adversely affected by federally assisted projects are guaranteed fair compensation, priority of reemployment if dismissed from work, first opportunity for new jobs created as a result of federal aid, right to collective bargaining, and, taken to the extreme, the right to be the sole provider of local public transit services. Today, most Section 13(c) agreements guarantee transit workers who are dismissed or demoted six years of compensation (or the length of employment, whichever is less). Few compensation payments have been made under 13(c), however, because the transit industry usually handles reduced labor through attrition rather than layoffs (Black, 1995). By the letter of the law, 13(c) protections apply to all affected transit workers, "whether or not they are employees of the recipient of the Federal aid" (Urban Institute, 1990). Occasionally, taxi drivers have filed complaints that federally funded paratransit services (e.g., for the elderly and handicapped) have deprived them of employment or worsened conditions of employment, thus violating 13(c) protections. After a 1977 dispute in Pittsburgh, the Department of Labor (DOL) ruled that a taxi company falls under the definition of transit if at least 15 percent of its revenues come from shared-ride services (Gilbert and Samuels, 1982); since local ordinances normally prohibit taxi ridesharing, most taxi drivers are effectively barred from 13(c) privileges. Since the late 1970s, federal policy has been to limit 13(c) protections to transit workers only (Jennings et al., 1978).

Ironically, the U.S. Congress originally passed the Section 13(c) amendment to the 1964 UMT Act to protect employees of *private enterprises* which, at the time, were rapidly being acquired by local governments. It was feared that public buyouts of private bus companies would harm private workers, although "in fact, most private operator employees in the late 1960's had low wages and were eager to become public sector employees" (Thompson, 1986). With most transit workers becoming civil servants, 13(c) labor protection rights were soon extended to the public sector.

Within the public transit industry, 13(c) is widely recognized as the chief tool used by labor unions to secure favorable collective bargaining agreements and suppress the privatization of public transit. Section 13(c) is often blamed for tying the hands of transit management during contract negotiations by giving labor the equivalent of veto power over federal grants. The section has also stifled efforts to contract out services to private bus and van companies and replace fixed-route with private dial-a-ride services. Many negotiations centered around 13(c) provisions have resulted in language written into contracts that effectively bar competitive bidding of both transit and paratransit services. These include labor's right to all new federally assisted work and clauses prohibiting new paratransit services from competing or displacing line-haul bus services. To avoid such conflicts, a handful of small California communities that have substituted dial-a-ride taxis for fixed-route bus services have avoided 13(c) problems by refusing federal funds altogether.[6]

Section 13(c) labor protection has without question stifled federal initiatives to promote competitive contracting of public transit services. Transit management complains, often off the record, about how debilitating and restrictive 13(c) is. However, an alliance between transit management and union officials has often tempered management's open criticism of 13(c). The section has benefitted both groups. Transit workers want to protect compensation packages and work rule bonuses they fought hard to obtain. Transit managers are usually compensated according to the size of their agency, not by the number of private contracts or measures of service productivity. Also, union clout is considerably more effective than transit management in lobbying for federal capital and operating subsidies. Inevitably, some degree of logrolling—unions help lobby for expanding federal transit programs in return for management limiting the amount of private-sector contracting—results.

Recent attempts to repeal 13(c) have met stiff political resistance and, despite high-pressure lobbying by APTA and others, have been unsuccessful.[7] Some observers expected the November 1994 election of a Republican Congress committed to reducing the federal deficit would open the door to 13(c)'s repeal. In mid-1995, a proposal to repeal 13(c) moved through the Transportation Subcommittee of the House Committee on Appropriations and under the Congressional "Corrections Days" Plan[8] was brought before the House of Representatives, but after vehement opposition from organized labor, the bill did not survive the floor vote. Early in the repeal process, many Washington insiders felt 13(c) would soon be laid to rest. Writes C. Kenneth Orski (1995, pp. 1-2), former associate administrator for UMTA: "For years, it was assumed that 13(c) labor protection provisions were cast in stone. The move to repeal Section 13(c) by the transportation subcommittee and its endorsement by the full House Appropriations Committee testifies to the transit unions' diminished clout in the Republican Congress." The obituary of 13(c) proved to be premature, however. Repealing 13(c) turned out not to be very high on the priority list of the new Congress, and in the wake of intense lobbying pressure from labor interests, Republican leadership of key House and Senate committees showed only lukewarm interest in rolling back labor protection legislation. Some observers now believe that current proposals to consolidate FTA with other agencies into a Surface Transportation Administration and devolve decisions over transit aid programs to state and local governments could eventually lead to 13(c)'s ultimate demise.[9]

Other Barriers

Other than 13(c), there are no significant barriers to private-sector provision of public transit services in the United States other than assorted rules and procedures that end up raising private sector costs. Federal rules, for example, discourage contracting of services to private companies that use their own vehicles; Section 9 funds will only cover up to 50 percent of depreciation costs for private-sector vehicles, whereas Sections 3 and 9 funds cover 80 percent of the capital outlays for publicly purchased vehicles.[10] Private operators receiving federal pass-through funds also face the same accounting and reporting requirements (e.g., Section 15, documentation of "Buy America" procurement compliance) as large public transit agencies.[11] Hiring a compliance administrator to meet federal reporting requirements can sharply raise overhead expenses for many small firms with skeletal staffs. Of course, other federal regulations, such as those related to worker safety and vehicle emission standards, impose compliance costs on private providers, although the resulting public benefits of safer working conditions and cleaner air justify these added expenses. However, because such standards are rarely enforced against independent van operators or unlicensed gypsy cabs, larger paratransit companies who are periodically inspected are placed at a competitive disadvantage. Lastly, private transit and paratransit operators have increasingly relied upon contracting to independents as a means to avoid having to pay worker's compensation and meet various worker safety and health standards. The employment status of drivers who lease vehicles, however, has been periodically called into question during audits by the U.S. Internal Revenue Service (IRS). The taxi and paratransit industries defend leasing to drivers on the grounds that drivers are independent contractors who are in compliance with IRS rulings and that the contractor status of drivers is protected by the "safe harbor provision" passed by Congress to grandfather in companies that have a long and reasonable history of treating their employees as independent contractors (LaGasse, 1991, p. 2).

Effects of Federal Privatization Initiatives

In spite of these barriers, through the force of the Reagan administration's privatization initiatives, contracting of transit services to private vendors picked up momentum during the mid and late 1980s. A 1986 survey showed that 11 percent of urban transit services were being provided by private companies or nonprofit organizations (White et al., 1986); in the same year, over a third of all demand-responsive services were under contract to private firms (Teal, 1988). Today, contracted firms provide all bus services in Honolulu, Phoenix, and Westchester County, New York. And four private management firms run 20 to 25 percent of all publicly owned systems (mostly small ones) (Black, 1995). Some states tried to extend federal privatization initiatives even further, such as in 1988 when Colorado's legislature ordered the Denver Regional Transportation District to contract out at least 20 percent of its bus services. Still, some private bus companies felt government mandates did not go far enough, complaining of unfair bidding and procurement processes, such as the inherent conflict of having public transit authorities serve as the solicitors, cobidders, reviewers, and judges of proposals to operate new bus runs.[12] Overall, the public transit industry in the United States has remained very public indeed. In 1992, only 3 percent of regularly scheduled, fixed-route bus services were operated by private firms (Federal Transit Administration, 1992). In contrast, private contractors provided almost 70 percent of specialized paratransit services for the elderly and handicapped and 30 percent of school bus services.

Early on, proponents held high expectations for transit privatization, hoping it would hold down costs, increase productivity, and spark service innovations. Over the years, dozens of studies have been published on the effects of privatization, and particularly competitive contracting, on public transit performance. The verdict is largely that, consistent with expectations, competitive contracting helped to contain operating costs, increase service output (e.g., revenue miles per operator), and stimulate modest service innovations. Roger Teal (1985) estimated that for fixed-route bus service, private contractors achieved cost savings ranging from

22 to 54 percent; for commuter bus services, cost advantages ranged from 25 to 58 percent. Others found similar rates of cost savings, particularly among big transit operators (Orski, 1985; Johnson and Pikarski, 1985; Cervero, 1988; Morlok, 1988; Downs, 1988). While cost savings accrued from using smaller vehicles, hiring part-time workers, better scheduling, and lower overhead, most savings came from hiring nonunionized workers and paying them less (Rosenbloom, 1988).

Studies also found, however, that the impacts of privatization were uneven, not always positive, and sometimes short-lived. Quite often, service quality (e.g., on-schedule performance, bus upkeep) fell following privatization. And over time, as their services expanded and their workforces enlarged, operating costs of some firms began to rise, approaching those of public transit services. This was partly because private-sector bus drivers organized into unions, bargaining for compensation packages that matched those of their public sector peers. With labor costs accounting for upwards of three-quarters of transit operating costs, the cost advantages of private contracting were being quickly eroded in such instances. In addition, after gaining work rule concessions from employee unions, public transit agencies sometimes won back services. This happened with Tidewater Regional Transit.[13]

In a study of 250 urban bus systems, James Perry and Timlynn Babitsky (1986) found that privately owned and operated systems were measurably more efficient than public ones—for example, averaging more daily vehicle miles per driver. However, they found few efficiency differences between private contractors and public bus operators: private contractors had little more interest in improving efficiency than their public-sector counterparts. John Donahue (1989, p. 48) concluded that "most privately run bus systems remain monopolies, with no competition to inspire innovation and efficiency improvements." Clearly, what matters most is not privatization for its own sake, but competition. A private monopoly is just as likely to produce services that are high cost and inefficient as a public monopoly.

In April 1994, the Bill Clinton administration rescinded the transit privatization policies introduced by the Reagan administration. While FTA continues to support, in concept, private-sector participation, the Clinton administration now views this as a local prerogative. Growing complaints of "unfunded Federal mandates" on both aisles of Congress, combined with the Clinton administration's close alliance with union interests and past disappointments with transit contracting, have apparently brought the privatization chapter of federal transit policy to a close.

COMMERCIALIZATION OF PARATRANSIT: OPPORTUNITIES AND BARRIERS

With regards to commercial transit and paratransit services, the federal government has been instrumental in deregulating interstate traffic and promoting commute alternatives under the aegis of air quality and congestion management programs. However, it has also been the chief architect of a system of highway and public transit financing that makes it all but impossible for many commercial paratransit operators to compete and survive. These issues are addressed in this section.

Federal Policies and Programs that Promote Commercial Paratransit

To date, Washington's permissive attitude toward interstate passenger services, including intrastate bus runs operated by inter-state operators, has done more than any federal initiative to promote commercial transit services. The Interstate Commerce Commission maintains jurisdiction over all interstate freight and passenger services in the United States, and its rules and regulations take precedence over those of state and local governments for operators certified as interstate carriers. Section 10526(2) of the Interstate Commerce Act, as amended, exempts taxicabs and vans that carry six or fewer passengers and that do not operate on fixed routes from regulatory controls, other than meeting minimum liability insurance and vehicle fitness standards. As noted in Chapter 3, private operators in the greater New York metropolitan area have taken advantage of these exemptions to provide frequent van and bus services between Staten Island, Manhattan, and northern New Jersey. Other metropolitan areas with fairly high volumes of interstate van services include greater Boston, Hartford, Philadelphia, Washington, D.C., Charlotte, Cincinnati, Chicago, Milwaukee, St. Louis, and Kansas City, Missouri. What effects the proposed demise of the ICC or the transfer of its functions to the Department of Transportation will have on interstate paratransit oversight is unclear; however, it seems unlikely that Washington will introduce tighter regulatory controls. More likely, federal control over cross-boundary paratransit traffic will be eased and potentially removed altogether.

The greatest boon to the interstate commercial bus and van industry was the passage of the Bus Regulatory Reform Act of 1982. Besides lifting entry, exit, pricing, and service controls over intercity bus services operated by interstate carriers (e.g., Greyhound), the act also provided for the preemption of state and local regulations that had previously burdened these services. Common carriers can now apply to the ICC for both interstate and intrastate operating authority, or for interstate authority alone. Certified carriers can pick up and discharge passengers between intrastate points over their interstate routes. Market entry is restricted to carriers that are "fit, willing, and able," defined as meeting minimum vehicle safety, driver qualification, and liability insurance standards. Entrants need not prove that an unfilled public need will be met. Anyone protesting the application bears the burden of proof that the proposed service is "not consistent with the public interest." In practice, this has proven to be next to impossible as long as applicants meet minimum standards. Of course, many intercity bus operators in the United States do not meet the 1982 act's interstate service requirements and thus cannot take advantage of the federal government's more permissive policies. Passage of the act, however, signaled congressional intent to liberalize, wherever possible, intrastate policies on initiating new bus services by allowing for federal preemption and shifting any burden of proof away from applicants (Reznick and Bardack, 1994). The act has also served as a model for states like Texas that have recently deregulated intercity bus and van services.

Recent federal initiatives like the 1990 Clean Air Act Amendments, 1991 national surface transportation act (ISTEA), and the Clinton administration's Empowerment Zone/Enterprise Communities (EZ/EC) programs have also helped to create a policy environment that is conducive to expanded commercial transit services. The 1991 act promotes multimodal transportation and allows for greater flexibility in expending federal transportation funds, although in practice few ISTEA dollars have gone to commercial transit operators other than through competitive contracts.[14] Under ISTEA, MPOs which are in a position to direct flexible funds to commercial paratransit are consensual organizations governed mainly by board members from public agencies, including transit authorities, who vehemently resist efforts to divert fiscal resources away from their constituents.

The CAAA includes in its list of 16 possible Transportation Control Measures (TCM) for air quality planning in nonattainment areas "programs for improved public transit" and "programs for the provision of all forms of high-occupancy, shared-ride services." So far, no nonattainment areas have aggressively pursued commercial paratransit, though some Employee Commute Options programs have included employer-financed, privately operated shuttle services. The EZ/EC program, approved in 1993 as part of the Economic Empowerment Act, provides special grants and tax credits to over 100 designated urban and rural areas across the United States, with emphasis given to job creation programs, including community-based paratransit that employs residents to drive and dispatch vans to suburban jobs and neighborhood retail centers. Supporting this program has been the Livable Communities Initiative launched by the FTA which targets federal transit dollars at, among other things, improving neighborhood transit services. Recent grants have gone to rehabilitating rail transit stations in Chicago, Cleveland, New York City, Baltimore, and St. Louis, including improving sidewalk connections and staging areas for shuttle vans and other paratransit feeder services.

A case can also be made that the 1990 Americans with Disabilities Act has been a stimulant to the commercial paratransit industry by recognizing the need for improved shared-ride, door-to-door services for certain segments of the nation's population. The act requires public transit agencies to offer complementary paratransit service to persons unable to use regular buses in areas served by fixed bus routes. The law also requires all common carrier vehicles purchased or leased after August 1990 to be readily accessible to and usable by those with disabilities, including people who use wheelchairs. The Act, however, includes several exemptions from the 100 percent accessibility rule that are important to paratransit providers: (1) automobiles are exempt; (2) if a new vehicle is to be used "solely in a demand responsive system," the vehicle does not need to be wheelchair accessible if it can be demonstrated that the entire system provides a level of service to the disabled that is equivalent to that provided to the general public; and (3) not all minivans (carrying seven or fewer passengers) need to be wheelchair accessible, even in fixed-route service, if it can be demonstrated that the entire system provides a comparable level of service.

Federal Policies that Inhibit the Commercialization of Paratransit

The most serious impediments to commercial paratransit are the federal (as well as local and state) subsidies that keep most public transit systems afloat. When local transit agencies operate bus services at fares that are subsidized by as much as 70 percent, private operators charging unsubsidized fares are hard pressed to compete. Experiments with legalized commercial jitneys in Los Angeles in the mid-1980s and Houston in the mid-1990s that went belly up just after a few months of service bear this out.

In 1993, average transit fares nationwide covered only 37 percent of operating costs and none of the billions spent on acquiring new buses, extending rail lines, and other capital purchases. Federal assistance made up around 11 percent of operating subsidies and 6 percent of total operating costs in 1993 (Table 8.1). This is considerably less than the 30 percent of operating subsidies and 17 percent of operating expenses covered by federal aid in 1980, the year the Reagan administration took office committed to eliminating federal transit subsidies. By allocating operating assistance according to formulas based mainly on population size and density, federal aid has done little to deter rising operating deficits and reward efficiency.[15] While federal subsidies today play a relatively small role in supporting public transit operators, one could argue that since federal aid helped induce inefficiencies and fiscal dependency, Washington bears a proportionally greater responsibility in eliminating the persistent distorting effects of subsidies.

It is on the capital side, however, where federal assistance is most strongly felt. In 1993, $2.42 billion, or 41.5 percent of all capital revenues to public transit, came from Washington; the federal government approved some $3.47 billion in new capital grants that year, the most ever. In all, federal dollars made up 24 percent of all subsidies and covered 15 percent of all transit operating and capital expenditures in 1993; federal aid amounted to $0.53 per unlinked passenger trip. While central government assistance to mass transit is prevalent around the world, in few other nonsocialist, industrialized societies is it as generous as in the United States. Since the 1970s, U.S. transit authorities have received more subsidies per passenger than in most Western European countries (Pucher, 1988; Button and Rietveld, 1993). Outside the Czech Republic, almost all European countries have sharply reduced transit subsidies in recent years, in particular countries like Great Britain, Italy, and Norway, but also in formerly socialist countries of Central Europe (Pucher and Kurth, 1995).

Table 8.1.
Government Subsidies to Public Transit in the United States, 1970-1993, by Level of Government and Type of Subsidy (in $millions, unadjusted)

	1970	1975	1980	1985	1990	1993
Operating Subsidies						
Federal	0	408	1,094	940	970	1,042
State	30	549	862	1,105	2,971	3,708
Local	288	944	1,749	3,874	5,327	4,964
Total	318	1,901	3,705	6,919	9,268	9,714
Capital Subsidies						
Federal	133	1,287	2,787	2,510	2,873	2,416
State & Local	67	322	647	996	2,063	2,397
State	—	—	303	568	697	1,335
Local	—	—	344	428	1,366	1,062
Total	200	1,609	3,434	3,506	4,936	4,813
Total Subsidies						
Federal (%)	26	48	54	33	27	24
State & Local (%)	74	52	46	67	73	76
State (%)	—	—	16	26	26	35
Local (%)	—	—	30	41	47	41

Sources: Pucher (1995b), American Public Transit Association (1995).

It is important to recognize, however, that subsidies to transit riders pale in comparison to those given to motorists. Roadway users in the United States pay only around 60 percent of the costs of highway construction, maintenance, administration, and law enforcement through fuel taxes and user fees. The remaining 40 percent (amounting to $30.7 billion in 1990) is subsidized through general government revenues (often hidden in the budgets for police departments to patrol highways, ambulance services to respond to roadside emergencies, and municipal utility expenditures for lighting highways) (MacKenzie et al., 1992).[16] In contrast, roadway user taxes exceed government roadway expenditures in every European country. The ratio of roadway taxes to expenditures range from 5.1:1 in The Netherlands to 1.3:1 in Switzerland, but most European countries collect at least twice as much from roadway user taxes as they spend on highways. European fuel taxes per liter range from five to ten times the tax rate in the United States, resulting in fuel prices that are two to four times as high; fuel tax rates in Canada are even twice as high as in the United States. Clearly, government taxation policies have made private car ownership and use much more expensive in Europe than in the United States, a key reason why transit carries 14 to 20 percent of all motorized trips in England, Denmark, Italy, and Switzerland, versus just 3 percent in the United States (Pucher, 1995a, 1995b).

Adding the social costs of externalities not borne directly by motorists, such as air pollution and highway accidents, raises the estimated annual subsidies given to America's highway users anywhere between $300 billion on the low end and $780 billion on the high end.[17] Among the negative externalities that have been attributed to motorists are air pollution (health and aesthetic impacts), noise pollution (reduced property values, stress, health impacts), emission of greenhouse gases that cause global climate change, foreign oil dependency, oil spill damage to the environment, vehicle and tire scrappage, loss of open space and wetlands, water pollution related to road salt use, and water run-off damage.[18] Federal policies account for a significant share of both direct and hidden subsidies to motorists. An estimated 72 percent of all vehicle miles travelled (VMT) occurs on federally funded Interstate and urban arterial roads, although these facilities account only for around 11 percent of the nation's total road and street mileage (Federal Highway Administration, 1995). The responsibility for failing to pass on to motorists such external costs as greenhouse gas emissions, expenses associated with the strategic petroleum reserve and maintaining a foreign military presence to secure oil imports, and oil spill damage to the environment also lies largely with the federal government.[19] James MacKenzie et al. (1992) place these costs alone at nearly $60 billion annually (in 1989 dollars).

Overall, huge subsidies to highway users and transit riders, direct and otherwise, have created market distortions that make it nearly impossible for commercial paratransit to compete to any significant degree. Until lasting changes are made in how both roadways and transit services are financed, commercial paratransit will have a difficult time gaining any kind of foothold in America's mobility marketplace.

DIRECTIONS FOR FEDERAL POLICY REFORMS

On balance, federal policies have suppressed the emergence of a viable commercial paratransit sector by heavily subsidizing its chief competitors—public bus services and the private automobile. On the regulatory side, the federal government has been a leader in liberalizing controls over bus services, though these actions have largely been limited to its interstate jurisdiction. Today, there are few federal regulatory barriers to initiating commercial transit or paratransit operations, whether intraurban or intercity. While a barrier to privatization, the Section 13(c) labor protection clause *is not* a significant barrier to the commercialization of transit.

Any federal policy reforms aimed at stimulating America's fledgling commercial paratransit industry must unavoidably look at ways of reducing the perverse impacts of existing subsidy programs. Efforts to do so, however, will inevitably meet with stiff resistance on many fronts. The Clinton administration's parking cash-out proposal, included as part of the 1993 Climate Change Action Plan, has been the most significant federal attempt to date to remove hidden subsidies to motorists. By giving workers the option of receiving a free parking space or a cash allowance and exempting up to $75 in employer-provided monthly transit passes and vouchers from taxable income, this initiative would promote transit and van riding by helping to level the urban mobility playing field. Because the program would only apply to parking spaces leased by employers from a third party, its effects would be somewhat diluted. As of early 1996, no legislative action had yet been taken to enact the federal cash-out program. Congress seems to be backing off of its get-tough-with-free-parking position, as few politicians seem willing to vigorously fight for higher parking charges, even if such charges promise to reduce automobile travel. A recent congressional plan to charge federal employees commercial rates for parking was abandoned in the face of strong opposition from employee unions. The proposal would have required more than 200,000 federal workers in the Washington, D.C., area to pay as much as $1,800 a year for parking instead of subsidized rates in government garages that are as low as $15 per month.

More effective than parking cash-out programs would be the passage of legislation that substantially raises federal motor fuel and excise taxes, closer to that found in Canada and Europe. In these countries, private car taxation has long been a valued source of general revenues, used to support a host of social programs, including expanded mass transit. Of course, diverting higher gasoline tax receipts to public transit agencies would do little to help commercial paratransit. Diverting them to transportation vouchers for the poor, however, would. Creating a national program of user-side subsidies, such as ridesharing vouchers, would not only prevent federal transfer payments from lulling public transit agencies into inefficient practices but would also stimulate competition and innovations in the marketplace as paratransit firms seek to win over voucher-holders. The UMTA experimented with user-side subsidy programs in the 1970s with varying degrees of success; however, provider-side subsidies to public transit systems today remain the rule of the land for political reasons (Kirby, 1981).

John Pucher (1995b) maintains that substantially higher motoring taxes in Europe gained political acceptance because they were implemented before private car ownership became widespread. The high cost of automobile ownership and use has become an accepted fact of life in Europe. In contrast, any attempt to increase motor vehicle taxes in the United States is viewed as an attack on the American way of life and is vigorously opposed by the vast majority of voters and by powerful automobile and oil industry interests. With fiscal conservatism sweeping the country, few politicians want to risk offending their constituents. Referenda to raise state motor fuel taxes by one to two cents per gallon in California, Arizona, and Washington state were handily rejected by voters in 1994 and 1995. By mid-1996, the U.S. Congress actually sought to lower federal gasoline tax rates to offset the price surges brought on by below-normal Middle Eastern supplies, underscoring just how politically volatile an issue fuel taxation can be. Perhaps the one element of fiscal conservatism that could eventually work in favor of higher motoring fees are recent Congressional efforts to redirect dedicated highway dollars to the general treasury to help offset the federal deficit. Over time, the use of motor fuel and excise tax proceeds to help balance the budget could end up increasing federal fuel taxes to make up losses to highway programs.

In sharp contrast to the optimism many held for the future of transit funding when ISTEA was passed in 1991, it now appears increasingly likely that coming years will bring substantial cuts in subsidy support from Washington. Congress's continuing efforts to reduce the deficit may result in the eventual phaseout of federal operating assistance altogether. For fiscal year 1995, Congress cut operating subsidies by 11 percent from the previous year, to $710 million annually; for fiscal year 1996, subsidies are fixed at $400 million, or 44 percent below 1995 allotments. Many transit industry officials portend a future of substantially higher fares, service cuts, and possibly even worker layoffs. While federal cuts will likely spur selective competitive contracting of bus runs, as long as America's motoring public continues to enjoy hundreds of billions of dollars in hidden subsidies each year, these trends will likely have minimal effect on stimulating commercial paratransit. To the degree that poor, inner-city neighborhoods suffer significant cuts in bus services, informal and unlicensed jitney and similar shared-ride services might expand in these areas.

Transit supporters often make the argument that transit aid serves as a countervailing subsidy, helping to offset the distorting effects of historically underpricing the private automobile (Sherman, 1972; Vickery, 1973); given the fact that highway programs have largely been spared of recent Congressional axe wielding, this argument retains some credibility. Economists argue that in an optimal world, neither highways nor transit would be subsidized since underpricing of both modes encourages excessive travel, leading to inefficient, dispersed land-use patterns (Walters, 1967; Gordon and Theobald, 1980; Wachs, 1981). As noted, the best (i.e., least distorting) way of directing federal transit aid would be in the form of user-side vouchers, targeted at the intended beneficiaries—the poor and transportation needy.[20] To the degree that provider-side transit subsidies remain (for political reasons), they should be refashioned so as to reward efficiency—for example, pegged to ridership increases. Indexing operating and capital assistance to service- and cost-effectiveness measures, like changes in annual transit trips per capita and riders per dollar outlay, would encourage some public agencies to competitively bid out more services to the private sector. This would still do little to stimulate free-enterprise, commercial paratransit, however. The best way to accomplish this would be to redirect federal aid to an impartial regional body that might be more receptive to commercial transit and paratransit, especially if it can increase federal receipts by raising ridership. Ideally, this regional authority would not be an MPO, whose board members normally include public transit officials. One possibility would be to form a regional transportation policy commission whose members are directly elected on the basis of their commitments to serving the mobility interests of the region at-large. To date, such commissions have largely been governed by political appointments and in several cases, they have been merged with transit operators.[21] Consolidated cities like Indianapolis have recently managed to wrestle away control over dedicated sales tax receipts from the local transit authority; the city plans to use these proceeds to competitively contract out jitney and commuter van services (see Chapter 6). Directing federal transit aid to regional transportation commissions or other nonoperating entities would likely spur local and state regulatory reforms that open the marketplace up to commercial paratransit providers. Until impartial regional authorities can be formed to apportion transit aid more effectively, implementing principles set by the Competitive Services Board that remove public transit agencies from the contract bid decision-making process may be the most realistic way of stimulating competitive paratransit.[22]

One could argue that capital subsidies earmarked for fixed-guideway systems should be eliminated altogether, in part to encourage more commercial paratransit; however, capital subsidies are likely to endure as long as there is political patronage and political capital to be gained. However, a different form of transit investment might be considered. The Federal Transit Administration could promote commercial paratransit by redirecting more Section 3 and Section 9 capital grant monies away from rail projects to High Occupancy Vehicle facilities, busway projects, and other investments that allow for different operations of more flexible forms of transit. In 1993, less than 1.5 percent of all federal transit capital grants went to HOV and busway projects. High Occupancy Vehicle lanes are essential toward making shared-ride modes time competitive with single-occupant vehicles. In Ottawa, express buses using over 30 kilometers of dedicated transitways and shared HOV lanes carry more riders per capita than any similar-sized transit system in North America, at one-third the capital cost per kilometer of comparable size Canadian light rail systems (Bonsall and Stacy, 1993). In Houston, carpools and vanpools comprise nearly two-thirds of all passenger traffic on its present 64-mile, five-corridor HOV network, the largest in North America (Sedlak, 1995). A survey of private paratransit operators in Southern California found stronger support for HOV lanes than congestion pricing or any other public policy that might reduce automobile dependency (Cervero, 1992).

The argument for directing more capital funds in the transit sector to HOV facilities is not new. More than 30 years ago, John Meyer, John Kain, and Martin Wohl (1965) concluded that: "Imaginative use of new technologies and facilities might bring about substantial economies in urban transportation. . . . Some of the more promising and immediate are reserved lanes for buses and small cars, special bus highways, and priority access for public transit vehicles moving onto controlled-access highways." Today, John Kain remains a passionate believer in the virtues of busways and HOV facilities over rail transit technologies, often arguing that most North American cities that turn to light rail investments are motivated more by politics than sound economics (see Kain, 1990; Kain et al., 1992).

Another policy shift that would benefit commercial paratransit over the long run would be to devote larger shares of ISTEA funding support for the Intelligent Transportation System (ITS) to programs that enhance paratransit service delivery, like automated vehicle locator and dispatching systems, real-time traveller information systems, and interactive on-line ride matching. To date, most ITS support has gone toward more futuristic uses of advanced communication technologies, such as in-vehicle navigation systems and collision avoidance systems. While the goal of making the private automobile smarter and safer is unimpeachable, unless similar strides are made in improving the performance characteristics of shared-ride vans, taxis, and minibuses, ITS programs could ultimately result in commercial paratransit losing market share. As to the potential of smart paratransit technologies to tap new market niches and attract legions of former motorists to shared-ride vehicles, we turn to Part 3 of the book.

NOTES

1. Prior to the passage of the 1964 act, the U.S. Congress debated the question of whether public or private providers are best suited for providing local transit services. A precursor to the 1964 act which set the foundation for encouraging private sector participation in transit was Senate Bill S.6 (88th U.S. Congress, 1st Session). In discussing the provisions of the bill, the principal author, Senator Harrison Williams, stated that "The public would not have to operate the transit facilities and equipment itself. It could provide for their operation by lease or other arrangements. Thus, every locality would remain free to choose public or private operation of its transportation system or any combination of the two" (U.S. Congress, Congressional Record, 1963).

2. Section 3 is a discretionary and formula capital grant program that provides funding for new rail projects (new starts), the improvement and maintenance of existing rail and other fixed guideway systems, and the rehabilitation of bus systems. The Intermodal Surface Transportation Efficiency Act (ISTEA) of 1991 made significant changes in the distribution of Section 3 fixed guideway funds, allocating them by formula rather than on a discretionary basis. New rail starts are still funded on a discretionary basis, according to benefit-cost criteria.

3. Section 9 provides capital and operating assistance to urbanized (50,000 or more in population) areas. Funds are apportioned by a statutory formula based on population and population density for areas under 200,000, and based on population, population density, and transportation performance factors for areas over 200,000.

4. Section 13(c) was recently renumbered as provision 5333(b) of the Federal Transit Act. However, this provision is still widely referred to as 13(c) within the transit industry; thus 13(c) is the term used here.

5. Until the 1960s, employees of private transit companies were guaranteed the right to collective bargaining under the National Labor Relations Act of 1935. When transit systems converted to public ownership, workers were no longer covered by this act, but rather by state laws that often denied public workers the right to organize. This prompted union leaders to seek federal protection. Section 13(c) states: "It shall be a condition of any assistance under Section 3 of this Act that fair and equitable arrangements are made, as determined by the Secretary of Labor, to protect the interests of employees affected by such assistance." "Arrangements" to protect mass transit employees include: (1) the preservation of rights, privileges, and benefits (including the continuation of pension rights and benefits) under existing collective bargaining agreements or other arrangements; (2) the continuation of collective bargaining rights; (3) the protection of individual

employees from a worsening of their positions with respect to their employment; (4) the assurance of employment and priority of reemployment; and (5) paid training or retraining programs (U.S. Department of Labor, 1993). Originally, 13(c) protections were afforded only to employees affected by Section 3 capital assistance. The protections were later extended to include operating assistance for urbanized (Section 9) and nonurbanized (Section 18) areas.

6. Besides the substance of 13(c) itself, the process of certifying compliance with 13(c) has become, in the minds of some public transit managers, so burdensome and unpredictable that many have felt forced to accede to the wishes of unions on almost any aspects of negotiations related to 13(c). 13(c) takes effect with the initial application for federal transit assistance. Before the Federal Transit Administration (FTA) can release funds, the U.S. Department of Labor (DOL) must certify that the applicant is in compliance with 13(c). Initially, DOL notifies unions representing transit employees in the service area of the project for which transit assistance is pending. Most 13(c) agreements are "recurring referrals," signifying that DOL has certified labor protection agreements with similar grants from the past and is proposing to certify the new project based on previous arrangements. Typically, DOL approves recurring referrals within two to four weeks. If there are no previously certified labor protection agreements, or one or both parties want to renegotiate existing agreements, DOL treats this as an "open referral." To facilitate negotiations, the American Public Transit Association and national labor organizations have developed a Model Agreement. While most transit operators and unions are signatories to the agreement, many are not. Once agreements are reached and signed into contract, labor protection guarantees are designed to last in perpetuity. The Model Agreement states: "Any signatory employer or labor organization may individually withdraw from the agreement . . . by serving notice of its intentions to withdraw; provided, however, that any rights of the parties . . . shall continue in full force and effect. . . ."

Normally, projects involving the contracting of transit services to private companies are treated as "open referrals" and there are no deadlines for certification. If unions and transit management cannot reach an agreement, DOL will mediate. If the parties remain deadlocked after good-faith bargaining and mediation efforts have been exhausted, DOL must decide based on the evidence at hand whether to certify compliance with 13(c). Rarely, however, do things ever go this far. Unions enjoy tremendous leverage under the open referral system. They can delay agreements to secure more favorable protections. Thus, 13(c) becomes a bargaining chip, and transit management often accedes to union demands in order to receive federal assistance in a timely manner.

Still, the certification process can drag on for a long time. A 1994 APTA survey found that around 25 percent of the 135 transit agency respondents experienced significant delays in the 13(c) certification process, with an average delay of 25 weeks. Transit agencies and APTA have openly complained about the opaqueness of DOL's rulings, claiming that "grantees are often in the dark as to the nature and scope of their 13(c) responsibilities, as well as to the liabilities and obligations that may be created by certain actions" (APTA, 1994). They complain that DOL's rulings are often concluding statements, with no rationale, no foundation for standards, and no clear precedence. Transit agencies and APTA have joined forces with FTA in seeking to set deadlines for 13(c) certification. Unions and DOL view deadlines as an unfair constraint on the negotiations process, a constraint which might weaken labor's position. Several joint FTA and DOL attempts to refine the certification process have failed. As FTA has moved from a quarterly funding cycle to funding on an as-ready basis, DOL has come under increasing pressure to act on 13(c) applications promptly.

7. In their February 28, 1995, testimony to the House Subcommittee on Transportation and Infrastructure, APTA officials recommended a gradual and, they hoped, politically feasible approach to reforming 13(c), taking the position that 13(c) should not be applied to grants for operating assistance, routine rolling stock replacement, or other projects that have no adverse impacts on workers or that are required to carry out federal mandates; labor protection agreements should "sunset," or expire, within a fixed period of time and should not carry over from contractor to contractor; the certification process should be transferred from DOL to FTA; a time limit of 60 days should be placed on certification; all certification decisions should have a legal basis; and the burden of proof that 13(c) protections have been violated should shift from applicants (e.g., transit agencies) to complainants (e.g., unions).

8. Under Corrections Days, "corrections" bills that repeal or modify existing rules and statutes deemed burdensome and unpopular are dealt with under a procedure patterned after the existing suspension calendar. Items brought up for floor consideration bypass the normal committee approval process. The Speaker of the House and committee chairs are allowed to place items on the corrections calendar.

9. In its appropriations bill, the First Session of the 104th Congress gave its blessing to the U.S. Department of Transportation to proceed with its reorganization plan of surface transportation. Consolidation would likely mean that transit operating and capital grant programs would be combined into a larger and more modally flexible "surface block grant" package. Elimination of 13(c) is unlikely under any reauthorization of the Federal Transit Act (the predecessor to the UMT Act). As part of a new surface transportation act, however, there might a window of opportunity for revising or repealing 13(c). Highway interests already complain of being overburdened by labor protection guarantees of the Bacon-Davis Act for road and bridge construction projects and would likely fight efforts to extend protections further for all surface transportation projects under the guise of 13(c).

10. Section 3 and Section 9 capital and operating assistance is technically available to private operators, though only if they are sponsored by a designated public recipient. Such sponsorship is rare, and if it does occur, it involves considerable red tape and precludes private firms from becoming both the administrator and provider of local transit services.

11. The Section 15 Uniform System of Accounts and Records also requires the reporting of nonfinancial data for contractors operating less than 50 vehicles. Surveys must be carried out to estimate revenue and passenger miles of service. Contractors operating more than 50 vehicles must file a complete and separate Section 15 submittal.

12. Instances of bidders complaining that transit agencies were conducting unfair and sometimes sham bidding processes were common. High insurance and bonding requirements set by transit agencies sometimes prohibited small- and medium-size firms from competing. Some Requests for Proposals set minimum compensation rates for drivers, thus equalizing labor costs between the agency and private bidders. Also, some agencies were accused of canceling solicitations and using initial outside bids to renegotiate internal wage packages and work rules. Other common complaints included: insufficient time to prepare for prebid meetings and RFP submittal; fixed, short-term contracts that discouraged private investment in new vehicles and equipment (given no assurances of long-term contract commitments); and the excessive time and cost involved in filing protests

against alleged unfair public-sector bids and, given that transit authorities review and act upon filed grievances, the minimal likelihood that protests would have much impact.

13. Tidewater Regional Transit (TRT), serving the Norfolk–Virginia Beach area, was one of the first U.S. transit agencies to introduce competitive contracting, beginning in 1979, and has been one of the few to contract out already-existing services. By replacing regular-size buses with privately contracted demand-responsive vans along low-density corridors starting in 1981, TRT reduced its subsidy per passenger for these corridors by 64 percent within two years. This prompted the TRT employees' union to file a suit, alleging infringement of drivers' section 13(c) protectionist rights; however, because cost savings were so significant and TRT was already certified as being in compliance with 13(c), the legal challenges did not hold up in court. Seeing the writing on the wall, during 1983–1986 contract negotiations, TRT's labor representatives agreed to two major concessions: one, a reduction in guaranteed pay from 8 to 7.5 hours, and second, the creation of a minibus driver position at a reduced salary, with no work rules and few benefits. Because of productivity gains, TRT's minibus paratransit division was able to win back dial-a-ride services from private taxi companies (Cervero, 1986). In the case of Houston Metro, express bus runs were returned to the public operator after private operating costs rose 40 percent between 1979 and 1984 (Cervero, 1988).

14. Over the six-year life of the $151 billion ISTEA authorization, over half of all funds are theoretically eligible for transit programs, including over $70 billion in "flexible" highway funds. Because of the tremendous highway construction and maintenance backlog across the United States, very few flexible highway dollars have been diverted to transit. Moreover, actual federal funding has fallen far short of the original authorizations of the ISTEA bill, which also has set aside over $6 billion in Congestion Management and Air Quality (CMAQ) funds that can be applied to transit service "which has been specifically developed for air quality benefits" as well as to "shared ride services." Overall, the actual subsidy levels of public transit represent only about one-fifth of the total ISTEA funding potentially available for public transit (including various flexible and transferable funds) (Pucher, 1995b).

15. Shrinking operating subsidies appear to have had some positive impacts on the transit industry. Since 1985, for example, labor productivity has risen and operating costs per vehicle mile have increased by less than the rate of inflation (Federal Transit Administration, 1992).

16. Of course, private taxi and paratransit providers receive these subsidies as well, though less on a per-passenger basis than most single-occupant private automobile trips. Among the hidden municipal service and administrative costs are: police efforts to reduce highway-related crime, such as stolen vehicles, court costs for litigation, emergency costs for responding to highway accidents by firefighters, paramedics, and police, and utility outlays for operating street lights and traffic signals. MacKenzie et al. (1992) place these municipal services costs at around $68 million annually (1990 dollars), or about 3 cents per vehicle mile, based on a study of vehicle-related service expenditures in Pasadena, California, by Hart (1985). Litman (1995) estimates these costs to be 1 cent per vehicle mile for urban areas based on work by Miller and Moffett (1993).

17. In their work for the World Resources Institute, an environmental advocacy organization, MacKenzie et al. (1992) estimate the annual social costs not internalized by motorists to be around $300 billion (in 1989 dollars). Lee's (1995) very methodical analysis puts the figure closer to $374 billion (in 1991 dollars). Miller and Moffett (1993) come up with a range, from $380 to $660 billion annually, depending on cost assumptions.

Litman's (1995) research claims American motorists receive $778 billion in subsidies annually.

18. The cost of motor vehicle pollution emissions remains a controversial subject. MacKenzie et al. (1992) report the annual costs of motor-vehicle-generated ozone, reflected in health effects, lost labor hours, and reduced agricultural revenues, to be $9 billion annually. Small and Kazimi (1994) place the average cost of air pollution at about 2 cents per VMT, nationally. The cost of vehicle-generated noise pollution are less documented; Hokanson (1982) estimated the effects of automobile and truck noise levels on lost property values to be around $9 billion annually. McPhee (1993) estimates that 3 billion scrap tires inhabit the United States and assigns $1 per tire for cleanup.

19. The strategic petroleum reserve is an underground petroleum storage facility maintained by the U.S. government, at a cost that includes interest on the net accumulated stock (568 million barrels at $15 per barrel) plus annual operating costs (Lee, 1995). Environmentalists have argued that the cost of maintaining a large military contingency in the Middle East region is tied to the demands for imported oil created by high levels of automobile and truck travel. In their work, MacKenzie et al. (1992) allocated half of the estimated $50 billion annually associated with the strategic petroleum reserve and maintaining a military presence in the Middle East to motor vehicles. Lee (1995) largely ignores these purported motorist subsidies. In coming up with a dollar figure for greenhouse gas emissions, MacKenzie et al. claim motorists should pay about $27 billion extra per year to reduce carbon-dioxide emissions so as to comply with international standards for reducing greenhouse gases.

20. Subsidies targeted at specific groups of users would allow individuals to patronize the transit provider of their choice, encouraging greater competition and thus over the long run more efficient, less costly services. In an evaluation of user-side demonstration projects implemented by several small U.S. transit systems, Kirby (1981) found them to be administratively feasible and cost-effective ways of targeting fare reductions and spurring competition among taxis, dial-a-buses, and fixed-route bus systems. The programs were discontinued, however, for political reasons. Granting total consumer sovereignty over how income transfers are spent weakens the donor's control over monies. Also, subsidy transfers to transit agencies, unlike vouchers for the poor, have greater visibility, reach a broader and more politically powerful constituency, and thus have greater political appeal. Some local politicians view transferring income to unionized transit labor as more advantageous than providing unemployed, inner-city residents another entitlement.

21. The Los Angeles Transportation Commission merged with the Southern California Rapid Transit District to form the Los Angeles County Metropolitan Transportation Authority (MTA) and the Orange County Transportation Commission merged with the Orange County Transit District to form the Orange County Transportation Authority (OCTA). These mergers were designed to reduce bureaucracy, to integrate transit planning, design, operations, and financing, and to create economies of scale.

22. The board has adopted the following principles: (1) operating agencies that contract out services should assign responsibility for recommendations on contracting to a branch or unit of government that is separate from the agency's own services unit, at as high a level as possible within the organization; (2) private operators, the MPO, and all interested agencies should be included in the analyses of which routes or services can be provided by the private sector; (3) states should consider establishing specialized offices to promote competition and private sector contracting in transit; and (4) flexibility in the

use of funds should be a factor in deciding which agency should contract services (see Urban Institute, 1990).

REFERENCES

Altshuler, A. 1980. *The Urban Transportation System: Politics and Policy Innovation.* Cambridge, Massachusetts: MIT Press.

American Public Transit Association. 1994. "APTA 13(c) Report." Washington, D.C.: APTA.

———. 1995. *1994–1995 Transit Fact Book.* Washington, D.C.: APTA.

Barnum, D., and J. Gleason. 1979. *Measuring the Influences of Subsidies on Transit Efficiency and Effectiveness.* Washington, D.C.: Urban Mass Transportation Administration, U.S. Department of Transportation.

Black, A. 1995. *Urban Mass Transportation Planning.* New York: McGraw-Hill.

Bonsall, J., and R. Stacey. 1993. "A Rapid Transit Strategy into the Next Century." Ottawa: OC Transpo.

Button, K., and P. Rietveld. 1993. "Financing Urban Transport Projects in Europe." *Transportation* 20: 251-265.

Cervero, R. 1984. "The Anatomy of Transit Operating Deficits." *Urban Law and Policy* 6(3): 477-497.

———. 1986. *Ripple Effects of Transit Service Contracting.* Houston: Rice Center for Urban Mobility.

———. 1988. *Transit Service Contracting: Cream-Skimming or Deficit-Skimming?* Washington, D.C.: Urban Mass Transportation Administration, U.S. Department of Transportation.

———. 1992. *Fostering Commercial Transit Alternatives in Greater Los Angeles.* Los Angeles: Reason Foundation, Policy Study No. 146.

Donahue, J. 1989. *The Privatization Decision.* New York: Basic Books.

Downs, C. 1988. "Private and Public Local Bus Services Compared: The Case of New York City." *Transportation Quarterly* 42(4): 553-570.

Federal Highway Administration. 1995. *Our Nation's Highways.* Washington, D.C.: U.S. Department of Transportation.

Federal Transit Administration. 1992. *National Transit Summaries and Trends.* Washington, D.C.: U.S. Department of Transportation.

Gilbert, G., and R. Samuels. 1982. *The Taxicab: An Urban Transportation Survivor.* Chapel Hill: University of North Carolina Press.

Gordon, P., and P. Theobald. 1980. "Urban Transit Subsidies and Vanpooling." *Transportation Research* 4A: 229-234.

Hart, S. 1985. "An Assessment of the Municipal Costs of Automobile Use." Altadena, California, mimeo.

Hilton, G. 1974. *Federal Transit Subsidies.* Washington, D.C.: American Enterprise Institute for Public Policy Research, Evaluative Study No. 17.

Hokanson, B. 1982. "Damage Costs Attributable to Motor Vehicle Travel." Iowa City: Institute of Urban and Regional Research, Technical Report 135.

Jennings, K., J. Smith, and E. Traynham. 1978. *Labor Relations in Public Service Industry: Unions, Management, and the Public Interest in Mass Transit.* New York: Praeger.

Johnson, C., and M. Pikarski. 1985. "Toward Fragmentation: The Evolution of Public Transportation in Chicago." *Urban Transit: The Private Challenge to Public Transportation*, C. Lave, ed. San Francisco: Pacific Institute for Public Policy Research, pp. 49-78.

Kain, J. 1990. "Deception in Dallas: Strategic Misrepresentation in Rail Transit Promotion and Evaluation." *Journal of the American Planning Association* 56(2): 184-196.

Kain, J., R. Gittell, A. Daniere, S. Daniel, T. Somerville, and L. Zhi. 1992. *Increasing the Productivity of the Nation's Urban Transportation Infrastructure: Measures to Increase Transit Use and Carpooling*. Washington, D.C.: Federal Transit Administration, U.S. Department of Transportation.

Kirby, R. 1981. "Targeting Money Effectively: User-Side Transportation Subsidies." *Journal of Contemporary Studies* 4(2): 45-52.

LaGasse, A. 1991. "Major Federal Issues Impacting For-hire Vehicle Fleets." *Taxi and Livery Management* (April): 14-20.

Lee, D. 1995. "Full Cost Pricing of Highways." Washington, D.C.: Paper presented at the Annual Meeting of the Transportation Research Board.

Litman, T. 1995. *Transportation Cost Analysis: Techniques, Estimates, and Implications* . Victoria, British Columbia: Transportation Policy Institute.

MacKenzie, J., R. Dower, and D. Chen. 1992. *The Going Rate: What it Really Costs to Drive*. New York: World Resources Institute.

McPhee, J. 1993. "Duty of Care: What to Do with Two Hundred and Fifty Million Old Tires?" *The New Yorker* 69(19), June 28: 72-80.

Meyer, J., J. Kain, and M. Wohl. 1965. *The Urban Transportation Problem*. Cambridge: Harvard University Press.

Miller, P., and J. Moffett. 1993. *The Price of Mobility: Uncovering the Hidden Costs of Transportation*. New York: National Resources Defense Council.

Morlok, E. 1988. "Privatizing Bus Transit: Cost Savings from Competitive Contracting." *Journal of the Transportation Research Forum* 28(1): 72-81.

Orski, C. 1985. "The Private Challenge to Public Transportation." *Urban Transit: The Private Challenge to Public Transportation*, C. Lave, ed. San Francisco: Pacific Institute for Public Policy Research, pp. 311-311.

———. 1995. "Transportation and the Changing Political Landscape IV." *Innovation Briefs* 6(4): 1-4.

Ott, D., and A. Ott. 1969. *Federal Budget Plans*. Washington, D.C.: The Brookings Institution.

Perry, J., and T. Babitsky. 1986. "Comparative Performance in Urban Bus Transit: Assessing Privatization Strategies." *Public Administration Review* 46: 45-59.

Peskin, R., S. Mundle, and S. Buhrer. 1992. "Transit Privatization in Denver: Experience in the First Year." *Transportation Research Record* 1349: 75-84.

Pickrell, D. 1985. "Rising Deficits and the Uses of Transit Subsidies in the United States." *Journal of Transport Economics and Policy* 19(3): 281-298.

Pucher, J. 1988. "Subsidies to Urban Public Transport in Western Europe and North America." *Transportation Quarterly* 42(3): 377-402.

———. 1995a. "Urban Passenger Transport in the United States and Europe: A Comparative Analysis of Public Policies: Part 1, Travel Behaviour, Urban Development and Automobile Use." *Transport Reviews* 15(2): 99-117.

————. 1995b. "Urban Passenger Transport in the United States and Europe: A Comparative Analysis of Public Policies: Part 2: Public Transport, Overall Comparisons and Recommendations." *Transport Reviews* 15(3): 211-227.

Pucher, J., and S. Kurth. 1995. "Making Transit Irresistible: Lessons from Europe." *Transportation Quarterly* 49(1): 117-128.

Reznick, S., and P. Bardack. 1994. "Reinventing Urban Transportation: A New Regulatory Vision." Philadelphia: Commonwealth Development Associates, consulting report.

Rosenbloom, S. 1988. "Role of the Private Sector in the Delivery of Transportation Services to the Elderly and Handicapped in the United States." *Transportation Research Record* 1170: 39-45.

Sale, J., and B. Green. 1978. "Operating Costs and Performance of American Transit Systems." *Journal of the American Planning Association* 4(2): 22-27.

Sclar, E., K. Schaeffer, and R. Brandwein. 1989. *The Emperor's New Clothes: Transit Privatization and Public Policy.* Washington, D.C.: Economic Policy Institute.

Sedlak, J. 1995. "Lessons Learned in the Development of Houston's HOV System." Houston: Metro.

Sherman, R. 1972. "Subsidies to Relieve Urban Traffic Congestion." *Journal of Transport Economics and Policy* 6(1): 22-31.

Small, K., and C. Kazimi. 1994. "On the Costs of Air Pollution from Motor Vehicles." Berkeley: University of California Transportation Center, Working Paper 237.

Smerk, G. 1964. "Three Experiments in Urban Transportation." *Business Horizon* 7(2): 39-47.

Teal, R. 1985. "Transit Service Contracting: Experiences and Issues." *Transportation Research Record* 1036: 28-36.

————. 1988. "Public Transit Service Contracting: A Status Report. *Transportation Quarterly* 42(2): 207-222.

Thompson, T. 1986. *Barriers to Private Sector Participation in Public Transportation.* Washington, D.C.: Urban Mass Transportation Administration, U.S. Department of Transportation.

Tye, W. 1976. "Problems and Potentials of Federal Transit Operating Subsidies." *Transportation Research Record* 573: 21-29.

Urban Institute. 1990. *Adopted Principles of the Competitive Service Board, 1986–1990.* Washington, D.C.: Urban Institute.

Urban Mass Transportation Administration. 1984. "Private Enterprise Participation in the Urban Mass Transportation Program." *Federal Register* 49, 205.

U.S. Advisory Commission on Intergovernmental Relations. 1961. *Intergovernmental Responsibilities for Mass Transportation Facilities and Services in Metropolitan Areas.* Washington, D.C.: U.S. Senate.

U.S. Chambers of Commerce. 1963. "Business Views on Local Transit: An Analysis of How 1,129 Chambers of Commerce View the Need for a Federal Subsidy Program." Washington, D.C.: Transportation and Communications Department, U.S. Chambers of Commerce.

U.S. Congress. 1963. *Congressional Record.* Washington, D.C.: U.S. Congress, House of Representatives.

U.S. Department of Labor. 1993. "Protections for Transit Workers." Washington, D.C.: U.S. Department of Labor, Fact Sheet No. OAW 93-2.

U.S. Senate. 1961. *Transportation Policies in the United States*. Washington, D.C.: U.S. Senate, Doyle Report.

Vickery, W. 1973. "Current Issues in Transportation." In *Contemporary Economic Issues*, N. Chamberlain, ed., Homewood, Illinois: Richard D. Irwin, pp. 219-300.

Wachs, M. 1981. "Pricing Urban Transportation: A Critique of Current Policy." *Journal of the American Planning Association* 47(3): 243-251.

Walters, A. 1967. "Subsidies for Transport?" *Lloyds Bank Review* 83: 22-33.

White, C., S. Edner, and K. Ketcheson. 1986. *Transit Agency Characteristics: An Industry Profile*. Washington, D.C.: Urban Mass Transportation Administration, U.S. Department of Transportation.

PART III

FUTURE RIDE: PARATRANSIT FOR THE TWENTY-FIRST CENTURY

CHAPTER 9

Smart Paratransit: Technologies for the Future

SMART PARATRANSIT: TECHNOLOGY AND SMALL VEHICLES

High-technology enhancements can greatly improve paratransit offerings, making them more cost-effective and time-competitive with the private car. To the degree that technology can lead to more door-to-door, short-wait, effortless-transfer service, the prospects for small-vehicle transportation are bright. The idea is to create new forms of mass transit that behave more like the automobile, but provide the benefits of collective-ride transportation. In a piece titled "The Marriage of Autos & Transit," Melvin Webber (1994, p. 31) writes:

> If it's true that the automobile owes its tremendous success to its door-to-door, no-wait, no-transfer service, and if it's true that the structure of the modern metropolis is incompatible with large-vehicle transit systems like trains, trolleys, or even 50-passenger buses, then it must also be true that workable transit systems in low-density sections of the metropolis must be those using automobile-like vehicles. I suggest that the ideal suburban transit system will take its passengers from door-to-door with no transfers, with little waiting—and that it will fit the small numbers of persons having the same origin, the same destination, and the same schedule. Only such a system can compete with the private car on its own grounds.

The marriage of technology and small-vehicle service that would create the competitive form of transit envisaged by Webber and others is what I have termed *smart paratransit*. The advent of vehicle-tracking systems, real-time scheduling and routing algorithms, automated communications systems, and on-board navigation aids make smart paratransit more than a pipe dream. Indeed, all of the capabilities are now in place to create intelligent forms of paratransit that closely mimic the service features of the private automobile. This chapter probes important advances that have been made in this arena, experiences with pilot projects, and the steps that need to be taken to move smart paratransit from an idea to a reality.

TECHNOLOGY AND THE SERVICE DOMAIN OF PARATRANSIT

There are a number of dimensions of paratransit services that bear on high-tech applications. This section maps out the different service features of paratransit that are most amenable to technological enhancements. Eight features, and the options available, are summarized in Table 9.1.

(1) *Scheduling.* As reviewed in Part 1 of this book, paratransit runs the gamut of scheduling practices, from prescheduled subscription buspools, to quick-response dial-a-ride van services, and to the more common unscheduled jitneys, commercial vans, shuttles, and shared-ride taxis. Technology can potentially enhance demand-responsive and unscheduled paratransit services by decreasing the time between trip request and actual pickup, and by optimizing the amount and sequencing of vehicles according to demand levels. Local context has a lot to do with the potential value of advanced scheduling technologies. In Mexico City, Manila, and other megacities, paratransit services are so thick that sched-

Table 9.1
Paratransit Service Features Relevant to Advanced Technologies

	FEATURES	*OPTIONS*
1.	SCHEDULING	· Fixed Schedule · Demand-responsive · Unscheduled
2.	ROUTING	· Fixed Route · Route-deviation · Flexible-route
3.	CLIENTELE	· Specialized · General Public
4.	CONTINUITY	· Transfers · No Transfers/Continuous
5.	OCCUPANCY	· Shared-ride · Exclusive-ride
6.	CONNECTIVITY	· Door-to-door · Checkpoint
7.	GEOGRAPHY	· One-to-one · One-to-many/One-to-few · Many-to-many/Few-to-few
8.	INFORMATION	· Real Time · Delayed

ules are neither needed nor used. With perhaps the exception of New York City, however, America's population densities are too low to support high-frequency paratransit services; thus scheduling enhancements stand to yield important benefits.

The private car and exclusive-ride taxis pose few scheduling challenges since vehicles are either accessed or promptly dispatched to serve the demand. It is the shared-ride nature of paratransit that generally makes scheduling more complicated. If a given day's requests are known, say, a day in advance (as with most dial-a-ride services), computerized scheduling algorithms can be used to determine the optimal dispatching and sequencing of vehicles in a fleet, subject to the constraints of passenger origins and destinations, the requested time of services, and possibly other factors (e.g., the need for vehicles equipped with wheelchairs). If real-time (immediate-response) requests are allowed, the scheduling problem becomes vastly more complicated, since each vehicle which could potentially serve waiting customers is subject to the constraints of on-board passengers plus those already scheduled to be picked up. If a scheduling algorithm has just computed optimal vehicle assignments, departure times, and routing based on all requests up to a particular time, there is no way to know the extent to which subsequent requests might render these suboptimal.

(2) Routing. Most paratransit services in the United States and abroad follow predefined routes, just as conventional buses. Some services, like van shuttles and circulators, have scheduled arrivals at given checkpoints; however, jitneys and most other forms of paratransit operating along specified routes have no time-tables. Unlike conventional buses and shuttles, moreover, jitneys and other loosely scheduled services often make slight detours at riders' requests. At the extreme, as with taxis, vehicles might go wherever demand takes it (e.g., flexible routing). As with scheduling, it is the shared-ride feature of paratransit that complicates efficient routing. It is this complex relationship between spatially and temporally varying ride-share requests and vehicle routing and scheduling that makes the development of cost-effective smart paratransit technologies so challenging.

(3) Clientele. Who the customers are has some bearing on the kinds of paratransit technologies that might be introduced. To date, most technological advances in scheduling and routing have been aimed at specialized markets, in particular ADA clients. Normally, the goal is to improve both the efficiency (e.g., lower costs per vehicle mile) and effectiveness (e.g., high average vehicle loads) of services. The fact that most ADA paratransit service requests are made at least 24 hours in advance has aided automated computerized scheduling, though most systems today do allow for unexpected scheduling changes. For general-public dial-in services, like airport shuttle vans, trip requests are more random and are less likely to be held to one-day advanced notice. That is, services must be more demand responsive. Moreover, for privately provided general-public services, operators' main goal is much different than that of specialized services—namely, profit maximization.

(4) Continuity. By their very nature, small-vehicle services normally involve transfers, such as from feeder vans to subways. Transferring is usually part and parcel of riding transit and (non-dial-a-ride) paratransit in the suburbs. There, activities are often too spread out to serve all trip origins and destinations in a single vehicle at a reasonable cost and without undue delay. Many middle-income travelers loathe making transfers, perceiving the time loss to be two to three times longer than it actually is (Wachs, 1976), which is a major reason why most drive. Automated technologies that help synchronize connections between vans, minibuses, and mainline services, thus easing transfers, can yield potentially big ridership payoffs.

(5) Occupancy. By definition, paratransit is a shared-ride service, though there are potential situations where single-occupant vehicles might transition into a collective-ride mode. One model that has been advanced is the formation of a "para-taxi" sector that would match up subscribers—those driving and those wanting a ride—on an instantaneous, real-time basis. To be worthwhile for the driver, the person (or party) requesting a ride would need to: (1) have the same approximate destination as the driver; (2) be in a location that is easy for the driver to swing by; (3) and be willing to pay the driver for the service. Unlike a taxi, the driver and passenger have the same destination. And unlike a carpool, casual or otherwise, the driver is compensated for carrying the passenger. The incentive to the passenger is a convenient trip by car at a reasonable price and without the hassle of parking. The incentive to the driver is supplemental income and perhaps the chance to use an HOV lane. Institutionally, residents of a city might subscribe to the service, and a broker, perhaps a large insurance company, might manage the program—for example, screen participants, collect subscription fees, indemnify the participants, and so on. Webber (1994) foresees technology one day allowing a "711" telephone number that, through a central computer, does real-time ride matching. Such a scheme would elevate paratransit service quality to perhaps the highest echelon possible.

(6) Connectivity. Paratransit that is time competitive with the private automobile must have high connectivity—that is, provide curb-to-curb services. Federal law now requires transit agencies or their agents to provide front-door pickup and drop-off for Americans with physical disabilities whose trip origins or destinations are more than three-quarters of a mile from a public transit corridor. Today, almost all dial-a-ride, door-to-door services in the United States cater to special clientele. It is because of the prospect of unacceptable time delays that the few general-public dial-a-ride services, namely airport shuttles, usually guarantee that passengers will endure no more than two side trips to pick up other fares while en route. On-board navigational aids and routing software packages might shave a minute here and there off door-to-door services; however, the low densities of most U.S. cities would still limit curbside services for the general public to a few passengers at most.

Vehicle occupancy can be increased by using checkpoints—designated pick-up locations—however, this is at the expense of travelers having to transfer (e.g., from one van to another) and sometimes change modes (e.g., from car to a sub-scription buspool at a park-and-ride checkpoint; from a feeder van to a subway at a rail station checkpoint). With the exceptions of dial-a-ride vans and shared-ride taxis (or parataxis), virtually all paratransit services rely on checkpoints—whether a jitney stop, a casual carpool pickup spot, or a storefront neighborhood car operation. Just as technology stands to marginally improve the routing of door-to-door services, it also offers some hope of enhancing checkpoint services, such as synchronizing transfers or providing passengers real-time information on expected vehicle arrival times.

(7) Geography. Automated technologies also have different potential appli-cations depending on the geographic alignment of trip ends—whether one-to-one (e.g., some rail feeder shuttles), few-to-one (e.g., airport shuttles), or many-to-many (e.g., some dial-a-ride vans). In general, the greater the number of trip ends, the greater the opportunities for automated technologies to materially enhance service quality. However, in reality, the constraints imposed by low population densities and most Americans' limited tolerance for delays restrict how many trip ends can feasibly be included in many-to-many (or even few-to-few) services.

(8) Information. Three groups—passengers, drivers, and dispatchers—stand to gain the most from improved information flows. Communications technologies can deliver real-time traffic and routing information directly to drivers, enabling them to bypass congestion hot spots. Information might range from radio mes-sages of downstream traffic conditions to on-board computer screens that display optimal travel paths given a present location, planned destination, and traffic conditions. While flexible-route services would probably benefit the most from this information, even drivers of fixed-route jitneys would gain from knowing whether connecting vans are encountering delays in reaching a timed-transfer point. Information about expected arrival times of vans and minibuses would allow passengers to time their activities so as to minimize waits—for example, display screens at shopping malls would enable patrons to browse and window-shop instead of idly standing by five or so minutes before a vehicle arrives. Lastly, those dispatching dial-a-ride vans would obviously find their jobs easier with real-time information on the location of vehicles and areawide traffic con-ditions.

CREATING SMART PARATRANSIT

So far in this book, the chief explanations given for why paratransit has been a small player in America's urban transportation scene, largely limited to special-ized services like ADA vans and airport shuttles, have been factors like mispric-ing, overregulation, and protectionism. However, it may be that paratransit has been equally limited by its technical inability to realize flexible routing, many-to-many coverage, real-time information acquisition, and other characteristics that would materially enhance service quality.

What leading-edge technologies would allow paratransit to take on such service features? This section proposes a general model of "smart paratransit" that, as diagramed in Figure 9.1, involves the integration of four key elements: (1) Automated Vehicle Location; (2) Automated Scheduling and Routing; (3) Database Systems; and (4) User Interfaces. Automated Vehicle Location (AVL) technologies give the dispatcher, central computer, or any other interested parties knowledge of the location of vans and minibuses in the field. Automated scheduling and routing technologies takes account of AVL and ride request information in assigning vehicles to waiting customers and recommending a "shortest path." Automated scheduling relies on real-time data on vehicle and customer locations, road conditions, and road configurations. This information is best stored in an easily accessible database system. Lastly, these three systems are useless unless there is a means of communications that connects the customer, the dispatcher, and the driver. Furthermore, any unforeseen conditions, like vehicle breakdowns or a traffic pileup, need to be communicated so appropriate adjustments can be made. By effectively linking these four subsystems, smart paratransit becomes technologically within reach.

Automatic Vehicle Location

The AVL technologies could truly revolutionize mass paratransit services in coming decades. Through technologies as simple as signposts or as advanced as the satellite-based Global Positioning System, it is now possible to monitor the real-time movement of vehicles, track on-time schedule performance, alert maintenance crews of vehicle breakdowns, control headways, and inform customers waiting at transit centers when vans and minibuses will arrive.

By pinpointing the location of each vehicle in a fleet, the greatest value of AVL to paratransit lies in providing information necessary to optimize scheduling and routing. Even for fixed-route paratransit, like jitney services, AVL would

Figure 9.1.
General Model of an Integrated Smart Paratransit System

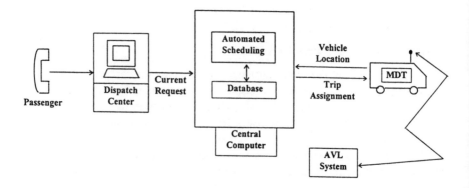

find value, such as in facilitating passenger transfers. For instance, if AVL determines that a bus is likely to arrive at a transfer point ahead of schedule, a message can be sent to the bus driver's terminal requesting a slowdown to ensure that passengers on a connecting van don't miss the bus. And for flexible and fixed-route services alike, AVL can increase service reliability by identifying the nearest backup vehicle in the field should a vehicle break down or have an accident.

Four specific AVL technologies that would support smart paratransit are fixed beacons, radio navigation location systems, global positioning systems, and on-board navigation and route-guidance systems. These are outlined below in the order of sophistication—namely, the ability to accommodate the considerable routing and scheduling challenges of flexible, demand-responsive paratransit.

Fixed Beacons

This scheme involves a series of signpost devices, mounted to utility poles along designated routes, that emit low-powered and uniquely identifiable signals (beacons) that can be detected by transmitters/receivers aboard vehicles. Vehicles, in turn, relay a signpost's identification to a central station, thereby informing the dispatcher which signpost has been passed at a point in time.[1] The main advantage of beacons is low cost. For paratransit, the main shortcoming is that beacons can only locate vehicles operating on fixed, predetermined routes. Still, most AVL systems currently installed in North American cities, including Toronto, Tampa, San Antonio, and Norfolk, used fixed beacons.

Radio Navigation Location Systems

Land-based radio navigation location systems, such as Loran-C, track vehicles by emitting low-frequency radio waves from a series of stations. Each station transmits pulses of timed signals, and receivers mounted on vehicles calculate distances traveled by comparing the time they receive different signals from different locations. This allows vehicles to be tracked within an accuracy of 500 meters. In greater Baltimore, the Maryland Transit Authority uses this technology to track 50 of its buses within a 650-square-mile service area.

For paratransit applications, the main advantage of radio location over a fixed beacon system is its flexibility—any vehicle equipped with a receiver can be tracked, regardless of route, as long as signals can be read throughout a service area. Its main disadvantage is that numerous sources can interfere with signals, including power lines and substations, tall buildings, and even fluorescent lights within vehicles.

Global Positioning Systems (GPS)

Global positioning systems overcome the interference problems of land-based radio location systems by using three or more satellites that pinpoint vehicle locations. Twenty-one satellites owned and operated by the U.S. Department of Defense, under the NavStar program, are available for commercial use.[2] The GPS can locate moving vehicles within an accuracy of around 60 feet, although field tests in Dallas have been accurate within 14 feet (Dailey and Lin, 1994). Most recent pilot ground transportation tests of AVL in the United States (including Des Moines, Denver, Milwaukee, Dallas, Chicago, Minneapolis, Tulsa, and Tampa) have employed GPS systems.

For paratransit applications, GPS needs certain capabilities. One is an acceptable accuracy. Timed transfers between jitney vans and mainline bus services that require close synchronization may need locational accuracies of 100 feet or less. In assigning the nearest available vehicle to a real-time ride request, accuracy standards can likely be relaxed—either one vehicle is far closer to a waiting customer or else it makes little difference which of several nearby vehicles is dispatched. A second necessary capability is the control of relayed information. A vehicle's GPS receiver can transmit locational information to a central dispatcher approximately every second. If dozens of vehicles in the field relayed information at this rate, the central dispatching computer would quickly become overwhelmed. A technique known as polling can be used to control the rate at which positional data are received. If there are 10 vans in the field and a sampling rate of once a minute for each vehicle is desired, then every six seconds one of the 10 vehicles will be "polled." Last, for the positional data to be of value to a dispatcher, it must be displayed in an easily decipherable manner. Ideally, the position of a vehicle is displayed on a digital map, geocoded according to U.S. Census Tiger files or a comparable commercial mapping program. For demand-responsive paratransit, dispatchers may need to zoom in on display images in order to identify street names and landmarks.

On-Board Navigation and Route Guidance Systems

A variation of the GPS approach to vehicle tracking is demonstrated by the ADVANCE (Advanced Driver and Vehicle Advisory Navigation Concept) project currently under way in the Chicago area. There, some 5,000 buses, vans, and cars have been equipped with a Mobile Navigation Assistant (MNA), a device that contains an on-board navigation computer, a GPS receiver, a digital road map stored on CD-ROM, and a transmitter/receiver for communicating with a Traffic Information Center (TIC) (Smith et al., 1992). Figure 9.2 depicts the overall architecture of an ADVANCE-type system. In effect, each vehicle acts as a probe of traffic flows by continuously sending data on its position (from GPS) and speed (from the time taken to traverse loop detectors) over a radio frequency network to the TIC. The TIC, in turn, is constantly creating a composite summary of areawide traffic conditions. This composite summary is then broadcast to each vehicle in the field, which in turn uses an on-board computer to combine information on traffic conditions, the areawide road network, and the desired destination so as to continuously update the best route to take.

Figure 9.2.
Automatic Vehicle Location: Schema for an On-board Navigation System

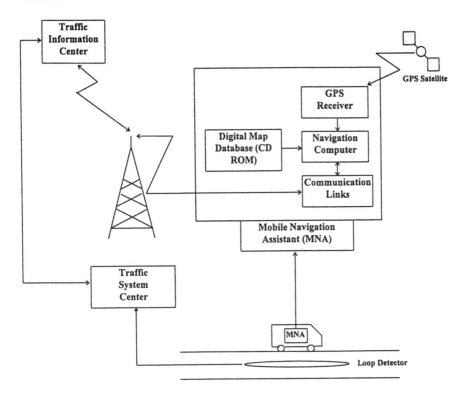

The ADVANCE-like systems distinguish themselves from GPS in that the "intelligence" resides in the vehicle itself, not in a centralized facility. For paratransit purposes, an atomistic system like ADVANCE allows vehicles to independently route themselves so as to minimize delays, though at an appreciable cost. Higher costs for in-vehicle systems, however, are partly offset by eliminating the need for human dispatching since real-time scheduling and routing is performed on board.

Automated Scheduling and Routing

America's taxi industry first adopted automated scheduling out of necessity. The formation of large taxi franchises in cities like Los Angeles and Denver during the 1970s created request volumes and fleet sizes that were too large for dispatchers to handle manually. Figure 9.3 sketches the components of a typical system used by taxi companies to automatically make a dispatch decision and relay the information to selected taxicab drivers.

Figure 9.3.
Schema for Computerized Scheduling of Taxicab Services

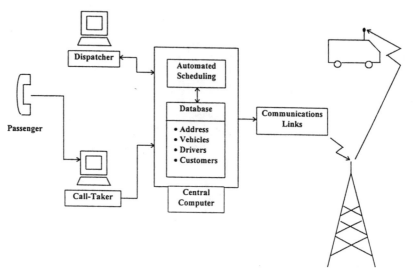

The requirements for automated scheduling for paratransit are more stringent than for taxicabs. Dial-a-ride vans, shared-ride taxis, and on-call shuttles require more advanced scheduling algorithms since multiple customers must be scheduled in logical sequence given the locations of vehicles, subject to budget and other constraints. Automated reservations and billing functions are also normally built into the system.

Figure 9.4 outlines the necessary components of an automated paratransit scheduling and routing system. First, a call taker enters a phone-in request into a central computer. An algorithm then optimally assigns a vehicle to serve the request and suggests a route that minimizes travel time, subject to constraints, including all previously scheduled pickups and deliveries, vehicle capacities, and the need for specialized equipment like wheelchair lifts. Normally, a dispatcher has the ability to override computer-recommended routes. With the combination of computerized scheduling and digital on-board terminals, changes in routing created by new trip requests can be easily displayed. The location of the next pickup or drop-off can likewise be broadcast.

Database Systems

The volumes of information on vehicle locations, traffic conditions, and travel requests feeding into and between a central computer and paratransit vehicle require that an effective database management system be in place. Database systems must organize two kinds of information: static and dynamic. Static data represent "permanent" information about roads (e.g., their locations, capacities,

Figure 9.4.
Schema for Computerized Scheduling and Routing of a Paratransit System

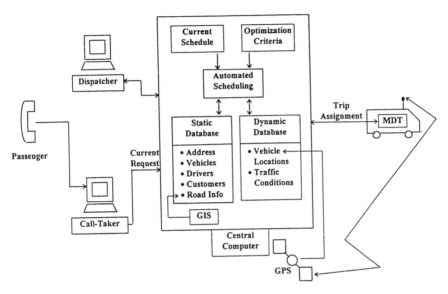

configurations),[3] vehicles (e.g., their capacities, equipment, top speeds), passengers (e.g., characteristics of regular patrons by names, addresses, typical destinations, special needs), and drivers (e.g., their names, years of experience). Dynamic data represent "temporary," ever-changing information about roads (e.g., current conditions, such as average speeds and construction delays), vehicles (e.g., their locations, scheduled assignments and routes), passengers (e.g., planned pickup and delivery times, special needs), and drivers (e.g., characteristics of the driver operating a particular vehicle). Thus, dynamic and static data can be combined to assign particular drivers in the field to a client (e.g., perhaps someone with experience in carrying toddlers as part of a "kids kab") and to optimize real-time scheduling and routing.[4] Normally, separate databases—commercial GIS packages (e.g., ArcInfo, Map Info) that organize and display static data about roads and commercial relational database packages (e.g., dBase, Oracle) that store all other data—are merged to create an integrated database system.

User Interfaces

Ultimately what determines whether a successful paratransit trip transaction takes place is a series of human judgments and decisions. User interfaces represent the mediums—voice messages, on-board displays, electronic mail, and so on—in which automated information is received and relayed by each person involved in the transaction: the passenger, the call taker, the dispatcher, and the driver.

The passenger initiates the travel request, usually by telephone, though for subscription services that provide a month or so of prearranged rides, correspondence might be via mail. In theory, requests can be made through a number of "videotex" modes, such as computer terminals (e.g., electronic mail) and checkpoint kiosks (as with the Ruf-Bus experiment in Germany, discussed in the next section). Customers also stand to benefit from real-time information on road conditions and anticipated vehicle arrival times. If traffic congestion is bad enough, for example, patrons might decide to delay a journey. The Ann Arbor Transit Authority has equipped 67 buses with a dead reckoning system that allows broadcasting of bus positions to passengers via cable television. In Hull, Quebec, and Halifax, Nova Scotia, signposts inform central computers where buses and vans are, whether they are out of schedule sequence, how fast they are going, and how soon they will likely reach a destination (or another sensor to update speed estimates). This information is transformed into digitally recorded phone messages that allow passengers to dial a telephone number reserved for each bus stop in the system to find out when the next two buses will be arriving at a stop, within 30-second accuracy. All households in Hull and Halifax have received by mail the respective telephone numbers for the two bus stops nearest their homes. Anyone who has ever stood outdoors longer than a few minutes during Canadian winters can surely appreciate the value of such real-time passenger information systems.

Once a ride request is initiated, the next person involved in the flow of information is the call taker (which for small systems, like kids kabs, is often also the dispatcher). The call taker confirms the request, types the parameters of the desired trip in a database form, and informs the caller of the expected time of pickup and delivery (either after a short pause or by a later call back). The central computer then either determines the driver assignment, schedule, and (possibly) route, or displays information that allows a dispatcher to make the decisions. Under the smart paratransit model, dispatchers' decisions would be guided by three kinds of display outputs: a digital road map of the service area overlaid with current locations of all vehicles in service; a text display of the passenger's origin, destination, requested times of departure and arrival, and other relevant information; and a text display of a recommended vehicle assignment, and an updated schedule and route for that vehicle. Thus, the dispatcher becomes the point person for information flows, relaying details about the ride transaction to the call taker (and ultimately the passenger) and driver in the field.

The assigned driver interfaces with the system by receiving and confirming the new passenger's address and updated schedule and route information. Information can be received as either a printout, display on a mobile data terminal (MDT), by a pager, or as direct voice communication from the dispatcher (or digital computer-generated voice). The MDTs offer the advantage of allowing the driver to scroll forward to see the routes and schedule that have been planned.

One other potential user interface medium is a smart card for paying smart paratransit fares. Besides expediting boarding and payment, smart cards provide convenience for both the rider and driver by eliminating cash transactions. Ultimately, paratransit riding might be covered by a universal transportation debit card system—a stored-value, magnetically encoded card that provides access to and automatically exacts charges for rides on any mode of transportation. A universal debit card would greatly facilitate intermodal (e.g., paratransit-to-subway) transfers. It would also allow more efficient pricing, like distance-based fares and peak-hour surcharges.

APPLICATIONS OF SMART PARATRANSIT TECHNOLOGIES

So far, smart paratransit largely exists in theory. Until there are successful real-world demonstrations, there will always be a healthy dose of skepticism about the practicality and feasibility of these concepts. Fortunately, some small but important steps have been taken in recent years that apply these automated technologies in ways that begin to resemble what a smart paratransit system might one day look like. Notably, three types of paratransit services either owe their existence to these technologies or have been substantially enhanced by them: specialized paratransit, general public paratransit, and the soon-to-be-implemented parataxi concept. This section examines experiences in applying automated technologies to these three types of services.

To date, the Winston-Salem Mobility Manager program in North Carolina has made the most inroads in adapting automated technologies to specialized paratransit services, specifically for ADA-eligible populations. The best example of technology-driven paratransit available to the general public so far is the Ruf-Bus/FOCCS system implemented in Germany. Both the Winston-Salem and German programs demonstrate the use of automated scheduling and routing, database management, and user interface systems. However, neither program applies advanced AVL technologies like GPS. This could change, however, with the introduction of a parataxi demonstration project in Ontario, California, that is now in the advanced planning stage and pilot projects currently under way in Des Moines, Iowa, and northern Virginia. Overall, these three cases provide the best insights yet into how effective automated technologies have been in meeting the varied and sometimes complex service needs of paratransit.

Winston-Salem Mobility Manager

The Winston-Salem Mobility Manager project is notable not only for its ambitious application of advanced technologies to ADA paratransit services but also for the thorough evaluation of resulting benefits and costs. To date, most pilot projects of high-tech applications in paratransit have been directed at ADA clients. Winston-Salem's program is widely viewed as the most advanced specialized application so far (Stone et al., 1994), building upon earlier successful experiences with automated dial-a-ride services in Orange County, California, and Rochester, New York (Teal, 1993).

Winston-Salem's paratransit service, called TransAID, is sponsored by the Winston-Salem Transit Authority (WSTA), which contracts out day-to-day operations to a private firm, ATC/Vancom, Inc. Services are door-to-door, and reservations made anywhere from several hours to several days in advance are accepted. In 1993, TransAID carried around 170,000 passengers from Winston-Salem and surrounding Forsyth County.

To date, the first of two phases of the Mobility Manager project has been completed. The first phase involved the use of computer-aided dispatch and scheduling (CADS) to enhanced TransAID services. The second phase intends to build upon the first one by incorporating AVL, MDTs, and smart card reader systems into all TransAID vans. The primary goals of both phases are to: improve the quality, timeliness, and availability of customer information; increase the convenience of fare payments within and between modes; increase service reliability; minimize passenger travel and wait times; improve schedule adherence and incident response; improve the timeliness and accuracy of operating data for service planning and scheduling; provide integrated information management systems; allow for greater variations in fares; and increase the mobility of users with ambulatory disabilities.

The Mobility Manager project has deployed new technologies in two steps. First, a computerized scheduling system, called PASS, was introduced and tested on 17 TransAID vans in late 1994. Several months later, three of the vehicles were equipped with AVL transmitters, on-board terminals (MDTs), and smart card readers. With these systems working in tandem, real-time vehicle assignments and scheduling/routing adjustments are today possible in response to on-demand requests for TransAID rides.[5]

Researchers from North Carolina State University (see Stone, 1995) have recently examined the impacts of the project's first-phase automated scheduling system, CADS, and have found the following:

- *Ridership:* The number of passenger trips during the six-month test period increased 17.5 percent, or by 71,910 riders over the same six-month period one year previously.

- *Total operating costs:* Operating costs for TransAID services rose 15 percent between the two six-month periods. This was mainly due to increased service; the client base doubled from around 1,000 to 2,000 with the expansion of the service area and the hiring of two additional dispatchers.

- *Unit operating cost:* The operating expense per vehicle mile of TransAID service dropped by 8.5 percent, to $1.93. On a per-passenger-trip basis, costs fell by 2.4 percent, to $5.64. And on a vehicle-hour basis, they fell by 8.6 percent, to $24.70.

- *Marginal unit costs.* Based on ridership gains and distributing the $100,000 capital cost of the CADS system over a five-year service life, the additional cost per passenger trip attributable to CADS is about 20 cents. This is about 3.5 percent of the total operating cost per passenger trip of $5.65.

- *Service coverage:* Vehicle miles per passenger trip increased from 2.79 to 2.94, or by 5.4 percent. Vehicle hours per passenger trip rose even more—from 0.21 to 0.23, or by 9.5 percent. These increases stem from the expanded service area, which encompasses some rural areas.

- *Service responsiveness:* During the six-month test period, about 10 percent of all ride requests were for same-day trips. Prior to this period, all trips were booked at least 24 hours in advance.

- *Service quality.* Average passenger wait times have fallen by more than 50 percent.

In addition, the CADS system is well liked by the "stakeholders"—passengers, receptionists, dispatchers, schedulers, and drivers—as well as by WSTA management. In particular, it has cut the amount of time required to process a call by more than half and has greatly facilitated the insertion of same-day trip requests into preset schedules.

In drawing conclusions about the effectiveness of Winston-Salem's project, some degree of caution is in order. While CADS has without question yielded benefits and seems to be a cost-effective investment, some of the recorded impacts could have been due to other factors, like the accrual of economies of scale from service expansion. Demographic trends, such as rising shares of population who are elderly, might also partly explain ridership gains (though only marginally, given the compressed time period of the evaluation). One way to control for such factors would be to introduce the service in selected areas only, and then compare trends in project versus nonproject areas (assuming they are otherwise comparable). Realistically, however, project evaluation is rarely a high priority in designing a pilot program like Winston-Salem's; usually more important are putting the program in place promptly and extending benefits to as many clients as possible so as to gain credibility and build political support. Regardless, CADS has clearly facilitated the process of making a paratransit trip transaction in greater Winston-Salem, from call taking to scheduling/dispatching, and accordingly has pleased virtually everyone involved.

German Ruf-Bus/FOCCS Systems

In 1977, city officials in Friedrichshafen, Germany, initiated a service called Ruf-Bus ("Call-a-Bus") to test the feasibility of demand-responsive transportation. The project explicitly incorporated all kinds of "buses"—large coaches, minibuses, and microbuses—in order to serve areas of different population densities and to promote intermodalism. Ruf-Bus was designed as a checkpoint-to-checkpoint service (rather than door-to-door) for use by the general public. Its target market was suburban areas where transit services were less frequent and transfers were more common.

Figure 9.5 sketches the key elements of Germany's Ruf-Bus system. Users initiated ride requests through a checkpoint kiosk, many of which were sited at

Figure 9.5.
Basic Architecture of Germany's Ruf-Bus System

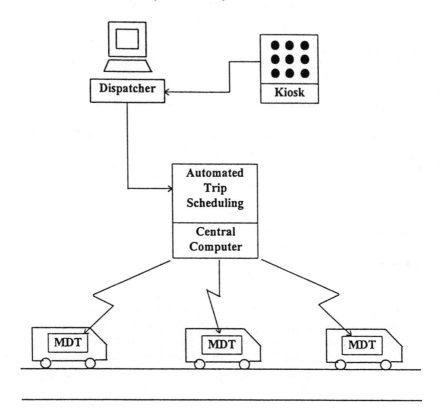

suburban rail (S-Bahn) stations. Using a machine mounted at the kiosk, patrons entered a three-digit code corresponding to the destination transit stop; entered the number of passengers in the party; inserted a 0.20 Deutsche Mark coin or a Ruf-Bus card; waited for a display of the bus number and scheduled arrival time; indicated whether they accepted or rejected the pickup offer; and removed the confirmation ticket if a pickup was accepted. Trip information for all accepted pickups were sent to a central computer, which in turn transmitted the information and an updated schedule to a computer terminal on-board the assigned vehicle. At each checkpoint where a pick-up or drop-off occurred, the driver simply looked at the display to determine the next checkpoint to go to. Overall, then, Ruf-Bus was a flexibly routed paratransit system that provided on-call service between fixed checkpoints.

The Ruf-Bus project was continuously expanded in the Friedrichshafen area over the first four years. By 1981, Ruf-Bus's ridership exceeded 44,000 per month, a 36 percent increase over the fixed-route bus service it replaced. How-

ever, the system operated at a financial loss, partly because of high operating
costs and partly because of the large share of Ruf-Bus patrons using discounted
monthly passes (Behnke, 1993).

In order to make Ruf-Bus more cost-effective, it was integrated with fixed-
route and route-deviation services in the early 1980s. The new system, named
FOCCS (Flexible Operations Command and Control System), relied on a mix of
buses, vans, and taxis equipped with data terminals. Unlike Ruf-Bus, vehicles
operated along fixed-route corridors between fixed checkpoints, with route deviations allowed depending on real-time demand. Normally, FOCCS vehicles operated in a fixed-route mode during peak hours, a route-deviation mode during the
midday, and in a demand-responsive (curb-to-curb) mode during evening hours
and on weekends. Compared to Ruf-Bus, FOCCS served an area four times as
large with nearly three times the population, had twice as many checkpoints, and
incorporated nearly twice as many vehicles.[6]

Table 9.2 reveals that both service and ridership levels fell with the replacement of demand-responsive Ruf-Bus services with the less convenient, checkpoint FOCCS services, but so did monthly operating costs. Compared to the
former line-haul service, both Ruf-Bus and FOCCS attracted far more riders. On
a vehicle-kilometer basis, however, Ruf-Bus and FOCCS were less utilized,
mainly because they concentrated on serving low-density areas. The infrastructure needed to support Ruf-Bus (e.g., kiosks) resulted in relatively high service
costs per passenger; however, on a per-kilometer basis, Ruf-Bus was actually
cheaper than the previous line-haul service. Because service levels were ratcheted
down, the cost per passenger for FOCCS was comparable to that of line-haul
service. Overall, by providing a quality of service that straddled between the
line-haul bus operation and Ruf-Bus, FOCCS's cost performance likewise straddled between those of conventional bus and Ruf-Bus.

Table 9.2.
**Comparison of Service, Ridership, and Cost Performance of Line-Haul Bus,
Ruf-Bus, and FOCCS Services, Friedrichshafen, Germany, 1977-1987**

	Type of Transit Service		
	Line-Haul Bus (1977)	Ruf-Bus (1981)	FOCCS (1987)
Aggregate Statistics:			
Vehicle kilometers per month	29,300	83,000	47,200
Passengers per month	32,600	44,300	37,800
Operating cost per month (1993 DM)	95,000	229,000	130,000
Performance Statistics:			
Passengers per vehicle kilometer	1.11	0.53	0.80
Operating cost per kilometer (1993 DM)	3.24	2.76	2.75
Operating cost per passenger trip (1993 DM)	2.91	5.16	3.44

DM = Deutsche Mark (1993, 1 DM = US$0.46)

Source: Adapted from Behnke (1993)

While FOCCS went through several other incarnations after 1987 (including attempts to install GPS receivers on-board vehicles), it has never managed to break even financially. As in the United States, transit and paratransit have lost ground in Germany because of rising automobile ownership and usage. Shifting government priorities, such as financing national reunification, have also prompted a curtailment of FOCCS services. Still, Germany's experimentation with technology-driven, demand-responsive transportation is the closest thing yet to the realization of smart paratransit, and overall the results provide some cause for optimism.

Parataxi: Real-time Ridesharing

If all goes according to schedule, a planned parataxi demonstration program in Ontario, California, could bring a form of smart paratransit into existence that closely matches the high-performance features of the private automobile. As noted earlier, the basic premise behind parataxi is that unused automobile seats can be filled by real-time matching of drivers and passengers. At first glance, this might seem a rehash of numerous failed attempts to get Americans to rideshare. However, parataxi differs from formal carpooling in two important ways: (1) use of technology to minimize delays and detours in picking up passengers and (2) financial compensation to drivers. A network of HOV lanes and universal parking charges would make parataxi all the more attractive.

The justification for compensating drivers comes from a survey conducted by the U.S. Department of Energy during the 1978–79 oil embargo, cited by Behnke (1993). The survey asked drive-alone commuters two questions: (1) at what level of compensation would they be willing to serve as vanpool drivers? and (2) how much would they be willing to pay to be vanpool passengers? The closest match was at 20 cents per mile (in 1991 dollars)—at this rate, 35 percent of those surveyed would be willing to drive and 35 percent would be willing to ride.

Because of concerns over cost escalation, the Ontario demonstration plans to couple drivers and passengers using two-way paging devices. Pagers will be linked to modems that transmit real-time requests to a central computer and that in turn receive "best match" feedback. The system will be fairly straightforward. Participants about to drive are to page in a message to the central computer, specifying trip origin, destination, and start time. Participants wanting a lift will page in their present location, trip destination, and desired time of pickup. If there is a critical mass of requests, the central computer can successfully make ride matches, informing all parties involved through a transmitted message to the paging device. Several electronic firms are currently developing paging devices that will support parataxi operations, which suggests there should be no supply-side constraints to implementing the concept. As to whether there will be sufficient demand to make the system work, however, we will have to wait until the results of the Ontario demonstration are in.[7]

Other Relevant Demonstrations

Several other projects in the preevaluation stage should shed additional light on the feasibility of smart paratransit. The Des Moines Metropolitan Transit Authority is currently testing a GPS-based system to improve timed transfers between 100 line-haul buses and 17 paratransit vans that offer door-to-door services for ADA customers (Kihl and Shinn, 1995). Paratransit ridership in Des Moines has historically been low, under 1,000 trips per day. The hope is that by tracking the location of vans at all times, paratransit-bus transfers can be better synchronized. This project will expand the boundaries of previous demonstrations by exploiting the ability of AVL to improve intermodal transfers.

Another promising demonstration is SaFIRE (Smart Flexroute Integrated Real-Time Enhancement System), recently introduced in Prince William County in northern Virginia by the Potomac-Rappahanock Transportation Commission. SaFIRE is unique in several ways. One, it is the first system in the United States that integrates AVL, automated scheduling, database management, and user-interface technologies for general-public paratransit. Second, it is a multimodal system, linking paratransit feeders to line-haul buses and intercity trains. Third, it makes flexible use of vehicles—vans and minibuses can be operated in fixed-route, flexible-route, or demand-responsive modes, as circumstances warrant. SaFIRE services have already begun along three major corridors, with vans and buses deviating up to three-quarters of a mile from the corridors' major boulevards to pick up and drop-off customers.

FROM IDEA TO IMPLEMENTATION

Ultimately, the challenge in implementing smart paratransit has more to do with institutions, politics, and money than with technology. Applicable technologies are already in place to launch successful smart paratransit services throughout the United States and other industrialized countries. What is still missing is an effective integration of individual "parts" into a workable system, along with a conducive institutional, political, and economic environment. Indeed, in a transportation marketplace free of huge, hidden subsidies, there would no doubt be commercial pressures to advance smart paratransit technologies. The travelling public would be willing to spend the kind of money necessary to finance high-technology paratransit in return for curb-to-curb, minimal-wait, easy-transfer service. Priority treatment of collective-ride services—such as through HOV lanes, toll-free bridge crossings, and preferential parking—would further stimulate the smart paratransit industry.

It is imperative that we move full throttle on creating smart paratransit systems, if for no other reason than billions of dollars are now being invested on making transit's and paratransit's chief competitor, the private automobile, much smarter. In the 150th anniversary issue of *Scientific American*, devoted to leading-edge technological innovations, I raised this concern:

In a decade or two, travel by automobile in some advanced countries may very well involve the kind of technology and intelligence gathering once reserved for tactical warfare. Onboard navigational aids, fed by satellite tracking systems, will give directions in soothing digital voices. In big cities, roadside screens will flash messages about distant traffic jams and alternative routes. Computerized control and guidance devices embedded underneath heavily trafficked corridors will allow appropriately equipped cars and trucks to race along almost bumper to bumper. Special debit cards will let motorists enter tollways without stopping, park downtown without fumbling for change, and hop on trains and people movers by swiping their cards through electronic turnstiles. Some experts even foresee customized tractor trailer-style "car-buses" that carry up to 20,000 cars per hour per freeway lane—10 times the current capacity. This constellation of new-age technologies is only a part of master plans drawn up in recent years in Europe and the U.S. For example, Detroit's "Big Three" automakers and the U.S. Department of Transportation have together spent or pledged several billion dollars through the remainder of this decade on R&D and commercialization of the Intelligent Transportation System. . . . New transportation technologies have stretched the envelope of urban development, raising per capita fuel consumption, consuming farmlands and open space, and dirtying air basins. . . . The so-called Intelligent Transportation System stands to worsen this state of affairs by orders of magnitude (Cervero, 1995, pp. 118, 120).

To the extent that transit and paratransit fail to keep pace with the increasingly intelligent auto-highway system, it is inevitable that more and more people will rely on their cars to get around. Public policies and demonstration grants, I would argue, should give funding preferences to improving the relative performance of efficient, environmentally conserving forms of transportation, including paratransit, through technological advances. As to other recommended public policy directions for the future, we turn to the final chapter.

NOTES

1. A variation has the transmitter/receiver attached to the vehicle operating in "transmit" mode, so that the vehicle's signal is detected by the signpost device, which relays its identification, along with the time the vehicle passed, to the central dispatch station (Kihl et al., 1993).

2. Each satellite moves at approximately 3.5 kilometers per second, continuously transmitting two types of data. The first type identifies the position of the satellite. The second type, called *range data*, corrects for the fact that the satellite will have moved from its transmitted position by the time that position is received on the ground. The GPS receiver mounted on vehicles uses these data to mathematically compute its own location within a certain margin of error. The location is then communicated to a central dispatching station (Dailey and Lin, 1994).

3. For the operational area of the vehicles, the road network is normally digitally represented by a collection of nodes and links. Nodes define key junctures and terminuses of the network (e.g., intersections, interchanges, end points). The physical location of each node is defined by its geographic coordinates (e.g., latitude and longitude). Connecting nodes are links, representing major passageways (e.g., collectors, arterials, expressways). The database maintains attribute information for each node and link of the network, including number of lanes, direction of lanes, link distances, speed limits, average link speeds and travel times by time of day and vehicle type, signal phasing for nodal

intersections, turn restrictions, height clearance restrictions, and any other important information that bears on traffic conditions. The two most common sources for defining networks are digital map files produced by the U.S. Census Bureau (e.g., Tiger files) and Quadrangle maps produced by the U.S. Geological Survey.

4. Optimization algorithms rely on dynamic data relayed from such sources as: AVL readings; loop detectors installed at regulator intervals; "probe" vehicles equipped with transmitter/receivers; and traditional sources such as radio reports from helicopters. The central computer's database system organizes the incoming information to allow dispatchers to query which vehicle can optimally serve the latest trip request, subject to constraints like prescheduled assignments.

5. Five individuals are involved in making a paratransit ride transaction in Winston-Salem: a client, receptionist, dispatcher, scheduler, and driver. Two layers of scheduling takes place. First, a "skeleton" schedule is created by the scheduler using PASS. This skeleton consists of regular trip requests (e.g., Mrs. Smith's therapy session every Thursday at 3:00 P.M.). Second, on-demand calls alter the skeleton. When a client phones in a trip request, the receptionist takes the call and enters the information into PASS. The dispatcher then uses PASS output to decide which vehicle should be assigned to the request. The receptionist then informs the client of the expected pickup time, and the dispatcher informs the driver of any schedule or route modifications. The PASS takes into account all constraints (e.g., current scheduling commitments, projected number of riders, availability of special equipment like wheelchair lifts), applying a linear-programming optimization algorithm to select a vehicle. The dispatcher is free to override this selection and sometimes does, based on knowledge about specific clients (e.g., grouping together kidney dialysis patients as a means of consolidating trip ends). The dispatcher then informs all drivers affected by schedule changes through radio contact, and PASS also automatically handles billing and data collection requirements generated by a trip request.

6. The service characteristics of FOCCS versus Ruf-Bus were as follows: service area size (in square kilometers)—300 vs. 75; service area population—100,000 vs. 36,000; number of checkpoints—180 vs. 90; number of call boxes—13 vs. 16; maximum number of vehicles—40 vs. 24 (Behnke, 1993).

7. Less formal approaches to real-time, or more accurately, interactive on-line, ride matching are also currently in the works. These systems enable employees to do their own carpool matching using computer bulletin boards accessible through desktop computers or through touchscreen kiosks located in company cafeterias and public lobbies. Employees can enter their names, telephone numbers, and carpool preferences into the database. The explosive growth in corporate electronic mail systems and local area computer networks (LAN) have made on-line, interactive ride matching possible. One of the largest initiatives has been undertaken by the University of Washington, called the SWIFT Smart Traveler system. It involves an array of communications technologies, including electronic mail, computer bulletin boards, touchscreen kiosks, and telephones (Orski, 1995).

REFERENCES

Behnke, R. 1993. *German "Smart-Bus" Systems: Potential Application in Portland, Oregon.* Washington, D.C.: Federal Transit Administration, U.S. Department of Transportation.

Cervero, R. 1995. "Why Go Anywhere?" *Scientific American* 273(3): 118-120.

Dailey, D., and P. Lin. 1994. *Investigation of GPS and GIS for Traveler Information.* Olympia: Washington State Department of Transportation, Report WA-RD-332.1.

Kihl, M., and D. Shinn. 1995. *Improving Interbus Transfer with Automatic Vehicle Location: Year Two, Final Report.* Ames: Iowa State University, Midwest Transportation Center.

Kihl, M., D. Shinn, B. Das, and N. Eltinay. 1993. *Improving Interbus Transfer with Automatic Vehicle Location: Year One Report.* Ames: Iowa State University, Midwest Transportation Center.

Orski, C. K. 1995. "Applying ITS Technologies to Travel Demand Management." *Innovation Briefs* 6(6): 1-3.

Smith, B., B. Clark, P. Pollock, F. Koppelman, C. Bhat, P. Nelson, and D. Rorem. 1992. "A Conceptual Overview of ADVANCE." *Proceedings of the IVHS America 1992 Annual Meeting.* Newport Beach, California: IVHS America, pp. 579-588.

Stone, J. 1995. *Winston-Salem Mobility Management: An Example of APTS Benefits.* Raleigh: North Carolina State University, Civil Engineering Program.

Stone, J., A. Nalevanko, and G. Gilbert. 1994. "Computer Dispatch and Scheduling for Paratransit: An Application of Advanced Public Transportation Systems." *Transportation Quarterly* 48(2): 173-184.

Teal, R. 1993. "Implications of Technological Developments for Demand Responsive Transit." *Transportation Research Record* 1390: 33-41.

Wachs, M. 1976. "Consumer Attitudes Toward Transit Service: An Interpretative Review." *Journal of the American Institute for Planners,* 42(1): 96-104.

Webber, M. 1994. "The Marriage of Autos & Transit: How to Make Transit Popular Again." *Access* 5: 26-31.

CHAPTER 10

Paratransit for the Twenty-first Century

PARATRANSIT AND POLICY OUTLOOKS

Today's most pressing and troubling transportation-related problems—traffic congestion, air pollution, and inaccessible neighborhoods—demand that bold and creative approaches to reducing reliance on the private automobile and improving efficiency in urban travel be introduced. In America's mobility marketplace, the automobile has reigned supreme because it is best suited to serving contemporary travel patterns—suburb-to-suburb journeys, multileg trips, spontaneous travel demand, and so on—in addition, according to some studies, to being substantially underpriced. Public transit's falling fortunes—declining market shares, soaring operating costs, diminishing productivity—stem, to a large degree, from the fact that traditional fixed-route, fixed-schedule, large-vehicle transportation is unable to effectively compete with the private car given today's settlement and travel patterns. We have experimented with publicly owned, operated, and subsidized traditional transit services in this country for some three decades now, and tens of billions of dollars later, the results have not been terribly impressive. Nationwide, ridership has remained fairly flat and service practices have remained more or less the same.

Might not it be time to try a radically different approach to transit service delivery in the United States, one which is more responsive to shifting travel patterns and public policy concerns? Commercial paratransit, I would argue, offers the kinds of service features and inherent adaptability that would make mass transit far more competitive with the private automobile. This has been demonstrated many times over in developing countries of Asia, Latin America, and the Middle East. Of course, there will always be a role for mainline bus routes and fixed guideway systems where high demand levels and economies of scale warrant them. However, such services should not be at the *exclusion* of alternative forms of mass transportation. In combination, widespread commercial paratransit services which complement mainline bus and rail systems—along with other policy initiatives, like higher motoring fees—could go a long way toward enhancing mobility in metropolitan America.

Without question, the bane of America's mass transit industry has been the continuing spread and dispersion of new growth into the suburbs, exurbs, and beyond. Low-density environs have never been traditional mass transit's natural habitat and never will be. Almost by definition, mass transit needs "mass," or density, to be successful. In light of this, there has been a growing interest in recent years in redesigning America's cities and suburbs so that they are more conducive to transit riding—that is, have higher densities, greater land-use mixtures, and more pedestrian-friendly site designs. Proposals for creating transit villages around rail stops and neotraditional villages linked by guideway systems embrace such thinking (for example, see Calthorpe, 1993; Katz, 1993; Downs, 1994; Bernick and Cervero, 1994). An inherent flaw of such initiatives, however, is that they put the transportation cart before the land-use horse. That is, they are built on the premise that cities should be planned and designed to support some preconceived notion of what is "good" transportation—namely, rail and bus systems. Transportation should be serving neighborhoods, towns, and regions, not vice versa. We don't consume transportation for its own sake, but rather for the sake of reaching jobs, schools, clinics, shops, and so forth. It is these places, and the joys, services, and personal gains we derive from them, that really matter, not transportation per se.

The problem with pursuing transit-oriented development planning as a means of reshaping travel demand and reducing automobile dependency is that it runs counter to the unshakable lifestyle and consumption preferences of the vast majority of Americans (accepting, of course, that artificially cheap automobile transportation has helped to feed such preferences). Surveys consistently show that 90 percent or more of Americans prefer large-lot, single-family living to apartments, condominiums, and high-rise development (Altshuler, 1980; Bookout, 1992). As urban development patterns continue to be market driven and cities continue to spread outward, building new rail systems and expanding traditional fixed-route bus services are unlikely to yield significant mobility dividends over the long run. Nor will transit village schemes and neotraditional development ideas find much political favor or market acceptance, short of dramatic increases in the cost of low-density, auto-oriented living.

Paratransit represents an entirely different paradigm for coping with suburban development patterns. It more or less accepts the low-density lifestyle preferences of most Americans and tries to effectively adapt to the suburban-exurban landscape. Thus, paratransit is a transportation response to established land-use patterns and preferences, not vice-versa. It remains the closest thing yet in the mass transportation field to a supply-side strategy that begins to mimic the operating characteristics of the private automobile.

PARATRANSIT FOR TOMORROW: SERVICES AND ORGANIZATION

While there is a tendency to dwell on the hardware characteristics of paratransit, such as sizes and types of vehicles, it is really paratransit's software, or service make-up, that is most distinguishing. As a hybrid of bus transit and the private car, paratransit offers a wide spectrum of service features that are consonant with the shifting nature of urban travel. As reviewed in this book, many of the travel attributes that are increasingly sought by Americans are provided by paratransit in one form or another:

- *direct, door-to-door service*—shared-ride taxis, dial-a-ride, vanpools, carpools, neighborhood cars

- *frequent service, short headways*—jitneys, vans, shared-ride taxis

- *demand-responsiveness*—dial-a-ride, shared-ride taxis, neighborhood cars

- *relatively few fixed-route stops*—jitneys, vans, shuttles

- *comfort, guaranteed seat*—carpools, vanpools, buspools, shared-ride taxis

- *no parking required*—shared-ride taxis, jitneys, shuttles, dial-a-ride, neighborhood cars

- *friendly environs*—jitneys, vans

Of course, paratransit can never match the service features of private automobiles in certain areas, like on-call availability and personal privacy. Accordingly, paratransit will never have the breadth of applications of a car. Inherently, then, paratransit is and always will be a *niche market* service.

One of the greatest values of commercial paratransit is that it stands to expand and enrich our travel *choices*. For many Americans, the choice of driving versus taking an exclusive-ride taxi versus riding a conventional bus is no choice at all. Expanding transportation service-price options would better reflect the ever-widening diversity in movement patterns and makeup of the travelling public itself. For example, it is commonly accepted that the privacy afforded by the private automobile is one of its great virtues. This, however, reflects traditional cultural norms. In Miami, New York, and other cities, some customers value jitneys and vans because of their congenial and homespun qualities. Many like travelling in vans and minibuses because they invite social interaction. While some urbanites avoid jitneys out of concern over safety, others feel more protected in jitneys since owner-operators are more careful about whom they allow on board.

One basic distinction in the commercial paratransit options examined in this book is whether services are immediate response or prearranged. Here again, paratransit's diversity is apparent. Immediate-hail services, like shared-ride taxis and neighborhood cars, begin to match the convenience and responsiveness of the automobile, though for this a premium fare is charged. Routine travel, such as for going to work or chauffeuring kids to after-school events, offers the opportunities to customize and economize on services. Private vanpools and "kids kabs" are examples of market responses.

Paratransit finds further variation in the organization of services. One aspect of organization is sponsorship. Some options, like jitneys and neighborhood cars, are pure entrepreneurial services that have no sponsors. Others, in particular shuttles and vanpools, are initiated and underwritten by employers or developers. Today, virtually all shuttles and most dial-a-ride services in the United States are contracted out on a competitive bid basis. Another organizational dimension pertains to owner and driver relationships. With many shared-ride taxi and jitney services, for instance, vehicle owners and certificate holders lease sedans and vans to drivers for a set daily or weekly fee. This arrangement encourages efficiency since the harder drivers work and the more productive they are, the more profit they make. In other instances, jitneys are owner-operator enterprises—such as in Atlantic City and the one-man jitney business in downtown San Francisco.

Another important organizational dimension of paratransit is the level of individualism versus cooperativeness. Ridesharing, for instance, runs the gamut from ad hoc, laissez-faire initiatives, like casual carpools in the Bay Area and northern Virginia, to regional brokerage services and TMAs. In areas like New York City and Miami, the jitney-van industry is highly atomistic, with independent owner-operators vying for customers and continually trying to out-maneuver each other. In Atlantic City, where a route association has existed for nearly 80 years, jitney services are centrally coordinated and controlled. Cooperatives enable paratransit services to be rationalized, allow for economies of scale, and promote self-regulation. In the absence of market competition, however, they can also become virtual cartels, charging inflated prices for services that are unresponsive to shifting travel demand. This has been the experience not only in the United States, but abroad as well. An open marketplace offers the best opportunity for striking a balance in levels of competition and coordination within the commercial paratransit industry.

PARATRANSIT FOR TOMORROW: NICHE MARKETS

The U.S. cases reviewed in this book reveal that the market for commercial paratransit services is segmented along two lines: spatially and sociodemographically. Spatially, paratransit markets vary in terms of trip-making patterns and geographic extent. At one extreme are the one-to-one services—such as commuter van runs between park-and-ride lots and office parks. At the other are many-to-many services—such as shared-ride taxis and dial-a-ride vans. Even within paratransit sectors, however, the spatial pattern of travel can vary greatly. In the case of jitneys, for instance, San Francisco's downtown jitney operates point-to-point whereas Miami's jitneys make multiple stops and willingly deviate from routes for an extra charge. Some paratransit, like shuttles and neighborhood cars, serves a small geographic area, whereas others, like vanpools and subscription buses, traverse 100 miles or more per trip. It is the inherent flexibility and adaptability of small-vehicle transportation that enables commercial paratransit to effectively serve neighborhoods and megalopolises alike.

Sociodemographically, commercial paratransit is segmented by income, stage of life cycle, and ethnicity and culture. Both income and stage of life cycle relate to what transportation planners classify as captive versus choice riders. Most immediate-response, fixed-route, and curbside hail services—shared-ride taxis, jitneys, dial-a-ride vans, neighborhood cars—cater to low-income populations and carless households. There are exceptions, however, like the casual carpools of San Francisco–Oakland, which serve mainly white- and pink-collar workers. The young and the old are also normally considered captive users, with highly specialized forms of paratransit, like "kids kabs" and dial-a-ride van services, today available to serve their unique travel needs. Discretionary paratransit users—that is, those with cars and the income means to drive if they really need to—have gravitated more toward prearranged, routine forms of commercial paratransit, like subscription vanpools and feeder shuttles. While it is apparent that commercial paratransit has segmented itself, to a certain degree, along class lines, as an industry it is no more stratified by income, race, and ethnicity than other forms of common carrier transportation.

The hallmark of commercial paratransit in the United States and abroad, then, is that it is a *niche market* industry. It fills in the gaps and expands the service options of urban transportation along the continuum between private automobile travel on one end and conventional fixed-route transit on the other. Its strength and promise lies in its diversity.

PARATRANSIT FOR TOMORROW: PERFORMANCE OUTLOOKS

Just as commercial paratransit occupies the middle ground between private cars and conventional transit with regards to services and markets, its relative performance also spans the extremes. In fiscal terms, some modes—like jitneys and shared-ride taxis—cost far less on a per-passenger basis than conventional bus transit. Cost savings of 20 to 70 percent per rider were found among the U.S. cases examined. For other services, notably dial-a-ride vans, it can cost as much as five times more to haul a passenger as on a fixed route bus. For jitneys, vans, and taxis, cost savings come mainly from lower-priced labor inputs. However, cost performance is also enhanced by high productivity, specifically high average loads and fairly rapid seat turnover. Some prearranged, regularly scheduled paratransit services, like subscription buspools, can be costly because of amenities, like the provision of comfortable padded seats and air-conditioning; however, full costs are recovered because discriminating customers willingly pay for such premiums. Other prearranged services, like employer-sponsored vanpools and carpools, economize on costs through free labor, specifically spreading driving chores among coworkers. With regard to cost performance, then, we again see that commercial paratransit engenders diversity.

Perhaps the most important financial advantage of commercial paratransit is that, unlike public transit, it generates profits instead of deficits. Given the fiscal cutbacks facing America's public transit industry today, the expansion of more entrepreneurial, commercial transportation services seems inevitable. While critics charge that the poor will suffer as a result, other remedies—like travel vouchers for the poor—are available for redressing inequities. Moreover, the history of commercial paratransit is certainly not one of ignoring poor neighborhoods. For jitneys and neighborhood car services, low-income areas have traditionally been their market base.

From a productivity standpoint, commercial paratransit consistently underperforms conventional transit on a per vehicle basis; however, this is due simply to lower passenger capacities. On a per-seat basis, most forms of (non-dial-a-ride) paratransit consistently hold a decisive edge over bus transit. In other areas, like service reliability, accident rates, and schedule adherence (where timetables are maintained), commercial paratransit is generally on a par with bus transit.

When transportation's "objective function" is broadened to include other considerations, like the effects on the environment and neighborhood accessibility, commercial paratransit generally receives high marks. Reducing tailpipe emissions and per capita energy consumption, for instance, is directly a function of diverting trips from low-occupancy to high-occupancy vehicles. Experiences in Miami with jitneys and numerous cities with successful ridesharing programs suggest that cost-effective paratransit services can draw customers from single-occupancy automobiles, rather than simply siphoning passengers away from other mass transit modes. Experiences with casual carpools and other forms of ridesharing likewise reveal that paratransit incentives, notably HOV lanes, coupled with drive-alone disincentives, like commercial parking rates and tolls, can induce even greater modal shifts.

Perhaps the least recognized but most enduring long-term social benefit of expanded commercial paratransit lies in enhancing the accessibility of inner-city residents. Proautomobile interests commonly argue that the negative externalities of the private automobile can be mitigated through various innovations, like pre-heated catalytic converters (that reduce cold-start emissions), lightweight synthetic materials (that reduce fuel consumption), and on-board navigational aids (that improve automobile performance and reduce congestion). No high-tech gadgetry, however, is available that might increase the accessibility of residents from isolated and disaffected inner-city neighborhoods. Among the supply-side approaches for effectively linking central-city residents to jobs, health clinics, retail centers, and other regional offerings, commercial paratransit is the most promising. The very existence of a thriving but illicit paratransit sector in many inner-city areas speaks to how badly some urban dwellers need and want improved mobility.

Of course, paratransit is not without its faults. From time to time, the industry has been plagued by excessive and ruinous competition, predatory behavior, overly aggressive driving, and poorly maintained vehicles. Inequities and inefficiencies still abound, like cream skimming from high-demand corridors that exhibit economies of scale and redlining of minority neighborhoods. For these and other reasons, there will also be a necessary and important role for government involvement in paratransit affairs. However, whether governments have overstepped their boundaries by introducing regulations and policies that suppress the commercial paratransit sector remains a source of considerable debate. Certainly, the promise held out for paratransit in the 1974 seminal study *Paratransit: Neglected Options for Urban Mobility* has gone largely unfulfilled: "Current urban goals for providing mobility with minimal congestion, pollution, and energy consumption strongly favor expansion of . . . paratransit services, and it seems likely that they will play an increasingly important role over the next decade" (Kirby et al., 1974, p. 278).

DEREGULATION AND COMPETITION

Trains, buses, and planes have largely been deregulated in the United States in recent times, with bipartisan support and generally good results. Government has gotten out of the friendly skies and off the busy roadways of this nation so that market forces can prevail. But while the cross-country rider now benefits from lively competition, the crosstown rider unfortunately does not.

The triad of arguments for restricting paratransit market entry—exploiting natural monopolies, eliminating cream skimming, and promoting cross-subsidization—are economic based. On closer inspection, however, these arguments lack credibility and relevance to the contemporary urban transportation scene. Public transit rarely exhibits economies of scale and there is little cream, or profits, that would be threatened by an expanded commercial paratransit sector. Commercial paratransit clearly works best in *niche market* roles—as feeders, circulators, service extenders, supplements—and is certainly not a replacement for conventional bus transit. It is a complement, not a substitute.

In reality, regulation and oversight of America's paratransit industry has always been driven by politics every bit as much as by economics, going back to the jitney bans of the First World War era. The attitude of protectionism has become so pervasive that free competition has all but vanished. Of course, commercial paratransit is no urban mobility panacea, and problems do exist. Jitneys and vans are not always reliable and their operators don't always play by the rules. Because of their smaller capacities, their proliferation in heavily trafficked corridors can worsen congestion (Vuchic, 1976). Clearly, controls over safety, driver qualifications, and operating practices (possibly including where vans and minibuses are allowed to go) are still in order, as in any other transportation sector. However, in most instances, there is no compelling reason why price and supply restrictions should be imposed on taxis, jitneys, vans, and minibuses.

Financially successful transportation systems around the world are marked by private ownership and healthy competition (Roth and Wynne, 1982). The marketplace has proven its prowess at responding to the many and varied preferences of American consumers in other areas, and there is no reason why the same would not hold for the urban transportation sector. What our cities need now more than ever is a robust and competitive transportation environment—one in which services and prices can be closely tailored to the diverse needs of America's travelling public. The call for deregulating paratransit as a means of enriching travel options is certainly not new. In reviewing Chicago's restrictive taxi and jitney laws a quarter century ago, Edmund Kitch et al. (1972, p. 347) noted: "The most pernicious consequence of the monopoly ordinance has been the significant constraint imposed on the city's public transportation policy. Except for the jitneys in South Park and the gypsies on the West Side, the automobile has had no role in mass transit in Chicago."

Decontrol would allow jitneys, shared-ride taxis, vanpools, and private minibuses to compete for parts of the travel market now largely monopolized by bus and subway operators. A competitive marketplace would force operators to restructure their services and price them more rationally. The riding public would benefit not only from a wider array of available travel options but also from a more integrated system of urban transportation.

Critics of paratransit deregulation point to some of the problems encountered with taxicab deregulation in the late 1970s and early 1980s across several dozen American cities. Instances of overcompetition and price gouging, especially at airports, were common, prompting some cities to later reregulate their industries. Similarly, experiences with across-the-board deregulation in Santiago, Chile, and parts of Great Britain led to incidences of fare escalation and excess competition. Many problems attributed to free entry, however, are actually problems of inadequate enforcement of regulations governing public safety and the behavior of paratransit operators. Paratransit deregulation without adequate policing and enforcement is a recipe for failure. Together, however, they can ensure a healthy dose of fair competition.

OTHER NEEDED POLICY REFORMS

Every day tens of thousands of Americans share rides to airports on commercial vans, enduring slight delays to pick up other fares in route. In greater Washington, D.C., and San Francisco–Oakland, at least as many get into cars with total strangers to take advantage of HOV lanes and shave 15 to 20 minutes off commutes. Both of these healthy and growing slices of paratransit activity in the United States provide insights into the kinds of policy reforms, beyond deregulation itself, that are required if commercial paratransit is to be a player in the twenty-first century urban mobility scene. The popularity of commercial van services to airports underscores the importance of market-rate pricing of transportation services. If air travellers could park for nothing or a nominal fee, as most do at their workplaces, far more would drive than share rides to airports. It is largely because of *commercial parking* rates that *commercial paratransit* has thrived at airports. Thus, in addition to deregulation and competition, market-based pricing should pervade America's urban transportation sector to the maximum extent possible. To the degree that transportation prices remain below socially optimal levels, as historically has been the case, second-best policy responses are in order. Incentives should reward travel behavior, like vehicle-pooling, that promotes the public interest. For example, preferential programs, like freeway on-ramp bypass lanes and convenient intermodal transfer facilities, can encourage ridesharing, whether on an informal (casual carpooling) or formal (employer-sponsored vanpooling) basis, by expediting travel relative to the drive-alone automobile.

From a policy standpoint, both deregulation and market-based pricing must go hand-in-hand. They are codependent. Recent experiences in Houston and Indianapolis make clear that opening up a *distorted* marketplace—one decidedly slanted to favor solo commuting and public transit riding—will do little to attract new paratransit businesses. Fortunately, deregulation and market-based pricing can complement one another quite well. Law enforcement agencies, for example, might receive some of the proceeds from congestion tolls to allow adequate policing of paratransit safety laws. A stronger commitment to enforcement might help allay the fears of incumbent taxi and bus operators about the effects of relaxing paratransit regulations. Besides enforcement, income from higher fuel taxes and congestion tolls might be used to buy back price-inflated medallions, underwrite insurance premiums for ridesharing, construct HOV lanes, create the infrastructure for a "smart" paratransit network, and provide travel vouchers for the poor. In a monograph titled *Road Use Charges and Jitneys*, Ward Elliot (1976) was one of the first to articulate the link between market-based pricing and commercial transit alternatives. In addressing Los Angeles's smog and traffic congestion problems, Elliot remarked:

The two most badly needed reforms in urban transportation are road-user charges (for smog and congestion) and legalization of jitneys. Together, these two reforms show good promise of cutting peak-hour traffic by about a quarter in cities like Los Angeles. This cut, which would reduce total daily traffic by about 5 percent, would reduce daily vehicular smog by at least 10 percent and eliminate most congestion, at a net savings to the public of at least $150 million a year. *No other transportation reforms remotely approach these two in combining high benefits and low costs. . . .* [emphasis added] (p. 1)

AN AGENDA FOR ACTION

While local governments are in the best position to introduce policies which stimulate the commercial paratransit sector, in reality political pressures and inertia have slowed and blocked progress. Higher levels of government, which are more removed from the day-to-day pressures exerted by transit unions and other special interests, arguably are better positioned to initiate reforms, both through example and "carrots and sticks." Thus, the action agenda proposed below for stimulating America's struggling paratransit sector starts with policy initiatives at the federal level. Washington might be an effective rallying point for redefining mass transit since, as noted in Chapter 8, transit has historically enjoyed broad ideological appeal and bipartisan support at the federal level. Runaway deficits and declining productivity, however, have seen this support steadily erode over the years. A national policy based on redefining and strengthening mass transit, centered around the commercialization of paratransit and other market-based principles, might find support on both aisles of Congress and the White House. Paratransit is one of the rare breeds of urban transportation strategies that simultaneously promotes efficiency and equity. The prospect of both enhancing mobility for white-collar office workers and improving job access for the inner-city poor makes paratransit unique.

The proposed trickle-down action agenda operates on the premise that a phased program of federal policy reforms would over time induce similar proparatransit initiatives at the state and local levels. It calls for generally limiting central government involvement in paratransit affairs to removing market distortions, encouraging healthy and fair competition, redressing inequities, and safeguarding public safety. Rather than a wholesale deregulation of the paratransit industry, the proposed action agenda calls for a rather carefully and measured set of policy adjustments that over time could reduce market distortions and promote more open competition in the urban transportation sector.

Federal Initiatives. The Federal government's principle role in stimulating commercial paratransit should be to eliminate modal biases, perverse subsidies, and other market distortions in the urban transportation sector. Past federal policies aimed at transit privatization failed to induce much competition; thus they fell well short of their targets. More effective would be policies that encourage selective commercialization of urban transportation and level the playing field. These should include:

- *User charges*: Fuel taxes and motoring fees should be raised to more closely approximate true social costs of automobility, such as in most other advanced, industrialized countries.

- *Assistance programs*: Funding support for mass transportation should shift to user-side assistance (e.g., as a form of income transfer) and urban transportation block grants.

- *Incentives:* Any provider-side assistance should promote efficiency and fairness. Allocations should reward states and metropolitan areas that set up impartial regional bodies for locally distributing transportation grants and that achieve a high level of productivity in the urban transportation sector.

- *Fairness:* Policies and rules which distort modal choices should be eliminated, starting with enactment of a federal cash-out parking program.

- *Demonstrations:* To the degree these programs encounter political resistance, "second-best" policies should be considered. One possibility is to provide commercial paratransit demonstration grants. Funds might "seed" community-based paratransit services under an "infant industry" logic, just as federal aid was originally granted in the 1960s to stimulate the public transit sector. Commercial paratransit demonstrations might be tied to the Federal Livable Communities and Empowerment Zone initiatives.

It is important to stress that few regulatory reforms are needed at the federal level to stimulate commercial paratransit. Policies of the ICC already promote interstate paratransit traffic. Nor is federal repeal of labor protection legislation, notably the 13(c) provision of the Federal Transit Act, particularly essential to stimulating commercial paratransit. As noted, 13(c) has historically formed a barrier to transit *privatization,* but not paratransit *commercialization.* Of course, a repeal of 13(c) would probably aid commercial operators to the degree that increased contracting allows them to expand their market domain. However, this should not be at the expense of getting embroiled in contentious labor protection battles, something which could sidetrack federal policy makers from more important tasks at hand—namely, removing modal biases and market distortions.

State Initiatives. States should follow the federal lead in revising urban transportation funding programs so as to level the urban transportation playing field. Perhaps their most essential role is to enact enabling legislation that encourages fairness and efficiencies in how lower levels of government regulate and promote urban transportation services. States should take the lead in the following areas.

- *Regional authorities:* Enabling legislation should be enacted that encourages the formation of impartial regional authorities, possibly Metropolitan Planning Organizations (MPOs), for distributing transfer payments and earmarked aid to urban transportation sectors.

- *Model ordinances and consolidation:* States should consider creating model county-wide paratransit ordinances. Regulatory consolidation across jurisdictions should also be promoted to enhance service coordination.

- *Liberalize intercity common carrier regulations:* More states should relax market entry restraints on inter-city carriers, following the lead of the federal ICC. Where "public convenience and necessity" requirements remain, states should shift the burden of proof from applicants to protesters.

- *Review uniform fitness and protection standards:* More flexibility should be considered in the setting of standards for fitness, such as the maximum age of common carrier vehicles. One-size-fits-all requirements should give way to more variable standards in line with the growing diversity in travel markets. Whether built-in margins of safety and fitness are too rigid or costly in some instances should also be examined.

Local Initiatives. City and county governments occupy the front lines of the battle to strengthen commercial paratransit, and thus ultimately are the governing bodies best able to effect change. As long as higher levels of government do their part, localities can concentrate on matters of setting service policies, policing standards, and enforcement, in addition to delivering needed public transportation services. Municipal and county governments can also play an important role in reforming parking policies and creating public-private partnerships.

- *Revise local paratransit and taxi ordinances.* Ordinances should be revised and crafted to promote healthy competition by removing market entry restrictions and relaxing controls over pricing and service practices.

- *Regional initiatives.* Consolidated regional paratransit regulations and oversight authorities should be created, as appropriate, for coordinating services and distributing public assistance. Local-source funding programs should be designed to further promote commercial paratransit. Regional transit services should be reconfigured to focus on areas where public transit enjoys natural advantages, such as mainline corridors. Market-based transportation programs, like road pricing, should be actively promoted.

- *Parking reforms.* Municipalities are best positioned to reduce what is arguably the most easily removable hidden subsidy to motorists—abundant, free parking. Local ordinances should discourage the oversupply of parking and require motorists to pay for parking, such as through cash-out parking programs.

- *Partnerships.* Localities should work closely with paratransit route associations, cooperatives, and other alliances to form mutually beneficial public-private partnerships.

Implementing this action agenda will be an uphill struggle. The institutional and political resistance to commercial paratransit in America is immense and will not be broken down easily. However, small victories—raising fuel prices, loosening jitney restrictions, opening HOV lanes—are possible. Now is the time to begin moving on such fronts. Future mobility and the sustainability of twenty-first century urban America will, to a significant degree, depend on it.

REFERENCES

Altshuler, A. 1980. *The Urban Transportation System: Politics and Policy Innovation.* Cambridge, Massachusetts: MIT Press.

Bernick, M., and R. Cervero. 1994. "Transit-based Development in the United States." *Passenger Transport* 12(2): 7-8.

Bookout, L. 1992. "The Future of Higher-density Housing." *Urban Land* 51(9): 1-5.

Calthorpe, P. 1993. *The Next American Metropolis.* Princeton, New Jersey: Princeton Architectural Press.

Downs, A. 1994. *New Visions for Metropolitan America.* Washington, D.C.: Brookings Institution.

Elliot, W. 1976. *Road Use Charges and Jitneys.* Claremont, California: Rose Institute of State and Local Government, Claremont Men's College.

Katz, P. 1993. *The New Urbanism: Toward an Architecture of Community.* New York: McGraw-Hill.

Kirby, R., K. Bhatt, M. Kemp, R. McGillivray, and M. Wohl. 1974. *Paratransit: Neglected Options for Urban Mobility.* Washington, D.C.: The Urban Institute.

Kitch, E., M. Isaacson, and D. Kasper. 1971. "The Regulation of Taxicabs in Chicago." *Journal of Law and Economics* 14(2): 285-350.

Roth, G., and G. Wynne. 1982. *Free Enterprise Urban Transportation.* New Brunswick, New Jersey: Transaction Books.

Vuchic, V. 1976. "Transit Regulation: Improve It, Decrease It or Eliminate It?" *Transit Journal* 2(4): 2-14.

Selected Bibliography

Armstrong-Wright, A. 1993. *Public Transport in Third World Cities.* London: HMSO Publications.

Banister, D., and R. Mackett. 1990. "The Minibus: Theory and Experience, and Their Implications." *Transport Reviews* 10(3): 189-214.

Black, A. 1995. *Urban Mass Transportation Planning.* New York: McGraw-Hill.

Cervero, R. 1984. "Revitalizing Urban Transit: More Money or Less Regulation?" *Regulation* 8(3): 36-42.

Cervero, R. 1991. "Paratransit in Southeast Asia: A Market Response to Poor Roads?" *Review of Urban and Regional Development Studies* 3: 3-27.

Chujoh, U. 1989. "Learning from Medium-and-Small-Sized Bus Services in Developing Countries: Is Regulation Necessary?" *Transportation Research* 23A(1): 19-28.

Davis, O., and N. Johnson. 1984. "The Jitneys: A Study of Grassroots Capitalism." *Journal of Contemporary Studies* 4(1): 81-102.

Dimitriou, H. 1995. *A Developmental Approach to Urban Transport Planning: An Indonesian Illustration.* Aldershot, England: Averbury.

Donahue, J. 1989. *The Privatization Decision.* New York: Basic Books.

Eckert, R., and G. Hilton. 1972. "The Jitneys." *Journal of Law and Economics* 15(2): 293-325.

Frankena, M., and P. Paultner. 1984. *An Economic Analysis of Taxicab Regulation.* Washington, D.C.: Urban Mass Transportation Administration, U.S. Department of Transportation.

Gilbert, G., and R. Samuels. 1982. *The Taxicab: An Urban Transportation Survivor.* Chapel Hill: University of North Carolina Press.

Gomez-Ibanez, J., and J. Meyer. 1993. *Going Private: The International Experience with Transport Privatization.* Washington, D.C.: The Brookings Institution.

Kirby, R., K. Bhatt, M. Kemp, R. McGillivray, and M. Wohl. 1972. *Paratransit: Neglected Options for Urban Mobility.* Washington, D.C.: The Urban Institute.

Kitch, E., M. Isaacson, and D. Kasper. 1971. "The Regulation of Taxicabs in Chicago." *Journal of Law and Economics* 14(2): 285-350.

Lave, C., ed. *Urban Transit: The Private Challenge to Public Transportation*. Cambridge, Massachusetts: Ballinger.

Poole, R., and M. Griffin. 1994. *Shuttle Vans: The Overlooked Transit Alternative*. Los Angeles: Reason Foundation, Policy Study No. 176.

Rimmer, P. 1986. *Rikisha to Rapid Transit*. Sydney: Pergamon Press.

Roth, G., and G. Wynne. 1982. *Learning from Abroad: Free Enterprise Urban Transportation*. New Brunswick, New Jersey: Transaction Books.

Susuki, P. 1995. "Unregulated Taxicabs." *Transportation Quarterly* 49(1): 129-138.

Thompson, T. 1986. *Barriers to Private Sector Participation in Public Transportation*. Washington, D.C.: Urban Mass Transportation Administration, U.S. Department of Transportation.

Urban Mobility Corporation. 1992. *The Miami Jitneys*. Washington, D.C.: Federal Transit Administration, U.S. Department of Transportation.

Walters, A. 1979. "The Benefits of Minibuses: A Comment." *Journal of Transport Economics and Policy* 15: 77-79.

Webber, M. 1994. "The Marriage of Autos & Transit: How to Make Transit Popular Again." *Access* 5: 26-31.

Index

About the Author

ROBERT CERVERO is a Professor in the Department of City and Regional Planning at the University of California-Berkeley. Dr. Cervero has published three books and many journal articles concerned with public transport, and has frequently served as a consultant in this area.

ISBN 0-275-95725-X

HARDCOVER BAR CODE